CLASSICAL STUDIES PRESENTED
TO BEN EDWIN PERRY

Ben Edwin Perry
21 February 1892—1 November 1968

CLASSICAL STUDIES PRESENTED
TO BEN EDWIN PERRY
BY HIS
STUDENTS AND COLLEAGUES
AT THE
UNIVERSITY OF ILLINOIS, 1924-60

ILLINOIS STUDIES IN LANGUAGE AND LITERATURE

58

UNIVERSITY OF ILLINOIS PRESS
URBANA, CHICAGO, LONDON
1969

FOREWORD

A committee, composed of persons who were students or colleagues of Professor Perry at some time during his thirty-six years of active teaching at the University of Illinois, has prepared this volume of studies in testimony of the warm-hearted encouragement and genial stimulation which he has always offered them. We speak here of his friendship. The studies, such as they are, can be but small return for his scholarship. It is sufficiently attested by the list of his published writings with which the volume opens, ranging as they do from a brilliant doctoral dissertation through critical but always courteous reviews and such memorable and pungently titled articles as "The Early Greek Capacity for Viewing Things Separately" to books like the monumental first volume of *Aesopica,* which won the coveted Award of Merit of the American Philological Association, or like his two learned monographs (and a share in a third) in the same Association's series, or the elegantly written and richly persuasive Sather Classical Lectures delivered at Berkeley in 1951 and recently published.

A native midwesterner, trained at Michigan and then Princeton, with time out for service in the first world war, Professor Perry represents American classical scholarship at its best. We his students and associates at Illinois are justly proud of his achievement. Our contributions will not add to his fame, but we hope they will show that we—and the many others who were privileged to learn from his teaching—have caught some small spark from the fire that burned in him. At the time our book was planned, Professor Perry was in good health and we had hoped to present it to him in token of our affection and admiration for him and his wife. *Sed dis aliter visum.* He had seen only the page proofs and that a few weeks before his death, after a lingering illness, on the first of November, 1968. In deepest sorrow we now dedicate this volume to his memory.

We thank the Editorial Board of Illinois Studies and the University Research Board for their generous support of our project to honor Professor Perry, and the editorial staff of the University of Illinois Press for their patience and skill in giving it material form.

CONTENTS

LIST OF ABBREVIATIONS

Names of ancient authors and the titles of their works or designations of papyri, if abbreviated, can be located in *LSJ, OCD,* or *TLL* (see below). Other abbreviations, if not immediately transparent, are explained in an early footnote of the article in which they occur. Acronyms used for the titles of serials or collections are as follows:

AJA	American Journal of Archaeology		(Liddell, Scott, Jones, McKenzie)
AJP	American Journal of Philology	*MPG*	Patrologia Graeca (Migne)
BCH	Bulletin de Correspondance Hellénique	*MPL*	Patrologia Latina (Migne)
BHR	Bibliothèque d'Humanisme et Renaissance	*OCD*	Oxford Classical Dictionary
BZ	Byzantinische Zeitschrift	*OGIS*	Orientis Graeci Inscriptiones Selectae (Dittenberger)
CIA	Corpus Inscriptionum Atticarum		
CIL	Corpus Inscriptionum Latinarum	*PAPA*	Proceedings of the American Philological Association (with *TAPA*, below)
CJ	Classical Journal		
CP	Classical Philology	*PW*	(Berliner) Philologische Wochenschrift
CQ	Classical Quarterly		
CR	Classical Review	*RE*	Real-Encyclopädie der classischen Altertumswissenschaft
CW	Classical Weekly (World)		
GHI	Greek Historical Inscriptions (Tod)		
HSCP	Harvard Studies in Classical Philology	*REB*	Revue des Études Byzantines
IG	Inscriptiones Graecae	*REG*	Revue des Études Grecques
IGRRP	Inscriptiones Graecae ad Res Romanas Pertinentes (Cagnat et al.)	*SEG*	Supplementum Epigraphicum Graecum
		SIFC	Studi Italiani di Filologia Classica
ILLRP	Inscriptiones Latinae Liberae Rei Publicae (Degrassi)	*TAPA*	Transactions of the American Philological Association
ILS	Inscriptiones Latinae Selectae (Dessau)	*TLL*	Thesaurus Linguae Latinae
JHS	Journal of Hellenic Studies	*TU*	Texte und Untersuchungen
LSJ	Greek-English Dictionary		

PUBLISHED WORKS OF BEN EDWIN PERRY

Marian Harman

BOOKS

1920. *The* Metamorphoses *Ascribed to Lucius of Patrae, Its Content, Nature, and Authorship.* (Princeton dissertation.) Lancaster, Pa. v, 74 p.

1934. *Index Apuleianus* (with W. A. Oldfather and H. V. Canter). (Philological Monographs, No. 3.) Middletown, Conn., American Philological Association. liii, 490 p.

1936. *Studies in the Text History of the Life and Fables of Aesop.* (Philological Monographs, No. 7.) Haverford, Pa., American Philological Association. xvi, 240 p.

1952. *Aesopica: A Series of Texts Relating to Aesop or Ascribed to Him or Closely Connected with the Literary Tradition That Bears His Name; Collected and Critically Edited with a Commentary and Historical Essay.* Vol. 1. Urbana, University of Illinois Press. xxvi, 765 p.

1964. *Secundus, The Silent Philosopher. The Greek Life of Secundus Critically Edited and Restored so far as possible.* (Philological Monographs, No. 22.) Ithaca, N. Y., American Philological Association. xiv, 160, 74, 96 p.

1965. *Babrius and Phaedrus. Newly Edited and Translated into English, Together with an Historical Introduction and a Comprehensive Survey of Greek and Latin Fables in the Aesopic Tradition.* (Loeb Classical Library.) London and Cambridge, W. Heinemann and Harvard University Press. cii, 634 p.

1967. *The Ancient Romances: A Literary-Historical Account of Their Origins.* (Sather Classical Lectures.) Berkeley, University of California Press. xii, 407 p.

ARTICLES

1923. "The Significance of the Title in Apuleius' *Metamorphoses,*" *CP* 18, 229–38.

"Some Aspects of the Literary Art of Apuleius in the *Metamorphoses,*" *TAPA* 54, 196–227.

1924. "On the Authorship of *Lucius sive Asinus* and Its Original," (abstract) *PAPA* 55, xxx.

1925. "On Apuleius' *Metamorphoses* II 31–III 20," *AJP* 46, 253–62.

"Petronius and the Comic Romance," *CP* 20, 31–49.

1926. "An Interpretation of Apuleius' *Metamorphoses,*" *TAPA* 57, 238–60.

"On the Authenticity of *Lucius sive Asinus,*" *CP* 21, 225–34.

1927. "On Apuleius' *Hermagoras,*" *AJP* 48, 263–66.

1928. "Chariton and His Romance from a Literary Point of View," (abstract) *PAPA* 59, xxvii.

1929. "Note on Apuleius' *Metamorphoses* II 30," *CP* 24, 93–94.

"The Story of Thelyphron in Apuleius," *CP* 24, 231–38.

"On Apuleius' *Metamorphoses* I 14–17," *CP* 24, 394–400.

1930. "Chariton and His Romance from a Literary-Historical Point of View," *AJP* 51, 93–134.

1933. "A Manuscript Fragment of the *Prochiron,*" *BZ* 33, 362.

"The Origin and Date of the Fables Ascribed to Syntipas," (abstract) *PAPA* 64, xliv.

"The Text Tradition of the Greek *Life of Aesop,*" *TAPA* 64, 198–244.

1934. "The Greek Source of Rinuccio's *Aesop,*" *CP* 29, 53–62.

1937. "The Early Greek Capacity for Viewing Things Separately," *TAPA* 68, 403–27.

1939. "Some Addenda to Liddell and Scott," *AJP* 60, 29–40.

1940. "The Origin of the Epimythium," *TAPA* 71, 391–419.

"Physiologus," *RE* 20, 1074–1129.

1943. "On the Manuscripts of the *Philogelos,*" *Classical Studies in Honor of William Abbott Oldfather* (Urbana, University of Illinois Press), pp. 157–66.

"Fable, Aesopic," *Dictionary of World Literature,* Edited by J. T. Shipley (New York, Philosophical Library), p. 229.

1953. "An Aesopic Fable in Photius," *BZ* 46, 308–13.

1955. "Literature in the Second Century," *CJ* 50, 295–98.

1957. "Babriana," *CP* 52, 16–23.

1959. "Fable," *Studium Generale* 12, 17–37.

"The Origin of the *Book of Sindbad*," *Fabula* 3, 1–94. (Reprinted separately 1960; Berlin, W. de Gruyter.)

1960. "Some Traces of Lost Medieval Story-Books," *Humaniora; Essays in Literature, Folklore, Bibliography, Honoring Archer Taylor* (Locust Valley, N. Y., J. J. Augustin), pp. 150–60.

1961. "Two Fables Recovered," *BZ* 54, 4–14.

1962. "Demetrius of Phalerum and the Aesopic Fables," *TAPA* 93, 287–346.

1963. "Aesop," *Encyclopaedia Britannica*, Vol. 1, 220–21.

1964. Foreword to *David of Sassoun: The Armenian Folk Epic.* Text translated by A. K. Shalian (Athens, O., Ohio University Press), pp. vii–ix.

1966. "The Greek Source of Some Armenian Fables, and Certain Closely-Related Matters of Tradition," *Polychronion: Festschrift für Franz Dölger* (Heidelberg, C. Winter), pp. 418–30.

"Some Addenda to the Life of Aesop," *BZ* 59, 285–304.

REVIEWS

1923. B. Lavagnini, *Le origini del romanzo greco* (Pisa, 1921), in *AJP* 44, 371–73.

1928. E. H. Haight, *Apuleius and His Influence* (New York, 1927), in *CP* 23, 84–85.

1929. *Petronius,* The Satiricon, Edited by E. T. Sage (New York, 1929), in *AJP* 50, 300–304.

1930. F. G. Allison, *Lucian, Satirist and Artist* (New York, 1926), in *CW* 23, 115–17.

1932. J. J. Chapman, *Lucian, Plato, and Greek Morals* (Boston, 1931), in *CW* 26, 46–48.

1934. J. E. Harry, *Greek Tragedy: Emendations, Interpretations, and Critical Notes* (New York, 1933), in *CJ* 30, 179–80.

1937. *Physiologus,* Edited by F. Sbordone (Milan, 1936), in *AJP* 58, 488–96.

J. Svennung, *Untersuchungen zu Palladius und zur lateinischen Fach- und Volkssprache* (Uppsala, 1935), in *CW* 31, 45–46.

E. H. Haight, *Essays on Ancient Fiction* (New York, 1936), in *AJP* 58, 245–46.

1938. E. V. Marmorale, *Petronio* (Naples, 1936), in *CP* 33, 327–29.
1939. Chariton. *De Chaerea et Callirhoe Amatoriarum Narra-tionum Libri Octo,* Edited by W. E. Blake (Oxford, 1938), in *AJP* 60, 497–99.

       S. Costanza, *La fortuna di L. Apuleio nell' età di mezzo* (Palermo, 1937), in *CW* 33, 78.
1941. M. Molt, *Ad Apulei Madaurensis* Metamorphoseon *Librum Primum Commentarius Exegeticus* (Groningen, 1938), in *CP* 36, 308–309.
1942. A. Hausrath, ed., *Corpus Fabularum Aesopicarum,* Vol. 1, fasc. 1 (Leipzig, 1940), in *CP* 37, 207–18.

       M. Braun, *History and Romance in Graeco-Oriental Litera-ture* (Oxford, 1938), in *CJ* 37, 537–40.
1945. A. Turyn, *The Manuscript Tradition of the Tragedies of Aeschylus* (New York, 1943), in *CP* 40, 259–60.
1948. *Apulée:* Les Metamorphoses, Edited by D. S. Robertson and translated by P. Vallette. (Paris, 1940–45), in *CP* 43, 192–99.
1949. B. J. de Jonge, *Ad Apulei Madaurensis* Metamorphoseon *Librum Secundum Commentarius Exegeticus* (Groningen, 1941), in *CP* 44, 38–42.
1950. R. Strömberg, *On Some Greek Proverbial Phrases* (Göte-borg, 1947) and *Grekiska Ordspråk: en Antologi* (Göteborg, 1949), in *CP* 45, 122–23.

       M. Richard, *Répertoire des bibliothèques et des catalogues de manuscrits grecs* (Paris, 1948), in *CP* 45, 199–201.
1957. A. de Lorenzi, *Fedro* (Florence, 1955), in *CP* 52, 267–69.

       K. Meuli, *Herkunft und Wesen der Fabel* (Basel, 1954), in *Gnomon* 29, 427–31.
1958. R. Strömberg, *Greek Proverbs* (Göteborg, 1954), in *CJ* 54, 38–40.
1960. S. Trenkner, *The Greek Novella in the Classical Period* (Cambridge, 1938), in *AJP* 81, 442–47.
1961. F. Geissler, *Beispiele der alten Weisen des Johann von Capua* (Berlin, 1960), in *Fabula* 4, 274–75.
1962. A. Wiechers, *Aesop in Delphi* (Meisenheim am Glan, 1961), in *Gnomon* 34, 620–22.

       E. I. Gordon, *Sumerian Proverbs* (Philadelphia, 1959), in *AJA* 66, 205–207.
1964. L. O. Sjöberg, *Stephanites und Ichnelates. Überlieferungs-*

geschichte und Text (Stockholm, 1962), in *Gnomon* 36, 722–24.

1968. *Paradoxographorum Graecorum reliquiae,* Edited by A. Giannini (Milano, 1965), in *AJP* 89, 119–21.

WORKS IN PROGRESS

Aesopica, Vol. 2–3, consisting of translations of many Near-Eastern fables; surveys of other medieval and early modern collections of fables; commentary on the texts; and a terminal essay on the literary tradition as a whole.

Johannes Georgides' prose anthology; a critical edition based on manuscripts not used in Boissonade's edition.

Physiologus; the oldest Greek text edited and translated.

Sindbad and the Seven Wise Masters; a critical edition and translation of the oldest version.

University of Illinois
14 March 1966

AESOP AND BRITO

Lloyd W. Daly

As a truly humble offering to an honored master I bring the following lines of verse:

> Ficus comedens sycofanta.
> Hic libet antiquam brevibus recitare fabellam.
> Dives erat cuius nequam fuit assecla.   Ficus
> Hic furtim cepit domini postquamque comedit.
> Infamans socium de ficubus impedit illum.
> Liberat insontem dominus pravumque clientem
> Cogit aquam bibere calidam, ficusque repente
> Evomit invitus.   Hinc est sycofanta vocatus.

The appropriateness of this offering will not, I hope, be obscure since the *fabella* repeats in a highly condensed and confused form an incident from the *Life* of Aesop.

The source of the verses is an unpublished treatise on Greek words which is to be found in Latin MS 62 of the *Bibliothèque Municipale* of Douai (fol. 245ᵛ)[1] and in MS *Lat. quart.* 2 in the *Stiftung preussischer Kulturbesitz, Tübinger Depot der Staatsbibliothek* (fol. 157). The treatise is ascribed in both manuscripts to Brito, who is to be identified as Guillelmus Brito, a thirteenth-century Master and Rector of the University of Paris, who also compiled a *Summa* or *Expositiones difficiliorum verborum de biblia* and *Expositiones* on Jerome's prologues to the books of the Bible.[2]

The *fabella* appears as the only such embellishment in the whole treatise. Clearly Brito was not a good storyteller. He has omitted the essential fact that the *socius* was dumb and that it was he who, to demonstrate his innocence, introduced the test of drinking warm

[1] I am indebted to the Institut de Recherche et d'Étude des Textes for the loan of microfilms of this manuscript.

[2] Cf. my "Guillelmus Brito and His Works," *The Library Chronicle* 32 (1966), 1–17.

water and submitted to the test himself. Although Brito normally makes a somewhat ostentatious parade of his authorities, he says nothing about his source for this story. A terse statement in the marginal commentary does say, "Ysopus fuit, ut dicitur," but that is all. Brito may have known the story from a wide variety of places, perhaps merely as an independent anecdote. Still the use of the word *fabella* suggests to me that some properly Aesopic source should be thought of. It seems most natural to suppose that Brito was familiar with a Latin version of the *Life*, for his knowledge of Greek, as evidenced in this treatise, was not such that he could be expected to have read it in Greek, even if that had been available to him in Paris. The Latin *Vita Lolliniana* may have been the source. There is nothing to prove or disprove this possibility so far as I can see. In this case the *Vita Lolliniana* would have to be at least as early as the last quarter of the thirteenth century although the unique manuscript, *Bellunensis Lollinianus* 26, is of the fourteenth century.[3]

This treatise of Brito is of some general interest as representing something of the knowledge and teaching of Greek at Paris in the late thirteenth century. Compared with Roger Bacon's *Greek Grammar* it is a very disappointing performance. Bacon does refer to Brito's other works, and it is possible that he is referring to this treatise when he says, "Britonem in tractatu suo de vocalibus (vocabulis?) grammaticis nolo sequi in aliquo, quia ubique errat, vel probaciones legitimas non affert, sui capitis stulticia obstinatus." [4]

The whole treatise in question runs to over 2300 lines. It begins by saying that the author will now treat in verse matters he has previously dealt with in prose, and much of the matter does duplicate what is to be found in the *Summa*. Then the author says that he will first offer information which will help prevent confusion between Greek and Hebrew words. There follow 121 lines devoted to explanation in alphabetic order of some fifty Hebrew words from the text of the Vulgate.

With the transitional lines (129–30),

> Partes preposui quasdam sermonis hebrei;
> Iam libet et grece quedam subiungere lingue,

we pass on to the main body of the work. First the letters of the

[3] Cf. B. E. Perry, *Aesopica*, I (Urbana, 1952), 30.

[4] *The Greek Grammar of Roger Bacon*, ed. E. Nolan and S. A. Hirsch (Cambridge, 1902), p. 37.

Greek alphabet are named in verse, with the addition of *ephisimon* (for *digamma* or *stigma*), *scopita* (for *koppa*) and *caractira* (for *sampi*). These last three are named in the same way as they are by Bacon and are explained as being numeral notations rather than letters. There follows a table giving the name of each letter, the letter itself and its numeral equivalent expressed in Roman numerals. Then five lines (148–52) are devoted to a brief explanation of the extension of the Greek alphabetic numeral system by the addition of subscript virgules to multiply by 1000. The rest of the treatise runs in alphabetic order through an extensive vocabulary of Greek words, giving their meaning, their Latin equivalent, etymological comments, lists of compound derivatives and various grammatical and orthographical comments.

The Greek words are spelled in Roman characters. Even so the work obviously gave copyists trouble. Lines 173–74 run as follows:

> *Ampho* dic grece, sed dicas ambo latine.
> Porto *fero,* circum notat *an,* portat *amphora* grecum.

Here *grecum* might seem a clear error for *circum,* but experience with the text leads to distrust of the author as well as the scribe. In this case the author appears to have had *amphora* in mind when he explained *ampho,* but if he did he was distracted by his misinformation about *an.* Such dubieties assail one at every point in the text. And yet correct information can be given straightforwardly, as in the following lines (175–77):

> Hec tibi verborum datur horum regula: verbum (grecum?)
> E commutatur in o, sic dic *foros* a *fero, stello*
> Dat *stolos,* et *lego* dat *logos,* atque *nomos nemo* format.[5]

In this work, as in the *Summa,* Brito not only depends entirely upon recognized authorities for his information but cites his authorities as fully as his verse will permit. In the course of the work he cites, in addition to books of the Bible, the following authorities: Aimo, Alain de Lille (*doctor Alanus*), Alexandre de Villedieu (*Doctrinale*), Augustine, Bene (*doctor Bene*), Bernardus Silvestris (*Bernardinus*), John of Damascus (*Damascenus*), Glosa, Horace, Huguitio, Isidore, Jerome, Juvenal, Lucan, Papias, Petrus Comestor (*Historiae*), Petrus Riga (*Petrus, Aurora*), Pliny, Priscian (*Priscus magister*), Rabanus, Remigius, Vergil. That the verse form was an embarrassment in this particular as well as in others is made clear

---

[5] Here again it is tempting to read *grecum* for *verbum,* and *grecum* is the last word in the preceding line where *grecum* seemed a possible mistake for *circum!*

by repeated apologies for atrocities he is conscious of committing, as in lines 544–45:

Hic modo subiungam Grecorum nomina quedam
Que metra vix capiunt, veniam peto si male sistunt.

But this is not the only sign of the author's consciousness of the inadequacies of his medium to his purpose.

In both the manuscripts rather generous margins are left and these are rather generously filled with commentary. The comments serve two purposes in general. First, they undertake to explain in more intelligible terms what has been said very briefly or enigmatically in verse. For example, on the verse 728,

Inde *galaxia* fertur capitumque *galama*

the comment is, "*Galaxia* est lacteus qui vulgo via Sancti Jacobi appellatur. *Galama* est velamen capitis candidissimum." Second, they add citations of authority. For example, on line 752,

Dico *geronta* senem sed *presbyterum* seniorem,

the comment is, "Gregorius in omel. lxxº, Greci valde seniores non *gerontas* sed *presbyteros* appellant, ut postquam senes esse insinuent quos provectiores appellant." In addition to the authorities cited in the verse the commentary also refers to Cicero, Donatus, Macer, Ovid, Persius, Rufinus, Statius and Theodolus.

This commentary must, I believe, be ascribed to Brito himself. That his reason for writing it was his keen awareness of the inadequacy of his verse to convey the information he had to offer seems to me evident. That the ascription is correct can be proved by a single Vergil reference on line 2091 where the commentary says, "Virgilius in viiiº Eneidos, Suspendive tholo, aut sacra ad fastigia fixi." The correct reference is not to the eighth book of the *Aeneid* but to IX. 408. In the *Summa* Brito repeatedly and consistently makes his book references to the *Aeneid* one number too low for all books beyond the fourth, and I know of no one else who does just this.

In his Grammar, Bacon reflects a contemporary pronunciation in his orthography, but Brito generally displays older conventional spellings. He does, however, display some of the vocalic changes characteristic of later Greek. For example, on *selenites* (1833) he comments, " sed melius dicuntur omnia ista a *selini*, quod est luna." So also he shows *min* for μῆν (1199), *pigi* for πηγή (1610), *scinos* for σχοῖνος (1819) as well as *zigon* for ζυγόν (2301) and *ke* for καί

(1028). Consonantal changes also appear occasionally, as in the comment on 2102,

> Grece *o autos* idem, *nauti* eadem, *to auto* idem
> in neutro. Profertur autem *oaphtos, eaphti,*
> *toaphto,* et forte a *thaphto* formaverunt Latini
> *tautologos.*

In the case of Bacon it is assumed that such contemporary pronunciation represents familiarity with Greek speakers. In Brito's case this seems less likely because he relies so exclusively on written authority, but it cannot be excluded as a possibility that he learned something from living informants.

Contemporary peculiarities of orthography appear everywhere: *y* for *i*, omission or addition of aspiration, *f* for *ph*, etc. This is to be expected but it is more than usually confusing in such a text. On aspiration he demonstrates more knowledge than his orthography would suggest in saying (805–807):

> Si, lector, grecam bene servas ortographiam
> Aspiras *hepta,* sic *hemis,* et inde creata;
> Vel dasiam muta, sic septem dicis ab *hepta.*

It is typical that utter confusion should seem to reign in a passage such as lines 708–713 where we meet *Phiton* (Python), *Phitius* (Pythius), *Fitea* (Pythia), *Fiton* (Python) and *Fitonissa* (Pythonissa), and that order should be introduced into such seeming chaos by the following statement (715),

> Aspiratum p, non f, caput hiis solet esse.

In the matter of distinction between Latin derivatives from Greek and Greek-Latin cognates Brito seems to be completely at sea, as when he writes (676–77),

> Utimur f vice phi per quod scripsere Latini.
> A Grecis sumpta sicut sunt fur, fuga, fama.

But he is here following what is for him best authority as he makes clear in his comment, "Priscianus dicit in principio maioris voluminis (I. 13), Greci, quibus in omni doctrina auctoribus utimur, Φ cuius locum F apud nos optinet, quod ostenderunt maxime in hiis dictionibus quas a Grecis sumpsimus, hoc est fama, fuga, fur, mutam esse confirmatur." He also recognizes the existence of what he classifies as hybrids (*notha*) in the following lines (1340–44):

> Sunt notha que greca modo dico modoque latina;
> Principium grecum retinent finemque latinum.

Nam finem vario declinans more latino.
Dico *noym* grece, mentem sensumve latine;
Noys cum diptongo vox est monosillaba recto.

On this point he cites no authority but is pretty clearly dependent either directly or indirectly on Isidore (*Etymol.* I. 7, 13) for his information, but not for his example.

Elsewhere, however, there is real and unmitigated confusion, as when he begins clearly enough (2172),

Tres vel ter dic *tris, trieris* venit inde triremis,

but goes on to list a large number of derivatives, including many Greek compounds indiscriminately assorted with such purely Latin words as *tridens, trimus, triginta, triquadrum, triplex,* etc.

Another striking feature of the treatise is its etymological lore. A fair example is to be found in the following lines (1586–90):

Quod de re purgas radisve *peripsima* dicas,
Et venit a *simo* vel *semo* cum *peri* iuncto,
Vel venit a verbo quod Grecus ait *perisevo.*
Alludunt voci grece plerumque Latini
De seco deque *peri* dicendo *peripsima* dici.

On the last two of these lines the comment is, "Ethimologia potius est quam dirivatio," and this kind of comment is to be found repeatedly. This kind of etymologizing is, of course, familiar from Varro and Isidore onward. It is not so clear just what Brito thinks he is doing and what he means by the comment. He undertakes to explain all this in the following passage (302–17):

Hec calamus grecum signat quod harundo latinum,
Et Campanorum flumen Calamum lego dictum,
Arbor aromatica sic est speciesque vocata,
Fistula vel [sic] stipula segetis, scriptoria penna.
Grecismi matrem linguam, non pono latinam;
Non tamen exerro nec in hoc preiudico greco,
Alludens grecis quia verbis scribo latinis,
Significatarum dum tango propria rerum,
Nec reputo greca variat que forma latina,
Sed notha sunt; prisci sic vult doctrina magistri.
Pellicanum quasi pelicavum dic pelleve canum.
Cur? Quia pellicanus pellem cavat est quoque canus.
A caleo calamum pro canna sic lego dictum,
Nam calet inmisso flantis spiramine crebro.
Sic dici petram tibi dico quasi pede tritam,
Sic fit et in reliquis quibus est allusio talis.

Again on line 308 there is the comment, "Quia non est dirivatio sed ethimologia."

If I understand this explanation correctly, it means something like the following:

The Greek *calamus* means what *harundo* does in Latin, and I read that a river of the Campanians is called the Calamus, an aromatic tree as well as the spice is so called, so also the reed or straw of the field and the writer's pen. I assert that the Greek language, not Latin, is the mother (sc. of *calamus*). Yet I am not making any mistake nor am I showing any prejudice against Greek because I write in Latin words in playing upon (*alludens*) Greek words while I touch upon the true significance of things; nor do I consider as Greek those words which are inflected in Latin, but they are hybrids (*notha*); such is the teaching of the ancient master. Say *pellicanus* as though it were *pellicavus* or *pellecanus*. Why? Because the *pellicanus* "*pellem cavat*" and is also *canus*. I read that *calamus* for *canna* is so called from *caleo*, for it takes on heat (*calet*) from the repeated insufflation of a blower. So I tell you *petra* is used as though for "*pede trita*". And such also is the case in other words in which there is such a play on meaning.

Thus Brito first lists meanings for the word *calamus*, then asserts that he takes it to be Greek in origin, forestalls criticism to the effect that it is Latin because it has a Latin ending by explaining that in this form it is a hybrid according to his definition, and then goes on to give three examples of *ethimologia*. The comment, "Quia non est dirivatio sed ethimologia," is apparently intended to apply to the word *alludens*. From this I believe it can be discerned that *ethimologia* is something to be taken less seriously than *dirivatio*. Etymology thus appears to be regarded as a legitimate kind of free associative play with the significance of a word. The aim of such play may be to provide a mnemonic device supposed to be useful in retaining the meaning of a word, a prime concern of Brito, or it may be intended to disclose hidden allegorical depths in the word, a procedure thoroughly familiar in contemporary Biblical interpretation. In any case this latter kind of play can be seen to good advantage in the explanation of the word *pandochium* (1489–90):

> Captio dicta *doche* sit, *pan* compone, domusque
> *Pandochium* fertur qua cuncti suscipiuntur.

In these lines the explanation is perfectly straightforward and acceptable, but the accompanying comment takes an altogether different line, without even suggesting that it is an alternative. It runs as follows, "A pando, dis dicitur hic et hec et hoc pandox, id est ebriosus, gulosus, qui pandit os ad omnem escam. Et inde dicitur *pandochium* lecacitas, ebriositas, taberna vel caupona." The moralizing tendency of the comment is obvious and probably should serve as sufficient notice that this is etymology in the sense above described as opposed to the *dirivatio* offered in the verse. Presumably the distinction would be clear enough to Brito's audience that he would feel no need to call attention to it in every case.

Thus the whole work is nearly incredible as a serious effort unless one tries to understand it in its setting. When Roger Bacon writes his *Greek Grammar* he intends it to be useful to those who wish to learn to read or translate Greek texts, and he criticizes contemporary knowledge of the language, or lack of it, from that point of view. A work like Brito's, however, does not have this aim. It is rather aimed at shedding some light on the Greek element in the contemporary Latin vocabulary and especially that element as represented in the text of the Vulgate. This was regarded as a legitimate end in itself, and in the light of what we know of the curriculum at Paris at this time it is not a surprising end. Bacon was a revolutionary, ahead of his time, whereas Brito was a traditional scholastic, concerned primarily with Scripture and with established written authority on the interpretation of Scripture.

In writing this treatise in this form Brito had good precedent. The *Grecismus* [6] of Eberhard of Bethune (died *ca.* 1212) was a standard school work dealing with similar material in a comparable verse form and was thoroughly familiar to Brito as is indicated by his frequent citation of it in the *Summa*. Brito also refers frequently in the *Summa*, as well as in this treatise, to the *Doctrinale* of Alexandre de Villedieu, and it likewise is a versified school text by a close contemporary.[7] Of a similar sort are the so-called *Corrogationes Promethei* of Alexander Neckham, a versified glossary on the Vulgate which follows the order of the books of the Bible.[8] Brito also cites this work repeatedly in the *Summa* and a closer study would probably show that he was considerably influenced by its style and technique.

Such, then, is the setting for my gem of Aesopic literature. If my description of the setting has outweighed the gem I throw myself

[6] Eberhard of Bethune, *Grecismus*, ed. J. Wrobel, *Corpus Grammaticorum Medii Aevi*, I (1887).

[7] Alexandre de Villedieu, *Doctrinale*, ed. D. Reichling, *Monumenta Germaniae Paedogogica*, XII (1893).

[8] Alexander Neckham, *Corrogationes Promethei*. This work is unpublished, but is known to me primarily from Digby MS 56 in the Bodleian Library.

upon the indulgent and merciful understanding of my master and friend, who has often been called upon to indulge my weaknesses.

University of Pennsylvania
16 November 1965

ADDENDUM

Examination of Brito's sources since the above was written makes it clear that the *fabella* from the *Life* of Aesop was taken by Brito from the *Derivationes* of Huguitio (Uguccione Pisano), a work of the late twelfth century. The following is the text of the pertinent passage as it appears on fol. 204 of Paris MS *Lat. nouv. acq.* 2042, which is dated 1274:

apud Grecos siccofanta, i.e. sicca comedens, a siccos, quod est siccum et fagin, quod est comedere, sed hac dictione siccofanta dicitur falsus calumniator, cuidam enim domino misse sunt ficus quas latenter quidam suus famulus comedit et cepit calumpniari et accusare alium quod eas comedisset. tunc dominus precepit aquam calidam ab eo qui comederat ficus, qua pota statim evomit ficus cum aqua. unde postea semper dictus fuit siccofanta, i.e. ficus comedens, et quia falso calumpniatus est socium comedisse eas, ideo inolevit consuetudo ut sicofanta diceretur falsus calumpniator.

Thus we have evidence of familiarity with the *Life* in north Italy in the late twelfth century.

LUCIANIC NATURAL HISTORY

Jerry Stannard

Interpretations of Lucian are many and diverse, ranging from satirist to moralist, and imaginative romancer to critical historian of his own times. Doubtless he is all of these, and more. While I have no intention of preparing a *catalogue raisonnée* of the many facets of his genius, it is, I believe, time to call attention to one aspect of his work that has been somewhat neglected. Lucian was not a naturalist, still less was he a scientist, but that does not mean that his writings are devoid of interest to the student of ancient science.[1] In calling attention to some passages of scientific interest, I shall try to show how Lucian made use of his knowledge of natural history. It will be suggested, moreover, that despite his readiness to admit to the charge of ψευδολογία some of his observations must be taken seriously.

Lucian's references to natural history are intentionally subordinated to the demands imposed by genre, style, meter, and vocabulary. But when one looks beneath the literary artifices which have constituted a not unimportant part of his enduring appeal, there can be found a wealth of materials relating to and drawn from the world of nature. The entire corpus of Lucian's writings, when looked at in this fashion, indicates that he was a master in the art of utilizing such material in the most effective fashion. They indicate, also, how sensitive he was to details, selecting precisely those which emphasized the matter at hand or pointed a moral in a telling manner. The conclusion that is forced upon a reader attentive to details is that Lucian took pains to be exact.

---

[1] A parallel is provided by a study of the medical references in Lucian by J. D. Rolleston, "Lucian and Medicine," *Janus,* xx (1915), 83-108. Cf. Adolf Braun, "Die Tragopodagra des Lukian," *Münch. med. Wchn.,* Nr. 36 (4 Sept. 1936), pp. 1477-78.

Exactness and fidelity to nature, stemming perhaps from boyhood when he modeled waxen figures of animals (*Somn.* 2), should not, of course, be confused with truth. Lucian's humor greatly depends upon his ability to fabricate and to populate the skies, the waters, and the nether world with bizarre creatures: ὧν μήτε εἶδον μήτε ἔπαθον μήτε παρ' ἄλλων ἐπυθόμην, ἔτι δὲ μήτε ὅλως ὄντων μήτε τὴν ἀρχὴν γενέσθαι δυναμένων (*Ver. Hist.* I. 4). Yet one must take seriously his earlier claim κἂν ἓν γὰρ δὴ τοῦτο ἀληθεύσω λέγων ὅτι ψεύδομαι (*loc. cit.*) No reader is apt to confuse his ἀεροκώνωπες (*Ver. Hist.* I. 16) with real insects or to suppose that the κύων addressed as ὦ βέλτιστε ἰχθύων (*Pisc.* 48) is really a dog fish. But it might be forgotten, momentarily at least, that Lucian's motives entail that *he* should not confuse the real with the imaginary; after all, says Momus, we all know that θεοὺς μὲν τοὺς θεούς, κυνοκεφάλους δὲ τοὺς κυνοκεφάλους (*Deor. Conc.* 11). The success of these fabled creatures lies in their author's tight control upon his fantasies. He exaggerated, but did not lose sight of those objects whose dimensions he playfully stretched, he compounded but without ignoring the structural details of the component pieces and, if he had traffic with legend, it was to smile at those who took it seriously. This was made possible by the fact that he, like his latter-day admirer Rabelais, first looked at Nature and acquainted himself with her uneven hues before he painted her in unseemly colors. To borrow a passage from him to whom this volume is dedicated, one might say of Lucian, as it was said of Chariton, " By being closer to legend [he] is closer to nature and reality." [2]

Much of the natural history contained in Lucian's writings consists in passing allusions to the world about him, πάνθ' ἁπλῶς ὁπόσα τρέφει ζείδωρος ἄρουρα (*Icar.* 12). Mention of the better-known members of the fauna and flora is often accomplished through the agency of analogy and other forms of comparison. Their meaning depends partly upon the reader's ready grasp of the point being expressed and this in turn depends upon Lucian's use of plants and animals which were known to all, e.g. καὶ ἀνεμώνη ῥόδῳ καὶ ἀνθρώπῳ πίθηκος (*Pro Merc. Cond.* 11). But they also depend upon the context and their appropriateness to or within that context.

The false followers of Aristotle, in an extended example of Lucian's art, are first likened to certain unidentified fish, described as ἀκανθώδεις καὶ τὴν ἐπιφάνειαν ἐκτετραχυσμένους. This analogy is realistically reinforced by adding ἐχίνων δυσληπτοτέρους—" harder to grasp than sea urchins " (Pisc. 51). While this is only one of many specimens of Lucian's technique, it demonstrates his ability to put data from the real world to the service of the story teller's art. Since sea urchins were regarded as delicacies and hence known to all, Lucian made his point without unnecessary elaboration.[3] By prolonging the analogy, a less skillful artist might run the risk of boring his audience—certainly an anathema to be avoided by a satirist. Examples could be multipled of Lucian's ability to incorporate those details, and only those details, which further the story without interfering with the plot or the reader's almost intuitive grasp of the situation. Capitalizing on his ability to portray graphically a situation in succinct terms, Lucian did not hesitate to include homely references to matters of common knowledge. The passing remark that a goose runs along the ground in order to gain sufficient momentum for flight (Icar. 10) is an example. There was, in this case, no essential reason to note such a mundane matter. But in doing so, a mood and associated images were invoked, based on Lucian's own observations as well as those of his audience.

It was not Lucian's purpose to describe animal life except as incidental to the descriptions of his fellow men. Not all men, in fact very few, lived the blameless life of Demonax. Some less-than-fatal flaw gave Lucian the opportunity of finding further defects. He was aided in his search by the proclivity of the human species to act like animals. Anacharsis, more bemused than shocked, wonders at the sanity of those athletes who ἐν τῷ πηλῷ συναναφύρονται κυλινδούμενοι ὥσπερ σύες (Anach. 1). Analogy is piled upon analogy in depicting the animal-like behavior of wrestlers: τὰ μέτωπα συναράττουσιν ὥσπερ οἱ κριοί . . . ὥσπερ αἱ ἐγχέλυες ἐκ τῶν χειρῶν διολισθαίνοντες (loc. cit.). Animal traits supply Lucian with a repertory limited only by his knowledge of natural history and the antics of those who may fittingly be so described. Gaping expectation is graphically illustrated by the action of birds ὥσπερ τὴν χελιδόνα προσπετομένην τετριγότες οἱ νεοττοί (Timon 21) while a milling crowd is depicted ὥσπερ ἐπὶ τὴν γλαῦκα τὰ ὄρνεα (Harm. 1).

Enough has been said to demonstrate the appropriateness of Lucian's analogies and comparisons. That they rest upon a fund

[3] For edible sea urchins, cf. Aristotle, Historia Animalium IV. 4, 530b2; V. 12, 544a16-18.

of observational evidence cannot be questioned. It remains to note, however, that information of this sort need not derive solely from personal observation. Lucian himself admits his indebtedness to Homer, Herodotus, and others, including those whose names have been lost through the accidents of history, and those anonymous writings which he may have consulted as sources (e.g., Αἰγύπτιαι βίβλοι, *Philops.* 31). To the Poet, not unnaturally, he most often refers and while he can "laugh at Homer and his nonsense" (ψυχρολογία, *Dial. Mort.* XVI. 5) he is not slow to exploit it. At the outset of *True Stories*, he states that he will avail himself of ψεύσματα as the most suitable means of replying to the monstrous fables and myth-mongering τῶν παλαιῶν ποιητῶν τε καὶ συγγραφέων καὶ φιλοσόφων (*Ver. Hist.* I. 2). This does not mean that the "ancient classics" were valueless for Lucian's purposes. A Celt, surprisingly well-read in Greek literature, describes the persuasive powers of the Trojan leader in flowery (εὐανθῆ) terms. Then, as an afterthought λείρια γὰρ καλεῖται, εἴ γε μέμνημαι, τὰ ἄνθη (*Hercules* 4), referring evidently to the *Iliad* III. 152. But Homer was no more exempt from criticism than was any other writer. Nigrinus' vaunted wisdom eclipsed Homer's sirens, εἴ τινες ἄρα ἐγένοντο, καὶ τὰς ἀηδόνας καὶ τὸν Ὁμήρου λωτόν (*Nigrinus* 3).[4] Liberties were taken with Homer's verse when, with a deft alteration, a comical effect could be produced. Lucian's favorite targets, the sham philosophers, are made more ridiculous by having their grave comments interspersed with mock-heroic and mock-Homeric verses:

Πρόσθε κύων, ὄπιθεν δὲ λέων, μέσση δὲ χίμαιρα.
(*Fug.* 30; cf. *Iliad* VI. 181)

Lucian's parody of the χίμαιρα or she-goat resembles his parodies of other writers whom he read. Herodotus' εἴματα ἀπὸ ξύλων (VII. 65), worn by the Indians and usually identified as cotton garments, are turned into ὑαλίνη μαλθακή—malleable glass (*Ver. Hist.* I. 25).[5] More of Herodotus' fabled creatures will turn up later. Exactly how much Lucian owed to the writings of his predecessors is difficult to determine. A case in point occurs in his *Dipsades*. In half-serious tones he concludes that his motive for writing was one of friendship for an unnamed person, but ταυτὶ οὐ μὰ Δία πρὸς Νίκανδρον τὸν ποιητὴν

---

[4] For the problems involved in identifying the plants of antiquity, cf. Jerry Stannard, "Hippocratic Pharmacology," *Bull. Hist. Med.*, xxxv (1961), 497-518.

[5] Identified as cotton (*Gossypium herbaceum* L.) by Friederich Kanngiesser, "Die Flora des Herodot," *Arch. f. Gesch. d. Naturw. u. d. Techn.*, iii (1910), 88. Cf. Herodotus III. 47 and III. 106.

φιλοτιμούμενος διεξῆλθον (*Dips.* 9). Whether this means that Lucian depended exclusively on Nicander must be left to the industry of the *Quellenforscher*. But there is no doubt that he availed himself of the former's *Theriaca*, as the list of venomous beasts indicates (cf. *Dips.* 3).[6] Occasionally, citations from other writers contain stray bits of natural history and appear to have been chosen advisedly. A verse from Archilochus on the cicada is chosen for a twofold purpose—the proverb itself points to the difficulty Lucian's critic may expect, but secondly, Archilochus' own penchant for invective will supply a precedent in keeping with a version of *la Querelle des Anciens* (*Pseudol.* 1).[7] More strained, perhaps, but none the less ingenious is Lucian's citation of a verse from Pindar concerning ποντίου θηρὸς πετραίου, the cuttlefish, and how it supplies a model for the mimic (*Salt.* 67).[8] That these and other passages testify more to Lucian's reading habits than to field work in natural history can be granted. What must not be overlooked, however, is that Lucian knew enough natural history to turn these passages to his own, original purposes.

Midway between Lucian's knowledge of natural history, based upon observation and everyday experience, and the literary exercises just discussed, stands another literary genre, the proverb. A few words are required on this topic for, as several scholars have shown, rudiments of ancient natural history survived well into the Middle Ages.[9] Frequently they were transmitted by the *exempla* which lightened many a medieval sermon even if they failed to enlighten the devout.

Proverbs, however mechanically they may be used, usually rest upon a factual basis. Even those whose meaning rests upon an inversion of nature, exaggerate but do not obliterate this basis; otherwise such a *cliché* as ὁ νεβρὸς τὸν λέοντα (*Dial. Mort.* VIII. 1) would be pointless. Instances of both types, those with straightforward and those with oblique meanings, occur in Lucian. They tend, moreover, to substantiate the claim regarding Lucian's knowledge of natural history. A miscast proverb is grotesque; yet, in order to illustrate gross stupidity, what could be more economical than

---

[6] All of the creatures mentioned in *Dips.* 3, save the φύσαλος (cf. *Philops.* 12) occur in the *Theriaca*. For their identification, see Nicander, ed. Gow and Scholfield (Cambridge, 1953), pp. 19-23.

[7] Archilochus fr. 143 Bergk[3].

[8] Pindar fr. 208 Turyn; cf. Turyn's notes *ad loc.* for further references.

[9] Cf. G. R. Owst, *Literature and Pulpit in Medieval England,* 2nd ed. (Oxford, 1961), pp. 190-209.

"mute as fish," (*Adv. Indoct.* 16) or "senseless as grasshoppers" (*Jup. Trag.* 31)?[10]

Whether it is analogy, parody, or proverb, Lucian's ability to use them nicely permits at least one generalization: he was alert to any information which had potential value, whatsoever its source or degree of credibility. A telltale example occurs in some questions Zeus casually asked regarding things on earth. He inquired first, said Menippus, "about the price of wheat nowadays in Greece and whether last winter's rainfall was violent and whether the vegetables require more rain" (*Icar.* 24). Mundane questions though these may be, they commanded a widespread interest because they were the common concern of all. We may imagine Lucian, in his rambles about town, alive to the trivia of shopkeepers, sailors, and peasants. κἂν ἰδιώτης ᾖς, he once remarks, ἤτοι σκυτοδέψης ἢ ταριχοπώλης ἢ τέκτων ἢ τραπεζίτης (*Vit. Auct.* 11), that does not preclude the possibility of a vital piece of information. Conversations with farmers, perhaps, lie in back of a series of observations about agricultural practices (*Hesiodus* 7). Lucian's willingness to listen, as well as to speak, gave him access to information which he could later weave into the texture of his compositions. There is, for instance, no awkwardness in putting into a boatman's mouth the rectification of one of the oldest fables of literary ornithology, viz. the harsh fact that swans have equally harsh voices (*Electr.* 5). Discussions with professionals from all walks of life undoubtedly opened Lucian's eyes to superstitions passing all belief (cf. *Philops.* 7).[11] But there were other sources too.

Religious rites, for instance, provided an opportunity for a rudimentary course in comparative anatomy. *On Sacrifices*, diatribe though it may be, contains sufficient material to reconstruct, in part, some of the sacrificial techniques and to identify some of the victims. In addition to the ox, goat, and lamb (*Sacr.* 12), Lucian records the unusual practice of sacrificing a boar (*Syr. Dea* 54) and even a horse (*Luctu* 14).[12] The actual procedure followed by the priest

---

[10] For the ichthyological background of the former proverb, see D'A. W. Thompson, *A Glossary of Greek Fishes* (Oxford, 1947), p. 62 s.v. ῞ΕΛΛΟΨ.

[11] Superstitious beliefs about animals were often transferred to the drugs derived therefrom. For almost exactly contemporary uses, cf. Stannard, "Materia Medica and Philosophic Theory in Aretaeus," *Sudhoffs Archiv f. Gesch. d. Med. u. d. Naturw.*, XLVIII (1964), 27-53.

[12] Whether the sacrifice of a boar is based on idolatrous or Semitic practices is a moot question. Cf. F. S. Bodenheimer, *Animal and Man in Bible Lands* (Leiden: Brill, 1960), p. 212, and *Hori Apollinis Hieroglyphica*, ed. Francesco Sbordone (Napoli: Loffredo, 1948), p. 120.

was to cut the throat, eviscerate the animal, remove the heart and then either burn the carcass (*Sacr.* 13, cf. *Necyom.* 9) or simply bury the animal without removing the entrails (*Sacr.* 15). How much Lucian learned from observing or participating in sacrifices is problematic. But that he had some experience with sacrificial equipment is proved by one of those realistic details necessary to support the superficial persiflage. Mnesitheus is censured by Zeus for failing to live up to his promise of a hecatomb. Instead, he sacrificed a single old cock and " four pieces of frankincense so rotted with mildew (εὐρωτιῶντας) that they failed to burn upon the coals and produced so little smoke that they could not be smelled at all" (*Jup. Trag.* 15). Lucian's word-magic is nowhere better illustrated than in the deft touch by which such a detail, insignificant in itself, spells the difference between a *tableau vivant* and an overworked commonplace. The point, however, is not Lucian's dramatic ability but the fact that he must have known that a mildewed piece of incense was worthless.

One other source deserves mention because its obvious modern parallel has provided similar information for the amateur naturalist. Athletic spectacles and bouts, no doubt, provided more amusement than edification. But when one recollects his own boyhood days and the circus, it is easy to recall that some natural history insinuated itself into the mind, and perhaps the nostrils as well. The craze for horse racing is mentioned several times by Lucian (*Nigrinus* 29, *Timon* 50) and may have provided the basis for his remarks about a horse's gait (*De domo* 10) and whether driving a team is a τέχνη or not (*Paras.* 8). A limited knowledge of horses obtained in this way, and perhaps from a horse-breeder as well (cf. *Timon* 23), will help us to understand why Lucian praised Zeuxis' hippocentaur as realistic. " The Centaur herself," he begins,

is depicted lying on fresh young grass with all the horse part of her on the ground. Her feet are stretched behind her. The human part is slightly raised up on her elbows. Her fore-feet are not now stretched out, as you might expect with one lying on her side; one foot is bent with the hoof drawn under like one who kneels, while the other on the other hand is beginning to straighten and is taking a grip on the ground, as is the case with horses striving to spring up. She holds one of her offspring aloft in her arms, giving it the breast in human fashion; the other she suckles from her mare's teat like an animal. (*Zeuxis* 4, trans. by K. Kilburn, *Lucian,* Loeb Edition, Vol. VI)

Gladiatorial shows must have supplied a further glimpse into the ways of strange or angered animals, but in the one passage where

Lucian describes such a spectacle, he merely states that he saw θηρία κατακοντιζόμενα καὶ ὑπὸ κυνῶν διωκόμενα (*Tox.* 59).

A complete study of those sources from which even a passive bystander might profit would, however, fail to do justice to Lucian's command of natural history. There are, that is, far too many passages that can be explained only by supposing that he actually consulted Nature as the final arbiter.

That *tour-de-force*, the epideictic *Muscae Encomium* is, as the title suggests, devoted to the most improbable of all subjects. The mockery of current rhetorical practices should not disguise the fact that Lucian's description of the fly ranks as one of the finest pieces of descriptive entomology in antiquity. After describing its flight and comparing the peculiar buzzing with the sound produced by other insects, he continues:

Regarding the remainder of the body, her head is lightly connected to the neck and easily turned about, not united as it is in the case of grasshoppers. The eyes are prominent and resemble horn. The thorax (στέρνον) is firm and compact and the legs grow out from the waist (τῇ ἐντομῇ) which is not constricted as it is in wasps. Its abdomen is armored, even as wasps, and resembles a corselet (θώραξ) by its flattened segments and scales. She defends herself, however, not by means of her tail-end, as wasps and bees do, but by her mouth and her proboscis (τῇ προβοσκίδι). As in the case of elephants, she has the means of foraging, seizing and holding fast in virtue of an organ attached at the end, resembling a sucker (κοτυληδόνι). Projecting from it is a tooth by which she bites and drinks blood (for she drinks blood as well as milk) though her bite is not very painful. She has six feet but uses only four in walking, while the two in front are used as hands. You may see her standing on four feet holding in her two hands a piece of food, very much like a person. (*Musc. Enc.* 3) [13]

Quite apart from the purpose behind the encomium, the details could only have been ascertained by a direct, personal examination.

It cannot be doubted that Lucian closely examined various objects. A simple yet effective experiment is recorded when it is noted that a decapitated fly continues to exhibit signs of life, including breathing (*Musc. Enc.* 6). It would be unfair to tax Lucian for failing to recognize this behavior as a reflex phenomenon, yet it is to his credit that he does not go beyond his evidence as Albertus Magnus did, a millennium later, when repeating a similar experiment on a cicada.[14] Another sample of personal in-

---

[13] I have translated Harmon's text (Loeb Library ed., Vol. I, p. 84), as Jacobitz' Teubner text (Vol. III, p. 135) appears to be defective.

[14] Albertus Magnus, *De Animalibus*, XXVI. 14, ed. H. Stadler (Münster, 1920), II, 1585.

spection concerns the habits of the social insects. Well before
Lucian's time, the communal activities of ants had served as a
model for Stoic moralizing.[15] And while Lucian, too, is unable to
resist the temptation, the following description reads as if it derives
from an actual observation. The organized way of life of ants
is introduced by these words: "One ant carries out dung while
another, having seized somewhere a bean skin or a piece of cracked
wheat, is running, bearing it off" (*Icar.* 19). Then, armed with a
ready excuse to animadvert upon the similarities between ants and
humans, he adds, "Doubtless, among them there are, according to
their way of life, builders and demagogues, councilmen, musicians,
and philosophers" (*Icar.* 19). This extrapolation in no wise lessens
our opinion of Lucian's curiosity and visual acuity. While poking
fun at Pythagoras and his notorious taboo against beans, the Pythagorean spokesman attempts to justify the master's *ipse dixit* regarding the divinity of beans.[16] They are, he announces, the generative
principle (τὸ πᾶν γονή), "and if you should open a bean while
it is yet green, you will observe its resemblance to the *membrum
virorum*" (*Vit. Auct.* 6). The structure in question, ἡ φυή, is
probably the hypocotyl of a typical dicotyledonous plant. Its recognition is not surprising in virtue of the important place of legumes
in the ancient diet.[17] Acquaintance with such staples explains other
botanical observations such as the tough integument of the lupine
seed (*Ver. Hist.* I. 14). Finally, but still within the vegetable king-
dom, comes a remarkably prescient hint of things to come. Demonax, always ready with a quick retort, was once asked how much
smoke would result from burning a thousand pounds of wood. The
answer, said he, little realizing the prophetic step he was taking
in plant chemistry, was simple: "Weigh the ashes, the remainder
will be smoke" (*Demonax* 39).[18]

A noteworthy feature of Lucian's natural history consists in the
numerous passages dealing with insects or, more precisely, Arthrop-
oda, for Lucian, like the ancients in general, did not distinguish

[15] Cleanthes fr. 515 ed. H. von Arnim, *Stoicorum Veterum Fragmenta*, I
(Leipzig, 1905), 116.
[16] Cf. Alfred C. Andrews, "The Bean and Indo-European Totemism," *American
Anthropologist*, LI (1949), 274-92.
[17] Cf. Jacques André, *L'alimentation et la cuisine à Rome* (Paris: Klincksieck,
1961), p. 39.
[18] The later history of the subject is treated by L. F. Kebler, "Dr. Francisco
Redi, A Pioneer in Plant Ash Studies," *J. Am. Pharm. Assoc.*, XXVI (1937), 240-44.

the classes Insecta and Arachnida. We have already commented on his description of the fly and the social behavior of ants.

It remains now to call attention to a few other passages pertaining to insects. No other insect, save possibly the bee, is mentioned so often by the Greeks as the τέττιξ or cicada. The frequency of citation is an index of its common occurrence and widespread distribution. For this reason, a large literature could be assembled on its life-habits as seen by the ancients. Lucian adds his share to *tettigologia*, not all of which is accurate, but then Aristotle shared the mistaken belief that the cicada feeds on dew.[19] The majority of Lucian's references pertain to its song which was so appreciated that it gave rise to proverbs and similes and reached a peak in the fad of keeping cicadas imprisoned in little cages (cf. *Bacch.* 7, *Imag.* 13, *Peregr.* 41 etc.).[20] More significant, however, is Lucian's observation on the membranous wing (ὑμενόπτερος), shared alike by grasshoppers (τὰς ἀκρίδας), cicadas, bees, and flies (*Musc. Encom.* 1; *Dips.* 3). Among the laity there has always existed some confusion between the cicada and the grasshopper, yet Lucian is clear enough on the distinction. The flight pattern (πτῆσις) of the fly is " not, as in the case of bats, a smooth, continuous motion of the wings, nor, as in the case of grasshoppers, a bounding spring, nor, as in the case of wasps, a whirring motion, but rather so flexible as to permit her to fly wherever she may wish (*Musc. Encom.* 2). The dozen or so other insect types mentioned by Lucian are of interest chiefly in indicating that no detail was too small or too trivial to warrant a place in his writings (e.g., *Sacr.* 9).

Proverbs referring to insects likewise are cited where the same point could be made, though perhaps not so economically, by describing some aspect of insect life. A minimal knowledge of insects on the part of his audience left Lucian freedom to refer to insects for illustrative purposes. The famous strong man Milo will, like all mortals, reach that time when he will not be able to lift a mosquito (ἐμπίς, *Contempl.* 8). Lynceus' vision is so pene-trating that he can descry a mosquito's nest (*Icar.* 12). In order to understand passages such as these, no especial information is re-quired nor is there any reason for supposing that Lucian was a field entomologist. It is evident, nonetheless, that he had an eye for detail and was capable of using empirical evidence, witness his remark about the dung beetle and its curious habit of " pill-rolling "

---

[19] Aristotle *Hist. An.* IV. 7, 532b14. . . . τῇ δρόσῳ τρέφεται μόνον.

[20] For insects kept in cages, cf. *Anthologia Palatina*, VII. 189-98.

(*Pseudol.* 3). That moths eat woolens (*Saturn.* 21), coleopterous larvae destroy papyrus rolls (*Adv. Indoct.* 1, 17), and weevils infest granaries (*Saturn.* 26) are but some of the pieces of common information that found their way into Lucian's writings. Other passages betray a literary source, though the Indian ants of Herodotus (III. 102) do not deceive Lucian (*Saturn.* 24; cf. *Gallus* 16). On the other hand, he lends support to a belief that persisted, in one form or another, to the time of the famous debate between Pasteur and Pouchet on spontaneous generation. A grim future is predicted for Simon the miser and his hoarded wealth, for μετ' ὀλίγον πάντα ταῦτα καταλιπόντα σίλφην ἢ ἐμπίδα ἢ κυνόμυιαν γενέσθαι (*Gallus* 31). If the belief in the spontaneous generation of insects is only implicit here, it is spelled out elsewhere. Regarding the fly, he writes, " it is not generated in the form just described, but rather as a larva (σκώληξ), either from dead men or animals. Then, in stages, the legs emerge, the wings grow and from a creeping animal comes a flying animal; it becomes pregnant and gives birth to a little larva that is the future fly " (*Musc. Encom.* 4).

Turning from insects to other flying creatures, it may be said that Lucian's ornithology follows much the same pattern as his entomology. His bird-lore, that is, is a blend of popular knowledge and fable, strengthened by observational bits and scraps, to which a dash of the fabulous adds flavor. There is one major difference, however. Lucian's birds are either demonstrably real, and hence capable of identification, or they are fictitious, invented for the purpose at hand. In the latter category a creature such as the γρὺψ ὑπόπτερον θηρίον (*Navig.* 44) may be relegated to myth in the same fashion as Herodotus' φοῖνιξ is dismissed (*Navig.* 44, cf. *Peregr.* 27).

When we turn from the world of fantasy to the real avifauna, we find that Lucian refers to and illustrates his writings with some twenty different species. Not all can be identified to the species rank because such a term as γύψ denotes not only the vulture but several other species as well. The common birds, such as the crow (κορώνη), jackdaw (κολοιός) and raven (κόραξ) account for nearly half of Lucian's references (cf. *Eun.* 8, *Electr.* 5, *Jup. Trag.* 31, *Gallus* 21, etc.).

Other species are cited only once or twice but always in such a manner as to suggest that Lucian knew enough about their appearance or habits to refer to them when they answered to his specific needs. Thrasycles' table manners, προαρπάζων ὥσπερ ἴκτινος τὰ ὄψα

(*Timon* 54) allude to the ferocious grasping habits of the common kite. Lucian's sojourn in Egypt was not without its rewards, for it added to his fund of information. Describing the desolate wastes of Libya, he calls attention to the few animal species capable of withstanding a xerophytic area. The monotony and fear of venomous serpents, scorpions, and the dreaded βούπρηστις is relieved by the ostrich (*Dips.* 2-3). Not only is it hunted for food, but its eggs provide nourishment and utensils alike for the nomadic Garamantes (*Dips.* 7). Egypt was also the home of the sacred ibis, pictured so often in tomb reliefs.[21] The half-human, half-animal Egyptian gods are held up for ridicule in several passages (*Jup. Trag.* 42, *Deor. Conc.* 10). Lucian takes delight in contrasting the anthropomorphic Greek gods with the zoomorphic Egyptian gods and the endless possibilities provided by a belief in human transformations (*Sacr.* 14). In one passage he ceases his raillery long enough to list some gifts sought from Egypt which are sufficiently credible to suppose that Lucian was acquainted with the desiderata: τὰ Νειλῷα ταῦτα ταρίχη τὰ λεπτὰ . . . ἀπ' Αἰγύπτου ἢ μύρον ἀπὸ τοῦ Κανώπου ἢ ἴβιν ἐκ Μέμφιδος (*Navig.* 15).

One could, of course, go on to enumerate all the mammals, fish, and plants, perhaps emboldened by relying on Lucian himself—κόρος οὐδεὶς τῶν καλῶν (*Dips.* 9). But enough has been said, I believe, to support the claim that Lucian knew what he was talking about.

University of Colorado
1 December 1965

---

[21] Cf. Otto Keller, *Die antike Tierwelt* (Leipzig: Engelmann, 1913), II, 198-202.

SOME FALSE FRAGMENTS

Aubrey Diller

Very little ancient Greek literature has perished since the thirteenth century. The Byzantine scholars who revived the study of the classics after the restoration of 1261 bequeathed their interest without intermission to the Greeks of the fourteenth century and the Italians of the fifteenth, and virtually all that they were able to rescue from the ruins of the thirteenth and earlier centuries has been preserved. In the twelfth century Eustathius had some works that have since perished (for example, Arrian's *Bithynica*) and Tzetzes also doubtless had some, although it is often hard to tell what he had. But in the following centuries such cases practically cease. In this light, excerpts and citations of lost ancient literature in the fourteenth century are improbable or, when they do occur, suspect. I wish to illustrate this rule by examining certain geographical excerpts, which sometimes still pass as fragments of lost ancient works.

In Codex Monacensis Graecus 287, a paper manuscript of the fourteenth century containing a large collection of astrological excerpts,[1] there are at the end (fol. 158ʳ-162ʳ) three excerpts entitled as follows: Διηγήματα Κτησία Κνηδίου [sic] περὶ τῶν ἐν τῇ οἰκουμένῃ θαυμάτων :—Διαφόρων ποιητῶν καὶ ἱστορικῶν περὶ τῆς τοῦ Νείλου αὐξήσεως :— ᾿Αρτεμιδάρου [sic] γεωγράφου περὶ τοῦ Νείλου :—

The first excerpt (158ʳ3-160ᵛ9) was printed by D. Hoeschel in his edition of Photius' *Bibliotheca* ([1601], pp. 932a-33b) for comparison with Ctesias in Photius' cap. 72. It was included in some older

---

[1] I. Hardt, *Cat. codd. mss. graec. bibl. regiae Bavaricae* (1806-12), III, pp. 198-210; F. Boll in *Cat. codd. astrol. graec.*, VII (1908), 8-24. There is a complete apograph (presumably) of the Codex Monacensis in Holkham Greek MS 110 (formerly 292) in the Bodleian Library; see S. Weinstock in *Cat. codd. astrol. graec.*, IX, 2 (1953), 65-77, and R. Barbour in *The Bodleian Library Record*, VI (1960), 612. I have a microfilm of Cod. Monac. gr. 287 fol. 158ʳ-162ʳ.

editions of Ctesias, but in the last complete edition C. Müller [2] rightly rejected the whole excerpt as a conflation of Photius' text of Ctesias' *Indica* (Phot. cap. 72, pp. 45a-50a Bekker) with some extraneous bits from other sources. As the excerpt vanishes as a fragment of Ctesias it emerges as a testimonium on the *Bibliotheca*. Now that we have an apparatus of variant readings on Photius' text in the new edition of the *Bibliotheca* [3] it is possible to go further and state that this excerpt was taken from Codex M of the *Bibliotheca* (Marc. gr. 451, s. XII).[4] Since Codex M is known to have been in Thessalonica in the fourteenth century, it looks as if that is where our Codex Monacensis was written. There are other excerpts in other codices taken from M in Thessalonica.[5] Our excerptor is not faithful. He sometimes misread Photius' text, viz. 45a30 τοῦ Βακτρίων καπήλου: τῶν Βακτρίων πυλῶν, 46a30 Αἴτνη, Ζάκυνθος, Νάξος: ἐν Αἴτνῃ καὶ Προύσῃ, 46b41 ποταμόν: πηγή, 47a5 ὀβολούς: κοτύλους, 47a37 σπιθαμή: δάκτυλον. He often interpolates something of his own, such as 46a34 (καὶ μάλα ἡδύς,) ἀλλὰ καὶ τοῦ Φάσιδος ποταμοῦ τὸ ὕδωρ ἐν ἀγγείῳ διαμεῖναν νυχθήμερον οἶνος ἥδιστος γίνεται,[6] and 47b8 (τοῦ ἐνιαυτοῦ) μῆνα ἕνα δηλονότι τὸν αὔγουστον ὅλον.

The largest interpolations, however, are at the beginning and end. Müller (pp. 86 f.) found the source for most of the first interpolation in Ptolemy's *Geography* VII. 2, 21 and 30. The Seres over two hundred years old would be from Strabo XV. 702D, rather than Lucian *Macr.* 5, but no source has been found for the men thirteen

[2] C. Müller, *Ctesiae Cnidii fragmenta*, in one volume with W. Dindorf (ed.), *Herodoti historiarum libri IX* (Paris: Didot, 1844), pp. 86 f., 105.

[3] R. Henry (ed.), *Photius: Bibliothèque*, Paris: Les Belles Lettres, 1959 ff.

[4] Our excerpt approaches M in the following readings: 45a29 οξ', 45b1 προχοαί, 17 χώραις, 25 δύο ἄνδρες, 36 μεῖζον, 46b11 οἱ βόες καὶ οἱ ὄνοι, 25 ἀργύρεα, 47a38 πάντα, 47b24 κυνῶν, 48a1 ἱμάτια φοίνικα, 49a26 ἐφ' δ, 28 πηλῷ, 49b25 πεπωλιωμένας, 29 γινομένων, 37 πάντα τὸν νῶτον, 50a1 εἰδότων. There is only one agreement with Codex A against M: 49b35 ὥστε.

[5] A. Diller, "Photius' *Bibliotheca* in Byzantine literature," *Dumbarton Oaks Papers*, XVI (1962), 389-96, with references to previous studies. I take this occasion to supplement my account of the Byzantine testimonia on the *Bibliotheca*. From I. Ševčenko (*Études sur la polémique entre Théodore Métochite et Nicéphore Choumnos* [*Corpus Bruxellense historiae Byzantinae, Subsidia* III, 1962], p. 172 n. 2) we learn that Theodore Metochites had read *Bibl.* cap. 61 and possibly cap. 265, and that Nicephorus Gregoras, his disciple, excerpted from capp. 190, 242, 250, 276, *et al.* in his notebook in Cod. Palat. gr. 129 fol. 98ʳᵛ, also from cap. 224 on fol. 31ᵛ; see H. Haupt in *Hermes*, XIV (1879), 60, 62. I had already found cap. 224 in a letter of Gregoras. Which of the two codices of the *Bibliotheca* they had remains to be determined, but probably they did not read Photius in Thessalonica.

[6] Compare Hippocr. *aer.* 15, Arr. *peripl.* 8, Procop. II. 30. 25 f.

cubits tall. The last interpolation, inserted just before Photius' concluding remarks, is printed by Müller as fragment 87 (p. 105). It begins with a bit taken from Photius' cap. 250, p. 456a (Agatharchides), but the rest of it is still quite unknown. In spite of Müller's warning, LSJ cite the word κροκόττας from Ctesias, fr. 87. The unknown bits are perplexing, as they do not look like fictions of the excerptor; but in any case they cannot be from Ctesias because they are not in Photius' text of Ctesias and they have nothing to do with India.

The second excerpt, on the floods of the Nile (160ᵛ10-161ᵛ3), was printed by Hardt in his catalogue. It is cited respectfully by E. Honigmann in *RE* xxv (1926), 176, referring to an earlier notice by H. Berger in *RE* iv (1896), 1515, on an unknown author named Asamon cited in this excerpt. Actually the excerpt is from Diodorus I. 37-39, with a single interpolation from PsPlutarch *De plac. philos.* iv. 1, 7 (p. 386 Diels). It agrees with Codex C of Diodorus (Vatic. gr. 130, s. X) in several variant readings.[7] Berger's *Asamon* should be *Nasamon* (Diod. I. 37, p. 64.23); in the manuscript the initial was not supplied in red as intended.

The last excerpt, Artemidorus on the Nile (161ᵛ4-162ʳ12), has been printed several times [8] and has received the most attention. It is perhaps the most problematical of the three. Nevertheless it is taken verbatim in the main from Strabo XVII. 786A-793C, where most of it is attributed to Eratosthenes, not Artemidorus. It cannot be from Artemidorus. It is quite unlikely that both Artemidorus and Strabo followed Eratosthenes' words so closely. Artemidorus' account of the three tributaries of the upper Nile is in Strabo 771A and 821D. It is oriented toward the coast of the Red Sea, whereas Eratosthenes' account is oriented toward the Delta. The excerptor seems to have read 771A and 821D,[9] but he has jumbled the accounts and attributed all to Artemidorus. Unfortunately there are no telltale readings in this excerpt to attach it to any particular manuscript of Strabo.

---

[7] F. Vogel (ed.), *Diodori bibliotheca historica*, i (Lipsiae; Teubner, 1888) 64.2 τρωγλοδυτῶν, 64.5 om. ἐκείνοις, 66.13 om. ἐκ τοῦ Νείλου, 67.14 μετεώρους. There are no agreements with Codex D against C. It is strange that Codex C of Diodorus has, on a guard-leaf, an excerpt from Phot. *Bibl.* cap. 70 taken from Codex A, not M.

[8] Among the fragments of Artemidorus treated by R. Stiehle in *Philologus*, xi (1856), 220-22 (fr. 90), and with a special discussion by W. Ruge, who takes it seriously, in his *Quaestiones Straboniae* (Diss. Lipsiae, 1888), pp. 99-102.

[9] The ἀπόσπασμα of the Astaboras is in 770D; the name Ἀστασόβας is preserved correctly only in 821D. In the printed text προσεισβολοῦσι is a misreading of τρεῖς εἰσβολοῦσι in the manuscript.

None of our excerpts bears scrutiny as a fragment of a lost work. They are all taken from extant sources. They offer nothing new that looks like pure coin. Twice a specific source is proved by textual evidence. The immediate sources are not given, however, but an ulterior ancient author is plucked out of the context and placed in the title. In this there is an element of deception. Moreover, there are interpolations from outside the main source, which do not belong to the author named at all. This is a fraud. The excerptor was probably not a deliberate liar, but his standard of honesty was not rigorous. He has succeeded to some extent in imposing on modern scholars. If he has not deceived them, at least he has given them some trouble. His excerpts are worse than worthless. We should, however, give him some credit for wide reading.

Indiana University
1 December 1965

A DIFFERENCE OF METAPHOR
BETWEEN PROPERTIUS AND OVID

John C. Thibault

"Sunt qui Propertium malint. Ovidius . . . lascivior. . . ." Critical appreciation of the poetry of Propertius and Ovid presumably existed before this brief but famous assessment of their merits by Quintilian (X. 1, 93); nor has it since faltered from the endless task, persuaded, perhaps, that the significance of great literature can never be exhausted, or, at least, that the schoolmaster's laconic judgment needed interpretation. The present exploration of a very limited area of contact between the two elegists—the metaphorical vocabulary and expressions employed by them to describe elegiac inspiration and the elegy—is a small extension of this ancient tradition and is further encouraged because metaphor from antiquity to the present has been considered the touchstone of poetry.[1]

To facilitate matters, the pertinent verses from Ovid and Propertius are listed below and are identified by numbers for subsequent citation in the text. Unless otherwise indicated, all references for Ovid are to his *Amores*. The Oxford text is used for both authors.

PROPERTIUS:

1.	unde meus veniat mollis in ora liber	(II. 1, 2)
2.	sed tempus lustrare aliis Helicona choreis	(II. 10, 1)
3.	nunc aliam citharam me mea Musa docet	(II. 10, 10)
4.	pauperibus sacris vilia tura damus	(II. 10, 24)
5.	sed modo Permessi flumine lavit Amor	(II. 10, 26)
6.	tum capiti sacros patiar pendere corymbos	(II. 30, 39)
7a.	Callimachi Manes et Coi sacra Philitae	(III. 1, 1)

[1] Aristotle (*Poet.* 22. 1459A. 5 ff.) says that a command of metaphor is the mark of genius and the finest of poetic gifts. And Cecil Day-Lewis (*The Poetic Image* [London, 1947], p. 17) maintains that "metaphor remains, the life-principle of poetry, the poet's chief test and glory." The same idea may be found elaborated by other critics and poets.

7b. in vestrum, quaeso, me sinite ire nemus	(III. 1, 2)
7c. primus ego ingredior puro de fonte sacerdos	(III. 1, 3)
7d. Itala per Graios orgia ferre choros	(III. 1, 4)
7e. dicite, quo pariter carmen tenuastis in antro	(III. 1, 5)
7f. quove pede ingressi? quamve bibistis aquam?	(III. 1, 6)
8a. et mecum in curru parvi vectantur Amores	(III. 1, 11)
8b. scriptorumque meas turba secuta rotas	(III. 1, 12)
9. mollia, Pegasides, date vestro serta poetae	(III. 1, 19)
10. mollia sunt parvis prata terenda rotis	(III. 3, 18)
11a. non est ingenii cumba gravanda tui	(III. 3, 22)
11b. alter remus aquas alter tibi radat harenas	(III. 3, 23)
12. contentus niveis semper vectabere cycnis	(III. 3, 39)
13a. talia Calliope, lymphisque a fonte petitis	(III. 3, 51)
13b. ora Philitea nostra rigavit aqua	(III. 3, 52)
14. Musarumque choris implicuisse manus	(III. 5, 20)
15. tota sub exiguo flumine nostra mora est	(III. 9, 36)
16a. mollia tu coeptae fautor cape lora iuventae	(III. 9, 57)
16b. dexteraque immissis da mihi signa rotis	(III. 9, 58)
17a. serta Philiteis certet Romana corymbis	(IV. 6, 3)
17b. et Cyrenaeas urna ministret aquas	(IV. 6, 4)

OVID:

18a. par erat inferior versus; risisse Cupido	(I. 1, 3)
18b. dicitur atque unum surripuisse pedem	(I. 1, 4)
19a. attenuat nervos proximus ille meos	(I. 1, 18)
19b. nec mihi materia est numeris levioribus apta	(I. 1, 19)
20. cingere litorea flaventia tempora myrto	(I. 1, 29)
21. sustineamque coma metuentem frigora myrtum	(I. 15, 37)
22. non estis teneris apta theatra modis	(II. 1, 4)
23a. blanditias, elegosque levis, mea tela, resumpsi	(II. 1, 21)
23b. mollierunt duras lenia verba fores	(II. 1, 22)
24a. venit odoratos Elegia nexa capillos	(III. 1, 7)
24b. et, puto, pes illi longior alter erat	(III. 1, 8)
24c. forma decens, vestis tenuissima, vultus amantis	(III. 1, 9)
24d. et pedibus vitium causa decoris erat	(III. 1, 10)
25a. altera, si memini, limis subrisit ocellis	(III. 1, 33)
25b. fallor, an in dextra myrtea virga fuit	(III. 1, 34)
26. sum levis, et mecum levis est, mea cura, cupido	(III. 1, 41)
27. mota dedit veniam. teneri properentur Amores	(III. 1, 69)
28. aut tenerum dotes carmen habere putat	(III. 8, 2)
29. (nec me deliciae dedecuere meae)	(III. 15, 4)
30. aurea de campo vellite signa meo	(III. 15, 16)
31. inbelles elegi, genialis Musa, valete	(III. 15, 19)
32. quid tibi praecipiam teneros quoque mittere versus	(A. A. II. 273)
33. clauda quod alterno subsidunt carmina versu	(Tr. III. 1, 11)

The figures in the preceding lines are restricted almost entirely to the three or four poems that each poet presents as his apology for writing elegy. A brief examination will show that Propertius employs all but a handful of his metaphors (Nos. 1, 4, 11b) for elegiac inspiration, whereas Ovid has only four symbols in this category (Nos. 20, 21, 25b, 30), the rest signifying elegy. Furthermore, Ovid, who uses metaphorical epithets for elegy in almost half of these citations from his poems, is far freer in this regard than is Propertius with only four (Nos. 1, 9, 10, 16a).

Doubtless, many of these metaphors and epithets are standard, traditional formulas for the elegy and the pentameter, a consideration that makes more remarkable the absence of any repetition between the two poets even in single words; though a synonym does occur—*mollis=tener*—as do similar metaphors. Traditional or not, an analysis of these words and metaphors should lead to some informative conclusions about the attitudes of the two elegists.[2]

The preferred, not to say sole, epithet of Propertius is *mollis* (1, 9, 10, 16a). According to the article in *TLL,* this Propertian word is a standard epithet of love poetry and is synonymous with *amatorius.* In these poems Ovid's nearest approach to this word in such a context occurs when he uses the verb *mollierunt* (23b) in its root-meaning 'to soften.' However, elsewhere in his works [3] he occasionally employs *mollis* in the same way as does Propertius. *Tener,* used four times (22, 27, 28, 32), and *inbelles* (31) are the only synonyms for *mollis* that characterize his poems in the *Amores.* *TLL* indicates that the latter word, like *mollis,* is also equivalent to *amatorius.* Both men concur then in recognizing that elegy is concerned primarily with love. Nevertheless Ovid, unlike Propertius, employs other descriptive words which have the effect of qualifying the nature of elegy's preoccupation with love. Three times *levis* (19b, 23a, 26) is used of elegy in the sense of something light and trivial. Another time Ovid says elegy is *lenis* (23b), that is, *blanda* or characterized by *blanditiis* (*TLL*) and, therefore, aimed at persuading or charming the reader. Again he calls his elegiac Muse *genialis* (31), which can only mean, in relation to elegy, that the poetry she inspires is designed to draw the sexes together in a union that is *hilaris* (*TLL*). Add his descriptions of Cupid laughing as he creates the pentameter (18a, 18b) and of the personified Elegy

[2] To say that the nature of language is to communicate thoughts and emotions is a truism. Nor is it less obvious that the very choice a man makes among words and images communicates information about him.

[3] *Ep. ex Pont.* III. 4, 85 *molles elegi; Tr.* II. 307 *versus mollis; Tr.* II. 349 *mollia carmina.*

whose locks are fragrant (24a), figure shapely (24c), clothing seduc-
tive (24c), with a lover's face (24c) and a flirtatious glance (25a), and
the respective attitudes of the two poets toward their medium becomes clearer. Propertius, on the basis of these epithets, conceives
of elegy as a genre dealing seriously with love, whereas Ovid, while
conceding that love is the theme, views elegy as a form of literature
whose goal is primarily to charm and to amuse others through a
playful treatment of love.

Turning from the epithets to the metaphors, Propertius ordinarily
describes elegy or, more properly, elegiac inspiration, through the
image of water (5, 7c, 7f, 13a, 13b, 17b), and the correspondence
between figure and reality could scarcely be closer. Poetic inspiration is a phenomenon that cleanses and purifies a person's faculties
at the same time that it feeds and restores them, the end product
being poetical expression that surpasses the ordinary level of that
person's creative capacity.[4] But water, surely, is commonly taken to
be a purifying agent as well as a source of life to man.[5] In other
words, Propertius, to judge by the frequency of this metaphor, holds
that elegy is not merely a genre devoted to the serious expression
of love but that it also requires the services of genuine inspiration
for effective and appropriate communication.[6]

The remainder of Propertius' metaphors for elegy reveal a pattern
either consonant with the above analysis or, at least, not inimical
to it. On one occasion he compares elegy to *vilia tura* (4). Elegy is,
then, a sacrifice, but a humble one. Five times Propertius pictures
elegy as some kind of conveyance in which he is being carried along
(8a & b, 10, 11a & b, 12, 16a & b) with little or nothing to say about
where he is going. The relation of these figures to inspiration which
sweeps the poet along so that he is not in full command of himself
is sufficiently clear.[7] In conjunction with the chariot metaphor

---

[4] E. R. Dodds (*The Greeks and the Irrational* [Boston, 1957], pp. 81, 99 f.,
n. 115, and 100 f., n. 120) gives instances of ancient and modern man's conviction
that such are the qualities of poetic inspiration.

[5] Cf. Philip Wheelwright, *Metaphor & Reality* (Bloomington, Ind., 1962), p. 125:
"Water as an archetypal symbol draws its universality of appeal from the combined properties of being a cleansing agent and a sustainer of life. Thereby
water comes to symbolize both purity and new life. . . ." Water, as well as
wine, was a traditional and conventional catalyst of poetic inspiration.

[6] Georg Luck (*The Latin Love Elegy* [London, 1959], p. 124) titles his eighth
chapter "Sacra Facit Vates." As the title implies, the idea is the theme of this
chapter about Propertius in which Luck attempts to demonstrate the poet's
intense preoccupation with the mystery of poetic inspiration.

[7] Whether one looks to Plato's statement that poets know not what they do
(*Apol.* 22c) or whether the revelations of the poets themselves are examined (cf.
n. 4, above), the experience of being swept along by a higher power is customary.

(8a, 16a) occurs the mention of wheels (8b, 10, 16b), another peren-
nial symbol for mankind.[8] When Propertius feels that elegy may be
likened to a meadow (10) or to a cluster of ivy berries (6, 17a) or to
a cithara (3) the notion of refreshment or inspiration seems upper-
most, a reinforcement of the inspiration motif found in his water
symbols. Negatively, there appears to be no contradiction or inconsistency in these metaphors in regard to Propertius' inclination to
see elegy from a subjective viewpoint as a serious and inspired
expression of his experience of love. With the consideration of
these *loci,* Propertius has apparently exhausted his references to
elegy.

Ovid's favorite metaphor for elegy is *myrtus,* which was frequently
used as the material for crowns worn by the participants in a
convivium as a sign of the good cheer and high spirits that marked
their festive gathering. The myrtle crown was also worn in the
lesser triumphal procession called the ovation. Above all, the
myrtle tree was sacred to Venus and stood as her symbol in the
same way that the laurel was Apollo's or the vine Bacchus'. It is
presumably for this sort of context and association that Ovid makes
myrtus his standard symbol of elegiac poetry. For Ovid, consequently, elegy is the delight and enjoyment of love to be shared
with others.

Twice he constructs warlike metaphors, when he portrays elegy
in terms of the golden standards of Venus planted in the field of
his own talent (30), and when he compares his poems to weapons
(23a). But there can be no doubt about the levity of his intentions,
since his poems are the weapons of his serio-comic campaign to win
past the infamous *ianua;* nor will anyone prove so insensible as to
maintain that the warfare waged by Ovid's Venus is other than a
pretty, if commonplace, conceit. Besides, he expressly calls his
elegies *inbelles* (31). All that has been considered so far about
Ovid's words leads to the belief that he was quite objective toward
elegy, looking at it primarily as a witty and clever appeal to others.

There remains from Ovid a group of references to the meter of
elegy whose counterpart is less frequently found in Propertius (III.
1, 8; III. 9, 44), references that do little more than mention metrical

---

[8] According to Wheelwright (pp. 125 f.), "Perhaps the most philosophically
mature of the great archetypal symbols is the Circle, together with its most frequent imagistic concretion the Wheel. . . . In its rotation a wheel has the property that when its axis is at rest the movement of its spokes and rim is perfectly
regular—a property which readily becomes symbolic of the human truth that to
find the quiet center of one's own soul is to produce a more tranquil ordering
of one's experiences and activities."

terms such as *numerus* (I. 1, 27), *pedes* (I. 1, 30), *modus, versus* (I. 1, 17; III. 1, 66), and so must be passed over with only the brief comment that their comparative lack in Propertius and their relatively abundant presence in Ovid suggest that the latter could not help expressing his interest and delight even in the technical aspects of meter: "Carmina laetum sunt opus" (*Tr.* V. 12, 3).

Of greater concern are Ovid's specific references via metaphor to the pentameter, five in number, that characterize this line chiefly as a defect (18b, 19a, 24b, 24d, 33), in one case due to theft (18b), in another due to loss of strength (19a) and in the other three due to physical malformation (24b, 24d, 33). Apparently, Ovid found it impossible to describe the pentameter's origin in any other than this humorous and somewhat negative way. In a meter that is so like the hexameter, but one foot shorter, the poet is to be commended for his fancy and inventiveness, even though it involves the rather grotesque imagery of a beautiful woman made more so by a crippling defect (24b, 24d).

There is, finally, a possibility that Propertius may, once at least, have tried to describe the elegiac couplet (11b). Whether or not he had the couplet in mind, these lines appear susceptible of the interpretation; though the commentators either pass over this verse in silence,[9] perhaps considering it unworthy of attention or too clear for comment; or, if they take note of it, they do so merely to describe it as a stale, trite metaphor.[10]

In this figure the open sea represents epic, the shallows elegy. Or, to look at it another way, the one stands for the hexameter, the other for the elegiac couplet. But it is also possible to understand the oars of III. 3, 23 as representing on the deep side the full stroke of the hexameter, on the shallower side where the oar scrapes the

---

[9] Petrus Burmannus et Laurentius Santenius (*Sex. Aurelii Propertii Elegiarum Libri IV* [Utrecht, 1780], p. 500) treat the textual emendation, but not the content, of the line. J. P. Postgate (*Select Elegies of Propertius* [London, 1885], p. 155) points out merely that the emphasis is on *harenas*. D. R. Shackelton Bailey (*Propertiana* [Cambridge, 1956]) and H. E. Butler and E. A. Barber (*The Elegies of Propertius* [Oxford, 1933]) pass over the verse in silence as does Iuliannus Bonazzi (*Propertius Resartus* [Rome, 1951].

[10] Jo. Antonius Vulpius, *Sex. Aurelii Propertii Libri IV* (Padua, 1754), II, 589 f.; G. A. B. Hertzberg, *Sex. Aurelii Propertii Elegiarum Libri Quattuor* (Halle, 1865), III,[2] 261; Max Rothstein, *Die Elegien des Sextus Propertius* (Berlin, 1898), II, 19; *Sexti Aurelii Propertii Opera Omnia in Usum Delphini*, ed. P. D. Huet (London, 1822), II, 835; these editors explain the line, or its predecessor (Hertzberg), at some length on the grounds that it is a customary, even proverbial, statement of the ancient practice of navigating along a coastline for safety's sake.

sand of the bottom, or of the beach, as the shorter stroke of the pentameter, whether the oarsman strokes both oars simultaneously (the couplet as a whole) or successively (hexameter followed by pentameter).

Had these few lines, in which each poet refers to elegy, been all that survived of their work, they would compel belief that Ovid's manner was, in Quintilian's words, *lascivior* (X. 1, 93), that is, wittier, more playful, more fanciful, aimed at titillating the reader, and they would demand assent to the proposition that for Propertius elegy was somewhat of a struggle, a sacrificial and inspired revelation of self. If these observations should be granted, they may serve in turn as valid premises for the further conclusion that the relative merits of the two elegists should be determined on the basis of criteria that take into account the diverse attitudes and purposes of the poets involved.[11]

University of Missouri
30 November 1965

[11] Cf. L. P. Wilkinson, *Ovid Recalled* (Cambridge, 1955), pp. 439–44; J. P. Sullivan, "Two Problems in Roman Love Elegy," *TAPA*, xcii (1961), 522–37 *passim*.

THE TEXT OF
SERGII DE ARTE GRAMMATICA
IN CODEX REG. LAT. 1587

Chauncey E. Finch

A partially unpublished work entitled *Sergii De Arte Grammatica* is contained in folios 16ᵛ–21ᵛ of Codex Reg. Lat. 1587 (henceforth designated R), copied in a Carolingian hand which can be dated in the early ninth century. The work in question consists of a brief introductory paragraph followed by sections entitled *De Littera, De Syllabis, De Accentu,* and *De Pedibus.*[1] H. Keil included the introductory paragraph of this work and the section *De Littera* in Volume vii of his *Grammatici Latini,*[2] basing his text on a Vienna printed edition which in turn is based on a single manuscript— Codex Vindobonensis 16 (olim Bobiensis), saec. VIII–IX. This material is followed in Keil by short essays entitled *De Accentibus, De Propriis Nominibus,* and *De Nomine,*[3] all to be found in various parts of Codex Vindobonensis 16 and possibly to be attributed to Sergius. The section in Keil called *De Accentibus,* however, is quite different from the portion of R entitled *De Accentu.*

The second sentence of the introductory paragraph of *De Arte Grammatica* is: *Haec his rebus continetur, litteris, syllabis, accenti-*

---

[1] This study is based on a microfilm copy of Reg. Lat. 1587 placed at the disposal of the writer by *The Knights of Columbus Vatican Film Library at Saint Louis University.* The best known among the various items contained in this manuscript is a copy of Cicero's *De Senectute* (folios 66ʳ–80ᵛ) dating from the tenth or eleventh century. This was first published by Atilius Barriera in his Paravian edition of the *De Senectute* in 1921 and has since that time been listed in critical editions with the symbol D.

[2] Henricus Keil, *Grammatici Latini,* vii (Leipzig, 1880; repr. Hildesheim, 1961), 537–39.

[3] Keil, pp. 539–41.

bus, pedibus, VIII partibus orationis, anomalis,[4] *vitiis, figuris, clausulis, metris, etymologia, orthographia, expositione historicorum et poetarum.* Since the first four items mentioned in this list of contents are identical with the items included in R, it seems probable that R has preserved the original text of these portions of the text of the work, whereas the sections added beyond *De Littera* in Keil are miscellaneous materials excerpted from Vindobonensis 16. Incidentally, the section *De Pedibus* in R is obviously incomplete, breaking off in the middle of the topic under discussion and being followed by a work entitled *De Nominibus Pedum* apparently in a different but contemporary hand. This suggests that the portion of *De Arte Grammatica* contained in R was copied from a mutilated manuscript of the work which retained the first three sections and a portion of the fourth intact.

In the preface to the part of *Sergii De Arte Grammatica* published in Volume vii of *Grammatici Latini* Keil made no mention of Codex Reg. Lat. 1587. In the preface to Volume iv of *Grammatici Latini,* however, in a footnote (p. liv) dealing with confusion in manuscripts between the names Servius and Sergius, this editor did take note of the fact that Reg. Lat. 1587 contains a work entitled *Sergii De Arte Grammatica* and went on to quote the first line of the work. In this same note, incidentally, Keil erroneously dated R in the tenth century. There can be no doubt but that the manuscript dates from the early part of the ninth century. The symbol $\dot{t}$ is occasionally used as an abbreviation for *-tur,* while $\overset{2}{t}$ is never used. This ordinarily points to a date before 820.[5] Other indications of a ninth century date are the clubbing of tall strokes, frequent use of open *a,* and *g*'s with both loops open.

The remainder of this paper will be comprised of a collation of the portion of R containing the introduction to *Sergii De Arte Grammatica* and *De Littera* with the printed text of Keil, followed by the full text of the remaining three sections of the work of Sergius contained in R. It will be noted that these three sections agree closely in general content with the corresponding sections of Donatus and his commentators, as would be expected. In the case of *De Syllabis* the verbal resemblances to parts of Servius' *De*

---

[4] On the basis of R the text should be revised to read *anomalia* at this point.

[5] See W. M. Lindsay, *Notae Latinae* (Cambridge, 1915), pp. 376–77, and E. K. Rand, "Prickings in a Manuscript of Orléans," *TAPA,* lxx (1939), 338–39.

Syllaba [6] are quite striking, with the literary examples chosen for purposes of illustration being almost identical in both. The portion of *De Pedibus* in R is little more than an epitome of the corresponding part of the *De Pedibus* of Donatus.[7] On the other hand, the texts ascribed to Sergius in R are quite different from the material published by Keil in Volume IV of *Grammatici Latini* (pp. 475–85) under the title *Sergii De Littera, De Syllaba, De Pedibus, De Accentibus, De Distinctione.*

COLLATION [8]

PAGE 537

Title: *Incipit Sergii De Arte Grammatica*
   1 *est** added before *institutio*   2 *anomalia**   3 *orthografia*

PAGE 538

   1 *de* om. (possibly erased or faded)   4 **DLITTERA**
   5 *eo* om.   *legentibus iter*] *iter legentibus*   *praestet*] *praestat**
  10 *litterae omnes*] *omnes litterae*
  12 *syllabam*   *et** added before *sine quibus*
  14 *sint*] *sunt*   *corripi*] *correpi*
  15 *acer*] *aoer* (corrected by a contemporary second hand)
  16 *cum* om.   *ε*] *ei*   17 *pro o*] *pro y*
  20 *Iuno*] *iono* (corrected by a contemporary second hand)
  21 *digammae*] *digamia*   22 *sed u cum*] *cum vero*   *aliam* om.
  25 *fiet*] *fiat*   25–26 *loco fungitur*] *fungitur loco*
  27 *consonae*] *consonantes**   *sono*] *sonos*   *miscentur*] *miscentes*
  28 *obnixae*] *obnoxiae*
  29 *hae*] *haec*   *vero*] *voro* (corrected by a contemporary second hand)
  31 *inchoant*] *incoant*   32 *nix*] *nox*   34 *quia in*] *quia n in*

PAGE 539

   1 *cygno*] *cizno*   3 *autem* present in R[9]   *g* present in R[10]
   4 *collidatur*] *elidatur*   6 *nam* added before *si*
  10 *admissae*] *admissa* (but with final *a* written over an erasure by a later hand)
  13 *vocales*] *vocalis*   *e*] *f* (twice)   *inchoarent*] *inchoassent*
  14 *respuit*] *respoit* (corrected by a contemporary second hand)

---

6 Keil, *Grammatici Latini*, IV (Leipzig, 1864; repr. Hildesheim, 1961), 423–25.
7 Keil, IV, 369–70.
8 References in the collation are to page and line numbers in the printed text of Keil, *Grammatici Latini*, VII, 537–39. An asterisk following a reading cited from R indicates that this reading should be adopted into the text.
9 *autem* is omitted both by Vindobonensis 16 and the Vienna edition, but is included by Keil.
10 *g* is omitted by Vindobonensis 16 but is included by the Vienna edition and Keil.

DE SYLLABIS [11]

Syllaba proprie [12] dicitur quae coeuntibus litteris procreatur, ut "post." Abusive autem quam facit una vocalis, ut "i." Syllabae ratio a vocali sumit exordium cui consonantes prosunt quae eam secuntur, ut "ars." Quae vero praecedunt in ipsa quidem syllaba vacant, ut "sto," "sedant." Elatae auxiliantur, ut "resto." Syllaba aut brevis est aut longa aut utrique communis. Brevis est ⟨cum⟩ correptam vocalem ⟨habet⟩ et non desinit [13] in duas consonantes vel in unam duplicem vel in "i" inter duas vocales locatam. Longa aut natura est aut positione fit. Natura, vel ex una vocali producta, ut "dos," vel ex dip⟨h⟩thongis, id est duabus vocalibus copulatis, "ae," "oe," "au," "eu," "yi," ut puta "Aeneas," "poena," "aurum," "Eurus," "⟨H⟩arpyia." Positione longa fit cum correptam vocalem duae consonantes quoquo modo sequuntur, ut "ars," "Acrisius," "arma," vel una duplex, ut "pix," "axis," vel una consonans, "i" vel "u," pro consonantibus positae, ut "at Iuno," "at Venus," vel "i" inter duas vocales sicut tractavimus collocata, ut "aio." Verum naturaliter longas et breves deprehendere cupiens hoc habeat fidele conpendium ut a principalibus inchoans et syllabatim per derivationes [14] declinationesque procedens primam et ultimam poeticis confirmare exemplis medias accentu cautus examinet. Nam tonum [15] paenultima [16] tunc habet cum longa est. Cum brevis, non habet ipsa, sed tertia in sermone dumtaxat Latino.[17] Ergo si quaeratur, verbi gratia "orationibus," quibus syllabis constet, dicimus primam longam. Legimus enim "tangere cura potest, oro." Secundam similiter longam quoniam cum dicimus "orator," invenitur paenultima [18] sine accentu. Quartam longam quoniam cum dicimus "orationes," invenitur paenultima [19] cum accentu. Quintam brevem quoniam cum dicimus "orationibus," invenitur paenultima sine accentu. Sextam brevem quoniam dativus et ablativus plurales "bus" syllaba terminati breves probantur, ut "omnibus [20] una quies." Sed de regulis ultimarum plenissime tractavimus in libro suo. Communes syllabae

[11] Sillabis in R (and so in most other cases in which the word is used). In the text that follows, my insertions are marked by angle brackets, without further annotation.
[12] propropriae R.   [13] desinet R.   [14] dirivationes R.
[15] R has tonum. This has been changed to thonum by a second hand.
[16] paene ultima R.   [17] Lotino R.   [18] paene ultima R.
[19] R has paene ultima here and in all the other instances which follow.
[20] The original reading of R appears to have been omnesbus, but this was changed to omnibus by erasure. See Vergil, Geo. IV, 184.

sunt quae brevium longarumque funguntur officio. His parcius est utendum dumtaxat in poemate longiore. Non enim laudem versibus pariunt sed impetrant excusationem. Fiunt autem modis VIII. Primus modus est cum correpta⟨m⟩ vocale⟨m⟩ sequitur subiecta consonantibus liquida. Est enim longa ita, "vasto Cyclopis [21] in antro." [22] Brevis ita, "vastosque ab rupe Cyclopas." [23] Secundus modus est cum correpta vocalis in unam desinit [24] consonantem sequente "h"; est enim longa ita, "terga fatigamus hasta." [25] Brevis ita, "quisquis honos tumuli." [26] Tertius modus est cum correpta⟨m⟩ vocale⟨m⟩ duae consonantes sequuntur quarum prior est "s." [27] Est enim longa ita, "unde spissa coma." [28] Brevis ita, "ponite. spes sibi quisque." [29] Quartus modus est cum brevis syllaba partem terminat orationis. Est enim longa ita, "nam tibi Thymbre caput Evandrius abstulit ensis"; [30] brevis ita, "hoc caput o cives." [31] Quintus modus est cum diphthongum [32] vocalis sequitur. Est enim longa ita, "Musae [33] Aonides." [34] Brevis ita, "insulae Ionio in magno." [35] Sextus modus est cum longa⟨m⟩ vocale⟨m⟩ sequitur alia. Est enim longa ita, "o ego infelix quem tu fugis." [36] Brevis * * * [37] ita, "sub Ilio alto." [38] Septimus modus est cum pronomen "c" [39] littera terminatum vocalis statim subsequitur. Est enim longa ita, "hoc erat alma parens." [40] Brevis ita, "solus hic inflexit [41] sensus." [42] Octavus modus est cum correpta⟨m⟩ vocale⟨m⟩ sequitur "z." Est enim longa ita, "Mezenti ducis exuvias." [43] Brevis ita, "nemorosa Zacynthus." [44] Sed primum modum noster usus retinuit; ceteros antiquitati reliquit sicut licentiam quam sibi in addendis retrahendisque consonantibus adsumit vetustas. Lucretius sic adicit, "nam quid Brittannis caelum differre putamus." [45] Idem sic demit, "an caelum nobis ultro natura coruptum." [46] Sane

[21] clyclopes R.   [22] Vergil, Aen. III. 617.
[23] Aen. III. 647. R has clyclopas.   [24] desinet R.   [25] Aen. IX. 610.
[26] Aen. X. 493.   [27] The reading of R is a.
[28] Cf. Terentianus Maurus 1103 (Keil, VI, 358).   [29] Aen. XI. 309.
[30] Aen. X. 394. R has abtulit.   [31] Aen XII. 572.   [32] dipthongam R.
[33] mose R.   [34] Cf. Servius (Keil, IV, 424, 1. 30).   [35] Aen. III. 211.
[36] Cf. Servius (Keil, IV, 424, 1. 33), who gives only the first three words of the quotation.
[37] It appears that est has been erased.   [38] Aen. V. 261.
[39] R has e for c.   [40] Aen. II. 664.   [41] infilix R.   [42] Aen. IV. 22.
[43] Aen. XI. 7.   [44] Aen. III. 270. R has zacintus.
[45] Lucretius VI. 1106. R has brittanis and putatis for putamus.
[46] Lucretius VI. 1135. R has ultra for ultro and corrupit for coruptum. Also in R the first a of natura is by a later hand. The significance of the texts of the two lines of Lucretius quoted here has been discussed by the author elsewhere (see now, CP, LXII [1967], 261-62).

propriis [47] nominibus pro necessitate frequenter abutimur.[48] Hinc est enim "quam magnus Orion" et "circumspicit Oriona." [49]

DE ACCENTU

Accentus est unius [50] cuiusque verbi moderator. Sonus hic gravis dicitur si minus viget; acutus, si celeriter promitur; circumflexus, si moram requirit. Sed acutus et circumflexus simul esse non possunt. Gravis utriusque consortium non refutat. Acutus in Latino sermone paenultimum [51] et antepaenultimum [52] possidet locum; circumflexus autem paenultimum [53] tantum. Monosyllaba est pars orationis. Sive brevis ut "nec," sive longa positione ut "ars," acuetur. Si vero naturaliter longa fuerit, circumflectetur ut "dos." In disyllabis uno modo circumflectitur: si et ⟨prior⟩ ipsa naturaliter longa fuerit et ultima naturaliter brevis ut "musa." Ceterum si ambae sint naturaliter longae ut "leges," sive ambae positione ut "princeps," sive prior sola ut "arma," sive postrema ut "amans," sive ambae breves ut "bonus," [54] omni modo acuimus priorem. In trisyllabis et quamvis deinceps syllabarum verbis ratio similis invenitur: ideo quod ultra tertiam a fine syllabam non ascendit accentus. Igitur antepaenultima duobus modis acutum habebit accentum: vel cum paenultima brevis est ut "Romulus" vel cum positione longa invenitur ex muta et liquida ut "tenebrae." Paenultima vero ipsa duobus modis acuetur: cum vel solida positione fit longa ut "Metellus" vel naturaliter longam postrema longa comitatur ut "Aeneas." Circumflexum vero sortietur accentum cum et ipsa naturaliter longa est et ultima naturaliter brevis ut "amicus." In Latino sermone ultima syllaba nescit accentum nisi cum discretionis aut pronuntiationis aut correptionis [55] necessitas cogit. Est [56] enim "poné" [57] ut adverbium sit, non verbum. Est "ergó" ut causam significet, non coniunctionem, et "quaré" vel "undé" ut ratiocinantes fiant, non interrogantes. Novissimae syllabae propter discre-

[47] *pripriis* R.
[48] The original reading of R was *abutitur,* but this seems to have been changed to *abutimur* by the first hand.
[49] *orona* R. The quotations are from *Aen.* X. 763 and III. 517.
[50] *uni* R.   [51] *paene ultimum* R.
[52] *ante paene ultimum* R. Final *e* of *paene* was written over an erasure by a later hand.
[53] *paene ultimum* R.   [54] *bonos* R.
[55] *correptiones* in R, but corrected by a later hand.   [56] *et* R.
[57] I have added accent in this instance and in the instances which follow.

tionem relidimus [58] accentum. Item cum interveniunt "que," "ve," "ce," "pse," "ne," omni modo in novissimam syllabam quam sequuntur istae particulae transferemus accentum pronuntiationis intuitu ut "virumque," "subiectisve," "huiusce," "eapse," "tantane." Syllaba etiam quae per corruptionem ex paenultima ultima facta est ipsa possidebit accentum ut "tanton" pro "tantone," "credin" pro "credisne," "adduc" pro "adduce," "edic" pro "edice." Nec interiectionibus insolitum est accentus ultimis syllabis dare more Graeco unde originem ducunt ut "papae," "attat," "hui," et his similia. Verba Graeca suis accentibus proferemus cum vel integra sunt ut "Helene" vel suo more flectuntur ut "Didus." Cum vero transeunt in nostras declinationes et aliquid de his vel inmutatur vel dimittitur, Latinos sortientur accentus ut "Helenae," "Didonis." In nominibus barbaris vel peregrinis [59] licet facili venia peccetur, tamen [60] ad rationem syllabarum melius dirigentur accentus. Dicimus igitur "acinaces," [61] "framea," "sarisa," "gaza," "magalia," "tucceta," et similia. Unumquodque [62] nomen uno regitur accentu, licet ex duobus sermonibus copuletur [63] ut "malefidus," "antetulit." Accentuum notae sunt quibus distincta [64] pronuntiatio gubernatur. Acutum significat accentum apex oblique in dexteram surgens; gravem, apex oblique in dexteram vergens; circumflexum, linea desuper circulata. Longam syllabam docet linea [65] aequaliter iacens; brevem, linea sinuata. ⟨H⟩yphen est linea subiecta versui qua simul promenda iunguntur ut "nocticola." [66] Diastole, apex ad imam litteram circumactus quo male cohaerentia dividuntur ut "laevas caetra tegit." [67] Apostrophus,[68] apex ad summam littera⟨m⟩ circumactus quo significatur detracta littera ut "tanton me crimine dignum." [69] Punctum est quo [70] discernitur sensus. Hoc, si ad mediam litteram conlocatur,[71] significat adhuc multa membra superesse lecturo ut "iam validam Ilionei navem." [72] Si ad imam, vicinum ammonet finem ut "et qua grandaevus Aletes." [73] Si ad summam, completam docet esse sententiam ut "vicit hiems." [74]

---

[58] *relidemus* R.   [59] *peregrinus* R.   [60] *tanem* R.
[61] *achinacis* R.   [62] *unumquotque* R.   [63] *coculetur* R.
[64] Final *a* of *distincta* was written over an erasure by a later hand.
[65] *linea* has been written over an erasure by a later hand.
[66] *nocticula* R.   [67] *Aen.* VII. 732. The text in R is *leva sceptra tegit*.
[68] *apostrofus* R.   [69] *Aen.* X. 668.   [70] *quod* R.   [71] *conlocetur* R.
[72] *Aen.* I. 120. R has *ilioni* for *Ilionei*.   [73] *Aen.* I. 121.
[74] *Aen.* I. 122. R has *hiens*.

DE PEDIBUS

Universi pedes centum viginti et IIII colliguntur. Disyllabi enim sunt IIII; trisyllabi, VIII; tetrasyllabi, XVI; pentasyllabi, XXXII; hexasyllabi,[75] LXIIII. Sed licet omnes erudita frequenter antiquitas ⟨notet⟩, nos tamen priorum XXVIII nomina et exempla referimus. Ceteris commune synzugiarum [76] nomen inponimus. Igitur disyllabi IIII hi [77] sunt: pyrrichius [78] ex duabus brevibus ut "fuga"; spondeus ex duabus longis ut "aestas"; iambus ex brevi et longa ut "parens"; trochaeus ex longa et brevi ut "meta." Trisyllabi VIII hi sunt: tribrachys [79] ex tribus brevibus ut "macula"; molossus [80] ex tribus longis ut "Aeneas"; anapaestus ex duabus brevibus et longa ut "Erato"; dactylus [81] ex longa et duabus brevibus ut "Maenalus"; amphibrachys [82] ex brevi et longa et brevi ut "carina"; amphimacrus [83] ex longa ⟨et⟩ brevi et longa ut "insulae"; bacchius ex [84] brevi et duabus longis . . . ut "natura." [85] Tetrasyllabi [86] XVI hi sunt: proceleumaticus ex IIII brevibus ut "avicula"; dispondeus [87] ex IIII longis ut "oratores."

Saint Louis University
3 December 1965

---

[75] *exasillabi* R.   [76] *synzygiarum* R.
[77] *hii* R.   [78] *phyrritius* R.   [79] *tribrachus* R.   [80] *mollosus* R.
[81] *dactulus* R.   [82] *amfibrachus* R.   [83] *amfimacrus* R.
[84] *ex* has been written twice in R.
[85] From a comparison with Donatus (Keil, IV, 370, l. 5–7), it becomes clear that a line has dropped out of the text of R which must have read *ut "Achates"; antibacchius ex duabus longis et brevi.*
[86] *tetrasillabis* R.   [87] *dispondius* R.

THE DEVELOPMENT OF ERASMUS' VIEWS ON THE CORRECT PRONUNCIATION OF LATIN AND GREEK

John J. Bateman

In March 1528 Erasmus published in a single volume his *Dialogue on the Correct Pronunciation of the Latin and Greek Languages* and his *Ciceronianus*, subtitled, *On the Best Kind of Speaking*.[1] The *Ciceronianus* immediately aroused a furor which was not to die away for a generation; the Dialogue on pronunciation was received, to Erasmus' chagrin, with silent indifference.[2] The *Ciceronianus* with its sharp attack on certain trends in contemporary Italian humanism and its criticisms of contemporary Latin stylists touched many a tender nerve. How one wrote Latin was a matter of intense personal concern and prestige; how one pronounced it hardly seemed to matter, unless perhaps one was a Dutchman whose uncouth accent provoked derision in cultivated Italians. And yet for Erasmus who twice had these two dialogues printed side by side, the way one spoke was something which could not be separated from the way one wrote, and both in turn from the way one lived.[3]

---

[1] *De Recta Latini Graecique Sermonis Pronuntiatione Des. Erasmi Roterodami Dialogus. || Eiusdem Dialogus cui Titulus, Ciceronianus, siue, De Optimo Genere Dicendi* (Basel: Froben, 1528). The former will be referred to as *Drp*. The Leyden edition of 1703-1706 in 10 volumes, identified as LB, will be cited for this and other works of Erasmus except the letters, which are cited from P. S. Allen's edition in 11 volumes (Oxford, 1906-1947), identified as OE.

[2] OE, VIII, 2088, 1-8. Erasmus also wrote two poems on barbarism about this time, Nos. 14 and 15 in Reedijk's edition. Cf. Rudolf Pfeiffer, "Die Wandlungen der 'Antibarbari,'" *Ausgewählte Schriften* (Munich, 1960), pp. 190-93 and 198-207.

[3] I take with a grain of salt Erasmus' statement to John Vlatten that it was the printers who kept the two works from being published separately (OE VII, 1975, 2 f.). See the remark in *Drp*, LB, I, 924D: "Scripturam enim ineptam eadem sequuntur incommoda, quae malam pronunciationem. Vel Ciceronis orationem

Manner or style was not separable from content. To disregard content in favor of style is a disease, Ciceronianism; to pronounce badly is a flaw of the same order as an uncorrected speech defect. Foolish writing and defective pronunciation are alike varieties of the same pestilence and require similar cures.

I should like to explore here not Erasmus' proposed cures for vicious pronunciation or the scholarly value of his reconstruction of the ancient pronunciations, interesting as that might be, but rather the events, feelings, and motives which brought him to write this dialogue and challenge contemporary complacency about pronunciation. What was this disease, this corruption of classical purity, which had to be fought even in such seemingly innocuous areas as style and pronunciation? Erasmus' all-inclusive term for it is *barbaries*.

In a letter to his friend Cornelius Gerard of Gouda which was probably written in June 1489 when Erasmus was in the Augustinian monastery at Steyn, he advances a historical view of the fortunes of the fine arts during the past millennium.[4] Surviving ancient poetry attests the flourishing state of painting, sculpture and the other arts in the classical world. Their products disappeared and were replaced by the clumsy art of the Middle Ages whose rusticity is only too apparent when one compares it to the successful work of contemporary artists. (Erasmus is doubtless thinking of Flemish art, but he does not indicate whether he had any particular artists in mind like Sluter, Jan Van Eyck, Van Der Weyden or Memling). Literature, he says, has had the same history. Eloquence was trampled down by the barbarians and ignorance reigned in the schools where each generation of teachers was worse than the preceding one. The rejection of ancient usage and precept led to the recent popularity of the follies and delusions of the modist grammarians. These new barbarians, completely incapable of uttering a single sentence in good Latin, were bent on destroying literary Latin altogether, had not Lorenzo Valla and Filelfo come to its defense and restored it to life during the past generation.

This view of the course of Latin learning and Latin eloquence, here reinforced by the evidence of the pictorial arts, is later expanded by Erasmus to include the entire cultural, intellectual and

scribe literis Gotticis, soloecam dices ac barbaram." *Scriptura* of course means handwriting and the *Ciceronianus* is concerned with style (*Dicendi*), but the principle is the same.

[4] OE, I, 23, 87-110.

religious history of Europe.[5] Inspired by this vision and the success of the artists and the early Italian humanists, he begins to proclaim the need to return to the sources, the pure fountains of classical Greek and Latin.[6] The next step was to elaborate this aesthetic view into an active movement to "restore" or "renew" contemporary society. In the vanguard of this movement are to be the "humanists," the experts in the classical languages.

In a letter written eleven years later in Paris in 1500 he appeals to a potential patron to support his own special contribution to renewal, an edition of St. Jerome's letters.[7] He speaks in this letter of the "tightest bond of charity" which binds the individual humanists scattered all over the world. He employs the religious language of the day to give an emotional reinforcement to his meaning. The community of scholars (*eruditorum societas*) is something "holy" (*sancta*), where scholar unites with scholar in a sacred pledge. The humanists are sanctified by their common endeavors for "good letters" (*bonae litterae*). This last phrase comprises for Erasmus the whole of literary scholarship. Its substance is the literature of antiquity, both pagan and Judeo-Christian, whose study makes a man spiritually good and free. (How a man does this is set out in the *Enchiridion Militis Christiani*.) Its purpose is not, however, the submergence of the modern man in the ancient world and

[5] In the *Antibarbari*, the first version of which was produced between 1489 and 1495, LB, x, 1695D-96C, 1696E-1700D. Cf. Pfeiffer (above, n. 2), 200-202. Pfeiffer warns against incautiously identifying statements of the interlocutors in the dialogue with Erasmus' personal opinions; nevertheless, since these are two of the passages Erasmus revised and expanded from the 1495 draft, I think we can assume that they represent his own beliefs. The speech of Batt certainly anticipates one element in the *Drp*.

[6] Cf., e.g., *De Ratione Studii*, LB, I, 522A: "verum ex instituto omnis fere rerum scientia a Graecis auctoribus petenda est. Nam unde tandem haurias vel purius, vel citius, vel iucundius quam ab ipsis fontibus?" The imagery of drinking pervades this essay and suggests how Erasmus conceived of the total absorption of ancient literature by the modern reader. The notion of going to the sources, a commonplace with Hellenizing humanists but formulated by Erasmus first with regard to pagan authors, becomes fundamental for Biblical studies; cf. OE, ii, 337, 609-834, 541, 141-45, iii, 858, 134-43, iv, 1183, 35-40. Its meaning here can be seen from OE, ii, 456, 76-82 and 225-54.

[7] OE i, 141. The implications of this letter for understanding Erasmus' attitude toward antiquity are well, though one-sidedly, exposed by Walter Rüegg, *Cicero und der Humanismus* (Zurich, 1946), pp. 72-75. But the best comprehensive study of Erasmus' attitude is still Pfeiffer's "Erasmus und die Einheit der klassischen und der Christlichen Renaissance" (*Ausgewählte Schriften* [Munich, 1960]), pp. 208-21, especially 212-14 and 219 f. For the immediate background and meaning of *eruditio* and its connection with *religio* see E. F. Rice, Jr., *The Renaissance Idea of Wisdom* (Cambridge, Mass., 1958), pp. 149-63 *et passim*.

certainly not the historical reconstruction of the ancient world, but the assimilation of the ancient to the modern and the renewal of the modern through the liberating study of classical, patristic, and Biblical writings. To contribute texts, treatises, exhortation and guidance to this movement is the essential aim of Erasmus' own scholarship.

Humanitas is opposed to *barbaries* as freedom to slavery. Erasmus sees his contemporary world enmeshed in the chains of economic, political, and religious institutions. The essential goodness of human beings has been maimed by the stupidity and ignorance of the barbaric centuries which have intervened between the present and the classical past. The Promethean spirit of the classical pagan can combine with the charity and piety of the Christian to produce a new man such as one might see ideally in St. Jerome in whom were met together *summa eruditio* and *optima religio*. The crust of barbarism which must be broken through includes scholasticism, superstitious ceremonies in religious practice, the moral viciousness and ignorance of the clergy, the brutality and savagery of monarchical power politics, insensate pride in noble rank and class distinctions, the hatreds these distinctions engendered, nationalistic prejudices and ethnic antipathies.[8]

These ideas may seem remote from the question of pronunciation, but they are associated in Erasmus' mind with his general view of contemporary European society. He sees himself as an integral part of this world, for after all he is a Dutchman (*Batavus*), a descendant of the barbarians who were responsible for this society. He was obviously sensitive on this point—not, I mean, his being Dutch in particular (of that he was often and rightly proud) but his being a "barbarian" by birth and a *Latinus* only by virtue of his learning.[9] There are many places in his writings where his irritation on this score breaks out, especially against the Italians who, understandably enough, often thus distinguished themselves from the hated Germans. In this situation he had a kind of mission. In a letter to Cardinal Wolsey in 1519 he asserts that he himself is being surpassed by others in literary studies. It is enough for me, he says, to be praised by being described as one of the number of

[8] Cf. Gerhard Ritter, *Erasmus und der deutsche Humanistenkreis am Oberrhein* (Freiburg, 1937), pp. 11-13.

[9] Cf. Johan Huizinga, "Erasmus über Vaterland und Nationen," *Gedenkschrift zum 400. Todestage der Erasmus von Rotterdam* (Basel, 1936), pp. 38-40 and 47 f.

those who have tried to drive away from Holland the thick-witted barbarism and shameful ineloquence (*infantia*) which Italy has been taunting us with. Later in the Dialogue on pronunciation he several times defends a "barbaric" practice by turning up an ancient precedent for it. Conversely, the pronunciation of the barbarians can be a powerful tool for describing the ancient sounds.[10]

P. S. Allen, in order to illustrate the remark to Wolsey about Italian taunts, cites a sentence from a letter of Aldus Manutius to his patron Alberto Pio, written in October 1499. Aldus is dedicating to Alberto his edition of Thomas Linacre's Latin translation of Proclus' *Sphaera;* he says of Linacre's work:

> Would that Linacre had also given me the Latin translation he is now most diligently working on of Simplicius' commentary on Aristotle's *Physics* and of Alexander's commentary on Aristotle's *Meteora,* so that I might send them to you along with the Proclus. And yet (as I hope) he will some day give me these and other most useful works on philosophy and medicine so that we Italians may accept the good arts speaking learnedly in true Latin from the same Britain from which once upon a time barbarous and unlearned letters journeyed to us and, having occupied Italy, are still in possession of our citadels. Thus with the help of the British we may put barbarism to flight and take back again our own citadels.

Allen's citation is not very apt for the particular passage of Erasmus; nevertheless, it illustrates in Aldus Manutius an attitude of mind and a feeling toward "barbarism" which would strike a sympathetic chord in Erasmus. While the ideals and outlook of the two men were by no means identical, they were sufficiently similar to allow them to work strenuously together for a short while in their common, humanistic fight to banish barbarism from the citadels of learning.

Erasmus' stay in Venice with Aldus from January to December

---

[10] OE III, 967, 46-52. The same subject is touched on in a letter of the same time to Cardinal Albert of Brandenburg, *ibid.* 968, 16-19. *Barbaries* is clearly on Erasmus' mind in the spring of 1519. (He had written his *Apology* to Masson a month or so earlier; cf. n. 17, below.) The seemingly barbaric practice of writing long vowels in Dutch with doubled letters is justified by Quintilian's statement that the Romans down to and beyond the time of Accius did the same thing (*Inst. Orat.* I. 7, 14 f.; *Drp,* LB I, 947c). The distinction of long and short vowels in Dutch and French is used to illustrate vowel length in Greek and Latin, and to show how long vowels could in fact be pronounced differently from short vowels (*Drp,* L.B, I. 946E-47B); see the Appendix ll. 121-45. Augustin Renaudet (*BHR,* XVIII [1956], 190) argues that one motive for the composition of the *Drp* was Erasmus' desire to demonstrate to the Italians his knowledge of prosody, metrics and phonetics, i.e., that he was as good a classical scholar as any Italian. As a personal factor this could be at best only a subsidiary motive.

of 1508 was of signal importance for the business of pronunciation of the ancient languages because it appears probable that Erasmus owes to Aldus the notion and perhaps many of the details of a reformed pronunciation of Greek and Latin.[11] Aldus had been interested in this question for at least the preceding eight years,[12] and seems finally in the winter months of 1507-1508 to have put the finishing touches to a treatise on various points of grammar including the pronunciation of Greek, Latin, and Hebrew. There is no actual evidence that Erasmus read this work though he may well have done so in manuscript. For some reason Aldus never got around to publishing it, and his manuscript apparently disappeared soon after his death in 1515.[13]

References to this treatise, called simply *Fragmenta*, are embedded in various of Aldus' works. They suggest that it contained a fairly complete discussion of pronunciation. Equally important, they suggest that most of his views were correct. He was especially concerned with the questions of vowel length and the enunciation of diphthongs. (It is necessary to remember here that vowel length was not phonemic in Greek or the romance languages at this time, and that the contemporary pronunciation of Greek did not retain a single one of the ancient diphthongs while that of Latin in most areas kept only the diphthong *au*, and not even this one remained in some of the dialectical pronunciations in Italy.) Aldus also devoted some space, it seems, to what we may call remedial pronunciation, that is, to drawing attention to the effects of vernacular sounds on the pronunciation of Latin and to eliminating them from learned speech. These are the aims which will recur in Erasmus' dialogue.

Aldus' motives in pursuing these studies and disputations cannot be recovered. Doubtless there was a strong urge to discover and restore the pristine purity of the classics (occasionally defined by

---

[11] Although this connection was known to Erasmus' contemporaries and in the next century (G. J. Voss and J. R. Wetsten, for example), it seems to have been generally ignored thereafter until pointed out by Ingram Bywater in his lecture, *The Erasmian Pronunciation of Greek and Its Precursors* (London, 1908). Cf. Engelbert Drerup, *Die Schulaussprache des Griechischen* (Paderborn, 1930), I, 48 f. Aldus' views are discussed by Bywater (p. 12 f.) and by Julius Schück, *Aldus Manutius und seine Zeitgenossen in Italien und Deutschland* (Berlin, 1862), 95-97.

[12] The earliest datable statements of Aldus on pronunciation occur in the second edition of his Latin grammar, *Rudimenta Grammatices Latinae Linguae* (Venice: Aldus, 1501), 1 4ʳ.

[13] Drerup (above, n. 11), p. 35.

him as an act of charity), for we can see such a desire at work in his choice of authors to print. In contrast to most other printers of the time Aldus' work is heavily in favor of classical authors. He had also long been interested in purely linguistic problems such as the phonetic features of the different Italian dialects. He writes once of the delight and fascination he took from studying the phonetic and orthographic mutations of the Greek verb. Clearly, Aldus was a born philologist and linguist, and his surviving major writings are grammars of Greek and Latin and studies of classical metrics.

We have the evidence of another member of Aldus' Society of Philhellenes, described by Erasmus at the end of his Dialogue on pronunciation, and a co-worker of Erasmus in Venice in 1508, that Aldus' views on pronunciation were a subject of discussion in that year. Jerome Aleander, who was later to be appointed papal nuncio to the Low Countries and Germany in order to combat Luther, and whose activity in this endeavor was to turn him into a bitter enemy of Erasmus, lived in Venice with Erasmus—in fact, they shared the same bed—, and with Erasmus' encouragement set out for Paris to teach Greek and make a fortune. However, Greek was not so much in demand as he had hoped. Aleander found that he had to start from scratch and build his own curriculum including the preparation of the necessary textbooks. One of the books he wrote is a primer of Greek entitled: *Extremely Useful Tables for Those Eager to Enter by a Shortcut the Shrines of the Greek Muses.*[14] The format of this little work is much like our own traditional schoolbooks. It begins with some instruction on the pronunciation of Greek which Aleander describes after the sound system of contemporary Greek. But he states, rather vehemently, that this pronunciation is erroneous, and he adds that the same is true for the current pronunciation of Latin. There is little doubt that these views derive from Aldus. Aleander, however, having made his point, immediately retracts it and says that we should follow current fashions. He means of course current Italian fashions. Erasmus, writing some sixteen years later, alludes to this remark and pokes fun at it.[15] The contemporary Italian pronunciation of Latin may be better in several respects than

---

[14] *Tabulae sanequam utiles graecarum musarum adyta compendio ingredi cupientibus* (Paris: Gourmont, n. d., probably 1512). This work was reprinted under various titles in France, Germany, and the Low Countries more than a score of times in the next decade. Cf. J. Paquier, *Jerôme Aléandre* (Paris, 1900), pp. 64-83.

[15] *Drp*, LB, I, 965B-E.

the German pronunciation, but after all, he implies, barbarism is barbarism. It prevails in Italy as much as in Germany and must be eradicated everywhere by the restoration of classical standards.

The statements of Aldus and Aleander were spread throughout Europe as their respective writings were reprinted in nearly every major city on the continent north of Spain and west of Russia. Scarcely anyone could go about learning Greek in the years between 1512 and 1528 without also becoming aware that the prescribed pronunciation of the language was different from the ancient and therefore, by an Erasmian definition, barbarous. Even so, few persons would apparently have been bothered by this fact if Erasmus had not lent the weight of his prestige and the power of his erudition and persuasion to a detailed investigation of the subject and had not associated it with his general appeal for social and religious reform.

How did the matter of pronunciation become a part of the attempt to eliminate *infantia?* Erasmus' driving interest in the years immediately after he left Italy in the early autumn of 1509 was the reform to be effected through the divulgation of good letters and the widespread reading and study of the New Testament. Compared to the grand vision of a regenerated Europe which fills Erasmus' mind in 1516 the pronunciation of Latin and Greek seems of little moment. But it is precisely in connection with this vision and the work on the New Testament that the question of pronunciation received the stimulus which was to issue ten years later in the writing of the *Dialogue on the Correct Pronunciation of the Latin and Greek Languages.*

Erasmus' first edition of the New Testament, published by Johann Froben in Basel in 1516, contained the Greek text, an emended version of the Vulgate, and some 400 pages of annotations. The idea for the extensive commentary seems to have first come from his discovery of Lorenzo Valla's hitherto unpublished notes on the New Testament. Erasmus edited and published Valla's work in 1505.[16] He evidently studied them very closely, for many of Valla's notes are the starting point of his own later ones. Such a note is the one on verse 26 in Chapter 14 of St. John's Gospel. The history of the text of this note gives us the evidence for the development of Erasmus' views on the pronunciation of Latin and Greek during the years 1516 to 1526 or 1527.

[16] OE, I, 182.

The verse runs in the Vulgate: "Paraclitus autem Spiritus Sanctus, quem mittet Pater in nomine meo, ille vos docebit omnia . . . ." Valla's note turns mainly on the syntax and the style of the two nominatives, *Paraclitus* and *Spiritus Sanctus*, and the ambiguity of reference in the Latin relative pronoun *quem*. But he tacks on a comment about the customary spelling of *paracletus* in Latin with an *i* in place of the Greek eta or long *e*, and the retention of the Greek accent on the antepenult with the subsequent shortening of the penult syllable. He notes that a similar thing has happened in the words *agapitus* (ἀγάπητος) and *eleison* (ἐλέησον) .

I have given Erasmus' note on this verse in my Appendix. In the 1516 edition it was at first a simple recapitulation of Valla's points. But Erasmus seemingly could not restrain his satirical impulse and expanded the comment on the accentuation of *paracletus* by remarking that those overly scrupulous persons who insist that the sum and substance of Christianity consists in the exact and meticulous utterance of prescribed prayers must consider the matter of pronunciation closely. He goes on to say:

Whenever they pronounce *paraclitus* with the penult syllable short, they cheat God if not of one syllable, certainly of one measure of time. According to the grammatical rule, a long syllable has two measures of time, a short syllable one. No attention should be given to those persons who are forever saying the quantity of a syllable is a small matter. You must consider whom you are cheating rather than how little you are cheating him. Still, to bring some assistance to their cause, insofar as it is permissible, I see that ancient speakers of Latin in borrowing Greek words altered the quantity of syllables to accord with the requirements of the Latin accent; Prudentius who is to be counted among the learned in any century did it in the word *idolum*. On the other hand, what they do in κύριε ἐλέησον is a good deal harsher. They cheat God's ears of two whole syllables in these words, repeated so many times daily, when they make a two-syllable word out of the trisyllabic *kyrie* and a three-syllable word out of *eleeson*. Seeing that this wicked deed is committed perhaps a hundred times every day, if someone were to reckon up the account and figure out the sum for forty or fifty years, I don't see how it would be a sufficient penance if he were to repeat nothing else for a solid year than κύριε ἐλέησον in seven distinct syllables.

It reads like a gibe though there is a serious principle behind it. But as nothing seemed to irritate his opponents and critics more than his mockery, so this note may have come in for criticism, especially because of the implicit attack on canonical prayers, which is one of the points on which his later critics charge him with heresy. I am unable to suggest any specific persons who may have been responsible for this criticism, but they would most likely be connected with the group in the University of Louvain hostile to Erasmus. We can perhaps see echoes of such criticism in Erasmus' reply to Jacques Masson's attack on his beliefs about the linguistic training of theologians.[17] Two passages from the *Apology to Masson's Dialogue on Languages* are especially interesting.[18] In one place Erasmus argues that a proper understanding and correct pronunciation and spelling of the countless Greek loanwords in Latin depend upon one's having a knowledge of Greek. He lists errors which Masson himself made in his work, and asks how we can consider it a matter of indifference how a word is pronounced or written when sometimes the way we write a single syllable changes a word's entire meaning. In the other passage Erasmus considers whether a student of law, mathematics, or medicine should know some Greek, and asks what we are to think of a professor of medicine who says *Therapentica* for *Therapeutica*. He remarks that our barbarism, no matter that it is customary usage, is nonetheless something foul. If one considers the matter in itself, it is as ridiculous to say *Therapentica* for *Therapeutica* as it would be to say *meusa* for *mensa* or *caudela* for *candela*.

[17] Jacques Masson, *De trium linguarum, & Studij Theologici ratione Dialogus* (Antwerp: Hillen, 1519), reprinted by S. Cramer and F. Pijper in *Bibliotheca Reformatoria Neerlandica*, III, 41-84. Masson seems to be attacking primarily Petrus Mosellanus, but he must also have had in mind Erasmus, and Erasmus himself certainly thought so. The details of this controversy and others which revolved around the establishment of Busleyden's *Collegium Trilingue* are set out in Henry de Vocht's *History of the Collegium Trilingue Lovaniense 1517-1550* (Louvain, 1951), I, 298-532. The quarrel with Masson, which began in October 1518, postdates of course the revision of the note on *John* 14:26 which could have been written at the latest during the preceding summer, but was probably written in late 1517 or early 1518. Erasmus was involved in the *Collegium Trilingue* from the start (November 1517). There may have been occasions then, otherwise unrecorded, which led him to reflect on the question of correct pronunciation (cf., e.g., OE, III, 876, 10-17). But there were rumblings on the larger question of the languages even before the publication of the New Testament in 1516. The best documented of these is the conflict with Martin van Dorp; cf. Henry de Vocht, *Monumenta Humanistica Lovaniensia* (Louvain, 1934), pp. 139-78. The views which Dorp expressed in his rebuttal of Erasmus' first reply to him (OE, II, 347) were undoubtedly circulated and kept alive at Louvain in the next few years, especially since Erasmus did not answer them directly. (To some extent Masson continues them.) The subject of correct pronunciation occurs in Dorp's letter in a quotation from Augustine *(Conf.* I. 18), ll. 80-92. Although I would not make too much of this passage, it does raise, obliquely, the real issue.

[18] *Apologia rejiciens quorundam suspiciones ac rumores, natos ex dialogo figurato, qui Jacobo Latomo Sacrae Theologiae Licentiato inscribitur*, LB, IX, 85A f. and 84A f.

It was doubtless considerations of this kind which had already led Erasmus to expand his note on *paracletus* in the second edition of the New Testament, the manuscript of which was finished by May 1518. The tone of the added sentences is no longer mocking; on the contrary, Erasmus gives serious thought to the question of a correct pronunciation. In this new material there is, first, a survey of some of the most obvious mispronunciations of Latin then current in the churches and universities, and next the statement: "After these men were lovingly (!) warned by the experts on this subject, since they could pronounce correctly as readily as they pronounce wrongly, if they persist in their bad habits and, after rejecting and spurning the advice of more learned men, they knowingly continue to err, I don't see how they can be excused from a serious charge." It is evident from the language here and in the rest of the note that the expert and adviser on matters of pronunciation was Erasmus himself. It is noteworthy that all the barbarous mispronunciations mentioned in this note are instances of the phonetic features of different Low German and Dutch dialects imposing themselves on the Latin. The most striking of these examples is *kyrie eleeson* which Erasmus describes as being pronounced [kíːrdzelæ̃jzon]. Since there appear to be no other written statements from Erasmus on pronunciation during the period from 1516 to 1518 (or to 1520), I think we must assume that these views were advanced in oral discussions in and around Louvain. In this regard we should recall the letter to Cardinal Wolsey, cited above, in which Erasmus wrote of his mission to expel barbarism from the Low Countries and Germany. There may also be some substance in the story reported by G. J. Voss as emanating from Rutger Rescius that, while the two men were living together in the Lily in Louvain from September 1518 to October 1520, Erasmus, responding to a joke being played on him by Henricus Glareanus, wrote his Dialogue on pronunciation. While it is clear that the Dialogue as we have it could not have been written at this time, there may have been some document which was later suppressed.[19]

Another attack on Erasmus' Biblical studies, his promotion of classical literature, and indeed his scholarship and integrity itself came from Spain in the form of a detailed critique of his annotations on the New Testament and a defense of the Vulgate by Diego Lopez

---

[19] G. I. Vossius, *Aristarchus sive De Arte Grammatica Libri Septem* (Amsterdam: Johan Blaev, 1662) I. 28, pp. 106 f., reprinted in Bywater (above, n. 11) p. 23 n. 4. Cf. Drerup (above, n. 11) pp. 58-64.

de Zuñiga, or in Latin, Jacobus Lopis Stunica.[20] Stunica was a member of Cardinal Ximenes' new university at Alcalá de Heneres, and had worked actively on the preparation of the Polyglot Bible. Vehement by temperament and orthodox by inclination, he was shocked by Erasmus' critical attitude toward the Vulgate and his philological method of commenting on the text. He wrote to expose what he believed were Erasmus' errors and vainglorious pretensions. But his critique is shot through with abusive attempts to deride and denigrate Erasmus. He calls him over and over a thick-witted Dutchman and a barbarian who writes while sodden with beer. Stunica's attack disturbed Erasmus deeply, and especially the attempt to stigmatize him as a barbaric Dutchman. He saw in this constant reference to his being Dutch a deliberate incitement of ethnic animosities, the very feelings and prejudices which were at that moment rending Europe with religious controversy and outright warfare. Furthermore, Erasmus felt that his own person and life were being caught up in this quarrel, which included the issue of pronunciation.

Erasmus in his note on *Romans* 15:24, where Paul says he is going to Spain (*Hispania* in the Latin text, *Spania* in the Greek), had commented: The Greeks deprive Hispania of the region's first syllable which Spaniards generally add to words of this kind when they say *espero* for *spero, especto* for *specto*. Stunica is outraged by what he takes to be a slur on Spanish accomplishments and treats his reader to a vigorous and lengthy encomium of Spain and Spanish valor, energy, and prosperity, all of which he contrasts to Dutch pusillanimity, sluggishness, and dull-witted barbarity. No small part of Spanish scholarship, he says, is the result of the Spaniards' being descendants of the ancient Greeks and Romans, unlike of course the Dutch. (There is doubtless some political and ethnic hostility latent here because of the Dutch and Germans who came to Spain with Charles V.) Erasmus' reply contains a countering praise of Holland and the Low Countries. But he also defends his note and insists that some Spaniards do in fact pronounce words beginning with *s* with an added *e*. So do some neighboring peoples in France. (He is referring to the Gascons.) Pronunciations of this kind are not peculiar to Spaniards. "Who does not know," he says, "that there are some features of pronunciation peculiar to the common people in practically every region. Thus the French elide their

[20] Cf. OE, IV, 1128 and Appendix XV, pp. 621 f.

s's, the English say *i* for *e*, the Florentines say *chorpus* for *corpus,* other Italians say *laldo* for *laudo."* These peculiarities of pronunciation all spring from the speech habits of the vernaculars. The implication perhaps is that though these pronunciations are barbaric, they are excusable on that score. All of these particular examples recur in the later Dialogue.

There is another kind of mispronunciation which even the learned make, and this is inexcusable. In the note on *Philippians* 1:1, Erasmus remarked that the name *Timothéus* is commonly pronounced with the accent on the penult syllable though its correct position is on the antepenult, *Timótheus.* Stunica attacked this remark as an absurd suggestion for changing traditional practice. Erasmus replies: "Stunica thinks it is irreligious to make any change in traditional practices in the churches. I on the other hand think it a matter of holiness to change many recent innovations [i.e., remove medieval barbarisms], though I myself make no changes but only suggestions. I know of course that in *Paracleta, Idola, Jacobus, Andreas,* and some other words, the Greek accent has been adopted and in some words the quantity too of the syllable has been changed, as Prudentius does in his poetry." Erasmus points out that these pronunciations have no bearing on the pronunciation of *Timotheus.* Anyone, he says, who wants to defend any and every current practice in the churches will be a popular champion in the eyes of the ignorant.

In these few lines aimed at Stunica, issues are adumbrated which are going to appear later in the Dialogue on pronunciation: the effect of the vernaculars on pronunciation, which is tantamount to the barbarization of the classical tongues; the degeneration of language, thought, and religion; the question whether the reform of pronunciation is peripheral or central in the "return to the sources"; and the role of Latin as a unifying element in Christendom, transcending nationalistic barriers. But to trace these ideas as they appear and ramify in Erasmus' thinking and writing in the six and a half years between the publication of the *Apologia ad Jacobum Stunicam* in September 1521 and the publication of the *De recta pronuntiatione* in March 1528 would involve us in a web of statements, hints, and allusions which I have not space to unravel here. Let us return then to the text history of the note on *Paracletus.*

Final form was given to the note in the fourth edition, which was published in March 1527.[21] Erasmus adds a dozen sentences which report virtually the content of the section on pronunciation in the Dialogue. He describes and illustrates the various vocalic sounds of Greek, and suggests ways of differentiating long and short vowels, diphthongs, and accents in both Greek and Latin. He adds also some remarks on the special features of the national pronunciations of these languages. The specificity of this material and its close similarity to the Dialogue lead me to believe that he must have been actively working on the Dialogue or even had already written it as early as the summer of 1526.[22] Of particular importance, however, are the three sentences with which he begins this addition to the note:

Since the elementary school has always been of central concern to the Church, provisions must have been made that children would acquire the genuine and true pronunciation of the Latin language, in view of the fact that the Fathers of the Church decided that the sacred rites were to be conducted in the churches only in Latin. Nowadays negligence in this matter is so great that an Italian does not understand a German when he speaks Latin, nor a German a Frenchman, nor in fact does a person from Low Germany understand the speech of someone from High Germany. To such an extent is the whole of pronunciation taken not from the rules of grammar but from the usage of the common people.

His purpose in bringing these admonitions, he says somewhat later on, is to assist the schoolteachers to bring about a gradual correction in what usage had depraved. In a final plaintive sentence, with his mind no doubt on the Stunicas of this world, he says: "In *paracletus* and *idolum* and similar words they unjustly forgive themselves who are so fierce against others if they should perhaps pronounce anything differently from themselves even though that pronunciation is the correct one."

However, it is not Erasmus' personal feelings, but the mention of the schools and schoolmasters, which is the important item in this addition. For it introduces the last of the operative elements in the Dialogue on pronunciation as we have it. The Dialogue is in fact directed to the schoolmasters of Europe, and the first third of it is a discussion of the social position, training, and educational task of the public school teacher. The setting of the subject of pronun-

---

[21] OE, vi, 1744, 137-39; 1749, 9-14; 1755, 15-17; all written in September 1526. Erasmus had begun work on the fourth edition by July 1524; cf. OE, vi, 1571, 19 and Allen's note.

[22] This would confirm Allen's suspicion, based on the sequence of works in the book, that the *Drp* was written before the *Ciceronianus*, OE, vii, 1959, introd.

ciation realistically in the school program and the joining it closely to the learning of reading and writing give Erasmus' book a direction and thrust wholly different from both earlier and later discussions of this topic. In his *Paraclesis,* which is an exhortation to Bible reading and study, written for the first edition of the New Testament and always reprinted in subsequent editions as well as separately, Erasmus puts the schoolteachers together with the princes and the prelates as the three ruling orders in society to whom the principal task of renewing and expanding Christianity is assigned.[23] Indeed, the schoolteacher, he says in the Dialogue on pronunciation, is in some ways more important to society than the bishop because the persons he works with and upon, the minds and characters of children, are so pliant and obedient to his will (unlike, that is, the recalcitrant adults); these children are the community's hope for the future.[24]

The New Testament appeared in 1516, and the expanded version of the *Method of True Theology* in 1519; these two works are addressed to the clergy and the professors of theology in the universities, and outline the basis for a reform of higher education. The *Education of the Christian Prince* appeared in 1516 with a revised edition in 1518; it is a treatise on political and social reform. Between 1517 and 1524 Erasmus issued the various *Paraphrases* of the individual parts of the New Testament; they are dedicated to prominent bishops and secular rulers and are prefaced by letters urging specific reforms appropriate to the addressee. All of these works agree in their ultimate aim—the renewal of contemporary society—and together constitute Erasmus' appeal to the leaders of his world to reform it.[25] The program of reform is carried on in the works on education which appeared between 1528 and 1531. One could almost say that Erasmus, despairing of success with the mighty, turned to the lowly teachers and from the adult world to the children. But the early statement in the *Paraclesis* on the teacher's role in the great plan makes it likely that even then Erasmus was contemplating a major work on education. The Dialogue on pronunciation is in part the product of this contemplation.

23 LB, v, 141B f.

24 LB, I, 916E.

25 Cf. Augustin Renaudet, *Études Érasmiennes* (Paris, 1939), pp. 65-121; Pierre Mesnard, *L'Essor de la Philosophie Politique au XVIe siècle* (Paris, 1951), pp. 86-140, and his "La Paraclesis d'Erasme," *BHR,* XIII (1951), 26-34, with which compare Jacques Étienne, *Spiritualisme érasmien et théologiens louvanistes* (Louvain, 1956), pp. 18-39.

For it is, as Ingram Bywater correctly described it, "its title notwithstanding, a complete treatise on a liberal education, as Erasmus understood it, the reformed pronunciation of Greek and Latin being only a section—though a considerable one—of the whole." [26]

I have tried to show how it happened that the correct pronunciation of Latin and Greek assumed such an important role in Erasmus' understanding of a liberal education, especially at the primary level. Most of us today would probably consider Erasmus' energy misdirected here.[27] The question of the pronunciation of the classical languages may be, as Bywater says, "one of great philological importance." Had Erasmus thought of it in this way, I very much doubt that he ever would have written his dialogue. He viewed antiquarian and philological researches as pleasant hobbies, but hardly essential to the serious business of living and salvation. On the other hand, if he had not come to see the need for a reformed pronunciation as a necessary first step in the banishment of barbarism and in the reform of future generations, the matter perhaps would not even be of "philological importance" today.

University of Illinois
8 December 1965

APPENDIX

The copy text of this excerpt from the *Annotationes In Novum Testamentum* is the Basel edition of 1527 printed by Johann Froben. The note on *John* 14:26 attains substantially its final form in this edition. I have collated against this text that of the Basel editions printed by the Froben firm in 1516, 1519, 1522, 1535, and 1540, all of which contain or could contain authoritative changes in substantives and accidentals. The results of this collation are reported in the critical apparatuses. Apparatus A gives all variants from the copy text which I have accepted; apparatus B gives the substantive or semisubstantive variants in the texts of the other editions. The second and fourth editions of 1519 and 1527 present considerable additions to the original note as well as some substantive changes in it. Variants in the third edition of 1522 are limited, with two exceptions, to changes in punctuation and spelling which may not all be due to Erasmus. No changes are made after the 1527 edition

---

[26] Bywater, (above, n. 11), 6; cf. also Renaudet (above, n. 10), pp. 190-96.
[27] Cf. Thomas Pyles, "Tempest in a Teapot: Reform in Latin Pronunciation," *Journ. of Engl. Lit. Hist.*, VI (1939), 138-64.

other than corrections and added marginalia. I have changed initial minuscule *u* to *v*, which was not contained in Froben's fonts, in accordance with Erasmus' own orthography. For the same reason I have omitted all the accents on Latin words. On the other hand I have kept the capitalization of proper names which is introduced into the third and fourth editions though Erasmus himself was not likely to have written these words with capitals.

1   Paracletus autem spiritus sanctus.) Duriuscule cohæ-
     rent duo nomina substantiua, præsertim cum prius sit
     masculini generis, posterius neutri, ὁ παράκλητος, et τὸ
     πνεῦμα. Proinde commodius reddidisset ad hunc mo-
5   dum, Cæterum paracletus ille qui est spiritus sanctus,
     quem spiritum missurus est pater in nomine meo, ad-
     duntur enim Græcis utrobique articuli ὁ et τό.   Et
     articulus postpositiuus, quem, Græcis non potest re-
     ferri nisi ad spiritum, est enim ὁ non ὄν. Porro quod
10   accentus huius dictionis paracletus offendit Vallam,
     potest nonnullum iniicere scrupulum quibusdam su-
     perstitiosis verius quam religiosis, qui cardinem, imo
     puppim simul ac proram, quod aiunt, Christianæ
     pietatis in hoc consistere putant, si rite ac legitime
15   persoluerint preces illas quas vocant horarias. Ad
     quod quidem præstandum, cum alia requiruntur in-
     numera, tum illud in primis, vt verba singula plene et
     articulate proferantur. At qui paraclitus penultima   Verba sacra
     correpta sonant, quoties quoties id faciunt, deum si   conuenit et-
                                                                 iam emendate
20   non una syllaba, certe uno fraudant tempore. Quan-   pronunciare.
     doquidem iuxta grammaticorum leges syllabæ longæ
     bina sunt tempora, breui vnicum. Neque vero sunt
     audiendi, qui dicere solent, minuta res est syllabæ
     tempusculum, cum magis spectandum sit, quem
25   fraudes, quam quantulo fraudes. Quanquam vt et
     horum causam nonnihil, quoad licet, adiuuem, video
     veteres Latinos in usurpandis Græcanicis vocibus syl-
     labæ quantitatem, iuxta rationem accentus Latini
     commutasse, id quod in idolo facit Prudentius, vir
30   quouis etiam seculo inter doctos numerandus. Cæ-   Kyrie
     terum illud non paulo durius, quod in κύριε ἐλέησον,   eleeson.
     quæ verba toties quotidie repetunt, diuinas aures dua-
     bus fraudant syllabis, ex domino trisyllabo dissylla-
     bum, et ex miserere quadrupede tripedem reddentes.
35   Iam vero cum id flagitii singulis diebus fortasse cen-
     ties aliquando committatur, si quis rationem sub-
     ducat quadraginta, aut quinquaginta annorum, et in
     summam redigat, non video, satis fore, si quis solidum
     annum nihil aliud iteret quam κύριε ἐλέησον, idque
40   septem distinctis syllabis. Nam par est, opinor, deo

restitui, si quid illum fraudauimus, quandoquidem
sexcentis legibus cauetur, ut homini reponat homo si
vel numulus subtractus fuerit. Etenim si sacrilegium
est, paululum auri tollere de sacro, quanto grauius
45 sacrilegium est, ipsum omnis autorem sacri, re longe
sacratissima fraudare? Iam vero non sacrilegum modo,
verumetiam contumeliosum ac blasphemum videtur,
quod assidue ex Christo, Cristum faciunt, nec alio
vocabulo regem suum compellant, quam quo galeæ
50 aut galli cristas essent compellaturi. An hanc con-
tumeliam laturus sit Christus maximus optimus, si
tam morosus esset, quam ipsi sunt in alios supersti-
tiosi, aut tam iniquus erga homines deus, quam ipsi
iniqui sunt homines in hominem? Non auderes apud
55 regem homuncionem verba faciens, pro Ferdinando
Perdinandum dicere, neque pro Philippo Pilippum, et
non vereris in arcanis illis sacris, ubi nephas est vel
iota deprauare, dicere Cristæ pro Christe. Vt ne quid   Cristæ, pro
interim cauiller de accentu ab ultima perperam in   Christe.
60 primam translato syllabam. Cum tantum habeat ea
res momenti, vt subita metamorphosi ex via facias
cantiunculam, si pro οἶμος pronuncies οἰμὸς, aut ex
portu monile, si pro ὅρμος, ὁρμός, aut ex opulenta ciui-   Quantum
tate pigrum hominem si pro ἄργος dicas, ἀργός. Neque   valeat ac-
65 vero conuenit eos, hæc vt iocosa ridere, qui aliis in   centus.
rebus his aliquanto leuioribus tam Iudaice sunt anxii.
Verum ego quidem istos, ne cui videar durior, lubens
excusarim a culpa duntaxat capitali, quandiu per im-
prudentiam errarunt. Cæterum posteaquam moniti
70 sunt amanter ab iis, qui hisce in rebus sapiunt, cum
eadem opera possint recte pronunciare qua perperam
pronunciarunt, si postea perstiterint in male solitis,
et reiecta spretaque doctiorum admonitione, scientes
iam errare pergant, non video sane quo pacto queant
75 a graui crimine excusari. Neque enim istis suffra-
gabitur similiter errantium turba. Siquidem deus
iudex, vt non corrumpitur, ita nec opprimitur. Iam
vero quid dicendum arbitramur de iis, qui cum plus
quinquaginta annis tam periculose errarint, et errarint
80 non in his solum, admoniti non solum non resipiscunt,
ac monitori gratias agunt, verumetiam Sardonio quo-
dam risu exibilant atque explodunt, pro hoste ducunt
benemerentem, conuitiis insectantur, hæreticum clami-
tant. Et tamen dictu mirum, qui hic tam fortes sunt,
85 quam sint infirmi, aut certe videri velint, in iis quæ
ipsi sibi persuaserunt. Nos superbos vocant, si quid   Superba
tale vel amice per occasionem admoneamus: ipsi   inscitia.
sancti ac modesti sibi videntur, qui malunt in confesso
errore persistere, ne quid ignorasse videantur, ac prius
90 habent fratrem benemerentem vel hæreseos labe asper-

gere, quam suum agnoscere lapsum. Atqui ab istis li-
benter exegerim, si quoties inciderit in canone missæ,
pro pater pronunciaret aliquis phater, pro filium
pilium, num laturi sint? Non opinor. Imo verberibus
95 citius exigerent patrem et filium. Atqui, tolle assue-
tudinem, per se grauius etiam est ex Christo cristam
facere, ex kyrie eleeson, kyrghelayson, et in tam paucis
dictionibus, tot modis peccare, vt plura sint errata
quam syllabæ. Quoniam autem ludus litterarius sem-
100 per ad ecclesiæ curam pertinuit, prouidendum erat et
illud, ut pueri germanam ac veram Latini sermonis
pronunciationem imbiberent, quandoquidem ita visum est patribus vt in templis non nisi Latine pera-
gantur sacra. Nunc huius rei tanta est negligentia, ut
105 Italus Germanum Latine pronunciantem non intelligat, nec Germanus Gallum, imo nec inferioris Germaniæ qui sit, intelligat superioris Germaniæ sermonem. Adeo tota pronunciatio petitur non ex gram-
maticæ regulis, sed ex vulgi consuetudine. Quod idem
110 accidit apud Græcos, apud quos idem sonant, iota,
η, υ, οι, ει, υι. Nec discrimen est inter ο, et ω. Et post
accentum acutum sæpe breuis videtur quæ longa est,
vt ταπείνωσις. Rursus idem accentus sæpe facit videri
longam quæ breuis est, vt θεολόγος. Atqui olim etiam
115 populus exibilabat histrionem, si syllabam longam sal-
tasset breuem. Hæc omnia restituere difficillimum
fuerit, quædam tamen ex vulgata pronunciatione restitui possunt. Apud Gallos adhuc audias diphthongum
οι et αι, ου, et ευ, in fide, facto, fulgure seu puluere
120 et duo. Itidem in lingua nostra, hollandicam dico, in
fœno, tenaci, sene, mendacio. Quin et quantitatis
manifestum habent discrimen, quoties vocalem sequitur consonans. Eam quum volunt significare longam, nec accentus id potest indicare, aut duplicem
125 scribunt vocalem, aut addita vocali scribunt diphthongum. Græci μῦς sonant acutam et breuem, at
Hollandi pronunciant longam et circumflexam, quemadmodum arbitror veteres pronunciasse, quasi diph-
thongo dicant μυῖς. Item quum album dicunt sonant i
130 breue, quum latum, i longum, quum solutum dicunt
sonant o breue et acutum, quum callidum, sonant o
longum et circumflexum. Id imitari facillimum esset
in dictionibus quæ desinunt in consonantem, vt in
καλὸς et καλῶς, vt ω sonetur quasi geminum οο. Hoc dis-
135 crimen obscurius fiet in mediis syllabis, et tamen hic
quoque seruari poterit, vt malum pro improbo, primam habeat acutam et breuem, malum pro pomi genere, eandem habeat longam et circumflexam, quasi
dicas máàlum. Et quemadmodum nos distinguimus ac-
140 centu et productione syllabæ, certum a sapiente, ita dis-

Pronuncia-
tio vitiata
vulgo.

tingui potest latine, vis et lis, a bis. Similiter fex et
lex, a nex. Galli quemadmodum acuunt omnes ulti-   Gallorum
mas, ita et producunt. Iesus bene sonant, sed animus   pronunciatio.
aut Christus non bene. Verum in his labentibus pub-
145 lica omnium consuetudo utcunque patrocinatur. In
hoc tamen admonui, vt litteratores paulatim emen-
dent quod deprauauit usus. In paracletis, idolis, et
similibus inique sibi ignoscunt, qui tam morosi sunt
in alios, si quid forte secus pronunciarint quam ipsi,
150 etiam si id rectius fuerit. Atque hæc obiter admonui,
non meo stomacho consulens, qui ne tantulum quidem alienis erroribus soleam commoueri, sed ipsorum
consulens saluti. Etenim si superbum est, non ferre
male errantem in rebus diuinis, multo superbissimum
155 est, in iisdem non ferre bene monentem. Nunc ad id
quod instituimus sese referat animus, sed si prius
vnum illud admonuerimus, in vocibus Græcis a nobis
receptis, vt simplicius ac facilius est, ita rectius quoque esse, si Latinum sequamur accentum, propterea
160 quod Græcus accentus pro eius linguæ legibus subinde
migret alio, velut ἰάκωβος ἰακώβου. Latinus non item.
Itaque qui nominandi casu sonet parácletus secunda
acuta, recte quidem pronunciet iuxta Græcos, verum
si idem faciat in paterno dandique casu, iam neque
165 Græce pronunciabit, neque Latine.

A: 5 modum, 19; ~. 16; ~: 22   6 meo, 16; ~. adduntur 19; ~. A~ 27
9 referri nisi 19; ~,~ 22   16 praestandum, 16-22   19 deum 16; ~, 22
21 leges 16; ~, 22   26 quoad 16 (quo ad), 19, 40; quod 22-35   27 vocibus 16;
~, 22   33 dissyllabum 16-22, 40; disyllabum 27   37 subducat 16; ~, 19
41 fraudauimus, quandoquidem 19; ~. Q~ 22   42 homo 19; ~, 22   62
cantiunculam 19; canciunculam 22   71 pronunciare 19; ~, 22   73 admoni-
tione 19; ~, 22   78 cum 19; quum 22   81 verum | etiam 19; verum etiam 22
98 errata 19; ~, 22   111 ω. 40; ~, 27   113 ταπείνωσις. 40; ~, 27   149 alios
35; aliis 27   149 quid 35; qui 27   159 Latinum 22; latinum 19, 27

B: Marg. add. 19 *usquead* Superba inscitia, *reliqua add.* 35   7 Et . . . ὄν
add. 19   12 imo 19; et 16   14 putant 19; putent 16   17 tum *add.* 19   23
res est 19; res, 16   34 quadrupedi 16   40 Nam . . . ὁρμός (63) *add.* 19
(Quando 19; Nam 22)   44 paulum 40   49 quam qua 40   63 aut . . . ἀργός
add. 27   66 Verum *ad fin. add.* 19 *excepto* Quoniam (99) . . . bene monentem
(155)   92 missæ *add.* 27   97 eleeson 27; eleison (!) 19   99 Quoniam . . .
monentem (155) *add.* 27   155 Nunc 27; Sed iam 19   162 secunda 22;
prima 19

THE *WANAX*
OF THE MYCENAEAN STATE

George E. Mylonas

Only one major Mycenaean site, Pylos, has yielded numerous tablets inscribed in Linear B Script. Thus far some 65 tablets have been found outside the Citadel and only 8 fragments in the Citadel of Mycenae; [1] none is known to have been found in Tiryns, and from Thebes we have but a handful of fragments. The more one works at Mycenae the more he wonders why we have such a scarcity of "written" documents in a site that seems to have been the greatest political and artistic center in the Mycenaean world.

It is generally assumed that since the great palaces of Mycenae and Tiryns were excavated in an early era of archaeological research, tablets that may have existed were not recognized and were thrown away or destroyed by the excavators. This may be so, but one should remember that the palace of Mycenae was dug by Tsountas, one of the most gifted excavators of his time, shortly before Evans' discoveries at Knossos, and that Schliemann's collaborator at Tiryns was Dörpfeld, whose attention to detail is indicated by his careful plans and observations. How would it have been possible to overlook tablets that are assumed to have existed in numbers when small pieces bearing letters were identified and carefully published? [2] We may assume that the archive rooms of these palaces were not preserved even at the time of the early excavations. At the palace of Pylos, however, tablets were found not only in the archive room, but, in smaller numbers or in isolated examples, in various other parts and sections. We would expect the same to be the case in

---

[1] *The Mycenae Tablets*, II, edited by Emmett L. Bennett, Jr. (Philadelphia, 1958) and *The Mycenae Tablets*, III, ed. by John Chadwick (Philadelphia, 1963. Publications of the American Philosophical Society).

[2] Ch. Tsountas, Μυκῆναι καὶ Μυκηναῖος πολιτισμός (Athens, 1893), pp. 213-16.

other palaces. It is true that only small sections of the palace at Mycenae were left to be excavated in times when the technique had improved considerably and by well-qualified excavators. The late Professor Alan Wace removed the fill below the south end of the Hellenistic temple which covered part of the south corridor and part of the main court of the palace. He cleared the preserved section of the so-called *pithos* room on the summit of the hill where he found, secured on the floor, the bases of *pithoi*. He partially cleared the northwest entrance to the palace and the guardrooms to the northeast of it. He cleared the "pillar room" and the rooms adjacent to the lobby of the southwest grand staircase. In none of these sections of the palace did he find remnants of tablets.

Following Professor Wace's example, we cleared the entire summit of the hill and the terraces on the east slope of the citadel and found here and there small areas of undisturbed fill; we cleared completely the northwest entrance; we revealed the north staircase and the roads leading to it from the Lion Gate and the Postern Gate; in 1962-63 we revealed again a large building on the northwest slope evidently connected with the storage arrangements of the north Cyclopean wall; in 1964 we revealed another large building in the northeast extension of the citadel with areas that then were being dug for the first time; in 1965 we revealed again what seems to be the east wing of the palace serving as the workshop and residence of the artists and craftsmen forming part of the royal household. Nowhere did we find even traces of tablets. It is true that most of the areas we explored had been dug before, but it is equally true that numerous small sections were found which had remained untouched since the destruction of the Mycenaean palace on the Citadel. Lord Taylour found eight fragments embedded in the calcined debris that rolled into the so-called "Citadel House" at some unspecified time.[3] I believe that this almost complete lack of tablets should not be explained away by assuming that they were not recognized in the early excavations, and were subsequently destroyed or thrown away. This may have been their fate, but still their scarcity is puzzling and may be attributed to other reasons.

We may now draw attention, despite the risk we run of drawing criticism as well, to what tradition and fact indicate regarding Pylos and Knossos where so many tablets were found. Tradition states that the rulers of Pylos in Late Helladic III times were foreigners

[3] Lord William Taylour, in *The Mycenae Tablets*, III, 40-41.

who by force established their rule over a native population, having ejected the native ruling class. Nestor's father Neleus established the foreign dynasty in Western Messenia. This tradition is preserved not only in epic poetry, but apparently was kept alive even to the days of Pausanias. For the *periegetes* records the arrival of Neleus in Messenia and adds that the Messenians were induced to give way to Kresphontes and his Dorians "by the suspicion which they felt for their rulers, as the Neleids were originally of Iolkos." [4] It seems that the Dorians took over the land by a political manoeuvre rather than by force.

Again, it is generally believed that during the period in which Linear B Script was in use mainlanders ruled over Knossos; [5] that is, foreigners had imposed by force their authority on the native population. The foreign rulers naturally had to keep a tight control over the economy and the activities of the people they had conquered. Perhaps this will explain why they probed "into the affairs of people in every gradation of society, from the highest officers of the state down to the slave of a manual worker." The impression left by the tablets, as Professor Page states so graphically, is that "not a seed could be sown, not a gram of bronze worked, not a cloth woven, not a goat reared or a hog fattened, without the filing of a form in the Royal Palace." [6]

Similar conditions do not seem to have existed in Mycenae where a refugee prince was asked by the people themselves to take over the office of the king when the native ruler was killed in battle. Nor did they exist in Athens and Thebes where we hear of a long line of native kings. It may be assumed that a tight control over the activities of the people was not established at Mycenae, Tiryns, Thebes, and Athens, and to this may be ascribed the scarcity of documents serving that control, the absence of many tablets. This reasoning, of course, is based on tradition, but it is also based on the scarcity of finds revealed by excavation and it may serve to caution the scholar against generalization based on evidence obtained in only one mainland site. This generalization is usually applied to the political and social systems of the Mycenaean states; as a rule, we forget the basic fact that the information contained

[4] Pausanias, IV. 3, 6-7 (Loeb edition, trans. Jones-Ormerod).

[5] Cf. S. Dow, "The Greeks in the Bronze Age," *XIᵉ Congrès international des sciences historiques* (Stockholm, 1960), pp. 13-16.

[6] Denys L. Page, *History and the Homeric Iliad* (Berkeley, 1959), pp. 180 and 182.

in the tablets is pertinent to the sites in which the tablets were found, that it may or may not be applicable to the entire Mycenaean world.

The evidence thus far unearthed in the mainland of Greece is applicable to Pylos only; but even that evidence is by no means full or even without ambiguities. There are many points in which scholars disagree and about which the tablets found thus far contain no complete data. It is generally accepted, however, that the supreme ruler and sovereign, the head of the Mycenaean state of Pylos was called *wanax*.[7] Some, if not all, of the prerogatives of the *wanax* are given in the tablets. He exercises supreme authority and for his benefit highly detailed accounts are kept; he is represented everywhere by a number of his appointed officials, important or less important, whose duty it was to see that his orders were carried out, that assessments were made, allocations of rations and commodities were fixed, that the obligations, imposed by him, were faithfully complied with. He had artisans in his household and royal servants; he owned land and besides he had a *temenos*.

The tablets do not state whether he was the commander in chief of the army, or the high priest, or the supreme administrator of justice. As far as the army is concerned there seems to have existed an official under the *wanax,* known as the *lawagetas,* who probably was considered as the leader of the army. In a community where military power was a controlling factor, however, the supreme leadership of the army is kept in the hands of the ruler who exercises supreme authority; otherwise his authority could be challenged by the man who has the army under his command. Consequently, we may assume that the *wanax* of Pylos was the Commander in Chief of the army, although a regular commander, the *lawagetas,* was the head of the officers' cadre of the armed forces. For the same reason, we may assume that the *wanax* exercised supreme authority in the administration of justice; here there is no evidence that there existed a special group of dignitaries entrusted with this administration. In fact, there are no tablets concerned with law or legal matters.

It is generally assumed that the *wanax* was also the high priest of his state.[8] This conception stems from the notion that the Minos

[7] M. Ventris and J. Chadwick, *Documents in Mycenaean Greek* (Cambridge, 1959), pp. 120-25; L. R. Palmer, *The Interpretation of Mycenaean Greek Texts* (Oxford, 1963), pp. 83 ff.; Page, pp. 183 ff.

[8] Palmer (pp. 83 and 92) even maintains that he was a sacral king who "would have represented in cult 'the' Young God." Cf. also Lord William Taylour, *The Mycenaeans* (New York, 1964), p. 69.

of Crete is also supposed to be its high priest, and the term priest-king applied both to the Minoan and Mycenaean states has become fashionable.[9] The evidence preserved in the documents indicates definitely that religious matters, even the properties of shrines and gods, were in the hands of priests and priestesses. There is no evidence that the *wanax* exercised any authority over these official representatives of the gods, that he was a " priest-king." Writing before Ventris' monumental achievement, Professor Martin P. Nilsson suggested that " certain sacral functions," performed by the ruler of a Mycenaean state in the sanctuary located in his palace, " were so firmly bound up with him and his title that the latter was not abolished when the kingship was," since " religious scruples forbade its discontinuance," but in later times was bestowed upon a functionary entrusted with the performance of religious rites and services. Thus one of the archons of Athens, charged with the care of sacrifices inherited from old times was known as βασιλεύς. Furthermore, he pointed out that according to Aristotle βασιλεῖς or πρυτάνεις were functionaries with a sacred office.[10] This reasoning, taken to have established as a fact that the Mycenaean chief of state was also its highest religious functionary, does not agree with the information the tablets have furnished.

The official title of the supreme ruler of Pylos and of Knossos in late Mycenaean times, the title of the official who resided in the palace with its shrine, was *wanax*. If the supreme ruler performed in his palace certain sacral functions which were so firmly bound up with his title that in later times the title was bestowed upon the official entrusted with the performance of religious rites and services, as it is assumed, then that official would have been called *archon wanax* and not *archon basileus*. Now we learn that in the Mycenaean age there was an official known as *pa₂-si-re-u*, who may be identified as a *basileus;* but he seems to have been a minor official, the lord of a locality, perhaps the governor of a small district, or even, as Professor Palmer has recently maintained, an "official responsible for royal bronze-smiths." [11] We may even assume that, at the end of the Mycenaean age when central authority seems to have collapsed, the local lord who survived, the *pa₂-si-re-u,* took for him-

9 See the concise thesis of E. Bennett against this notion in Κρητικὰ Χρονικά, 15-16 (1962-63, A), pp. 327-30.

10 Martin P. Nilsson, *The Minoan-Mycenaean Religion*, 2nd ed. (Lund, 1950), pp. 485-87.

11 Palmer (above, n. 7), pp. 227 ff. and 442.

self the prerogatives and duties of the *wanax* including the assumed exercise of religious functions; and that this was remembered at Athens in the historic period. The difficulty in accepting this assumption lies in the fact that the Mycenaean state of Athens was not destroyed; consequently its *wanax,* staying on the Acropolis, was not superseded by a minor official, by a *pa₂-si-re-u.* In short, if the *wanax* were a high priest in the Mycenaean Age he would have continued in that office until the authority of a supreme ruler, both that of the *wanax* and that of the *pa₂-si-re-u,* was abolished. The office therefore would have been remembered from tradition as that of the *archon wanax;* that is not the case and thus the claim based on the dignitary of Athens falls easily.

But it may be pointed out that a shrine is to be found in the palaces of the Mycenaean Age and this gave rise to the assumption that the Mycenaeans believed that their divinities, who occasionally dwelt in these shrines, lived with the *wanax* who was their high priest and was considered divine. The well-known verses in the *Iliad* and the *Odyssey* regarding Athena's relations to Erechtheus would seem to strengthen this notion: Athena placed the mythical king of Athens "in her own rich temple" and to Athens the goddess went and "entered the well-built house of Erechtheus," when she left Alkinous' domain.[12] However, it has often been stated that these verses were interpolations added in Peisistratid days by jealous Athenians who tried to glorify their city whose role in the Trojan War was not so exalted. Moreover, a shrine found in a simple house in the settlement of Asine and another in a house in the site of Berbati would indicate the fallacy of the assumption;[13] because if it were true, we would have to assume that the owners of those houses too, who were not *wanaktes,* were considered hosts of gods and goddesses, high priests, and divine personalities.

It has also been pointed out that temples of the Olympian gods were built over the ruined palaces of Mycenae, Tiryns, and Athens. One wonders, however, whether "the reason why the temples are built upon the ruins of the Mycenaean palaces is the sacred character of the king's palace, which remained always attached to the place through the tenacity of religious tradition," [14] as it is maintained. We have to remember that over the ruins of the palace both

[12] *Iliad* II. 549 and *Odyssey* VII. 81-82 (Loeb editions, trans. A. T. Murray).
[13] Nilsson, pp. 110 and 115.
[14] Nilsson, p. 487.

at Mycenae and in Tiryns small houses were also built in geometric times, used by the descendants of those who survived the catastrophe. It was natural for those people to build the temple of their god in the area in which they had their homes, and that was within the limits of the palace. The fact that temples were built over the palaces of Mycenae and Tiryns does not prove the sacred character of a Mycenaean king's palace nor his sacerdotal eminence.

There is current another notion about the *wanax*. It is assumed that he was considered divine, that he was believed to be the earthly embodiment of the divine *wanax*, of god.[15] This notion is based on the following two considerations:

1. It is based on the title *wanax*. The issue here, however, is not clear. The title *wanax* seems to have been given to a god as well as to the supreme ruler of the state of Pylos and it is not always clear whether the person mentioned in a tablet is the ruler or the god. The choice is left entirely to the reader who may decide in accordance with his preferences and theories. Thus Palmer states that because of its scale the recipient of the offering recorded in tablet Un2 (Ventris-Chadwick, *Documents* No. 97) "is more likely to be divine than the earthly *wanax*."[16] Equally, in the oil tablets the choice is left to the reader.[17] Wherever the earthly *wanax* is definitely indicated, no offerings or acts of worship are connected with him. Palmer, however, cites one tablet (Un 219) in which the *wanax* is closely associated with the goddess Potnia and this association proves, to his satisfaction, the divinity of the Mycenaean ruler.[18] That tablet contains "a list of names in the dative against which are booked commodities of various kinds . . . ; the recipients are both (a) gods and (b) their associates." In lines 7 and 8 of the tablet we read:

wa-na-ka-te TE I *po-ti-ni-ja* [
e-[ra] UI *e-ma-a₂* UI PE [

It is assumed that the *wanax* of the tablet is the earthly *wanax*. In fact there is no evidence to indicate whether the *wanax* of the tablet is a god or the ruler. It is noticeable, however, that this *wanax* is mentioned at the head of a number of well-known divinities: of

---

[15] T. B. L. Webster, *From Mycenae to Homer* (New York, 1959), pp. 11, 22, *et passim,* and in *Companion to Homer* (London, 1962), p. 455; Palmer, (above, n. 7), p. 267.

[16] Palmer, p. 258.

[17] For the oil tablets see Emmett L. Bennett, *The Olive Oil Tablets of Pylos* (suppl., *Minos*, 2, 1958); M. Lang, AJA, LXII (1958) and LXVII (1963); Palmer, pp. 240-45.

[18] Palmer, p. 259.

potinija, of Hera, and of Hermes. The position of honor at the head of the group of divinities such as the ones mentioned must have been occupied by a god, by the divine *wanax* mentioned in so many other documents. Consequently the tablet offers no indication, let alone proof, of an association between the earthly *wanax* and *potinija;* this association was based on subjective and arbitrary notions.

Perhaps here we may add that there is no evidence contained in the tablets to prove the *Wanax*-God was a young god, the son and consort of the Great Goddess.[19] This conception is entirely based on imagination. It has been stated that the title *po-ti-ni-ja* when given without qualification may "refer to the local potnia, who needs no further specification." The same could be maintained for the title *wanax;* it also may refer to a local divinity that "needs no further specification." That divinity may be assumed to have been Poseidon, the most popular god of the Pylian tablets. However that may be, the fact remains that there is no indication in the tablets to prove that the earthly *wanax* was considered as the embodiment of the god. In Mycenaean times perhaps the title indicated only that the right to rule was granted the bearer by the god who was the real *wanax;*[20] it stood for the principle of the divine right to rule explained in the *Iliad* by the story of Agamemnon's scepter.[21]

There can be no doubt that the title was given to a god as well as to the earthly ruler of the state. In a similar manner in epic poetry the title was given to the gods but also to mortal rulers and especially to Agamemnon; and no one could maintain seriously that Agamemnon was considered as the embodiment of a god by the members of the Greek army which marched against Troy.

2. The notion advocating the divinity of the earthly *wanax* is based on the information that the ruler of Pylos had a *temenos.* "The words wanax and temenos suggest that the Mycenaean ruler was divine. . . ." states Professor Webster.[22] In Pylos tablet Er 312 we read

wa-na-ka-te-ro te-me-no
to-so-jo pe-ma WHEAT 30
ra-wa-ke-si-jo te-me-no WHEAT 10
Vacat

[19] Palmer, pp. 83, 249-50; also *Mycenaeans and Minoans* (London, 1961), pp. 123-25 and 232. But see *contra,* Mylonas, *Hesperia,* xxxi (1962), 292-94.

[20] Cf. J. Puhvel in *Minoica* (Berlin, 1958), pp. 327-33.

[21] *Il.* II. 100-108.

[22] In Webster, *A Companion to Homer* (above, n. 15), p. 455. For the balance of this statement see below.

The tablet definitely proves that the *wanax* had a *temenos*. The same tablet, however, informs us that the *lawagetas* also had a *temenos,* though smaller in dimensions; this forced the conclusion that this official too was considered "in some sense divine." This conclusion, however, opens the possibility that a number of personalities are to be considered as divine. For it is generally accepted that only a portion of the tablets produced has been preserved and there is no way of proving that on what was lost more *temenea* were not recorded as belonging to other officials. But in what has been preserved no evidence whatever exists to prove that in Mycenaean times the term *temenos* had a religious connotation exclusively, that it meant more than a slice or cut of land given perhaps to the *wanax* as a royal prerogative and to the one *lawagetas* of Tablet Er 312, as a tribute for special services rendered. Until such evidence from the tablets is disclosed we are justified in maintaining that the term *temenos* means simply a cut of land given to the two officials to enjoy. Yet Webster maintains that the words "wanax and temenos suggest that the Mycenaean ruler was divine, and Homer remembers this when he calls him wanax and gives him a temenos (e.g. Alkinous in ζ, 291)."

There is no evidence in the tablets to justify Webster's assumption; an examination of Homer's statements will lead us to the same conclusion. In epic poetry we find that both gods and men have *temenea.* Zeus had a *temenos* on " the many-fountained Ida, mother of wild beasts," at Gargaros (*Iliad* VIII. 47-48), Demeter at the "flowery" Pyrasos (*Il.* II. 695-96), Spercheios in Phthia (*Il.* XXIII. 148), Aphrodite at Paphos in Kypros (*Odyssey* VIII. 362-63). In three of these *temenea* altars are mentioned, and, of course, all were considered sacred. *Temenea* were given to mortals for two main reasons. The *temenos* in Homeric times seems to have been the prerogative of kingship. Thus the *temenos* Hephaistos placed on the shield of Achilles is called βασιλήϊον (*Il.* XVIII. 550). Alkinous, the king of Phaiakia, had a *temenos* (*Od.* VI. 291); a *temenos* was given to Bellerophon, " to possess and enjoy " when the king of Lykia " gave to him . . . the half of all his kingly honor " (*Il.* VI. 191-92). The words spoken by Achilles over the body of Iphition (*Il.* XX. 389 ff.) seem to indicate that a *temenos* could be inherited, since he calls it πατρώϊον. And perhaps the *temenos* of Sarpedon and Glaukos (*Il.* XII. 313) was πατρώϊον, the *temenos* of their grandfather Bellerophon. In no case does the possession of a *temenos* granted to a king indicate that divine honors were paid to him.

A *temenos*, moreover, was given by the people or was promised to valiant warriors not because they were divine, but because of services rendered or to be rendered. This is clearly indicated by the case of Meleager who was implored by the elders and the best priests of the gods to go forth and defend his compatriots against the Kouretes; if he did so, he would be given μέγα δῶρον, " a great gift, . . . where the plain of lovely Kalydon was fattest, there choose him out a fair *temenos* of fifty acres, . . ." (*Il.* IX. 574 ff.) . This *temenos* was to be given to Meleager not because he was divine or the embodiment of a god, but for services rendered. As a matter of fact, ultimately the *temenos* was not given to him because he refused to listen to the prayers of the elders and of the priests and despite the fact that he went out and fought against the Kouretes when his " spirit was stirred " by the wailing of his " fair-girdled wife."

A second example from epic poetry is equally instructive. In the last phase of the Trojan drama Aineias strides forth against Achilles, who, in regular heroic manner, asked Anchises' son why he had " sallied far forth from the throng " to stand and face him. Is it, he asked, because he hoped to become the king of Ilios or because the Trojans have meted out to him a " *temenos* pre-eminent above all, a fair tract of orchard and of plough-land " that he may possess and enjoy if he should slay Achilles? (*Il.* XX. 184 ff.). That *temenos* would have been given to Aineias not because he was considered divine, but because of services rendered. In a similar manner a *temenos* could have been given to a *lawagetas* for services rendered. One may also stress the fact that a *temenos* could be πατρώϊον, an inherited property acquired by descendants who may or may not have succeeded their parents in the office of the king. The giving of a *temenos* to kings and heroes seems to reflect a Mycenaean custom, but there is no indication that divine honors accompanied the gift either in Mycenaean or in Homeric times.

In epic poetry we find that the title ἄναξ is given to gods and men. Occasionally it is given to some of the leaders of the Greek and Trojan forces; consistently it is given to Agamemnon who is referred to as the ἄναξ ἀνδρῶν.[23] Yet from the *Iliad* it is apparent that he

---

[23] A cursory survey seems to indicate that the title is given to Agamemnon 49 times and very sparsely to other leaders (Menelaos, 2; Diomedes 3; Idomeneus 3; Achilles 4, etc.) either because the meter required it, or in order to flatter them, or to indicate that they were in absolute control of their own contingent (cf. *Od.* I. 392 ff.). Of the Trojans, Priam is called "wanax" 8 times, Sarpedon 3, Aineias 1. Professor Page (p. 188), citing Finley, points out that the title *basileus*

was not considered as the embodiment of a god, that he was not given divine honors. It will be sufficient to recall Achilles' angry words in the very assembly of the Greeks to realize that it will prove almost impossible to substantiate the assumption of the divinity of Agamemnon. Οἰνοβαρές, κυνὸς ὄμματ᾿ ἔχων κραδίην δ᾿ ἐλάφοιο, δημο-βόρος, κερδαλεόφρον, μέγ᾿ ἀναιδές, ἀναιδείην ἐπιειμένε—one after the other these epithets were hurled against the ἄναξ ἀνδρῶν. It is true that often enough the gods used hard words and epithets against each other; however, the words of Achilles were not spoken in private or in a convention of equal kings and elders, but in the presence of the entire Greek army, the men who presumably would offer divine honors to their king and who regarded him as the embodiment of a god. When Diomedes before all the Achaeans stated that the "son of the crooked-counselling Cronos . . . did not give Agamemnon valor," in other words accused the supreme commander of cowardice, the "sons of the Achaeans shouted aloud," applauding the words of the young king from Argos.

Perhaps it has become evident that in Homeric poetry the terms ἄναξ and τέμενος do not indicate divine honors bestowed on the men possessing them. Before we admit that these terms reflect a tradition of older times in which the rulers were considered divine we have to prove that the Mycenaean *wanaktes* were so considered. There is not a particle of evidence to indicate that this was the case in the states of Pylos, or Knossos, or Mycenae.

In Homeric poetry, however, we find expressions and terms which have been interpreted as reflecting a tradition of divine honors accorded to kings in the past. "All men gaze upon us as on gods," says Sarpedon to Glaukos (*Il.* XII. 312); this is supposed to indicate that certain leaders and men were "regarded as gods," sometime in the Heroic Age. Yet this and other similar expressions are applied to men of doubtful quality and merit. Eurymachos, the son of Poly-bios, one of the suitors of Penelope, is looked upon by the people of

in Homeric times was of increased importance, and that the Mycenaean distinction between *wanax* and *basileus* became confused. Indeed it is evident that the title *basileus* became more important but it seems to me that the *wanax* remained in its exalted grade. It is the especial title of the king who exercised supreme authority in that expedition; in this it parallels the title given to the ruler exercising supreme control over the state. The *basileis* of Homeric poetry came under the "anax" the way the other officials of the Mycenaean state came under the *wanax*. In this we find another Mycenaean usage that was well remembered in Homeric poetry. It is interesting to recall that even Achilles admits that the host of the Achaeans will give heed to the word of Agamemnon (*Il.* XXIII. 156; cf. also XIX. 68 ff. and Nestor's words in IX. 69 ff.).

Ithaka "as on a god" (*Od.* XV, 520). Perhaps more instructive is the passage in the *Odyssey* (VIII. 170 ff.) where Odysseus, smarting under the insult of Euryalos the young Phaeacian, describes various types of gifted men; one of these is "gazed upon as on a god" because of his eloquence and modesty.

The expression "honored as a god" is assumed to reflect an old custom of awarding divine honors to the king. In the *Iliad* (IX. 149 ff.) Agamemnon promises to give Achilles, among other things, seven cities whose men shall honor him "as though he were a god." Agamemnon "ruled mightily over all the Argives and was honored of the folk even as a god" (*Il.* X. 33). Odysseus tells the psyche of Achilles that "of old, when thou wast alive, we Argives honored thee as the gods" (*Od.* II. 484). Such expressions are found in a number of passages, but should be considered as poetic exaggerations. We must recall again Diomedes' word that Agamemnon, as befits the commander in chief of the Greek army, was honored above others, but was not accorded divine honors. Odysseus' statement to Eumaios the swineherd (*Od.* III, 199 ff.) that by lineage he came from Crete the son of a wealthy man, who was "honored as a god among the Cretans for his good estate and his wealth and his glorious sons," is decisive. The old man of Crete was honored as if he were a god because of his wealth!

Sarpedon and Glaukos whom the people of Lykia "gaze upon as on gods" are honored above all, "with seats, and messes and full cups" (*Il.* XII. 311). These certainly are not extraordinary, divine honors. We get an equally good illustration of what the expression in reality means in the *Odyssey*. In Book V. 36, Zeus tells Hermes that the Phaeacians will honor Odysseus as a god: "these shall heartily show him all honor, as if he were a god." This came to pass and Odysseus tells Penelope that her husband is in the land of Phaeacians who "heartily showed him all honor as if he were a god" (*Od.* XIX. 280). We have a very detailed description of Odysseus' stay among the Phaeacians and of the gifts given to him. In no instance was anything resembling divine honors bestowed upon him. He was treated like any other gifted stranger that should arrive in Scheria. As a matter of fact he was even taunted by Euryalos. Neither he nor Alkinous and Arete claim that divine honors are due them. Odysseus explains simply his status (*Od.* IX. 19-20): "I am Odysseus, son of Laertes, who am known among men for all manner of wiles, and my fame reaches into heaven." Alkinous' description of his guest is equally sanguine (*Od.* XI. 367 ff.). Not a word of his being divine, or godlike, or that he should be given honors due a god. Indeed, Arete states clearly that gifts should be given him not because he was divine, but because Odysseus was the special guest of the royal family and also the guest of the Phaeacians, whose "halls are filled with treasures by the favor of the gods" (*Od.* XI. 336 ff.) Odysseus calls them "gifts of friendship" and they were not extravagantly many, coming from the people of Scheria as well as from its kings. This will become evident if we compare these gifts to the fictitious gifts of friendship Odysseus enumerates to Laertes as received from one host (*Od.* XXIV. 270 ff.).

In a similar manner we can find that terms like διοτρεφής, διογενής, δῖος, ἀντίθεος, θεοειδής, θεοῖς ἐναλίγκιος, etc., are poetic epithets that embellish a verse but convey no special status, no reflection of past honors vaguely remembered. Let us, for example, look for a moment at the epithet ἀντίθεος. Odysseus is called *antitheos* in *Odyssey* II. 17 and elsewhere, but all the Phaeacians are so called (*Od.* VI. 241): all the companions of Telemachos in his trip to Pylos and Sparta, the sailors and rowers, simple people not even aristocrats, are called *antitheoi* (*Od.* XVII. 54). Odysseus' fictitious companions who followed him to Egypt—all of them—are called *antitheoi.* Yet those were the people who, "yielding to wantonness" wasted the lands of the Egyptians, carried off women and little children and slew them savagely (*Od.* XIV. 246-47; 261-65). Even Polyphemos the Cyclops is *antitheos* (*Od.* I. 70), although he was a "monster with his heart set on lawlessness," "a savage man" (*Od.* IX. 428, 494).

To Odysseus and Mentor, to Achilles and Hektor, to all the Achaeans the epithet δῖος is given; but the same epithet is also given to the swineherd Eumaios (*Od.* XV. 301, *et passim*). I think it is apparent that these and other terms in the *Iliad* and the *Odyssey* are poetic exaggerations which can be paralleled by modern examples, and do not reflect the reality or the memory of past and traditional honors paid to leaders and kings.

We may now sum up our conclusions. The archaeological remains thus far brought to light in the mainland of Greece give us a glimpse into the political system of the state of Pylos only. Whether or not the same system prevailed in all the other states of the Mycenaean world cannot at present be established for lack of definite evidence; nor can it be determined whether or not similar systems varying in details were current beyond the confines of Messenia. At Pylos the supreme ruler was called the *wanax*. He had certain privileges and exercised a tight control over the activities of his people; but no evidence exists to prove that he was given divine honors, that he was considered the embodiment of a god. May we hope that future excavations and discoveries will add fuller details to the picture of the Mycenaean state which has been outlined so brilliantly by the discoveries in Messenia and in Crete.

Washington University
18 December 1965

EPICURUS AT MONTICELLO

Henry C. Montgomery

Modern estimates of Jefferson's reliance on ancient philosophy are, with good reason, unanimous in considering him independent of any one system but with strong leanings toward the two moral systems of Stoicism and Epicureanism.[1] First of all, he had no taste for metaphysics—including representatives of it such as Plato—because it was not susceptible to precise researches.[2] It is true that Jefferson spoke of himself as an Epicurean and it is just as true that although attracted by certain elements of this philosophy, he was emphatically at odds with its basic ascetic principles. Conversely, although he never speaks of himself as espousing Stoic morality, many of his philosophic comments and, surely, his devotion during his whole life to the service of his fellow men are eminently Stoic qualities. Therefore, his direct testimony and some of his attitudes may be considered Epicurean; his way of life and the implied testimony in many of his comments mark him a Stoic. The quotations from classical authors in his literary commonplace book[3] are mixed with the Epicureanism of Horace and Stoic principles in the excerpts from Euripides and Cicero. In a letter to John Page, written July 15, 1763, Jefferson said:

> The most fortunate of us, in our journey through life, frequently meet with calamities and misfortunes which may greatly afflict us; and to fortify our minds against the attacks of these calamities and misfortunes, should be one of the principal studies and endeavors of our lives. The only method of doing this is to assume a perfect resignation to the Divine will,

[1] Adrienne Koch, *The Philosophy of Thomas Jefferson* (Columbia diss., New York, 1943), p. 2; Gilbert Chinard, *Thomas Jefferson, The Apostle of Americanism* (Boston, 1929), p. 26; James Truslow Adams, *The Living Jefferson* (New York, 1936), p. 38.

[2] Gilbert Chinard, *Jefferson et les idéologues* (Baltimore, 1925), p. 222.

[3] Gilbert Chinard, *The Literary Bible of Thomas Jefferson* (Baltimore, 1928).

to consider that whatever does happen, must happen; and that by our own uneasiness, we cannot prevent the blow before it does fall, but we may add to its force after it has fallen. . . .[4]

From the literary jottings and this letter to Page it has been concluded,

If at this early period Epicureanism seemed to provide the good life, Stoic discipline was the method for attaining it. It is true that Jefferson derived more personal inspiration from the Greek and Roman Stoics than from the Epicureans . . . but Jefferson, even in his early period, is properly to be regarded as loyal to both Stoic and Epicurean principles. Both were rich for him in the integrative devices of individual morality.[5]

Even more properly, Jefferson's early philosophy is probably nothing more than the philosophy—if such it is—of adolescent moods and internal struggles inherent in his highly sensitive nature. If it happened to be Epicurean, or Stoic, it is more likely a matter of coincidence than a deliberate knowledge and derivation from either, or both, of these philosophic systems.

As Jefferson approached middle age equipped with a broader knowledge of philosophy and having reached a definite stand in his attitude toward religion, his philosophy becomes more clearly defined and definable. Since he was a professed Epicurean the testimony for this philosophy may be considered first. In the Notes on Virginia (1782) he says:

Millions of innocent men, women and children, since the introduction of Christianity, have been burnt, tortured, fined, imprisoned.[6]

This is an echo, at least, of the *tantum Religio potuit suadere malorum* of Lucretius.[7]

On June 27, 1813, Jefferson wrote to John Adams:

The *summum bonum* with me is now truly epicurian, ease of body and tranquility of mind; and to these I wish to consign my remaining days.[8]

These lines were addressed to Charles Thompson, January 9, 1816:

If I had time, I would add to my little book Philosophy of Jesus the Greek, Latin, and French texts, in columns side by side. And I wish I

---

[4] *The Writings of Thomas Jefferson,* ed. A. A. Lipscomb and A. Bergh (Washington, 1903), IV, 10; hereafter cited as Lipscomb and Bergh.

[5] Koch, pp. 7 f.

[6] *The Writings of Thomas Jefferson,* ed. Ford (New York, 1892–99), III, 265; hereafter cited as Ford.

[7] Lucretius, *De rerum natura,* I, 101.

[8] Lipscomb and Bergh, XIII, 279.

could subjoin a translation of Gosindi's [Gassendi's] Syntagma of the doctrines of Epicurus, which, notwithstanding the calumnies of the Stoics and caricatures of Cicero, is the most rational system remaining of the philosophy of the ancients, as frugal of vicious indulgence, and fruitful of virtue as the hyperbolical extravagances of his rival sects.[9]

Since Jefferson's Epicureanism is so close, as he himself says, to that of Pierre Gassendi (1592–1655), it is appropriate to comment briefly on the Epicureanism of this eclectic but generally empirical philosopher. Gassendi was attracted to Epicurus and the atomic theory early in his career. He agreed with Epicurus that the atom was a-tomic and capable of movement. He also agreed that no natural power could create or destroy a single atom. But although in agreement as far as purely natural forces are concerned, Gassendi believed that the atoms were created by God and that God was not only the source of movement of the atoms, but that also He could destroy them. Gassendi also rejected the ancient idea of the swerve of the atom and substituted a divinely guided dynamism from weight. The Epicurean-Lucretian concept was, as far as he was concerned, mechanistic, geometric, and inert.

Anyone interested in Epicureanism is also interested in liberty, and Gassendi was no exception. Yet he was primarily concerned not with physical or civil liberty, but with liberty in an inward and moral sense. We can always safeguard our liberty, he felt, in that when, on the point of acting, it is always in our power to suspend action, to consider things so as to distinguish the true good from the apparent good. For what is the good, he asked, of prudence, reflection, and counsel if all is regulated in advance?

Jefferson summed up his analysis of Epicureanism in a long letter to William Short (October 31, 1819): [10]

As you say of yourself, I too am an Epicurian. I consider the genuine (not the imputed) doctrines of Epicurus as containing everything rational in moral philosophy which Greece and Rome have left us. Epictetus indeed, has given us what was good of the Stoics; all beyond, of their dogmas, being hypocrisy and grimace. Their great crime was in their

[9] Lipscomb and Bergh, xiv, 386. Claude G. Bowers (*Jefferson in Power* [Boston, 1936], p. 48) summarizes a passage from the *Diary of John Adams* (i, 317) where Adams is reporting a dinner conversation, ". . . and he [Jefferson] suggested that 'the Epicureans' philosophy was nearer to the truth than any other ancient system. It had been misunderstood and misrepresented. He referred enthusiastically to the work of Gassendo upon it, lamenting that it had not been translated, since 'it is the only accurate account of it extant.' Adams reminded him of Lucretius. 'Only a part of it,' rejoined Jefferson—'only the natural philosophy.' The moral philosophy could only be found in Gassendo."

[10] Lipscomb and Bergh, xv, 219-23.

calumnies of Epicurus and misrepresentations of his doctrines; in which we lament to see the candid character of Cicero engaging as an accomplice. Diffuse, vapid, rhetorical, but enchanting. His prototype Plato, eloquent as himself, dealing out mysticisms incomprehensible to the human mind, has been deified by certain sects usurping the name of Christians; because in his foggy conceptions, they found a basis of impenetrable darkness whereon to rear fabrications as delirious, of their own invention . . . Of Socrates we have nothing genuine but in the Memorabilia of Xenephon; for Plato makes him one of his Collocutors merely to cover his own whimsies under the mantle of his name; a liberty of which we are told that Socrates himself complained. Seneca is indeed a fine moralist, disfiguring his work at times with some Stoicisms . . . yet giving us on the whole a great deal of sound and practical morality . . . Epictetus and Epicurus give laws for governing ourselves . . . I have sometimes thought of translating Epictetus (for he has never been tolerably translated into English) by adding the genuine doctrines of Epicurus from the Syntagma of Gassendi. . . . You are not a true disciple of our master Epicurus, in indulging the indolence to which you say you are yielding. One of his canons, you know, was that "the indulgence which prevents a greater pleasure, or produces a greater pain, is to be avoided" . . . debility of body, and hebetude of mind, the farthest of all things from the happiness which the well-regulated indulgences of Epicurus ensure; fortitude, you know, is one of his four cardinal virtues . . . I will place under this a syllabus of the doctrines of Epicurus . . . which I wrote some twenty years ago . . .

Syllabus of the doctrines of Epicurus

Physical—the Universe eternal.
> Its parts, great and small, interchangeable.
> Matter and Void alone.
> Motion inherent in matter which is weighty and declining.
> Eternal circulation of the elements of bodies.
> Gods, an order of beings next superior to man, enjoying in their own sphere, their own felicities; but not meddling with the concerns of the scale of beings below them.

Moral—Happiness the aim of life.
> Virtue the foundation of happiness.
> Utility the test of virtue.
> Pleasure active and In-do-lent.
> In-do-lence is the absence of pain, the true felicity.
> Active, consists in agreeable motion; it is not happiness, but the means to produce it.

Thus the absence of hunger is an article of felicity; eating the means to obtain it.
> The *summum bonum* is to be not pained in body, nor troubled in mind, i.e. In-do-lence of body, tranquillity of mind.
> To produce tranquillity of mind we must avoid desire and fear, the two principal diseases of the mind.
> Man is a free agent.
> Virtue consists in 1. Prudence. 2. Temperance. 3. Fortitude. 4. Justice.
> To which are opposed 1. Folly. 2. Desire. 3. Fear. 4. Deceit.

While proclaiming himself an Epicurean Jefferson spoke disparagingly of its rival system in antiquity, Stoicism. Nor does he ever speak positively in favor of the Stoic philosophy, but his persistent efforts toward something much more than temporal, transitory values, his creative endeavors applied to enduring institutions,[11] and his refusal to return evil for evil by answering, or prosecuting, the grossest acts of libel—all these are reminders of Stoicism whether he intended them to be or not. He wrote to Alexander White, September 10, 1793:

So many persons have of late found an interest or a passion gratified by imputing to me sayings and writings which I never said or wrote, or by endeavoring to draw me into newspapers to harass me personally, that I have found it necessary for my quiet & my other pursuits to leave them in full possession of the field, and not to take the trouble of contradicting them in private conversation.[12]

On May 26, 1800, Jefferson wrote to James Monroe:

I am so broken to calumnies of every kind, from every department of government, Executive, Legislative, & Judiciary, & from every minion of theirs holding office or seeking it, that I entirely disregard it. . . .[13]

And to the Attorney-General, Levi Lincoln, he wrote, March 24, 1802:

While a full range is proper for actions by individuals, either private or public, for slanders affecting them, I wish much to see the experiment tried to getting along without public prosecution for *libels*. I believe we can do it. Patience and well doing, instead of punishment, if it can be found sufficiently efficacious, would be a happy change in the instruments of government.[14]

Toward the end of his second term as president Jefferson wrote to his grandson, Thomas Jefferson Randolph, November 24, 1808:

I have mentioned good humor as one of the preservatives of our peace and tranquillity. It is among the most effectual, and its effect is so well imitated and aided, artifically, by politeness, that this also becomes an acquisition of first rate value . . . I never saw an instance of one of two

---

[11] For example, at the very time when he was most voluble in his praise of Epicureanism he was preparing to launch one of the greatest of his projects, the University of Virginia.

[12] Ford, VII, 174.

[13] Ford, VIII, 448.

[14] Ford, VIII, 139. To Thomas Seymour, February 11, 1807, he wrote, "I have never therefore to protect the freedom of the press even contradicted the thousands of calumnies so industriously propagated against myself" (Lipscomb and Bergh, XI, 155).

disputants convincing the other by argument . . . [my opponent's] error does me no injury . . . It is his affair, not mine, if he prefers error.[15]

Jefferson's efforts to be "obscurely good" in anonymous benefactions to churches and sufferers from various types of disasters are proverbial—and Stoic.[16]

Jefferson rejected the Pythagorean theory of the transmigration of souls as he rejected every kind of supernatural philosophy not measurable by some kind of natural reason. Without specific reference to Pythagoras—for his letter was in answer to one from the Reverend Isaac Story—he wrote, December 5, 1801:

It is not for me to pronounce on the hypothesis you present of a transmigration of souls from one body to another in certain cases . . . I have for very many years ceased to read or think concerning [such speculations] and have reposed my head on that pillow of ignorance, which a benevolent Creator has made so soft for us, knowing how much we should be forced to use it.[17]

On Socrates Jefferson wrote to John Adams, October 13, 1813:

An expression in your letter of September the 14th that "the human understanding is a revelation from its maker," gives the best solution that I believe can be given of the question, "what did Socrates mean by his Daemon?" He was too wise to believe and too honest to pretend, that he had real and familiar converse with a superior and invisible being. He probably considered the suggestions of his conscience, or reason, as revelations or inspirations from the Supreme mind, bestowed, on important occasions, by a special superintending Providence.[18]

While Jefferson made no secret of his almost fanatical dislike of everything—and almost everyone—connected with organized religion, there is no question as to his belief in and adherence to the moral teachings of Christ. He was himself able to make a synthesis of Christian morality and ancient moral philosophy and was greatly interested when anyone else attempted to do so. In an essay on Religion he said:

As the Antients tolerated visionaries & enthusiasts of all kinds so they permitted a free scope to philosophy as a balance. As the Pythagoreans & latter Platonists joined with the superstition of their times the Epicureans & Academicks were allowed all the use of wit & railery against it. Thus matters were balanced; reason had play & science flourished. These contrarieties produced harmony.[19]

[15] Lipscomb and Bergh, xii, 198–200.
[16] Cf. to Col. Thomas Newton, March 5, 1804 (Ford, viii, 298).
[17] Lipscomb and Bergh, x, 298 f.
[18] Lipscomb and Bergh, xiii, 391 f.
[19] Notes on Religion, October, 1776 (?) (Ford, ii, 95).

During some of the most strenuous days of the presidency Jefferson became much interested in a treatise by Joseph Priestley comparing Socrates and Jesus.[20] He wrote about it to Edward Dowse, April 19, 1803:

> though I concur with the author in considering the moral precepts of Jesus as more pure, correct, and sublime than those of the ancient philosophers, yet I do not concur with him in the mode of proving it. He thinks it necessary to libel and decry the doctrines of the philosophers; but a man must be blinded indeed by prejudice, who can deny them a great degree of merit . . . Their philosophy went chiefly to the government of our passions, so far as respected ourselves, and the procuring our own tranquillity. . .[21]

Only two days after this letter to Dowse, Jefferson wrote a letter to Benjamin Rush together with a treatise of his own, a *Syllabus of an Estimate of the Merit of the Doctrines of Jesus, Compared with Those of Others*.[22] In the *Syllabus* are these comments:

> In a comparative view of the Ethics of the enlightened nations of antiquity, of the Jews and of Jesus, no notice should be taken of the corruptions of reason among the ancients, to wit, the idolatry & superstition of the vulgar, nor the corruptions of Christianity by the learned among its professors.
>
> Let a just view be taken of the moral principles inculcated by the most esteemed of the sects of ancient philosophy, or of their individuals; particularly Pythagoras, Socrates, Epicurus, Cicero, Epictetus, Seneca, Antoninus [i.e., Marcus Aurelius].
>
> I. Philosophers. 1. Their precepts related chiefly to ourselves and the government of those passions which, unrestrained, would disturb our tranquillity of mind.
>
> 2. In developing our duties to others, they were short and defective. They embraced, indeed the circles of kindred & friends, and inculcated patriotism, or the love of our country in the aggregate, as a primary obligation: toward our neighbors & countrymen they taught justice, but scarcely viewed them as within the circle of benevolence. Still less have they inculcated peace, charity & love to our fellow men, or embraced with benevolence the whole family of mankind. . . .
>
> [On Jesus]. 1. Like Socrates & Epictetus, he wrote nothing himself. 2. But he had not, like them, a Xenephon or an Arrian to write for him

---

[20] Joseph Priestley, *Socrates and Jesus Compared*, printed, 1803, for J. Johnson, London, and P. Byrne, Philadelphia.

[21] Lipscomb and Bergh, x, 376.

[22] Jefferson had written to Priestley, April 9, 1803, stating some of the principles in this Syllabus (Lipscomb and Bergh, x, 374), and later (January 29, 1804) he wrote congratulating Priestley on his projected comparison of Jesus and the ancient philosophers, a work which, apparently, Priestley's death left unfinished (Lipscomb and Bergh, x, 445).

. . . 5. They [i.e., the doctrines of Jesus] have been still more disfigured by the corruptions of schismatising followers . . . perverting the simple doctrines he taught by engrafting on them the mysticisms of a Grecian sophist [i. e., Plato]. . . .[23]

In this wise, Jefferson distinguished between the Christian and ancient pagan moral philosophies. Had he been less a confessed Epicurean, hence a less energetic opponent to Stoicism, he might have found in this latter philosophy many of the qualities that he ascribed to the Christian teaching alone. The philosophy of Jefferson was, indeed, with reference to ancient philosophies, a mixed one.

If, as he himself asserts, his specific bent was toward Epicureanism, it was scarcely toward a literal interpretation of the creed. Certain aspects, however, of the philosophy were obviously attractive to him as they were to others before him and contemporary with him among Europeans, particularly and especially the French. Thomas Jefferson was perhaps not influenced by Epicureanism, but the individualistic features of it were in accord with the mood and temper of his age. He found attractive, therefore, the forceful expressions of Epicurus and his interpreters in his own attitude toward a world that was just embarking on significant political and social revolution.

Miami University
5 January 1966

---

[23] Lipscomb and Bergh, x, 381.

NAUSIKAA'S SUITORS

Richmond Lattimore

I take off from Woodhouse's proposition [1] that underneath Homer's story of Odysseus and Nausikaa there lies an older simple fairy-tale romance in which the poor vagabond ultimately married the princess, and that the wreckage of this story as it was before Homer fitted it into the *Odyssey* can be seen through his account, though there is not much left.

When Odysseus made his landfall on Scheria, the island of the Phaiakians, he was at the bottom of his fortunes; he had lost all his ships, all his men, the spoils of Troy, his raft, his provisions, and every stitch of clothing. He was thus ready to fill the frame of a story which would be, in the words of Woodhouse, "that of a castaway who comes on the scene in wretched guise, a mere wreck, or man of no account. In the sequel he is revealed in his true character, as a prince, foremost in manly exercises, in which he defeats all rivals, and wins the prize of marriage with the daughter of the king to whose land he has thus come incognito." [2] Odysseus spent the night after his landing under a bush in a pile of fallen leaves, near the outlet of a clear river. Athene came in a dream to Nausikaa, only daughter of King Alkinoos, and inspired her to go in the morning with a wagon and her maids to wash the family laundry in that very stream near which Odysseus was sleeping. Nausikaa was a princess, beautiful, young but grown up, and unmarried, and what else but marriage should be the next step in her young life, and what else should she be thinking about? Athene mentions

---

[1] W. J. Woodhouse, *The Composition of Homer's Odyssey* (Oxford, 1930), pp. 54-65. Since I composed the original draft of this paper, it has been called to my attention that Woodhouse was anticipated in several important points by van Leeuwen. See J. van Leeuwen, *Commentationes Homericae* (Leyden, 1911), pp. 56-63.

[2] Woodhouse, pp. 54-55.

this in the dream vision: "you will not be single for long; all the best Phaiakian young men—and you are Phaiakian too—are already courting you" (VI. 34-35). When Nausikaa woke and asked her father for the wagon and the mules, she was too bashful to connect the laundering with marriage, but her father knew what was in her mind (VI. 66-70). Throughout the episode, while Nausikaa is present, her marriage keeps coming up in one way or another.

The poet moves on to the encounter. When the girls have done the laundry, they have a game of ball, in which the princess moves pre-eminent like Artemis among her nymphs. Odysseus wakens and approaches the girls. He is naked and screened only behind a branch of greenery. All are terrified but Nausikaa stands her ground, and Odysseus entreats her for protection and guidance and " some rag of clothing" (δὸς δὲ ῥάκος ἀμφιβαλέσθαι, VI. 178) in a beautiful speech of flattery. He is given clean clothes, food and drink, and oil to anoint himself with after he has washed privately in the stream. He is accepted as a suppliant.

The situation is unique in epic, and loaded with romantic overtones. To express it, the poet has used, along with a mixture of formula and unique phrasing, something that looks like an adaptation of the *Iliad's* martial simile. Athene, in charge of the situation, sees to it that Odysseus wakes before the girls go away. Her action is indicated by the line (VI. 112)

ἔνθ' αὖτ' ἄλλ' ἐνόησε θεὰ γλαυκῶπις 'Αθήνη—

a formula used several other times in the *Odyssey* to introduce this goddess's activities,[3] and through its form suggesting improvised action on the impulse of the moment, though surely here the sequel has been planned from the outset and carefully led up to. When the girls squeal over a ball thrown in the water (αἱ δ' ἐπὶ μακρὸν ἄϋσαν, VI. 117), Odysseus wakens and wonders, as he wondered over the Kyklopes (IX. 175-76) and will again when he wakes on Ithaka (XIII. 201-202), what sort of people he will encounter (VI. 120-21)

ἦ ῥ' οἵ γ' ὑβρισταί τε καὶ ἄγριοι οὐδὲ δίκαιοι,
ἦε φιλόξεινοι, καί σφιν νόος ἐστὶ θεουδής;

The squealing of the girls becomes a " female battle cry," θῆλυς ἀϋτή

---

[3] Od. II. 382, 393; IV. 795; XVIII. 187. Cf. also V. 382. The formula is also adapted to others whose names with epithets have the same metrical dimensions as θεὰ γλαυκῶπις 'Αθήνη: so ποδάρκης δῖος 'Αχιλλεύς, Il. XXIII. 140, 193 (the only instances in the *Iliad*); 'Ελένη Διὸς ἐκγεγαυῖα, Od. IV. 219; περίφρων Πηνελόπεια, Od. XVI. 409.

(VI. 122).⁴ Odysseus resolves to advance upon them. With his heavy warrior's hand, χειρὶ παχείῃ,⁵ he rips off a branch and holds it before him, much as Sarpedon storming the Achaian wall held his shield before him (Il. XII. 294-97), but not to guard life and vitals from weapons but his modesty from female eyes, ὡς ῥύσαιτο περὶ χροΐ μήδεα φωτός (VI. 129). Onward go both Odysseus and Sarpedon, both like lions (and carried partly on the same phrases

$$\beta\hat{\eta} \; \delta' \; \text{ἴμεν} \; \text{ὥς} \; \text{τε} \; λέων \; \text{ὀρεσίτροφος}, \; ἀλκὶ \; πεποιθώς$$
$$\_ \; ῥ' \; \cup\cup \; \_ \; \cup \; \cup\_ \; \cup\cup\_ \; \cup\cup, \; \; ὅς \; τ' \; ἐπιδευής),$$

Both lions are urged by spirit and hunger (VI. 130, Il. XII. 299)

$$μήλων \; πειρήσοντα \; καὶ \; ἐς \; πυκινὸν \; δόμον \; ἐλθεῖν.$$

But while for Sarpedon's lion this last undertaking comes after (Il. XII. 300)

$$κέλεται \; δέ \; ἑ \; θυμὸς \; ἀγήνωρ,$$

for Odysseus' lion it is κέλεται δέ ἑ γαστήρ⁶ (VI. 133), and though, like Menelaos in the Iliad, he is ἀλκὶ πεποιθώς,⁷ all this is in defiance of, not armed men and dogs, but just the weather, "though he is rained on and windblown," ὅς τ' εἶσ' ὑόμενος καὶ ἀήμενος (VI. 131). It is only unarmed girls on whom he is advancing, but bits of martial phrasing continue to occur. He faces them γυμνός περ ἐών (VI. 136) as Euphorbos would not face Patroklos γυμνόν περ ἐόντ' (Il. XVI. 815). At sight of him the girls τρέσσαν δ' ἄλλυδις ἄλλη (VI. 138) as before Aias the Τρῶες δὲ διέτρεσαν ἄλλυδις ἄλλος (Il. XI. 486). T. E. Shaw says: "[Homer] sprinkles tags of epic across his pages. In this some find humor. Rather I judge that here too the tight lips of archaic art have grown the fixed grin of archaism." ⁸ The judgment, though shrewd, seems dated; perhaps we have out-grown the "tags of epic" which are no such thing but truly the way the epic poet thinks and composes; in any case, there must here be consciousness of what these phrases mean in other more usual contexts, since for formula, as for all poetry, context is all. And if not humor, there is wit, that wit that elsewhere so neatly

⁴ ἀϋτή comes naturally after αἱ δ' ἐπὶ μακρὸν ἄϋσαν in VI. 117, but in the Iliad it is regularly "battle cry" or even simply "battle," e.g., XVII. 167, see also Od. XI. 383.

⁵ Normally of warriors, but also of Penelope, Od. XXI. 6, cf. XVIII. 195.

⁶ γαστήρ in the sense of "hungry belly" or simply "hunger" is used mostly of Odysseus, often by himself, e.g., VII. 216; XV. 344. On the appetite of Odysseus, see Scott, The Unity of Homer (Berkeley, 1921), pp. 192-93.

⁷ Il. XVII. 61.

⁸ T. E. Shaw, The Odyssey of Homer (Oxford, 1932), Translator's note (no page number).

flips ὃ γὰρ γέρας ἐστὶ θανόντων (XXIV, 190, Il. XVI, 457) over into ἡ γὰρ δίκη ἐστὶ γερόντων (XXIV. 225). Perhaps it is not too much to say that here the poet has found in mock-heroic with a hint of self-parody a certain lightness of touch which gives the scene, and everything about Nausikaa, its elusive charm.

From his embarrassing position, Odysseus appeals to Nausikaa in a speech full of winning flattery. Is she a goddess, Artemis most likely, or is she a human girl? If so, how lucky is the man who wins her. And may she have the man she wants, and a blissful married life. Between these flatteries comes his prayer for his bit of clothing, and guidance. He is her suppliant. Nausikaa does not reply directly to these allusions to her nobility, but confines herself to friendly, dignified pieties, and in the same vein rallies her maids. She is the King's daughter, and she will give the suppliant stranger his rights. Phaiakians have nothing to fear, the gods love them, nobody attacks them. But after Odysseus has gone off and bathed and dressed with scrupulous decency, Athene glorifies him, in the same way that she is to glorify him after his housecleaning and before his reunion with Penelope (VI. 230-35 = XXIII. 157-62). It is then that Nausikaa, struck in turn by Odysseus' "godlike" appearance, voices to her maids that famous wish that such a man—well, *this* one—would be her husband (VI. 244-45):

αἲ γὰρ ἐμοὶ τοιόσδε πόσις κεκλημένος εἴη
ἐνθάδε ναιετάων, καὶ οἱ ἅδοι αὐτόθι μίμνειν.

(These two lines are athetized by Aristarchus but were known to Alcman).[9]

This, of course, is to the girls only, but some of the feeling gets into the following speech to Odysseus, which I will try to summarize thus:

> Let me go on ahead
> so we shall not be seen together
> since there are disagreeable people about
> who would say I picked you up and meant to
>   marry you
> so wait and give me time to get home, etc.

The suggestion of marriage to Odysseus in this speech is indisputable (that part is also athetized),[10] and Woodhouse has well-particularized

[9] See the Scholl. on VI. 244, Dindorf I, 314, especially (H.Q.) ἄμφω μὲν ἀθετεῖ Ἀρίσταρχος, διστάζει δὲ περὶ τοῦ πρώτου, ἐπεὶ καὶ Ἀλκμὰν αὐτὸν μετέβαλε παρθένους λεγούσας εἰσάγων " Ζεῦ πάτερ, αἲ γὰρ ἐμὸς πόσις εἴη (= Frag. 81 Page).
[10] Scholl. on VI. 275, Dindorf I, 317 (H.Q.) ἀθετοῦνται στίχοι ιδ' ἕως " ἀνδράσι μίσγηται " ὡς ἀνοίκειοι τῷ ὑποκειμένῳ προσώπῳ.

the details.[11] I believe, however, there might be a double motive, and I will return to the speech a little later. "Motive" itself briefly raises a problem. In a sense, as Waldock [12] has pointed out, a fictitious character can have no motive. Our Nausikaa is not a real person being reported; she is only words assembled, remembered, and at last set down. This merely converts our motive-seeking into a reading of Homer's mind. Despite the dimness of our concept of an authentic Homer—for plainly here there is a mind at work—we cannot really help ourselves. Or put it in another way and suppose this speech were not made. Some reason has to be given to prevent Nausikaa from coming home hand in hand with Odysseus and saying brightly to her parents, "Look what I found." Or else, I suppose, Odysseus would have had to marry her, and the home-coming would be lost.

Odysseus obeys instructions in letting the princess go on ahead, and when he himself has made his way into the palace, he again obeys instructions, namely " to go right past Father and supplicate Mother " (VI. 310; VII. 142). He asks for conveyance home, and sits down humbly among the ashes: πὰρ πυρί· οἱ δ' ἄρα πάντες ἀκὴν ἐγένοντο σιωπῇ (VII. 154). There is a pause. This adapted formula may indicate an embarrassed silence, but more probably (this time) serves to punctuate and stress a momentous speech.[13] At last Alkinoos, prodded by a counselor, raises the suppliant, orders more drinks, and announces that he will give him conveyance in the hospitable tradition of the Phaiakians. Odysseus ends his speech of acceptance with the wish that before he dies he may see once more his property, his servants, and his house (VII. 225)

κτῆσιν ἐμὴν δμῶάς τε καὶ ὑψερεφὲς μέγα δῶμα.

We ask in passing whether δμῶάς τε means male or female servants. It would have been nicer, a scholiast remarks,[14] if instead of κτῆσιν ἐμὴν δμῶάς τε he had begun the line with πατρίδ' ἐμὴν ἄλοχόν τε. The fact that Pandaros in the Iliad (V. 213) did say just that may indicate conscious care in the adaptation of a formula. Odysseus has not yet mentioned his wife to any Phaiakian. After the other guests are gone, Arete (who in fact was addressed first but who has said nothing hitherto) rather abruptly declares that she wishes to clear

11 Woodhouse, pp. 57-58.
12 A. J. A. Waldock, Sophocles the Dramatist (Cambridge, 1951), pp. 11-24.
13 The regular formula, beginning with ὡς ἔφαθ', appears some fifteen times in the two poems.
14 Scholl. on VII. 225, Dindorf I, 344 (P.Q.).

up one point (VII. 237) : " Who gave you those clothes " (VII. 238) :

τίς πόθεν εἰς ἀνδρῶν; τίς τοι τάδε εἵματ' ἔδωκεν;

The first half of this line is serviceable formula for all strangers, the second half unique and particular. The regular close after τίς πόθεν εἰς ἀνδρῶν; is of course πόθι τοι πόλις ἠδὲ τοκῆες; (I. 170; XIV. 187; XV; 264) .[15] I note in passing another new ending on a formulaic start. Nausikaa driving her mules used the whip, as did, for instance, Iris driving the divine horses of Ares (Il. V. 366, compare Od. VI. 82) but after μάστιξεν δ' ἐλάαν, instead of the eager flight of horses, τὼ δ' οὐκ ἀέκοντε πετέσθην, we are greeted by either a clatter of hooves or a startled heehaw from the mules (VI. 82), μάστιξεν δ' ἐλάαν, καναχὴ δ' ἦν ἡμιόνοιϊν.[16]

The answer of Odysseus to Arete is long and roundabout though, as he remarks, it is true (VII. 297; he lies only once to the Phaiakians). Still, he never answers the first question (his name and address); not till tomorrow night; moreover, in reporting that Kalypso wanted to keep him and make him immortal (VII. 254-58), though he censors the story a bit, he may be unconsciously implying that he is still marriageable, since goddesses, unlike gods, generally wanted permanent relationships with those they favored. At last he gets to Nausikaa (VII. 290-97). Alkinoos remarks that the girl should have brought her own suppliant home herself, and Odysseus defends her with his one lie. She invited him; he thought it better to come by himself; Alkinoos might have taken offense (VII. 307):

δύσζηλοι γάρ τ' εἰμὲν ἐπὶ χθονὶ φῦλ' ἀνθρώπων.

Nausikaa's hint (VI. 274) about the disagreeable Phaiakians is adapted, but kept by the elegant and tactful εἰμέν just within the limits of politeness, to Alkinoos himself. It wins him. His reply is prompt and to the point, essentially thus: " No, I should not have been angry, I am not that sort of man. How I wish in fact—for you and I could get on with each other—that you would stay here and marry my daughter. Say the word, and I will make a settlement "[17] (VII. 308-15) .

[15] The formula is Odyssean. In the Iliad I find only the first part, and only once, XXI. 150.

[16] καναχή with kindred verbs seems to mean the sound of hard substances elsewhere in Homer (the teeth of Achilleus in Il. XIX. 365) , but Pindar uses it of flutes, Pyth. 10, 39.

[17] " For you and I could get on with each other " paraphrases τά τε φρονέων ἅ τ' ἐγώ περ. The last person who had said this to Odysseus was Agamemnon,

Stage by stage, this proposal (athetized, or disapprovingly suspected, by Aristarchus)[18] has been led up to by everything said
since Arete noticed the clothes. But that is all, nothing happens.
"This is if you want to stay; god forbid that any Phaiakian should
keep you against your will" [19] (VII. 315-16). A line and a half
serves as fishplate between the first half of Alkinoos' speech and the
second, for he now goes rambling on for a dozen more lines, at the
end of which he is praising his people's seamanship. So we end with
conveyance and this makes it easy for Odysseus to accept conveyance
home. He has not had to accept or reject the proposal. It is gone
by default.

And that is all. Nothing more is said about this marriage. Next
day, after the games, Alkinoos alludes to the wife and children of
Odysseus (VIII. 243 παρὰ σῇ τ' ἀλόχῳ καὶ σοῖσι τέκεσσιν). How he
came by this not quite accurate information, we are not told. Or
did he merely assume, when Odysseus failed to snap up Nausikaa,
that the man must be married?

Next day, instead of sailing off, Odysseus is entertained by a series
of athletic contests. After the regular events, Laodamas, one of the
King's sons, invites Odysseus to have a try in competition. He
declines; he is tired; he only wants to go home. A friend of
Laodamas, one Euryalos, winner of the wrestling, then tells Odysseus, in substance: "I thought not. You do not look like an athlete;
more like a merchant, bent on profit" (VIII. 158-64). After an angry
reply, stating that the young man's brains, or manners, come far
short of his physical magnificence, Odysseus snatches up a discus
far bigger and heavier than the one the Phaiakians had been using
and, applauded by a disguised Athene, throws it so far beyond
expectation as to endanger the spectators. He then challenges all
comers (except Laodamas, his host's son) to any event (except,
perhaps, the footrace). There are no takers. There follows the same

_Il._ IV. 361. It should be added that many have thought Alkinoos is meant to be
a figure of fun. See A. Shewan, _Homeric Essays_ (Oxford, 1935), pp. 253-58, with
abundant reference to the earlier literature; further, Woodhouse, p. 59; G. S.
Kirk, _The Songs of Homer_ (Cambridge, 1962), p. 370. This may well be; I am
not yet absolutely convinced.

[18] Scholl. on VII. 311, Dindorf I, p. 350: τοὺς ἐξ Ἀρίσταρχος διστάζει Ὁμήρου
εἶναι. εἰ δὲ καὶ Ὁμηρικοί, εἰκότως αὐτοὺς περιαιρεθῆναί φησι. πῶς γὰρ ἀγνοῶν τὸν
ἄνδρα μνηστεύεται αὐτῷ τὴν θυγατέρα καὶ οὐ προτρεπόμενος, ἀλλὰ λιπαρῶν. But this
last is wrong; the fact is that Alkinoos breaks off and does not insist.

[19] VII. 315-16:

ἀέκοντα δέ σ' οὔ τις ἐρύξει
Φαιήκων· μὴ τοῦτο φίλον Διὶ πατρὶ γένοιτο.

pause as followed his first speech in the house of Alkinoos (VII. 154 and, in the *Iliad,* Hektor's challenge to the Achaians), and, this time it is an embarrassed silence (234):

ὣς ἔφαθ᾽, οἱ δ᾽ ἄρα πάντες ἀκὴν ἐγένοντο σιωπῇ.

Alkinoos changes the subject. There follows an entertainment by Demodokos, the famous song about Aphrodite and Ares (VIII. 266-366), then an exhibition ball-dance by two of the King's sons (VIII. 370-80). The end of the games merges in a proposal (not the first) for gift-giving to the stranger. The rude Euryalos is made to give Odysseus a special gift. The games are over.

What will follow, ultimately, will be the identification of Odysseus; his account of his wanderings; his return to Ithaka in a Phaiakian ship. These do not concern me here. There are certain points about the games.

The motive for having games at all is given by the poet. Alkinoos has noticed that the minstrel's song about an episode at Troy has for some reason saddened his guest; he improvises the games to divert, amuse, and impress Odysseus (VIII. 94-103). But Woodhouse has seen here an adaptation of an older tale in which the unknown stranger excelled in contests for the hand of the princess.[20] He makes the song of Ares and Aphrodite a kind of wedding song, though it is hard to think of anything more discouraging for a bridegroom. The following points about the games may be noted.

Cornford has argued that the original event in the Olympic games was " the foot-race for the bride "[21] which also distinguished the chief Kouros in the community. Certainly the footrace was traditionally *the* Olympic event par excellence. This is plain from Xenophanes, Pausanias, Diodorus, the Oxyrhynchos victor-list, etc.[22] The footrace is mentioned first in Pindar's account of the original complete games held by Herakles at Olympia,[23] just as it comes first among Homer's Phaiakian games (VIII. 120) though not in those for Patroklos. The status of the victor as chief Kouros might help (at least) to explain the curious emphasis of Homer on speed of foot as a distinctive quality of heroes.[24] Also, in the nature of things

20 Woodhouse, pp. 59-62.

21 F. M. Cornford, in J. E. Harrison, *Themis* (2d. ed., Cambridge, 1927), pp. 231-35. Cornford's essay, "The Origin of the Olympic Games," forms Ch. 7 of Miss Harrison's book.

22 Xenophanes 2, 1, 17-18 Diehl; Pausanias V. 7, 4; 8, 3; *Ox. Pap.* 222. Diodorus regularly lists the winner of the footrace as "the winner."

23 Pindar, *Ol.* 10, 64.

24 So the formula θοός περ ἐὼν πολεμιστής, *Il.* V. 571; XV. 585. Compare the

a short race is the most efficient and most dramatic ἅμιλλα or way of deciding without tedious complication who is best of a large number of athletes (or suitors) .[25] So Antaios of Libya married off his daughter, in a way suggested by, but not identical with, the way in which Danaos disposed of his forty-eight daughters, and conceivably the way in which the Lemnian women chose their own second husbands.[26]

Nausikaa had five brothers. Two were married, three were bachelors (VI. 62-63) . Only three competed in the games, and one may suppose that these were the three bachelors. Two were winners, Klytoneos in the footrace (mentioned first), Laodamas in boxing. " In literal fact," says Cornford, " it (sc. the footrace) seems to have been a contest to determine who should represent the male partner in the sacred marriage with the victor of the virgins' race." [27] Though it is not recorded that Nausikaa had won any such race, only outshone all others in a ball-dance (VI. 100-109), one must admit the possibility that, in some earlier version (if there was any), the νόμοι of the Phaiakians, as of Aiolos' family (X. 5-7), allowed brother-sister marriages.[28] It is more likely that only young marriageable men were competing, and sedate young husbands had no motive for showing off.

Odysseus, a great wrestler (IV. 343 = XVII. 134; Il. XXIII. 708-39) , was also, or had been, a runner (Il. XXIII. 754-97) . According

---

praise of Antilochus, Od. IV. 202. Ares alone of the gods has the epithet θοός (Il. V, 430, etc.) , and he (not, e.g., Hermes) is the swiftest of the gods, Od. VIII. 331. Aias is as strong as Achilleus but less swift, Il. XIII. 325, and in fact speed is the characteristic epithet of Achilleus.

[25] While the footrace seems specially appropriate, other competitions might sometimes have settled the issue. Sophocles leaves the nature of the struggle between Herakles and Acheloos obscure and confused (Trach. 507-22); but the broken horn suggests wrestling, see Jebb ad loc. Theseus boxed with the Minotaur (Apollodorus, Epit. 1, 9) so that Ariadne (like Deianeira, but unlike her own mother) might not have to marry a bull. Was Euryalos (see below) the monster from whom Alkinoos and Arete hoped their Nausikaa would be saved?

[26] For Antaios and Danaos, see Pindar, Pyth. 9, 105-25. The Argonauts ran a race on Lemnos; it seems to have been staged by Hypsipyle and the Lemnian Women (Pindar, Ol. 4, 23-31). Pindar says nothing about the choosing of husbands, but the analogy between the Lemnian Women and the Daughters of Danaos suggests that this might once have been in the story.

[27] Cornford, p. 233.

[28] Arete and Alkinoos seem to be made brother and sister, VII. 54-55; so too Hesiod (frag. 73 Rzach) according to the scholiast on this passage. But further on (VII. 56-66) they seem to be uncle and niece. See G. Murray, The Rise of the Greek Epic (Oxford, 1907), p. 117.

to Pausanias (III. 12, 1) he won the hand of Penelope by outracing the other suitors in a race arranged by Ikarios, though I know of no evidence that Homer knew this story. Concerning the red-figured amphora which shows Pelops driving away in his chariot with Hippodameia, Conford remarks: " Hippodameia stands erect, look-ing much more like a goddess than a ravished bride." [29] The scene could also illustrate the story told by Pausanias (III. 20, 10-11) about Odysseus driving away with Penelope, against her father's wish; or again, Pindar's word-tableau of Thrasyboulos driving with Nike standing beside him in his chariot (*Pyth.* 6, 17-19).[30] When Odysseus, after his great discus throw, challenges any Phaiakian (except Laodamas) to any event, he mentions footracing (VIII. 206), but ends by half-withdrawing this part of the challenge. He would not expect to win in a race and gives the curiously modern-sounding (but genuine) reason: " I couldn't keep my legs in shape on shipboard " (VIII. 230-33). If he does not quite decline to com-pete, he at least declines to win. Competition would have set him as a challenger against Klytoneos (VIII. 119; 123), Nausikaa's brother and, on one unlikely view, her prospective husband; but the implication of competing against one of his host's sons is not mentioned in connection with Klytoneos, only with Laodamas (VIII. 207-11). That would be boxing (VIII. 130, and note the word μάχοιτο, VIII. 208). Homer knew well what a boxer like Epeios (*Il.* XXIII. 689-99) or Odysseus himself (XVIII. 90-99) could do to an opponent.

It was Laodamas who first invited Odysseus to compete, in terms at least technically courteous (VIII. 145-51). " Come and try, ξεῖνε πάτερ." It may be unfair, but it is possible, to read some under-meaning in the scene. Odysseus in his doubtful forties stands be-tween the two generations, Kouroi and Gerontes. "Do you count yourself a Kouros or not? You'll have to show us." A modernizing translator would add (not without justification) " daddy-o." And at least Odysseus does say: " Laodamas, what are you people trying to make me do? You're having a game with me " (VIII. 153):

Λαοδάμα, τί με ταῦτα κελεύετε κερτομέοντες;

When Odysseus declines, Euryalos takes up the question much more rudely (VIII. 158-64). " You bear no resemblance to an ath-

[29] Cornford, pp. 226-27.
[30] Or Peisistratos riding into Athens with Athene; Aristotle, *Ath. Pol.* 14, 4 (Herodotus, I. 60, 4-5, does not actually put her in the chariot).

lete (he says this twice) but are more like a traveling merchant bent on profit." Elsewhere in Homer respectable acquisitiveness brings no rebuke. But in the constant Hellenic competitive drive for status, the respected man of property will be naturally older than the dependent young gentleman who must win κλέος by personal show of strength and skill.

Odysseus replies in effect that there is another way to win status, by public intelligence and just dealing. He draws a brief picture of such a man, unblest with looks and stature, but for his virtue idolized by his fellow-townsmen (VIII. 166-73). Hesiod, in the *Theogony*, describing a just βασιλεύς blessed by the Muses (80-97), uses remarkably similar language. Compare VIII. 171 ὁ δ' ἀσφαλέως ἀγορεύει with *Theogony* 86, ὁ δ' ἀσφαλέως ἀγορεύων; VIII. 172 and *Th.* 92 with identical αἰδοῖ μειλιχίῃ, μετὰ δὲ πρέπει ἀγρομένοισιν; and finally VIII. 173,

$$\text{ἐρχόμενον δ' ἀνὰ ἄστυ θεὸν ὣς εἰσορόωσιν}$$

and *Th.* 91,

$$\text{ἐρχόμενον δ' ἀν' ἀγῶνα θεὸν ὣς ἱλάσκονται.}$$

Without being able to say which of these two passages is the earlier or which borrows from which,[31] I would note that, while Hesiod is drawing no contrast, Homer sets a standard of general humanity recognized by both poets against the aristocratic idea of ἀρετή expressed through proficiency and strength later produced by the Pindaric pair, πόνος and δαπάνη, which Homer also seems to have known, but in which Hesiod shows no interest.[32]

Odysseus follows this speech with his discus-throw and his challenge. No one takes up the challenge. Alkinoos compliments his guest, who has proved his ἀρετή, and withdraws his claims for Phaiakian excellence in athletics. "We are not flawless boxers nor wrestlers (you do not need to prove yourself against Laodamas or Euryalos)." "We do run well" (VIII. 246-47). (Odysseus did not chose to run). After the dancing and singing, Euryalos is directed to apologize with word and gift for his ill-timed utterance (VIII. 396-97).

---

[31] Wilamowitz, for instance, and Bethe have argued for the priority of Hesiod; see U. von Wilamowitz-Moellendorff, *Ilias und Homer* (2nd ed., Berlin, 1920), p. 477; E. Bethe, *Homer*, II (Leipzig and Berlin, 1922), 239. For the priority of Homer, see P. Cauer, *Gött. Gel. Anz.* (1917), p. 532; *Grundfragen der Homerkritik* (3rd ed., Leipzig, 1923), pp. 653-55; F. Solmsen, *TAPA*, LXXXV (1954), 1-15.

[32] πόνος and δαπάνη, Pindar, *Isth.* 6, 10-11; μόχθος and δαπάναι *Isth.* 5, 57; μόχθος = πόνος, *Nem.* 7, 16 and 74.

Euryalos promptly does so, with the gift of a sword, but in doing so he makes three points. This sword, he says, Odysseus will find worth a great deal, πολέος δέ οἱ ἄξιον ἔσται (VIII. 405) : harmless (compare *Il.* 23. 562), were it not for his own earlier remarks, about the acquisitive trader (163). He approaches Odysseus with χαῖρε, πάτερ ὦ ξεῖνε (VIII. 408), almost formulaic,[33] polite, yet perhaps significant when combined with the third point, " I do hope you get home to rejoin your wife," σοὶ δὲ θεοὶ ἄλοχον ἰδέειν καὶ πατρίδ' ἱκέσθαι / δοῖεν (VIII. 410) . " For doubtless," he adds, " you feel out of place here" (VIII. 411). δηθὰ φίλων ἄπο πήματα πάσχεις is formulaic,[34] but will scarcely do for one who might like to settle down— with the king's daughter.

It is perhaps an ordinary pattern of story that the hero should have his taunting challenger. Unferth rudely challenges Beowulf, out of jealousy, since Unferth himself is unequal to dealing with Grendel.[35] Sir Kay taunts Beaumains, an intruder in the tradition.[36] But Woodhouse has already seen in Euryalos a rival for the hand of the princess " in the old tale." [37] Indeed, Euryalos is the only young Phaiakian outside of the royal family to be described, and he is outstanding (VIII. 115-17; 176-77) . But overbearing and cantankerous (a suitor type in the *Odyssey*) . Nausikaa, we remember, spoke of overbearing people among the Phaiakians, μάλα δ' εἰσὶν ὑπερφίαλοι κατὰ δῆμον (VI. 274) , who will suspect the worst if she goes home openly with Odysseus. In this speech, her syntax is disorderly. The sentence beginning " when we come to the city," αὐτὰρ ἐπὴν πόλιος ἐπιβήομεν (VI, 262), does not reach its natural conclusion, "sit down and wait until I have time to get home" (VI. 295), until after thirty-three lines and a whole new start. So when she uses the plural about "some people" it could be a feminine, adolescent, or emotional plural, vague or exaggerating, and she could well be talking about Euryalos alone, for he is the only Phaiakian who behaves that way. Then in hinting to Odysseus that he is impressive and she is marriageable, sought after, but still fancy-free (so Woodhouse), she is at the same time taking pains so that, if she fails to have Odysseus, she will not lose her second string. If we permit ourselves the illusion that Nausikaa is a real person with a history and a

---

33 *Od.* XVIII. 122; XX. 199.

34 Odysseus actually said it of himself, VII. 152.

35 *Beowulf* ll. 499-528. Like Euryalos, Unferth atones for his rudeness with a gift when his opponent has proved himself (*Beowulf* 1455-72; 1807-12).

36 Malory, *Morte Darthur* VII. 1-4.

37 Woodhouse, p. 61.

future, Euryalos, who else, will marry her. If she is her mother's daughter, she will be able to handle him.[38]

At the end of the games, Odysseus has been established as a married man who will be escorted home by a Phaiakian crew. After this point, he sees Nausikaa once more. He has bathed and dressed and is on his way to join the men at their wine, when he meets Nausikaa, who has come to stand by the pillar (VIII. 458):

στῆ ῥα παρὰ σταθμὸν τέγεος πύκα ποιητοῖο.

The line recalls other scenes, of Penelope coming into the presence of the suitors (several times) [39] but the context of the formula highlights the difference. Penelope comes (I. 331-35):

οὐκ οἴη, ἅμα τῇ γε καὶ ἀμφίπολοι δύ' ἕποντο.
ἡ δ' ὅτε δὴ μνηστῆρας ἀφίκετο δῖα γυναικῶν,
στῆ ῥα παρὰ σταθμὸν τέγεος πύκα ποιητοῖο,
ἄντα παρειάων σχομένη λιπαρὰ κρήδεμνα ·
ἀμφίπολος δ' ἄρα οἱ κεδνὴ ἑκάτερθε παρέστη.

These lines in turn recall another lady's progress, that of Helen to the gate tower (Il. III. 141-45). Helen also goes (III. 143)

οὐκ οἴη, ἅμα τῇ γε καὶ ἀμφίπολοι δύ' ἕποντο.

And she is also veiled (III. 141). But Helen was going out of the house. Helen at home in the Odyssey (IV. 120-37) makes a quite different entrance, attended, it is true, but by a devoted procession in a scene at once majestic and cozy. She is not veiled and she needs no protection. Penelope is veiled in her own house, and firmly flanked by guarding attendants. Nausikaa sleeps at night behind locked doors with a maid on either side (VI. 15-19), but when she meets Odysseus she seems to have given her maids the slip, and unlike Penelope she seems not to be veiled (VIII. 459)

θαύμαζεν δ' 'Οδυσῆα ἐν ὀφθαλμοῖσιν ὁρῶσα.

The parting speeches are brief and delicate: "goodbye, stranger [she does not say ξεῖνε πάτερ]. Remember me. I am your first savior." "I will think of you as if you were a goddess, all the rest of my days. You gave me life."

---

[38] I am aware that Hellanicus, Aristotle, and Dictys had her marry Telemachos. See Hellanicus, frag. 170. c Jacoby = Suïdas s.v. 'Ανδοκίδης, whose family claimed descent from this union; Aristotle, frag. 506 Rose; Dictys 6.6. Another candidate for the honor of marrying Telemachos is Polykaste, daughter of Nestor, who gave him a bath, Od. III. 464; thus the Hesiodic Catalogue 17. 1 Rzach²; Scholl. on Od. XVI. 118 Dindorf ii, 625 (Q). Still another is Circe, according to the Nostoi, p. 144 Allen. See Wörner, in Roscher, Lexikon d. Mythologie, s.v. Nausikaa.

[39] I. 333, see also XVI. 415; XVIII. 209; XXI. 64.

Her name does not appear in the *Odyssey* again.

"Nausikaa shapes for a few lines like a woman. Then she fades unused." [40] This can stand for the modern poet or novelist complaining about the failure to exploit further a character so engaging, all the more that Greek literature is not rich in vivacious ingenues. Not used, we may say, in the sense that the story has not married her to Odysseus, nor had her involve him in a desperate and sticky illicit love affair (to satisfy the moderns), nor left her to pine away and die after his departure like the fair Elaine at Astolat (to satisfy the Victorians).[41] Homer, I feel, would always have been quite clear about the fact that these two attractive and mutually attracted people did not belong to each other. He was not for her nor she for him; they could only look and admire. Odysseus could get home, where he belonged, to his wife, who belonged to him and to whom he belonged, only by meeting and proving himself in a series of trials, both tasks and temptations, by terror and by seduction, in which he proved his stamina and resourcefulness, and his fidelity and moral fibre. The last and subtlest of these temptations was Nausikaa.

Before I conclude, let me raise briefly the question whether this account seems to be all by the same hand. We noted three important atheteses: first, Nausikaa's wish expressed to her maids that Odysseus would stay and marry her (VI. 244-45), praised by Ephorus, athetized, with doubts, by Aristarchus; second, Nausikaa's description of the jealous scandalmongers (VI. 275-88), athetized as *aprepes* and out of character, probably by Aristarchus; third, Alkinoos' proposal to Odysseus (VII. 311–16), questioned and disapproved of by Aristarchus. If these three passages are taken out of the text, all outright reference to Odysseus as a possible husband for Nausikaa vanishes.

Motives for athetizing lines seem to include:

1. Suspicion that certain repeated lines would be more appropriate in other contexts. This consideration does not apply here.

2. Aprepeia, of various sorts.

3. Scientific concern when lines contained in some copies were

---

[40] Shaw, *loc. cit.*

[41] Later ancient traditions involved Odysseus in affairs with several girls: Kallidike, queen of Thesprotia, Apollodorus, *Epit.* VII. 34-35; the daughter of Thoas son of Andraimon (*after* his return to Ithaka) VII. 40; and Euippe of Thesprotia, Eustathius 1796, 35 (*Cyclus* p. 144 Allen). Eustathius cites the authority of Sophocles and the historian Lysimachus for Euippe. See Pearson, *Sophocles, Fragments,* I, 146; II, 106. Pearson identifies Kallidike and Euippe. The story is found in Parthenius 3.

missing from others, and the conclusion that such lines were later additions not included in the earliest complete text, i.e. (according to Bolling), the Peisistratid recension or something like it. This is the only principle which Bolling really allows.[42]

If, as I doubt, Bolling was right and Aristarchus athetized solely on the grounds of what he found missing in his texts, the interesting result is not so much the rock-ribbed honesty of Aristarchus, still less the fundamentality of the Peisistratid recension, but the fact that this all points to the existence of some sprightly genius who was tampering with the text at quite an early date; before Alcman, in fact, and that is pretty far back, and long before Peisistratos.

But Bolling I suspect is wrong; Aristarchus has given himself away. He wanted to strike out Alkinoos' proposal as unworthy of Homer, even if by Homer.[43] Yet he did not. I see Aristarchus as a cheerless man who checked his sense of humor, if he had one, in the cloakroom before he went into the library; but at least he confined himself to querying these lines instead of striking them out.

What has here been demonstrated? At best, I think, this: that the language of *Odyssey* VI-VIII is frequently sophisticated, artful, careful, and self-conscious. It may not then be going too far to assume that the storyteller was aware that his material was full of possibilities, mostly unexploited, of untold potential stories. I have tried, by deliberately overinterpreting certain points (but the points are there) to show that there was a validly possible connection between, for instance, athletic contests and marriage, or again rescue and marriage (Kalypso would prove this). Without then having to postulate any previous model story which has been disarranged (though this of course remains a possibility), one might be content to think that such a storyteller in such a mood would be constantly aware of these possibilities, and would find this suggested imperfect and impossible romance something affecting to his hearers and himself.

Bryn Mawr College
7 January 1966

[42] G. M. Bolling, *The External Evidence for Interpolation in Homer* (Oxford, 1925), pp. 44-56.

[43] Scholl. VII. 311, Dindorf ɪ, 350 (P). See above, n. 18, and see M. H. A. L. H. Van der Valk, *Textual Criticism of the Odyssey* (Leiden, 1949), pp. 186-88.

A NEW MANUSCRIPT FRAGMENT OF
CONSTANTINUS AFRICANUS,
COMPENDIUM MEGATECHNI GALENI

L. R. Lind

In the summer of 1959 I discovered in Zeitlin and Ver Brugge's book shop in Los Angeles a parchment manuscript (now listed as No. 46 in Catalogue 209, dated 1965) used in the covers of a copy of Vitruvius, *De Architectura* (Florence: anonymous publisher, 1496). When removed, the manuscript proved to be two bifolia (four leaves, eight pages) of a codex eight by six inches in size with generally thirty-nine lines to each page, a total of three hundred and three lines of text in a hand of the thirteenth or fourteenth century; page seven has thirty-eight lines and pages three, four, five, and six only thirty-seven lines.

Mr. Richard J. Durling, of the History of Medicine Division of the National Library of Medicine at Bethesda, Maryland, found that the fragment formed part of the *Compendium megatechni Galeni a Constantino compositum,* printed as *Megatechni* in the *Omnia Opera* of Isaac Israeli, edited by A. Turinus and sold by Bartholomew Trot (Lyon: Johannes de Platea, 1515), fol. CXCVIII^v, nona particula, col. 1, extending to fol. CC^v, decima particula, col. 2. The manuscript fragment is thus a Latin translation of Galen, *Methodus Medendi,* which in C. G. Kühn's text (Leipzig: C. Cnobloch, 1821–1833) extends from Lib. IX. cap. 4, p. 611, with gaps, to Lib X. cap. 3, p. 678. Numbering each of the eight pages, the order in which they appear in the printed text is as follows (it is clear that the two bifolia were inside a quire): (1) notum est ei . . . ; (2) aspiciens nullam . . . ; (3) -teriam minuere . . . ; (4) frigidissimum. aut cum . . . ; (5) alium laborem et . . . ; (6) et in septimo . . . ; (7) oportet infirmum . . . ; (8) ad cor uelociter. . . .

Constantinus Africanus or Afer was born at Carthage and appears at Monte Cassino around A.D. 1056 to 1060. He lived for a time at Salerno and died there in 1087. He has been called "the first great translator from the Arabic into Latin." [1] Francesco Puccinotti [2] has discussed Constantinus and his school as well as his manuscripts in Italy; other writers have contributed considerably to our understanding of his importance in the history of medicine.[3] His services as a translator are concisely handled by Moritz Steinschneider.[4]

At least sixty-nine manuscripts of this translation of Galen are extant [5] and it has not therefore seemed practical to attempt a collation of them all for the purposes of this publication. It is difficult, moreover, to determine whether all of them are by Constantinus or have been revised in part at least by other translators. By way of an experiment I have collated from microfilm BM Royal 12. C. XV, 13th cent., fols. 118r–145r and find that it agrees mainly with the manuscript or manuscripts used by Turinus for his printed edition. I have decided to treat the printed edition as another

[1] By George Sarton, *Introduction to the History of Science,* I (Baltimore: Williams & Wilkins, 1927), 769.

[2] Francesco Puccinotti, *Storia della Medicina,* II (Livorno, 1855), 292–304; 306–308.

[3] See Paul Oskar Kristeller, "The School of Salerno, Its Development and Its Contribution to the History of Learning," *Bulletin of the History of Medicine,* XVII (1945), 151, with full bibliographical notes.

[4] Moritz Steinschneider, *Die europäischen Übersetzungen aus dem Arabischen bis Mitte des 17. Jahrhunderts* (Graz: Akademische Druck und Verlagsanstalt, 1956), p. 10, first published in *Sitzungsberichte der phil.-hist. Klasse der kais. Akad. der Wissensch.* (Wien), CXLIX, 4 (1905), 9–12.

[5] H. Diels, *Die Handschriften der antiken Ärzte. I. Teil. Hippokrates und Galenos* (Berlin: Verlag der königl. Akademie der Wissenschaften, 1905), pp. 92–93. Strangely enough, Diels omits Berlin 897, which is listed by Valentin Rose in his *Verzeichnis der lateinischen Handschriften* (2. Band, 3. Abteilung [Berlin, 1905], 1058). This manuscript is wrongly listed as Bern 897 by Lynn Thorndike and Pearl Kibre, *A Catalogue of Incipits of Mediaeval Scientific Writings in Latin* (Cambridge, Mass.: The Mediaeval Academy of America, 1937; 2nd ed., 1963), col. 596; cols. 970, 1163, 1282, 1417. They list, of course, only a few of the manuscripts. Berlin 897 is now lost, according to a letter from Dr. Hans Lülfing, of the Deutsche Staatsbibliothek, Berlin, having been removed to safety during World War II and never returned. It may now be at Marburg or Tübingen; see Paul Oskar Kristeller, *Latin Manuscript Books 1600* (New York: Fordham University Press, 1960), p. 78. Unfortunately, the information given by Diels is not complete, often lacking the book numbers for the *Methodus Medendi* and folio numbers for the manuscripts. Hence nothing short of a complete collection of microfilms could serve as basis for a collation; not all of these, moreover, would contain the excerpt given in LA. Most of the manuscripts listed by Diels are of the thirteenth and fourteenth centuries.

manuscript and to collate the present fragment (which I propose to name LA) with it.

The manuscript fragment deals with a discussion of the care and cure of fever, an excerpt from Galen's *Methodus Medendi,* also known by the early Renaissance variant titles as *Megatechne* or *De Ingenio Sanitatis,* one of the earliest of his works to be translated into Latin. It appears in the first collected edition of Galen, published at Venice in 1490. The highlight of the fragment is a rather exciting story in which Galen tells how he took over the treatment of a young man who had fallen ill with fever due to imprudent overexertion and untimely bathing and drinking of water. Having saved the patient by his own regimen, Galen did not neglect the opportunity to upbraid the other attending physicians for their ignorance.

TEXT OF THE LOS ANGELES MANUSCRIPT (LA) OF CONSTANTINUS AFRICANUS

The readings of the printed text which vary from those of the manuscript are given in square brackets immediately after those of the manuscript. Words which appear in the printed text but are missing in the manuscript are given in angle brackets. Words omitted in the printed text which appear in the manuscript are given in parentheses. The abbreviation *rev.* indicates that the two words immediately before it are reversed in their order in the printed text. Marginal and interlinear notes and glosses are presented with numbered footnotes. Since only two texts are involved, an *apparatus criticus* heavily laden with variant readings is obviated by this method of presentation and all variations are apparent at a glance.

Fol. CXCVIII verso, Nona particula, column 1 (page 1 in LA):

notum est ei sinocham esse de oppilatione propter multitudinem sanguinis ortam et prohibitionem dissolutionis propter crassitiem [grossiciem] sanguinis [corporis] et multitudinem carnis. At postquam febris sicut [sic] fuerat in illa nocte permansit. conueniunt medici una (*rev.*) ad flebotomandum [phlebotomandum] eum, sed discordati sunt ad quam horam debeant eum flebotomare [phlebotomare], unde permansit non flebotomatus [phlebotomatus] usque in [ad] alium diem et duricies febris augmentata est. Ad tertiam autem noctem passus est intolerabilem incensionem ⟨et⟩ extensionem ⟨et⟩ in toto corpore, dolorem in capite, uigilias
10   et angustiam, unde pre [ex] angustia coactus eger uoluebat se de uno

latere in aliud et de forma in formam mutabatur. In octaua (uero) hora
noctis (rev.) uenit ad eum Galienus pulsumque et cetera sicut diximus
putredinem non ostendere repperit, nam equalis erat pulsus, urina satis
[sane] uicina, calor multus et fumosus [fumus] et non pinguitudinis
15 [pungitiuus] et animaduersus est eum confestim et non tarde debere
flebotomari [phlebotomari]. Timuit (enim) tarde [tardare] flebotomiam
[phlebotomiam] ne putrefactis humoribus febris in putridam conuerte-
retur, unde flebotomauit [phlebotomauit] eum et dimisit sanguinem
fluere usque ad defectionem; deinde curam circa eum habuit quia secun-
20 dum racionem et experimentum notificatum est ei sanguinem usque ad
defectionem in his auferre utilissimum esse si uirtus tollerabilis erit quia
non solum purgat sed ⟨etiam⟩ propter defectionem corpus refrigerat, unde
febris aut cessat aut refrigeratur quo circa uel uomitus uel egestio colica
[cholerica] eos sequitur totumque corpus sudore infunditur. Taliter
25 autem huic egro contigit, unde quidam ex famulis dixerunt Galieno:
Inclite uir, multum subito febrem ⟨domini nostri⟩ abstulisti. Transactis
uero horis duabus (rev.) dedit ei parum cibi iussitque ut quiesceret et
dormiret. In quinta quidem hora reuersus inuenit ⟨illum grauissimo
somno teneri, exiccare enim cepit eius sudorem et ipse non sentiebat, qui
30 famulis ut sudorem tergerent precipiens abiit, sensit enim Galienus febrem
cessatam esse. Sed in decima hora reuersus inuenit⟩ eum dormientem.
Abiit ergo (et) in prima hora noctis veniens repperit eum dormientem
et excitans illum [eum] dedit ei tipsanum [ptisanum]. Deinde per totam
noctem eum dimisit. Mane autem [uero] missus in balneum sanus factus
35 est. Alter uero iuuenis qui febrem continuam ⟨habuit⟩ cum putredine
(habuit); causa fuerat fortis laboris per totum diem. (Nam) [Is] is ⟨enim⟩
postea lauit se cum aqua frigida parumque comedit citoque ⟨febre⟩ in illa
nocte (febre) uexatus est, sed febris in nocte ac die confortata fuit quem
in alio [alia] die Galienus uidens perpendit totas [omnes] qualitates
40 ⟨eius⟩ esse ⟨similes⟩ prioribus nisi tantum [tamen] quia putredinem
denotabant ex incensione febris et morsione pulsusque inordinatione et
urine ⟨multa in⟩ innaturalem mutationem [mutatione], quem mox flebotomauit [phlebotomauit] sanguinem usque ad defectionem dimittens;
aliquanto autem spacio transacto dedit ei mellicratum et post ⟨unam⟩
45 horam tipsanum [ptisanum]. Sed bonum est dari si febris est (rev.) acuta
ydrozaccaram [hydrozaccaram] cum aqua rosata maxime in calida regione
quem inquit postquam (eum) aspexi arbitratus sum esse sinocham (rev.)
cum putredine que ita fuit (rev.). Postea uero in tertia noctis hora (rev.)
magnitudinem eius (page 2 in LA) aspiciens nullam suarum qualitatum
50 minutam habentis (rev.) non ultra dubitaui. Sed tamen uolui ⟨eam⟩
inuestigare an in tempore accessionis terciane confortaretur et tempus
accessionis terciane erat in vii [septima] hora noctis ad quam horam
rediens inueni sicut arbitratus fueram quia tamen [tantum] non augmen-
tatam sed parum minoratam (quam ad primam horam noctis fuerat repperi.
55 In media autem die palam inueni eam minoratam), unde certissime [cer-
tissimam] eam esse sciui (printed text: sciui eam esse) quandam speciem
sinoche quae dicitur apagmasticus [epaumastica]. Nutriui ergo eum
[illum] in illa hora sicut prius feci. In quarta autem nocte inueni eam

ualde declinatam. Cibaui (uero) eum cepitque declinationis [declinatio]
60 ⟨et⟩ (augmentatio apparere et secundum mod[um] (space in LA) declinationis) digestio in urina apparebat [apparere], quare certissime praeuidi
febrem in vii [septima] die determinatam [terminandam] quod sicut
consideraui contingit (euenit is written above contingit and also appears
in the printed text). Porro oportet (te) intelligere quia quaedam sunt
65 (rev.) febres quarum putredo in prima die apparet et ⟨quedam⟩ quarum
apparet in tertia et etiam (rev.) in quarta nisi eger flebotomatus [phlebo-
tomatus] fuerit et nullus febricitans ex [et] opilatione [oppilationem]
sine putredine et flebotomatus [phlebotomatus] conuersus est in putredinem. Proper hoc dico (nichil) in hac febre ⟨nihil⟩ flebotomia [phlebo-
70 tomia] utilius esse (rev. utilius esse flebotomia) et extractione sanguinis
⟨et⟩ si etas uirtusque [utriusque] sustinuerint [sustinuerit] usque ad
defectionem sit. Sinautem minuamus sanguinem duabus apoforesibus
quantum in una minuere debemus quibus nisi ⟨ministrando⟩ flebotomia
[phlebotomiam] succurratur ueniant [uenient] in magnam molestiam et
75 timorem nisi uis nature eis fortunata fuerit cum nimio sanguinis fluxu
per nares uel multo sudore [per nimium sudorem]. Sufficeret autem
stultis medicis ut ex hoc quod in hoc morbo aspiciunt fieri (ex) actione
nature castigarentur [curarentur] neque flebotomiam [phlebotomiam]
formidarent [facerent] et fugerent. In quo (neque) experimentum nec
80 racionem aspiciunt. Rursus oportet te intelligere putredinem quia [nam]
si fuerit in totis maioribus uenis fit febris continua. Si uero in quibusdam
membris fit continua periodica oportet etiam (te) non dimittere quin
flebotomes [phlebotomes] eos qui febrem patiuntur (rev.) ex fumis propter
negligentiam ⟨exercitiorum⟩ ceterorumque iam dictorum (exercitiorum)
85 non dissolutis et minue secundum posse uirtutis et secundum quod uides
ruborem coloris et plenitudinem uenarum ⟨et⟩ extensionem membrorum.
Tunc enim nisi hoc [hec] feceris subito morientur aut in nimiam molestiam
et timorem ueniunt [uenient] nisi fortuna ex ui nature eis fauet sicut
diximus cum fluxu sanguinis ex naribus uel sudore nimio. Necesse est
90 etiam ut in his plenitudinem in uenis habentibus sanguis putrefiat nisi
purgati fuerint quia pori eorum non sufficiunt in excludendo ⟨ex eis⟩
tantam sanguinis habundantiam [abundantiam] (ex eis) et fumi quanta
excludi conueniat, unde oportet ex eo quandam minui quantitatem ut
fumus minuatur et uene et natura permaneant custoditiue sue complexi-
95 onis (permaneant) dissolutione ex inflammatione et refrigeratione ex
sanguinis detractione adquisitis [acquisitis]. Tunc enim confortatur[1] . . .
(page 3 in LA and fol. CXCIX verso, Decima particula, in the printed text)
teriam minuere quae causa sue incensionis est neglexerimus; febris tunc
extinguetur, sed postea cum incensione reuerteretur [reuertitur] et ali-
100 quando maior quam (ante) fuerat. Huiusmodi etiam (rev.) ordo[2] est causa
sue longinquitatis et suspectionis perituri infirmi. Quod [Quia] si in
putredine minuenda studium impendamus [impenderimus] et (in) extin-
guenda febri minime[3] non omni febri expediet. Quia ⟨si⟩ aliquando

1. scilicet natura. 2. in febricoso *supra;* ordo. id. est. febrim extinguere et non
minuere materiam ipsius id est putredinem communem humorum istud est
causa prolixi morbi. sepe inde moriuntur infirmi *in margine.* 3. pro non.

febris [4] adeo fortis est ut infirmus pereat ⟨nisi citissime et fortissime febri
105   extinguende occurramus quanto magis ergo confortamus eam et augmen-
tamus eam cum rebus calefactiuis? Quocirca huiusmodi ordo non expedit
nisi illi febri que est non tante uiolentie ut pereat infirmus⟩ in illo tempore
cum putredinem minuere satagimus. Idcirco [Ideo] oportet nos studiose
curare quod magis ex utrisque necessarium [5] est (necessarium est ex utrisque
110   rev.) neque illud [6] [ideo] aliud curare negligamus. Quia plurime inuenimus causam incensionis febris fortiorem. Unde magis necessarium est ut
tollatur ⟨et⟩. Raro febrem reperimus in seipsam tantam habere uiolentiam
ut timeamus egrum esse periturum nisi fortissime et uelocissime ⟨ei ut⟩
extinguatur succurramus [occurramus]. Sed cum [7] hoc fuerit necessitas
115   nos compellit [compulit] ut eam mitigemus, deinde putredinem detra-
hamus [decrescamus]. Propterea oportet te perpendere [intelligere] significationes magnitudinis febris et quantitatis putredinis et uirtutis et his
perspectis [expertis] uirtutem custodiri [custodi]. Deinde illa utraque [8]
curare satage et compara uirtutis quantitatem ad magnitudinem febris et
120   ad tempus putredinis, quae [9] si conueniunt festinanter quod faciendum
est utiliter fac. Si autem ⟨in his⟩ aliquid contrarii ⟨esse⟩ uideris succurres
[succurre] ad faciendum quod magis necessarium est. Alia [10] tamen ne
praetermittas quia plurime ⟨plurimum has⟩ sicut diximus significationes
inuenimus nobis causam incensionis febris (esse) expellendam ostendentes
125   et causam uirtutis custoditiuam et confortatiuam magis esse necessariam.
Unde debes haec rationabiliter perpendere quia si uirtus [uirtutem]
permanere uidetur [uideris] cum putredo [11] minuta est matura [12] eicere
[ejiciet] eam. Quod [Quia] si defecta [13] non sustinet [sustineat] euacua-
tionem humorum uel cibi abstinentiam (rev.) seu alia similia putredinem
130   expellentia, primum confortetur deinde ad putredinem excludendam
conuertite [expellendam conuertere]. Ergo si febris tantae magnitudinis
est ut secum multa et pessima habeat accidentia prius ad eam mitigandam
studeamus, deinde ad ⟨id⟩ quod necessarium est. Porro effimerarum [ephi-
merarum] febrium quaedam sunt in quibus quod solitum est dissolui
135   inseparabiliter latitat et quaedam cum quibus ⟨constant⟩ plurime et
nonnulle ⟨e⟩ quibus raro ⟨sunt⟩. Ille uero ⟨cum⟩ quibus dissoluenda
inseparabiliter sunt fiunt ex lauacro aluminoso et ceteris stipticis aquis
uel frigidissimis aut conclusione pororum. Hec [He] uero cum quibus
plurime consistunt fiunt ex assiduitate solis. Cetere uero cum quibus
140   dissoluenda raro existunt fiunt ex ira, tristicia, uigiliis [uigilia] (et)
saturitate et apostemate in inguine (in inguine apostemate rev.). Sed omnibus his febribus dissolutio et pororum apertio conuenit (page 4 in LA)
⟨Hec etiam omnes non nisi in spacio xxiiii horarum permanent neque hoc
tempus transierint nisi cum error in dieta est aut cum tempus⟩ frigidis-
145   simum (fol. CXCIX verso, decima particula) aut cum cataplasma[ta] uel
epitima[ta] in exterioribus corporis applicantur. Cessatio quoque earum [14]

---

4. aliqua. 5. periculosius. 6. id est. minus periculosum. 7. id est uiolentia
caloris febris. 8. illa utraque calorem febris et putredinem. 9. quae dicta sunt
sed. 10. scilicet quando sunt magis periculosa. 11. id est. cum minus febris
digesta est. 12. id est. festina. 13. uirtus. 14. febrium.

uel fit cum sudore uel (fit) cum aliqua alia [15] (rev.) dissolutione et sentit
eger suam cessationem. Delicati etiam et nobiles transacta hac febre
balneum ingrediuntur et unguntur.[16] Deinde comedunt et dietam seruant.
150 Vulgi uero absque balneatione et unctione comedunt. Palam ergo intelli-
gimus effimereriam [ephimeram] febrem ⟨cessare⟩ cuius causa, id est, calor
solis cessata est. Est et alia cuius occasio cum ea [17] permanens est [per-
manet] sicut uiarum [18] conclusio que duobus modis est aut propter oppila-
tionem an [aut] propter conclusionem. Conclusio uero aliquando est
155 propter siccitatem sicut aque [19] uel aeris frigidissimi, aliquando (autem)
propter stipticitatem ut [sicut] aluminosarum aquarum et aliquando propter multitudinem humorum uel eorum uiscositatem. Que autem propter humorum multitudinem est utilis et laudabilis est [eius] curatio
flebotomia [phlebotomia] erit. Que uero propter humorum uiscositatem
160 causa [cura] inciditiua, attenuatiua, et mundatiua curetur. Inuestigare
etiam uirtutem in effimereria [ephimera] febre non multum necessarium
[necesse] est. In ea [20] que multarum dierum est uirtutem perpendere
necessarium (et utillimum) est maxime si prolixa [21] est, unde si uirtus
permaneat ne dubites [dimittas] quin purges [22] in febribus que paucorum
165 dierum (sunt). Si autem contraria, id est, defecta fuerit [23] conuerte[re] ad
purgationem secundum (quod) eius defectio[nem] (est). Raro etiam
uirtutem in prima uel secunda die defectam inuenimus. Quod si sic fuerit
non est propter aliud nisi propter malam complexionem infirmi uel
etatem sicut senium et puericiam. Aliquando (etiam) accidit infirmo
170 nimius labor propter deambulationem per solem, (propter) angustiam,
uigilias, (et) ieiunium, cui si omnia coadunata fuerint et uespere illius die
priusquam ⟨eger⟩ comedat febricitauerit et in ea nocte uigilauerit neque
propter febrem comederit uirtus eius necessario dissoluitur [dissoluetur]
maxime si calidissima [24] est et eger in sanitate macer erat. Unde hanc
175 similitudinem que Galieno contigit [contingit] tibi ostendam: [25] Quidam
iuuenis xxv annorum macilentus (uenosus), lacertosus, calidissime et
siccissime nature ⟨existens⟩ quoddam castellum egressus est ⟨et⟩ quadam
coactus legatione ad ciuitatem quandam abiit, unde per totum diem
laborando fessus est; postea balneatus cenauit. In nocte uero propter
180 cogitationem legationis (rev.) quae sibi nuntiata [data] fuerat uigilauit et
mane facto uelociter perfecit [per siccum] iter et calidum solem ambulauit.
Ingrediens autem urbem quedam [quandam] uidit unde ⟨et inde⟩ animus
eius (gauisus) quieuit. Tunc ire uolens ad balneum per locum palestrense
[palestre] ⟨transiuit et quendam magnum laborem ludere cepit, postea
185 autem transeundo quosdam certantes separauit. Quare uenit in⟩ (p. 5 in
LA) alium laborem et exercitium et pre [propter] garrulitatis et ire
motione[m] nimis fessus est. Rediens autem ad mansionem nimium eius

15. ut soluet uentris fluxus rigans per nares etc. 16. id est. unguento competen-
ter. 17. id est. cum febre. 18. magnarum uenarum. 19. balneum aquae frigidis-
simae uel aer frigidissimus inducunt siccitatem. 20. febre. 21. id est. cronica.
22. id est. putredinem. 23. uirtus. 24. complexio, id est, uel febris. 25. The story
told here is from Galen, *De Ingenio Sanitatis*, fols. 416ᵛ–417ʳ in Galen, *Opera
Omnia* (ed. Diomedes Bonardus; Venice: Filippo Pintio de Caneto, 1490), later
known as *Methodus Medendi* (Vol. x, Kühn, 3, 671–79).

corpus desiccatum atque [et] fatigatum est et angustia captus,[26] unde
bibit aquam. [a] Qua ebibita augmentata est angustia donec eam uomendo
190 (rev.) reddidit, qui cum se taliter sentiret propter timorem et suspectionem
febris ne ei ueniret [27] manducare noluit. In lecto ergo se prostrauit (et)
in illius diei uespere febrem habens per totam noctem propter febrem
uigilauit (uigilauit propter febrem rev.). Mane autem cepit dormire (neque
expergefactus est) usque ad medium diem ut uigilias quas in nocte passus
195 est restauraret [neque expergefactus est]. Tunc quidam ex illis medicis
ad eum uenere qui dixerunt [dicunt] non debere febricitantibus uictum
dari [dare] nisi post tercium diem. Cui [28] dixerunt: (o amice) in hac
hora non est bonum dare tibi ad comedendum. Nos autem uespere (te)
uidebimus. Uespere uero [autem] redeuntes febrem declinare uiderunt
200 neque horam cibandi oportunam [opportunam] aspexerunt. Sed quidam
⟨ex illis⟩ uolens ei [29] uictum dare ab illis increpatus est; dicebant enim si
febris fuisset [esset] omnino ablata bonum esset ut comederet, sed febre
adhuc existente comedere molestum (est). Quem [30] dimittentes altero die,
id est, (in) tercio summo mane uenerunt neque licentiam ei (rev.) come-
205 dendi dederunt, [ex] (s)pectabant enim horam terciane que [quia] erat
in fine diei. At in illa hora Galienus ad eum ueniens sicut ypocras [Hippo.]
in pronosticum [31] dicit illum repperit: habebat [habentem] nares acutas,
oculos concauos, timpora [tempora] plana et cetera. Unde certissime
notum est ei quod in ecticam [ethicam] et post in ptisin [phthysim]
210 esset uenturus (rev.) nisi confestim uictum [cibum] acciperet. Festinanter
ergo sibi ius uiscosum (rev.) tritici tribuit. Accessione uero [autem]
incipiente (et) pedes et manus (manus et pedes rev.) infrigidari conspexit
adeo (ut) diu morarentur [moraretur] ad calefaciendum, pulsum etiam
paruum (et) defectum. Unde arbitratus ⟨est⟩ eum esse periturum nisi ab
215 eo cibaretur. In quarto quidem die mane et sero illum cibauit et cognouit
uirtutem eius paulatim excitari et corpus humefieri, quia figura eius
⟨prius erat⟩ siccissima quasi siccum corium (erat). Cumque in quinto
[quinta] die febrem [febris] sicut ⟨prius⟩ fuerat conspexisset miscuit
[misit] in illo iure grana malorum grana(torum). Iste enim cibus his
220 infirmis bonus (est), quia stomacho eorum multa colera [cholera] domi-
natur et mala granata eum confortant et coleram [choleram] extinguunt
⟨et⟩ prohibent (etiam) ne cibus in stomacho conuertatur in fumositatem
uel in acetositatem et ut non natet in ore stomachi. Mala enim granata
in his omnibus ualent. Continet [32] [Continent] (enim ius) ⟨etiam et in
225 stomacho⟩ illud quoad paulatim digestum erit; tipsanum [ptisanum]
quoque cum malis granatis [malisgrana mixtum his bonum est.] ⟨Accessio
iterum in quinta die eodem modo uenit et cibauit illum in vi et vii
similiter⟩ (p. 6 in LA) et in septimo accessio (rev.) similiter aduenit [uenit].
Tunc (Galienus) [ergo] uoluit [noluit] errorem (illorum) medicorum in
230 uulgis [uulgi] notificare egrum [egro] quin manducaret prohibentium
qui [33] tantam [quintam] febris molestiam aspicientes [febrem molestam

26. id est, iuuenis. 27. id est. febris. 28. febricitanti. 29. patienti. 30. patientem.
31. Hippocrates, Prognosis, ed. E. Littré, II (Paris, 1840), 115; translated by John
Chadwick and W. N. Mann, p. 113, (Oxford, 1950). 32. continet in se ius tritici
propter uiscositatem quia non cito dissoluitur nec digeritur et ita plus nutrit
quam ptisanum. 33. fatui medici.

accipientes] sciebant ⟨egrum⟩ ad illum diem (non) esse uenturum nisi in
tercio die Galienus ⟨illum⟩ cibasset [cibaret.] Illi similiter dicebant
Galienum non bene fecisse eo quod febre nondum mitigata egrum [eum]
235   cibasset. Nam Galienus noluit eum[34] tradere sed liberare et medicos
illos uituperare. Cumque ante accessionem ⟨eum⟩ unaquaque die cibasset
et ex pulsu aliquid fortitudinis etsi debilis[35] erat sensisset nequiuit garru-
litatem illorum [eorum] amplius ferre. Dixit ergo familie infirmi: Cito
[Scito] certissime (noscetis) quia iste hodie non uiueret nisi dieta mea
240   [per dietam meam] (esset) quam ⟨et⟩ hii[36] [hi] garruli uituperant. Tunc
in illo die non dedit (ei) uictum ⟨et⟩ expectans quousque accessio transiret.
Incipiente autem accessione cessauit pulsus et eger deficiens non loque-
batur neque sentiebat eum quo tangebatur. Tunc Galienus clamauit
familiam et medicos illos. Famuli ⟨illi⟩ (uero) pre dolore ⟨tumultuose⟩
245   super (medicos) illos irati sunt, sed Galienus confisus ⟨quia⟩ ex eo quod
fecerat eger non moreretur nichil [nihil] timoris habuit. Illi autem
cognito sui [suo] errore fugere uolebant, quos Galienus ui tenebat et
clamando dicere cepit: Modo apparet ille qui uitam huius (rev.) usque
modo custodiuit et liberabo eum a morte. Securus enim erat Galienus
250   quod ipse ex hac [ista] accessione et abstinentia non moreretur eo quod
actenus [hactenus] eum nutrierat. Iterum quia senserat per pulsum
aliquantulam uirtutem neque cibum propter aliud nisi [sed] propter [ad]
uituperium eorum (rev.) prohibuerat etsi eger aliquam (tamen) passus est
molestationem. Dixit quoque ad eos: Modo ⟨uos intelligere⟩ (intelligite)
255   oportet non solum ante accessionem febricitantibus cibum dari sed ⟨etiam⟩
in accessione. Deinde ⟨igitur⟩ os egri (rev.) aperuit,[37] mittens in eo [illud]
tipsanum [ptisanum], post mediam autem horam uinum subtilissimum
album eque [aque] mixtum, unde eger suos aperuit oculos et cepit uidere,
audire, et loqui, et scire eos qui undique stabant. Ante enim uelut
260   mortuus fuerat. Postea uero dedit ei panem in uino infusum (rev.) unde
tota uis (eius) conuersa est. Tunc (Galienus) [ergo] conuersus (est) ad
suam primam dietam cibans eum ante accessionem, quare (in) terciade-
cima [decimatertia] die facilius eger accessionem sustinuit. In quartade-
cima [xiiii] die autem dedit ei cibum (in) prima hora diei et in octaua
265   balneauit eum dedit (que) ei grossius nutrimentum. Inicium enim accessionis in fine diei uenturum erat et tribuit ei uinum[38] et seruauit hanc
dieatam (sic LA) usque in septimam [xlii] decimam.[39] Cumque febris
alleuiari (rev.) cepisset eum uelut ab egritudine conualescentem dieta
custodiuit.[40] Unde per eum multi castigati sunt et didicerunt (cibum)
270   ⟨debere dari⟩ (page 7 in LA) oportet infirmum ab eo tangi[41] ne constipet
eum et incensiuos fumos egredi prohibeat. Iterum [Item] quia ex poris
(cutis) non uenit frigiditas ad cor sicut ex pulmone, unde oportet egrum
[ut] cooperias et a frigido aere defendas[42] et solummodo eum[43] [cum]
olfatum [olfactum] frigidum aerem attrahere dimittas. Huiusmodi enim
275   ordo[44] ecticam [ethicam] febrem habentibus utilis est, maxime ei[45] cuius

34. infirmum. 35. per quamuis. 36. fatui medici. 37. Galienus. 38. lymphatum.
39. diem. 40. i.e. per dietam i.e. Galienus. 41. scilicet ab ultima medicina.
42. praeterquam ab olfatia. 43. pacientem. 44. curandi. 45. pacienti.

[cui] febris [46] causa cordis fuerat. Frigiditas etiam [uero] ⟨quae est⟩ per [propter] flatum cito ad cor ducitur sicut utilius citiusque refrigeratur stomacus si ⟨in⟩ initium ectice [ethice] ab ipso [eo] stomacho extitit cum cataplasmatibus ⟨et⟩ cibis et potibus quia hec cito sicut sunt [47] ad
280 stomachum ueniunt, ad cor uero tarde ⟨et⟩ postquam conuersa sunt.[48] Aer similiter sicut est uelociter cum flamine [49] ⟨cum flamine uelociter *rev.*⟩ ad cor attrahitur. Epari [Epati] uero non ualet olfacio [olfactio] aeris et iuuamen ei [50] ex frigido [cibo] et potu minus quam stomacho contingit,[51] sed tamen non multum ⟨minimum⟩. Cataplasmata uero
285 utrosque [52] equaliter iuuant, porro ⟨si⟩ ectica [ethica] plurime fit propter passionem ⟨horum⟩ membrorum, id est, cordis, stomachi, ⟨et eparis⟩ et oris eius et aliquando ex mala complexione calida et sicca in pulmone. Sed tamen hoc membrum quia humidum est (*rev.*) et tenerum non sunt preparata [53] [parati] ut fortiter febricitent.[54] Nonnumquam etiam ecticam
290 et (*ambo uerba in ras.*) [ethica] tisis [phthysis] fit [sequitur] de mala complexione pulmonis [pectoris], meseraice, intestini ieiuni, colon, matricum ⟨et renum⟩. De diafragmate uero nunquam ptisim [phthysim] fieri uidi (*rev.*). Ecticam [Ethicam] autem consequi passionem diafragmatis [diaphragmatis] multociens [multotiens] aspexi et completa et perfecta
295 fuit. Vidi etiam ⟨ea⟩ multociens [multotiens] quosdam perire (*rev.*) priusquam perficeretur, quia si nimium calorem diafragma patitur, sequitur anhelitus et alienatio unde perit eger priusquam ectica [ethica] perfecta fiat [sit perfecta]. Scientia uero huius febris si de diafragmate fuerit facilior est [55] quia significatio (eius) aperta est. Nam pulsus durissi-
300 mus furcula (uentris) circa superiora multum mouetur anelitus inordinate induratur nunc paruissimus et [nunc] spissimus, nunc magnus et rarus, nunc tardus, (nunc) ⟨et⟩ ortomosus, et aliquando ⟨hec aerem⟩ una attractione (bis aerem trahunt) [attrahunt] et aliquando (bis eum) [hec aerem] emittunt (et) aliquando totum pectus una cum spatulis et diafragmate
305 [diaphragmate] seorsum eleuatur, et interdum flatus eorum est paruissimus et aliquando maximus, quod fit cum alienationem patiuntur sicut dictum est in libro de anhelitu titulato.[56] Sed plurime aer ualet ptisicis [phthysim] propter cor patientibus, omnibus etiam tisicis [57] [phthicis] febribus. Impossibile est enim [iterum] (ptisim esse sine febribus. Impos-
310 sibile uerum est ptisim) [phthysim] corde non febricitante generari, unde aeris frigiditas (page 8 in LA, fol. CC *verso*, second column, in printed text) ad cor ⟨quia⟩ uelociter penetrans [penetrat] magnum ⟨ei⟩ prestat iuuamentum. Quod si hec passio fuerit propter pulmonem (fiet) frigidus aer magis ceteris [cunctis] membris iuuatiuis. [iuuatiuus] Cataplasmatus
315 uero oportet te eligere [intelligere] quedam que sine multa stipticitate (*rev.*) refrigerant [refrigerent]. Si enim multum fuerint stiptica non solum corpus desiccant, sed (etiam) frigiditas eorum usque ad corporis interiora (non) penetrat nam claudit [penetrat] et [co]adunat superficiem

---

46. id est caloris innaturalis. 47. aliquo medio et sine mutatione. 48. in alios humores. 49. stomacho scilicet. 50. epati. 51. id est, ualet. 52. scilicet stomachum et epar. 53. scilicet corpora. 54. propter humiditatem ipsius membri. 55. quam de aliis membris. 56. Galen, *De uoce et anhelitu,* a treatise of three pages in the Giuntine edition of 1625. 57. ualet aer.

320 carnis et cutis (cutis et carnem *rev*.). Meliora ergo [uero] eligamur
[eligantur] que et frigida sine stipticitate sunt [sint] et subtilem (habent)
substantiam; frigidissima tamen cum subtili substantia inuenire non
possumus namque (acetum) etsi subtilius sit [fit] omnibus ⟨etiam frigidis-
simis⟩ frigidis rebus quas ego scio non est uere frigidum. Nam quiddam
caloris cum eo mixtum est et corpus desiccat et [etsi] uisualiter [58] humidum
325 appareat. Proinde non oportet in hoc loco [hunc locum] solum apponi
in quo frigidum et humidum necessarium (est) sed cum eo (tantum) aque
frigide (*rev*.) ⟨tantum⟩ decet misceri quantum [quam] una uice bibi
poterit. At quoniam res frigidissimas ⟨rev.⟩ et subtilissimas inuenire non
possumus de horum genere que meliora sunt eligamus [eligimus] que in
330 libro simplicis medicine scripta inuenies.[59] Nos etiam pauca hic (*rev*.)
[his] nominamus [nominabimus]. Hec est medicina que refrigerat et
humefacit cera scilicet punica [pumica] et oleum rosarum [rosatum] ⟨et⟩
eliquefacta [liquefacta] in uase in aqua calida posito [ponatur]. Olei
uero pondera tria ⟨pumice⟩ (uel) quattuor (ponas) cere [60] (*rev*.), id est,
335 que in mortario nimium moueantur et quanto agitata fuerint tanto ex
aqua frigidissima rorentur et⟨si⟩ parum aceti subtilissimi et clarissimi cum
eis misceas bonum est. Que corpori apposita cum tepefieri ceperint
eleuentur et alia frigidissima apponantur que sepe sepiusque frigidissima
ne calefiant inducantur (*rev*.) Aut accipe subtilissimum ordei pollinem
340 que cum suco herbe acetose aut cum suco euxinos [61] [oxinos] an [aut]
porfire [porphire] an [aut] solatri ⟨miscebis⟩, deinde in panno lineo
(*rev*.) spisso et duplicato posita corpori inducantur [inducatur]. Similiter
faciendum est cum suco semperuiue an [aut] cum suco uue agrestis an
[aut] lente [lentis] aque an [aut] tribulonum an [aut] uirge pastoris
345 uel lactuce uel endiuie. Hec omnia (an) cum farina ordei aut ipsa ⟨sola⟩
apponantur neque super totum uentrem sed ubi incensio est applicentur.
Loca enim refrigeratione non indigentia non oportet refrigerari neque
(dimittas) ea quousque necessaria esse uideris quod nequaquam facere
poteris nisi cum in loco quo necessaria fuerunt ea posueris. Timendum
350 enim est ne ipsa in loco quo (non) expediunt applicata alia generent
accidentia. Uidi enim quosdam frigida sub diafragmate apponere [ponere]
unde cito in hanelitum [anhelitum] ducti sunt et alii in tussim, sed causa
ablata liberati et ad suam naturam (end of page 8 in LA). . . .

University of Kansas
13 January 1966

58. per quamuis. 59. Galen, *De simplicium medicamentorum temperamentis et
facultatibus,* xi, xii, Kühn, translated by Constantinus Africanus (?). 60. olei trias
partes uel quattuor quoniam . . . quinta. 61. iouis barbe.

ON THE NAMES OF
OLD AND YOUNG MEN IN PLAUTUS

William M. Seaman

From only a casual examination of the plays of Plautus, it is apparent that some of the personal names are "appropriate," that is, they identify the character, type or role of the people who are either engaged in the action or mentioned in the dialogue, by the etymological meaning of the names. Lessing [1] called this a *redender Name,* a term which German scholars have sometimes rendered as *nomen loquens.* Thus, for example, Erotium, "Lovey," and Philematium, "Kissy," are suitable for courtesans; as are Gelasimus, "Laughable," and Peniculus, "Brush," for two of the parasites. Others of the more obvious examples include Misargyrides, "Hate-Silver," for a moneylender; Pyrgopolinices, "Great Conqueror of Citadels," for a *miles gloriosus;* and Pseudolus for a "tricky" slave.

But what of the ordinary citizens in the plays, men such as Menaechmus, Callicles, Demipho, Philocrates and others, whose names are seemingly not "telltale" or coined for comic purposes, but many of which are found in such lists of actual Greek names as those of Fick-Bechtel, Pape-Benseler, and the Corpus of Greek Inscriptions? [2] Did Plautus, or possibly the author of the original which he was following, apply these names also with some idea of appropriateness?

From the large body of material which I have gathered for a study

---

[1] Lessing, G. E., *Sämtliche Schriften,* hrsg. von Lachmann und Muncker (Stuttgart, 1894), x, 165 (= *Hamburgische Dramaturgie,* 2, 90 for 3 March 1768).

[2] The collections cited in this article include: A. Fick und F. Bechtel, *Die griechischen Personennamen nach ihrer Bildung* (2. Aufl., Göttingen, 1894); J. G. W. Pape, *Wörterbuch der griechischen Eigennamen* (3. Aufl. von G. E. Benseler, Braunschweig, 1863–70), 2 vols.; F. Preisigke, *Namenbuch* (Heidelberg, 1922).

of Plautine nomenclature [3] I have chosen to examine here the names
of only two groups of people, who are clearly intended to represent
ordinary Greek free citizens: the *senes* and *adulescentes*. For convenience let us consider only those old and young men who partici-
pate in the action as *personae*, excluding those who are mentioned
but are not seen on the stage.[4] This gives a total of twenty-eight
senes and thirty *adulescentes* to examine. All of these names are
Greek in form, with the exception of Hanno in the *Poenulus*, who
is a Carthaginian and has, quite properly, a Phoenician name with
the significance of "merciful" or "mild." [5]

Of the twenty-eight old men, twenty are found to have actual
Greek names, nearly all of them common in Attica (Fick-Bechtel,
Pape-Benseler, and *IG*). It has been noted by Gatzert that, with
few exceptions, all names of *senes* in New Comedy are Attic.[6] In the
case of Hegio in *Captivi*, in which the scene is laid in Aetolia, the
fact that this is not an Attic name is not surprising. Those which we
find to be actual Greek names are: Antipho (*Stich.*), two instances
of Callicles (*Trin.* and *Truc.*), Callipho (*Pseud.*), two instances of
Charmides (*Rud.* and *Trin.*), Demaenetus (*Asin.*), two instances of
Demipho (*Cist.* and *Merc.*), Dinia (*Vid.*), Euclio (*Aul.*), Hegio
(*Capt.*), Lysidamus (*Cas.*), Lysimachus (*Merc.*), Nicobulus (*Bacch.*),
Philoxenus (*Bacch.*), Philto (*Trin.*), two instances of Simo (*Most.*
and *Pseud.*), and Theopropides (*Most.*).

One recognizes in this list the common elements *demo, kallo,
macho, niko* and *philo* which were favored by the Greeks in name-
forming. They are stems which contain in them ideas of the civic
and personal virtues desirable in a good citizen, applied to a child
at birth as a good omen.

The remaining names of this group are found only in Plautus:
Alcesimus (*Cas.*), Apoecides (*Epid.*), Daemones (*Rud.*), Megadorus

[3] W. M. Seaman, "The Appropriate Name in Plautus," unpublished doctoral
dissertation, University of Illinois (1939). This is one of several dissertations
written under the guidance of Professor W. A. Oldfather on the subject of the
appropriate name. The only one published is that by J. C. Austin, *The Significant Name in Terence* (Urbana, 1921).

[4] Amphitryon is not considered here because it is the name of a person in a
myth which existed, with its own implications, before the playwright made use
of it.

[5] Peck, *Harper's Dictionary of Classical Literature and Antiquities*, s.v. *Hanno*.

[6] K. Gatzert, *De nova comoedia quaestiones onomatologicae* (Inaug. diss.,
Giessen, 1913), p. 57. Gatzert gives "Cnemo(n)" as one of the exceptions, but
Knēmōn in the recently discovered *Dyscolus* of Menander shows that this is
also an Attic name.

(*Aul.*), Megaronides (*Trin.*), Periphanes (*Epid.*), and Periplectomenus (*Mil.*). But even if these are not known to be actual Greek
appellations, they are very much like those which are attested and
most of them could easily be good Greek forms. There are many
known examples derived from *alkē*, 'strength, aid,' from which
Alcesimus is derived (e.g., Alkaios, Alkibiades, Alkibios, et al.).
Periphanes, 'brilliant,' is modeled on such names as Pericles and
Aristophanes. Megadorus, 'great gift,' has a counterpart in an actual
Megistodōros (*IG* 3, 1142, 1165, 1171). Apoecides is a reasonable
patronymic which could be derived from the known *Apoikos*,
'colonist' (Pape-Benseler, s.v.). Megaronides, 'son of a Megarian,' is
a likely form, comparable to a Megareus listed in Pape-Benseler.
But Periplectomenus, supposedly from peri+plekesthai, 'to devise,
intertwine,' is the only one of this group of names which seems to
be invented by the playwright. The form presents somewhat of a
problem, because it is actually a middle or passive participle. In
comedy such forms may be used as titles of plays, as in the case of
Perikeiromenē, but not usually as names of *personae*.[7]

It is apparent, then, that the old men are given names which
identify them as belonging to a certain class of society, that is, the
respectable free citizens of Athens or of another Greek city. If we
desire, however, to establish a more direct appropriateness of name
to the man, in some cases this, too, can be plausibly argued. Euclio,
'man of good reputation,' is a respected member of the community
(hominem hau malum, *Aul.* 172; civem sine mala omni malitia, 215).
Megadorus in the same play shows himself to be a man of 'great
gift' in his generosity toward Euclio and his family. Alcesimus, 'the
helper,' in the *Casina* does aid his friend Lysidamus in an escapade
(521 ff.). Demipho in the *Mercator* had led an exemplary life,
worked hard on a farm, gone into business and made a fortune (61
ff.). He was a 'man of the people' and respectable up to the time
of his intended escapade in the play. Of Charmides in the *Rudens*
we may say that he is aptly named 'the cheerful one,' for he exhibits
such a nature in his role.

On the whole, however, Plautus does not suggest by pun or word-
play that the names of old men are anything but suitable to types
of a certain social class. In some instances the appropriateness of a
fine-sounding name can be said to be due to irony, or *kat' anti-*

---

[7] K. Schmidt, "Die griechischen Personennamen bei Plautus," *Hermes*, XXXVII
(1902), 377.

phrasin, for the actual behavior of supposedly respectable citizens is in great contrast to their reputations, or to what might be expected of them. Examples of this sort are Demaenetus in the *Asinaria,* who is by no means worthy of the name 'praised by the people'; Nicobulus in the *Bacchides,* who should be a 'man of superior wisdom,' but is deceived by a slave; and Lysidamus, with the appellation 'one who frees the people,' but actually not so honorable a man in the *Casina.*[8]

From scattered bits of information we gather a description of the *senex* type in Plautus. He is usually a father, somewhere between fifty and sixty years of age, as, for example, Periplectomenus, who is fifty-four (*Mil.* 629) and Demipho, who is sixty (*Merc.* 524). He is sometimes described as *decrepitus, vetulus, vetulus vervex,* or *edentulus* (cf. *Asin.* 863; *Cas.* 535, 550, 559; *Epid.* 186, 666); he may have white hair (*Bacch.* 1208, *Cas.* 518, *Merc.* 305, *Trin.* 874); he is apt to be fairly wealthy, but not necessarily extremely rich, as Duckworth points out; [9] he is often a pillar of society (*senati columen, praesidium popli, Cas.* 536). In many cases the *senes* are married to shrewish wives whom they attempt, usually without success, to deceive, as we see in Simo of the *Mostellaria,* who slips away from his unattractive but wealthy wife (690 ff.). Other examples are Demaenetus in the *Asinaria,* whose wife also has money (*Asin.* 87) and finds him out in an attempted deception, and Lysidamus in the *Casina,* who has a brief return to youth, becomes infatuated with a young girl, hopes for adventure, and is finally disappointed and shamed.

It is notable that there are few men of what we might call middle age in the comedies. Amphitryon, who is called *senex,* exhibits, however, none of the attributes of an old man and must be considered rather to be in the prime of life.[10] Other than that, the men in Plautus are either young or old, the distinction being, in most instances, that a young man is unmarried. The reason for this

[8] Lysidamus perhaps should not be considered as a name, since the character is unnamed in the text. The name was probably inserted in the scene headings at a later date. See G. E. Duckworth, "The Unnamed Characters in the Plays of Plautus," *CP,* xxxiii (1938), 279 ff.

[9] G. E. Duckworth, *The Nature of Roman Comedy* (Princeton, 1952), p. 273.
I wish to express my appreciation to Professor Duckworth for reading this paper and offering some valuable suggestions which have been included in the present text.

[10] P. E. Legrand, *The New Greek Comedy* (English trans. by J. Loeb; London, 1917), p. 142, n. 2.

divergence of ages lies in the well-known sociological fact that Greek men, particularly as we know them in Athens, did not marry until late, usually at the age of thirty or later.[11] Thus a father will be at least fifty when his son, who, like Philolaches in the *Mostellaria*, has seen military service, is twenty or so.

Turning now to the young men's names, we find that a smaller percentage than those of old men are actual Greek forms. Of the thirty, only eight can be regarded as common in the standard lists and four others are found but rarely. Those which are genuine and of frequent occurrence are: two instances of Charinus (*Merc.* and *Pseud.*), Eutychus *(Merc.)*, Menaechmus *(Men.)*, Mnesilochus *(Bacch.)*, Nicodemus *(Vid.)*, Philocrates *(Capt.)*, and Sosicles *(Men.)*. Less common occurrences are found for Chaeribulus *(Epid.)*, Lyconides *(Aul.)*, Lysiteles *(Trin.)*, and Strabax *(Truc.)*. The remaining eighteen names of young men are found only in Plautus.

One notes that in no case are the names of young men used for old men. This might lead erroneously to a ridiculous assumption that men changed their names on reaching a certain age to appellations which were more fitting. But apparently comic playwrights considered certain names typical of old men, others typical of young men, even when they were names actually existing and not coined for the play. Among the young men's names are a number which relate, quite properly, to the military: Mnesilochus, 'mindful of the company,' Philocrates, 'fond of power,' Menaechmus, 'mighty with the spear,' Aristophontes, 'killer of the best,' Stratippocles, 'famed for army and horse,' and Philopolemus, 'fond of war.'

Several of the young men's names contain the element *hippo*, while none of our old men are thus identified with horses. The frequency of such forms indicates the importance of riding, driving and breeding of horses in the life of Greek young men of means. That there was a connotation of aristocracy in "horsy" names may be inferred from the passage in Aristophanes' *Clouds* (63 ff.), where the aristocratic wife of Strepsiades insists upon giving her son a name containing *hippos*—Xanthippos, Charippos, or Kallippides. She finally compromised on Pheidippides.[12]

The names of Plautus' young men, while in general appropriate to them as a class, since they are those of Attic or Greek free citizens, have in addition a more direct application to role or character than

---

[11] Walter Miller, *Greece and the Greeks* (New York, 1941), p. 69.

[12] On this aristocratic passion for horses, see G. Meautis, *L' Aristocratie athènienne* (Paris, 1927), pp. 42 ff.

was noted for old men. Argyrippus, 'silver horse,' although not known to us as a genuine name, could well be so, from the analogy of Chrysippos, Melanippos, Xanthippos, Leukippos, and the like. But there is a very intrinsic fitness in the frequent use of *argentum* for money throughout the *Asinaria,* and especially in the "horse-play" scene (699 ff.), in which the slaves compel Argyrippus to play horse before they give him the twenty minas of silver (vehes pol hodie me, si quidem hoc argentum ferre speres, *Asin.* 699).

Aristophontes, which means literally 'killer of the best,' is a form found nowhere else, although similar to such names as Bellero-phontes and Argeiphontes. Its significance lies in the fact that by his stupidity he condemns Tyndarus, who is clearly the "best" man of those in the *Captivi,* to almost certain death in the quarry.[13]

Philopolemus, 'fond of war,' also in the *Captivi,* identifies a man who is a soldier, although further than that his character is not well defined, and certainly nothing warlike is to be found in him. Yet Philopolemus is an Aetolian and few tribes of Greece, in the days of Plautus and the writer of his original, were engaged in more warfare than the Aetolians. Philopolemus is an excellent name for any soldier, but unusually suitable for an Aetolian.

Stratippocles in the *Epidicus* has a name which is unusual in that it violates the general practice of name-forming whereby the personal name has no more than two members.[14] For this contains *strato,* 'army,' + *hippo,* 'horse,' + *klēs,* 'fame,' and would mean something like 'a man famous for war and horses.' A Stratippos (Pape-Benseler and *CIA* II, 2121, 784A) and a Stratoklēs (Preisigke, 396) are known as actual names, but Stratippocles combines the three elements found in the two. Thus we may be sure it is a high-sounding, coined name and excellently suited for a youth of aristocratic position who is a soldier returning from the wars in this play. But our warrior's ability in battle consisted entirely in losing his arms to the enemy (29–31).[15]

Pamphilippus of the *Stichus* has another of these three-element names. Pamphilus, which is suitable for a lover (e.g., Pamphilus in the *Andria*), here has the aristocratic *hippos* added to it. No special significance is attached to the name, however, except that he is a

[13] W. M. Seaman, "Some Names in the *Captivi,*" *CW,* xxxv (1942), 197.
[14] Fick-Bechtel, p. 4.
[15] C. J. Mendelsohn, *Studies in the Word-Play in Plautus* (Philadelphia, 1907), p. 52.

young Athenian and married to a girl who is called, appropriately, Pamphila.

Pleusicles, 'noted sailor,' in the *Miles Gloriosus,* has a most appropriate designation because he wins his beloved while dressed in the guise of a sailor (1177 ff.). The name is not, so far as we know, a real one, but plausibly coined from the verb, *pleō,* 'to sail,' or from *pleusis* 'sailing,' with the addition of the stem *klēs,* which is so frequent as an ending that it loses virtually all of its etymological sense.[16]

Philolaches, the lover in the *Mostellaria,* shows in his name, which is not known to be genuine, the idea of love in the first syllable *phil.* Since the girl he loves is Philematium, the pairing of the two similar names, as also in the two noted above in the *Stichus,* is obviously intentional, revealing the fondness for names displayed by the playwright.

In the *Truculentus* Strabax, 'the squinter,' is a country fellow (*agrestis . . . adulescens,* v. 246), described also as *horridus* and *squalidus* (933). This is a genuine Greek personal name (*CIA* II, 1155 and Pape-Benseler, s.v.). Here it is used appropriately of a certain type, the sort of word applied in derision of rustics, such as Grumio, 'Clodhopper,' in the *Mostellaria.* (Cf. Pollux, II, 51: οἱ στράβωνες ἐν τῇ νέᾳ κωμῳδίᾳ.)

Several of the names of young men have just a slight trace of appropriateness in their basic meanings. Diabolus, 'slanderer,' in the *Asinaria* may be so named from the blame which he places on Demaenetus for the loss of his girl. Lyconides, 'son of the wolf man,' had wronged the daughter of Euclio in the *Aulularia;* the name may thus refer to his wolfish act of pouncing on the helpless sheep. Pistoclerus in the Bacchides has a name combining *pisto,* 'faithful,' and *klēros,* 'lot.' The emphasis appears to be on the first part, for he shows himself to be faithful to his friend. Lesbonicus of the *Trinummus,* by his exhibition of licentiousness, reveals this quality in his name, 'little Lesbian.' Callidamates, interpreted by Fay in his edition of the *Mostellaria* as 'lady-killer,' is a lover who may be identified also as a dandy from the *kallo* element in his name. Agorastocles in the *Poenulus* must have been called the 'buyer' because of the business transactions relating to the purchase of Adelphasium.

From the examples just cited we can conclude that the names of

---

[16] K. Schmidt, pp. 354–55.

young men are appropriate in describing them, just as we have seen with respect to old men, as members of a particular class. Especially when they are actual Greek personal names, they identify their possessors as free citizens. But it is clear from the direct application of the etymological significance of the word to the *persona* that the playwright selected or invented names with this purpose in mind.

One is prompted to conjecture how much the Roman audience of Plautus' productions understood of the significance of these Greek names. The better educated, we may infer, would know enough Greek to catch the import of these designations. But the appropriateness was probably lost on the majority of listeners. To the latter they must have been merely foreign-sounding, much as T. S. Eliot uses Mr. Silvero, Limoges, Hakagawa, Madame de Tornquist and Fräulein von Kulp for individuals identified only as foreigners (*Gerontion*). A Roman, and even a Greek, probably did not think primarily of 'son of' for the meaning of the patronymic ending *ides*, nor of 'fame' for the ending *klēs*.[17]

That Plautus himself understood the meaning of Greek names, of course, is evident from his puns and other references to the names. The probability is, however, that the names existed in his originals and that the wordplay there was more obvious. To expect that every name was appropriate according to its exact etymological formation is not reasonable. The astonishing thing is how thoroughly the principle was followed.

In his study of the social attitudes in Middle and New Comedy Dunkin takes the position that the slave in Plautus is the hero, while the Rich Man, represented by *senex, adulescens, leno,* and *miles,* is the dupe.[18] His theory is that Plautus used the plays as attacks on the rich and pleaded the cause of the poor. It is not our purpose here to enter into a controversy over the social attitude which the playwright had in mind, but since we have said that the names themselves are an identification of a social class, it may be in order to make a comment in passing.

To be sure, Plautus shows sympathy for the slave and seems to speak for his sad lot in life. Toward the free man he is also sympathetic, not bitterly antagonistic. "The perception of the comic," said Emerson, "is a tie of sympathy with other men" (*The Comic*).

17 C. W. Peppler, *Comic Terminations in Aristophanes and the Comic Fragments* (Baltimore, 1902), pp. 44 ff.
18 P. S. Dunkin, *Post-Aristophanic Comedy* (Urbana, 1946), p. 93. See the review of this by G. E. Duckworth (*AJP,* LXVIII [1947], 419–26) for opposing views.

It is well to remember that these plays are primarily comedy, often burlesque; they are not problem-plays, concerned with preaching a social lesson. The question then arises, whether or not the entire social class of free citizens is being indicted when certain old and young men are made the objects of ridicule by Plautus. Lucilius, quoted by Cicero (*De Senectute* XI. 36), speaks of *comicos stultos senes* as *credulos, obliviosos, dissolutos.* Just as Cicero explains that these are not the faults of all old age, but only of a certain type of old age, so we should understand that the old and young men portrayed in Plautus are *comici,* not necessarily typical of all Greek citizens.

The late Professor W. A. Oldfather once said, "the stage portrays chiefly the actions of but two classes of people, the very rich and the very poor, since these are the only people who have the leisure or the freedom from moral restraint to indulge in the interestingly abnormal behavior that seems appropriate to the stage." [19]   In the slave economy pictured in New Comedy, the upper middle-class, moderately well-to-do persons also would have the same leisure and freedom. The ordinary middle-class individual, who lives a normal, decent life without any aberrations, provides rather dull material for a play, particularly a comedy. The errant *senex,* the helpless young lover, and the brash slave are therefore more likely subjects for comedy, without implications of social significance.

In the plays of Plautus the names of *senes* and *adulescentes* show that they were chosen for these *personae* primarily to designate them as belonging to a certain class of society and that they were by general reputation respectable free citizens of a Greek community. The contrast between such a reputation, as shown in the names themselves, and their actual behavior on the stage is in itself a comic element.

Michigan State University
14 January 1966

---

[19] A statement made in a conversation and incorporated in my dissertation.

THE GRAPHIC ANALOGUE FROM MYTH IN GREEK ROMANCE

Grundy Steiner

The Emperor Tiberius would often remark (Suet. *Calig.* 11), as he noted the brutality of the young Caligula, "I am rearing a water-snake for the Roman people and a Phaethon for the whole world!" In so speaking he was joining company with Socrates, who had said to Euthyphro (15B), "You are the Daedalus who makes your arguments walk away!" and with Trygaeus in Aristophanes (*Pax* 76-77), who had patted his dung-beetle and said, "My little Pegasus! Noble winged steed!" and even with the Dionysius of Chariton's romance (V. 2, 8), who remarked, "There is many a Paris among the Persians!" This incongruous set of speakers possesses one point in common: each had found in myth a vivid analogue to something he saw before him. Tiberius implied that Caligula, like Phaethon, would careen wildly across the world, doing untold damage; Socrates, that Euthyphro could move his shifting arguments as Daedalus his walking statues (*Meno* 97DE); Trygaeus hoped that his beetle would convey him Olympusward as Pegasus had carried Bellerophon; and Dionysius, traveling with his beautiful wife toward the Persian court, was justifiably fearful that he himself would prove to be a Menelaus beset by many equivalents to Paris.

These analogues were not hard to come by. The presence of myths in almost all phases of ancient art and literature reflects their widespread popularity, hence their availability. But they were more than merely available. Innumerable tellers had reshaped them from time to time, consciously or unconsciously altering details and motivations, to make them ring true in terms of human nature and the patterns of human conduct. As a consequence they tended, with the passage of time, more and more to become symbolic stories available as examples in all kinds of situations.

In some authors these examples are chiefly moral—patterns of behavior to be imitated ("If Niobe could eat in her sorrow, or Meleagros control his temper, so can you"). Sometimes they are taken as evidence for what is likely to follow under given circumstances ("If Menelaus had a bad time of it in Sparta, what can you expect here?"). While both these types (and others) are found in Greek romance, most of the examples employed are essentially illustrative (although often with moral or evidential overtones). At their best they provide the vivid parallel—the graphic analogue—that enables the reader to visualize almost as if physically present either the person or the situation with which the author is concerned.

The purpose of this essay is to present briefly typical analogues [1] from myth found in the five extant Greek romances, to note how they are used, and to examine difficulties about the appropriateness of some of them. Since almost all are largely decoration in admittedly light literature, it would scarcely be appropriate to try to read much more than their obvious significance into them; therefore they are presented mostly as samples of the way mythology could be used for relatively unpretentious readers in perhaps the first, and certainly the second and third centuries A.D. Since, however, such examples could scarcely be effective without some thought by the authors, and attention to artistic and other considerations, this examination inevitably yields some general conclusions about the writers themselves.

I

The most universal class of analogues in the five authors involves the motif of physical beauty so far beyond that of mortals that its possessor is mistaken for a god, or, at the least, is said to resemble pictures of some hero. Chariton introduces both forms at the start of his romance, for Callirhoe's (I. 1, 2) loveliness was hardly human;

---

[1] There is no attempt here at completeness in listing the examples from any author. This brief sampling can only suggest what might emerge from a longer study.

All excerpts are presented in translation alone, except for the occasional word or phrase of the original that can have some special significance, or where there are textual difficulties. All passages from Chariton, except V. 2, 8 (cited above) are from the version by W. E. Blake (University of Michigan Press, 1939). All other passages were translated by the author.

"it was divine, . . . not that of a mere nymph of the sea or the mountains, either, but of Aphrodite the Maiden." And Chaereas (I. 1, 3) resembles "the statues and pictures of Achilles and Nireus and Hippolytus and Alcibiades." Chariton obviously preferred the divine analogue, for he used it in every book of his story except the seventh. This apparent omission may be accidental, for there are large lacunae in that book, but possibly it is deliberate, for Chariton seems almost apologetic when he resumes the motif in the last book, saying (VIII. 6, 11) that the Syracusan women thought Callirhoe seemed more lovely than before, "so that *in all honesty* (ἀληθῶς) you would have said that it was Aphrodite herself whom you saw arising from the sea." [2]

The last excerpt may suggest that Chariton took the idea from art; [3] yet he is more obviously indebted to Homer. Homeric tags and excerpts abound in his work, but three passages actually link the poet and the analogues: First, Callirhoe's "gleaming face and uncovered arms" are said (IV. 1, 8) to make her seem "more beautiful than the Homeric goddesses 'of the white arms and fair ankles.' " Second, Babylonian men hear that she is "the masterpiece of Nature, 'like unto Artemis or golden Aphrodite' " (IV. 7, 5, quoting *Od.* XVII. 37). Third, when the Persian King thinks how wonderful it would be to have the girl along on the chase, he visualizes her (VI. 4, 6) in terms of *Od.* VI. 102-104, "even as Artemis the archer" moving down Taygetus or Erymanthus. And behind these three passages stands the fact that Homer himself used the motif, for example, when (*Od.* VI. 149-52) Odysseus suggested that Nausikaa resembled Artemis.

The other authors of romance make similar uses of the divine analogue. In Xenophon of Ephesus (I. 2, 7) Anthia is so beautiful that "when the Ephesians saw her in the sacred precinct, they prostrated themselves as before Artemis." [4] Egyptian spectators in Heliodorus (I. 2, 6) keep saying that Chariclea is "some goddess, in

[2] For the same notion, cf. Chariton I. 10, 7, I. 14, 1, II. 2, 6, II. 3, 6, II. 4, 8, III. 2, 15, III. 2, 17, III. 3, 5, III. 9, 1, IV. 7, 5, V. 2, 6, V. 9, 1, VI. 3, 4, and VI. 3, 5.

[3] So also Callirhoe's visit to the temple (III. 8, 5-6) where she held the child in her arms and "thus presented a most charming sight, the like of which no painter has ever portrayed, nor sculptor fashioned, nor poet described . . . ; for no one of them has created an Artemis or an Athena holding a child in her arms."

[4] Cf. Xenophon of Ephesus I. 1, 3, I. 2, 8, and I. 12, 1 for other uses of this motif.

particular, Artemis or the native Isis." [5] But while Chariton's Callirhoe was more beautiful than "a mere nymph of the sea," Longus, exercising his "cultivated taste and understanding," [6] says only that Daphnis (I. 24, 1), upon seeing Chloe "wearing fawnskin and pine garland and holding out her milk pail, would think that he was looking at one of the nymphs from the cave." Daphnis himself, however, is compared with Dionysus by the women at the vintage (II. 2), and Longus observes (IV. 14), after the young herdsman has been scrubbed up to meet his master, that "If ever Apollo herded cows for Laomedon as a slave, he looked the way Daphnis looked now." The divine analogue seems to have appealed only slightly to Achilles Tatius, although a messenger does say of Leucippe (VII. 15, 2), "I've never seen another like her, except for Artemis!" [7] Heliodorus and Achilles Tatius, however, both had use for the Homeric Achilles as the type of masculine beauty.

Heliodorus says (IV. 3, 1) Theagenes at the race in panoply "was an impressive sight and admired by all—just the way Homer portrays Achilles contending during the battle along the Scamander." Rattenbury in his Budé commentary, ad loc., protests the comparison as "arbitrary" since Theagenes and Achilles share no exploits in common. Now while it is true that Theagenes' career is very different, Heliodorus has two good reasons for making Achilles his analogue: Achilles is commonly a type of the handsome, as in Chariton (I. 1, 3) and Lucian (Dial. Mort. 18). Theagenes claims descent from Achilles. For Heliodorus these two reasons blend into one, as may be seen in the words of one speaker (IV. 5, 5) who says Theagenes "traces himself back to Achilles as his forefather, and I even think he speaks the truth, *if one should judge from physique and beauty that testify to noble descent from Achilles.*" [8] Since heroic or divine ancestors are commonly (as in Od. IV. 62-64) symbolic of some

[5] Cf. Heliodorus I. 2, 1, I. 7, 2, V. 31, 1, and X. 9, 3-4, but also II. 23, 1 where beauty of character is involved.

[6] Ben Edwin Perry, "Literature in the Second Century," CJ, L (1955), 298.

[7] Cf. also the episode of the panpipes (VIII. 6, 7) where (following Knox's, hence Gaselee's οἴαν εἰς θεοὺς ἐγκρίνειν) the maiden is so " beautiful that one could accept her among the gods," or (following Vilborg's οἴαν εὐχὴν κινεῖν) so " beautiful that she could arouse prayer." The second, although less graphic, should mean about the same as the first.

[8] So again in Heliodorus II. 34, 2-8 and II. 35, 1 physical appearance alone is considered. When Chariclea describes her beloved to her physician in IV. 7, 4 by quoting Il. XVI. 21: "Oh Achilles, son of Peleus, far the bravest of the Achaians," she is doubtless speaking as a lovesick young girl who would call any man brave.

moral, as well as physical, quality in their descendants, and since Heliodorus knew this point (to judge from the argument, III. 14, 2-15, 1, that Homer's genius reflects his descent from Hermes), it seems safe to assume that he intended Achilles as an analogue solely to Theagenes' appearance, both in the context of the race in armor and in those passages where the ancestry is actually mentioned. Whether this was the best use Heliodorus could have made of the analogue is an entirely different question.[9]

Achilles Tatius also took up Achilles as the type of beauty, but to achieve quite another effect: The virtuous Clitophon, a very reluctant (albeit helpful) bridegroom, and his over-eager, presumably widowed, bride, Melitte, are surprised by the return of Melitte's lost husband. Melitte arranges to get Clitophon out of the house disguised in her own clothing. As she finishes dressing him to resemble herself (VI. 1, 3) she gazes at her handiwork, kisses him, and says, "You've become much more lovely in this dress! You're just like the Achilles I saw once in a painting!" The brave Achilles, type of youthful, manly beauty, has traveled far as an analogue! The author, tongue in cheek, need offer no explanation, for his readers would inevitably smirk as they recalled the story of Achilles in the girls' school on Scyros.[10]

One more heroic analogue merits brief notice. To compare Achilles and Theagenes is not entirely satisfactory, and Heliodorus (cf. p. 130 below) had perhaps more difficulties with analogues than the other writers; but he should receive credit for working out one which, however fanciful, is not just decoration but, rather, a firm element in the dramatic framework of his story. Chariclea, the Ethiopian princess, turns out to look exactly like the fair, white Andromeda (actually a distant ancestor, IV. 8, 3) because at the moment of her engendering, her mother's eyes had rested upon a painting of Andromeda (IV. 8, 5 and X. 14, 2). As a consequence the picture of Andromeda is here not so much an analogue—an

[9] In the charming realism of his pastoral romance Longus (e.g., I. 2, 3, I. 7, 1, III. 32, 1, IV. 20, 2, IV. 30, 4, and IV. 32, 2) often lets the good looks of Daphnis and Chloe serve as evidence that their parents were more than simple peasants, but he does not provide them with heroic ancestors as analogues. This is a subdued and plausible use of the motif of ancestry. Cf. also Chariton II. 1, 5 (the truly beautiful must be free-born).

[10] Achilles Tatius also tries his hand at an analogue between a legendary beauty and his heroine, Leucippe. The wording of the passage (I. 4, 3), however, is uncertain, and should the reading Σελήνην of certain manuscripts stand, a routine divine analogue would replace the contextually more appropriate Europa.

illustration—as the "determining pattern" that marks the child, causing her to look exactly like the subject of that painting.

II

But myth used only to suggest the physical beauty of heroes and heroines would quickly wear thin. Much more interesting, intellectually and artistically, are analogues to situations and events, for in them greater variety is possible. Most are still largely illustrative, but in so far as some sound more like evidential or moral examples the usage seems less purely ornamental.

Chariton, again in his opening pages, reveals much of the pattern for this treatment of myth: The wedding of Callirhoe (I. 1, 16) is very "like that of Thetis, which, as the poets sing, took place in Pelion. Yet here, too, was found a demon of envy just as there, they say, was the goddess of strife." To compare Callirhoe's wedding with that of Thetis recalls a host of pictures from the poets, but Chariton's comment, *"Yet here, too,* was found a demon of envy . . ."* implies that this story, like that from the epic tradition, will probably involve a series of difficulties. The analogue, therefore, serves both as an *illustration* of what took place and as a ready symbol, adumbrating the course of events to come.

This course of events is long and involved and adorned with numerous other analogues from myth.[11] Jason, for example, is the type of the unjust husband and Medea of the mother that slays her children to get revenge, when Callirhoe, in captivity, ponders aborting her child but reconsiders in these words (II. 9, 3-4): "Are you planning to kill your child? . . . Is there a Jason who is brutally insulting you, that you should consider the revenge of a Medea?" Then the comparison takes a moral turn as she examines how her situation departs from that of her chosen analogue: "you will seem even more cruel than the savage Scythian, for she considered her husband as her enemy, while you wish to kill the child of Chaereas and thus leave behind not even a remembrance of our famous marriage." Ariadne, again, plays three traditional roles: (1) She is the type of the sleeping beauty when (I. 6, 2) Callirhoe, laid out in her bridal garments, is compared by all to "the sleeping Ariadne." (2) She is the stolen bride when (III. 3, 5) Chaereas asks beside Callirhoe's empty tomb: "Which one of the

---

[11] Cf. Chariton II. 6, 1, V. 5, 9, and VII. 3, 5 for passages with Homeric echoes, and II. 4, 8, IV. 7, 2-7, V. 10, 1 and VI. 3, 2.

gods . . . has become my rival and has carried Callirhoe away and now holds her by his side . . . ? This, then, is why she died so suddenly, that she might not be disfigured with disease! So once Dionysus robbed Theseus of Ariadne and Zeus stole Semele." (3) She is also the forgotten bride when (VIII. 1, 2) Chaereas unknowingly, after the capture of Aradus, is about to sail away leaving Callirhoe behind, "and that, too, not like the sleeping Ariadne, to be the bride of a Dionysus, but as the spoil of his own enemies."

While these analogues serve basically to illustrate the situations in which the actors find themselves, nevertheless Callirhoe reasons through a moral interpretation when she likens herself to Medea, and Chaereas tries to use myth evidentially when (III. 3, 5-6) he concludes that a god must have stolen his bride since deities have committed such thefts in the past. Then he applies the argument to his own situation (ibid.): "can it be that I had a goddess as my wife and did not know it, and she was beyond my human station? But, even so, she should not have disappeared so quickly from the sight of men, however good her excuse. Thetis, too, was a goddess, but she remained with Peleus and bore him a son, while I have been deserted in the very perfection of my love . . . ." Since the goddess Thetis remained to bear a son, he reasons, Callirhoe, even if a goddess, should also have remained to do so.

Callirhoe likewise knows how to reason from myth when (II. 9, 5) she worries about the fate of her child who is apparently going to be born a slave. She consoles herself with the stories about gods and kings "who had sons that were born in slavery and later regained the rank of their fathers, like Zethus and Amphion and Cyrus! My child," she adds, "some day you too shall sail back to Sicily . . . ." [12]

Xenophon of Ephesus, as epitomized, offers only a single analogue to any event in his story. The canopy above the bridal bed (I. 8, 2-3) for his hypervirtuous young hero and heroine is adorned with symbolic pictures of Aphrodite and Ares. While Xenophon apparently regards his analogues from divine beauty as serious, the symbolism here could certainly be less than straightforward, in view of the lily-pure motives of the bride and groom bedded beneath a portrayal of the (adulterous) Ares, "not armed, but dressed as if to meet his beloved Aphrodite, wearing a garland and a light cape."

[12] Note Callirhoe's attempt to justify the noise of the grave-robbers as the sounds of the gods below when (I. 9, 3) she regains consciousness in the grave.

Conceivably in the original form of the passage [13] the canopy served, not only as an analogue to the passion of the night (as it still may in the epitomized version), but also as a symbol of the interlopers who tried to separate the young couple. Yet the silence of the epitomator makes this unlikely.

The canopy, however, is perhaps no more astonishing than the first analogue to role and situation in Heliodorus (I. 10, 2) : The passionate stepmother, upon seeing Cnemon, exclaims, " Oh, my young Hippolytus! " Maillon, ad loc., complains about the poor taste whereby not the author, but rather the stepmother herself, sees the analogy with Phaedra. Humor, which might justify the choice, is scarcely possible in the context. Rather, several considerations (here presented in ascending order of probability) could offer some justification for the analogue: (1) Conceivably the woman, whose advances are extremely overt ("she was beside herself," says Cnemon, "and no longer artfully concealed her love, but with obvious passion ran up and kissed me "), has committed a " Freudian slip " in calling her handsome stepson " Hippolytus." (2) Indignant Cnemon may be editorializing. Perhaps he has replaced some endearing nickname from the lady with this most damaging analogue, hoping thereby to portray her as utterly tasteless and abandoned. (3) Possibly both Xenophon (if the canopy signified only passion) and Heliodorus are reverting to a free ability to take things separately, long enjoyed by their predecessors. Countless generations of Greeks had been able, in *worship*, to contemplate Zeus as a mighty god of power and righteousness, and in *myth* to tell stories about him as a henpecked and immoral husband. Possibly, then, the present mention of Hippolytus was intended only to imply his youthful beauty (as in Chariton I. 1, 3) and nothing more. (4) While the last word cannot now be written on this, since the text appears corrupt, the name of Theseus seems probably to follow that of Hippolytus in the words of the stepmother, " ὁ νέος Ἱππόλυτος, † ὁ Θησεὺς ὁ ἐμός †." [14] Although this tends to compound the *gaucherie* of the analogue by making the stepmother all the more conscious of her moral turpitude, it also suggests that Helio-

---

[13] Dalmeyda, ad loc., follows Burger (Hermes xxvii) in arguing that even the very text of this analogue shows signs of abridgment.

[14] This is the Budé text. Lumb's translation of the unemended text, ap. crit. ad loc., ibid., "qualis hic iuvenis, qualis pater ejus!", is certainly consonant with the interpretation here suggested. Rattenbury's argument, that a gloss, ὁ Θησεύς, has intruded, avoids the problem, but also implies that a *glossator* had recognized the same very natural interpretation. (Cf. R. M. Rattenbury, CQ, xix [1925], 178.)

dorus wanted his readers surely to think of Hippolytus in terms of *the son of Theseus* and not merely as a handsome young man. And if this reminded the reader of the Euripidean Phaedra, so much the better. Euripides' Phaedra torments herself (*Hipp.* 337-41) by groveling in her own moral failings after the pattern of her family: "Oh, wretched mother," she says, "what a love you loved! . . . And you, unfortunate sister, the bride of Dionysus! . . . And I, the unlucky third, how I meet my destruction!" The Euripidean Phaedra (and the Senecan, too) knows that she is acting wrongly. It is therefore quite natural that Heliodorus' Demaenete, her spiritual descendant, should also be frank in recognizing her own wrongdoing.

Heliodorus, of course, uses other analogues. The aged Calasiris (II. 21, 6) echoes the story of Midas' barber (but without mentioning any names) by saying that, had he not met Cnemon, he would have told his troubles "even to these reeds, as the myth goes." A little later (II. 24, 4) Cnemon finds the old man with his digressions like Proteus, "not turning yourself into a false and changing guise, but rather trying to lead *me* astray." (The minor readjustment in the story may mean that Heliodorus felt an inappropriateness in the analogue, hence clarified its application through the speaker, but the slight inconcinnity and its correction do produce an effect of great naturalness that may be deliberate.) Certainly the author once more skirted difficulty when, groping for a typically fearful object, he suggested (IV. 7, 11) that the girl "screamed as if she'd seen the Gorgon's head." (The usual form of the story with instant petrifaction might be expected to preclude any noise.) Finally, the conventional metonymies of divine names are near in the hymn to Thetis (III. 2, 4) when Achilles is called "the Ares of warfare," and a measure of the allegorical interpretation of myth figures in the suggestion (IV. 2, 3) that Eros is portrayed as winged in art to symbolize "the speediness of those subdued by love." [15] While his analogues often seem slightly malapropos, Heliodorus had surely learned well the theory of applying myth to persons and situations.

Longus, as usual, displays a fine sense of the charming and of what is appropriate to a pastoral setting. Daphnis argues (I. 16, 3-4)

[15] Chariton (IV. 7, 6-7) expresses much the same idea about the attributes of Eros, while Longus says (II. 7, 1) that Eros takes pleasure in youth and beauty and gives wings to souls because he is young, beautiful, and winged. Clitophon (Ach. Tat. I. 17, 1) thinks it perfectly natural that Eros should excite birds since he is winged himself.

his own worth from a series of analogies: "A goat suckled me—
and one suckled Zeus. . . . I don't smell of goats—neither does Pan,
and yet he is mostly goat. . . . I don't have a beard—neither does
Dionysus. I'm dark—so is the hyacinth. But Dionysus is better than
the Satyrs, and the hyacinth is better than lilies. . . ." (This
goatherd would have done well in the rhetorical schools of the
Empire!) But the episode (III. 34) which perhaps gave the author
his greatest pleasure involves an apple left at the tree top. Daphnis
climbs to get it for his beloved Chloe (after the news that they may
marry) and says, as he presents it, "This was what Aphrodite received as prize; this I present to you in your victory. You both have
similar judges: *he* was a shepherd; *I* am a goatherd." And lest any
reader lose the pretty analogy, Longus adds how, in return, Chloe
kissed Daphnis—"a kiss that was better than even a golden apple." [16]

The analogues in Achilles Tatius tend to be more vigorous.
Clitophon suggests (II. 6, 2-3) that some god has sold him to Leucippe "like Herakles to Omphale." When Clitophon's servant,
Satyrus, drugs Leucippe's guard, Conops, he rushes in to say (II.
23, 3), "You've got your Cyclops lying asleep; see to it that you
become a brave Odysseus!" Later, Clitophon, immobilized through
anguish at the sham sacrifice of Leucippe (III. 15, 6), likens himself
to Niobe. In Egypt a painting serves to warn the pair as they start
toward a banquet where Leucippe is to be kidnapped. They take
the subject of the painting (the rape of Philomela) as a portent
which a friend, one Menelaus, interprets for them, incidentally
encouraging the habit of looking for analogues (V. 4, 1-2): "The
interpreters of signs say that one should look closely at the stories
of pictures, if we meet up with any as we set out on business, and
to conclude that what is going to happen will be like the plot of
the story. You see therefore how loaded the picture is with woes:
unlawful love, unabashed adultery, the misfortunes of women. For
this reason I tell you to hold off on the trip."

But perhaps his treatment of Tantalus is most representative of
the attitude of Achilles Tatius, who obviously possesses a satiric
vein. Tantalus plays various roles in ancient literature, being any-

[16] Gnathon (IV. 17, 6-7) argues from analogy somewhat after the pattern
followed (I. 16, 3-4) by Daphnis. And cf. Lamon's fear (IV. 8, 4) that his master
will hang him "though an old man, from a pine, just like Marsyas!" This
analogue appealed also to Achilles Tatius, who suggests (III. 15, 4) that Leucippe
was strapped to the ground "the way the modellers of figurines portray Marsyas
bound from the tree."

thing from a guilty malefactor, justly punished for presumption
(e.g., Pindar, *Ol.* 1, 54-64; Eurip. *Or.* 4-10; Plut. *Mor.* 607F) or even
for idleness (Dio Chrys. 64, 7), to an unjustly maligned equivalent
of a Brahman, denigrated by the poets because he was a good man
who revealed divine truths (Philostr. *VA* 3.25). Typologically he
serves, for example, as symbol for unlimited wealth (Plut. *Mor.*
759E-F), for the *avarus* unable to enjoy his property (Hor. *Sat.* I. 1,
68-72; Phaedrus *App.* 7.7-9; Petron. 82), for the wealthy man too
busy to make use of his possessions (Plut. *Mor.* 498A), and for the
superstitious man, ever expecting some object of dread to fall upon
him (Lucr. III. 978-83). This somber figure Achilles Tatius uses as
the type of frustration in love—both homosexual and heterosexual.
Clitophon (II. 35, 4-5) says of the quickly evanescent beauty of
youths, "it seems like Tantalus' drinking water, for often it escapes
in the very act of drinking, and the lover goes away without having
found anything to drink. That which is being drunk is snatched
away before the drinker is sated." This studied parallel, which
sounds almost like part of a school declamation, is matched by the
anguished words of the eager Melitte (V. 21, 4). After a most
frustrating night during which she had passionately hoped that
Clitophon would at long last consummate their marriage, she asks,
"What day are we waiting for now? How long are we going to sleep
as if in a temple? Though you have placed a wide river at my side,
you keep me from drinking. Though I've had water all this time,
I'm thirsty, sleeping by the fountainhead itself! I have a bed like
the food of Tantalus!"

Finally, Achilles Tatius seems to have enjoyed suggesting analogues by supplying only a few details from their stories. When, for
example, before an engagement, the general, Charmides, tries to
seduce Leucippe, he says (IV. 7, 5), using the divine metonymies,
"Love's embrace would be a good omen before joining battle. Let
Aphrodite send me to Ares." The Homeric story (*Od.* VIII. 266-366)
of the two gods is not mentioned; yet inevitably the reader recalls
it and sees that Charmides visualizes himself as Ares and Leucippe
as his Aphrodite.[17]

[17] For other stories touched only lightly, often without identifying proper
names, cf. Achilles Tatius VI. 2, 3 (the hind for Iphigenia), VI. 7, 3 (the amber
tears of Phaethon's sisters). Perhaps V. 7, 4 and VIII. 16, 2 are intended to echo
the dismemberment of Absyrtus. The text of VIII. 13, 2-3 (the words of
Clitophon as Leucippe enters Pan's cave) contains only the common noun for
" Panpipe " as printed by both Gaselee and Vilborg: δέδοικα μὴ δευτέρα καὶ σὺ

This story is not serious in Homer; so the present treatment does no violence to its intent. However, the humorous propensity of Achilles Tatius, as we have seen, did not discourage him from readjusting numerous tales to fit a satiric purpose.[18]

III

As already suggested (p. 124), their analogues from myth may possibly reveal a little about the several authors themselves. Biographical data are rare and untrustworthy. There is treacherously little evidence to establish the order in which the men wrote, but a purely subjective judgment based upon their usages of myth seems to warrant a few generalizations: (1) Chariton seems to be fresh and enthusiastic—apparently delighted with the game of finding analogues—and only toward the end does he seem to grow self-conscious about their repetition. It is tempting, therefore, to think that he belongs early in the sequence of authors. (2) Longus writes in the spirit of bucolic poetry at its most charming, and his examples from myth are gracious and right in context, while Achilles Tatius seems almost to belong to the tradition of travesty upon myth. The two authors are most unlike in their tastes and attitudes; yet they create one impression in common: both seem to be writing for an audience familiar with the old motifs and the well-worn episodes. The reader constantly expects Daphnis to have more serious trouble than he does, and recognizes that Clitophon and his beloved are facing perils treated more solemnly elsewhere. (3) Xenophon of Ephesus and Heliodorus are more difficult to assess. Both seem to lose interest in myth as their works progress. Unless the epitomator is responsible for the distribution of the analogues, it looks almost as if Xenophon, on starting to write, had decided to use myth generously, then had forgotten the idea in midstream (or had tired of it). Heliodorus, however, seems to have restricted himself more to analogies between life and the stage in the latter part of his work. Possibly he preferred this motif, and it tended to draw

---

σύριγξ γένη. In view of Clitophon's concern about the φιλοπάρθενος god and the clear reference to Syrinx in the next sentence, a more emotional pointing of the sentence seems in order: δέδοικα μὴ δευτέρα—καὶ σύ—Σύριγξ γένη (" I'm afraid that you—even you!—will become a second Syrinx!") In the next sentence ἐκείνη would then mean, "the former Syrinx," causing the passage to flow along more smoothly.

[18] For the argument that Achilles Tatius is writing parody, see D. B. Durham, "Parody in Achilles Tatius," CP, XXXIII (1938), 1-19.

him from the uses of myth which had figured generously in the first half.[19] If the inappropriateness latent in some examples from these authors has any significance, its ultimate source may lie in their disinterest in a type of adornment that they nevertheless felt obliged to use. In any event they sound as if they belong neither at the eager start, nor the jaded end, of the sequence, for then they might have felt obliged, like Longus and Achilles Tatius, to furbish up the tired old techniques through what appear to be innovations in point of view.[19a]

This use of myth (as would appear from the first paragraph of this essay) is not limited to the writers of Greek romance. Plato's "Proteus" for one shifty in argument (*Euthyphro* 15D); Horace's "bravest of the daughters of Tyndareus" (*Sat.* I. 1, 100) for a freedwoman with an ax, and "Proteus" (*Epist.* I. 1, 90) for changing public taste; Juvenal's "Clytemnestra in every street" (VI. 656) for wives who slay their husbands; Alciphron's unsuccessful fishermen (*Ep.* I. 2, 1) who style themselves "Danaids"; Aelian's "Hippolytus" (*Ep.* 12) for a confirmed hunter; Philostratus' remark to a reluctant girl (*Ep.* 47), "Danaus was your father and you have the well-known hand and homicidal will"; Eunapius' sophist (like Aristides' Demosthenes) styled as "the type of Hermes the Eloquent" (*VS* 490); Lucian's habitual reference to Peregrinus as

[19] The allusions to myth in Heliodorus are so unevenly distributed that there are about five *loci* in the first four books to every two in the last six. Allusions to the stage, on the contrary, give the impression of being more frequent in the later books. The distribution of passages cited in J. W. H. Walden's "Stage-Terms in Heliodorus's Aethiopica" (*HSCP*, v [1894], 1-43), however, suggests that while terms from the stage are used a little more frequently in the first books than in the last, their employment remains relatively constant. In any event, their relative importance, vis-à-vis myth, is greater toward the end of the work.

[19a] Since this paragraph was written, Ben Edwin Perry, *The Ancient Romances* (Berkeley, 1967), has become available, with its valuable summaries of the evidence about the dates of the authors (pp. 343-52) and its useful classification of the romances (p. 350). Had these data and suggestions been accessible as this paper was written, the remarks above would doubtless have taken a different form. The distinctions drawn between the work of Chariton and those of Achilles Tatius and Longus are, of course, confirmed from a new point of view. The remarks about Xenophon of Ephesus would remain almost the same, for there is little by which to judge when one approaches him from myth. Only about Heliodorus (now apparently last in the sequence) is much revision called for. Perhaps his "interest in analogies between life and the stage" should rather be taken as an effort "to furbish up tired old techniques," but that ought to be judged at leisure. In any event papyrus discoveries in the past have upset many previous opinions, and conceivably yet (to quote Terence, *An.* 314, for the spirit of coincidence common in the romances) *interea fiet aliquid*—although, of course, Byrria's reply may be the final judgment: *id 'aliquid' nil est.*

"Proteus" (e.g., *Mort. Peregr.* 1); Petronius' "little Ulysses" for a boy hiding by clinging beneath the webbing of a bed (97)—these scattered samples attest to the widespread vitality of the idea. A fine set could also be gleaned from the *Metamorphoses* of Apuleius where, for example, the ass's rider (VII. 26. 3) qualifies as a "Bellerophon," and Meroe (I. 12. 4) calls her sleeping lover, Socrates, her " Endymion " and then adds that he is a " Ulysses " and herself a desolate " Calypso." Since two analogues ("Dirce " for the old woman dragged behind the runaway ass (VI. 27. 5) and "Pasiphae" for the rich woman who spends the night with the ass (X. 19. 3 and X. 22. 4) have their counterparts in the Λούκιος ἢ Ὄνος (23 and 51), one might suspect Lucian as the source for the analogues in Apuleius. But Apuleius was perfectly capable of finding them for himself with a genuine measure of appropriateness, as when (*Apol.* 23) he assigned the nickname " Charon " to the ugly-looking Aemilianus who had grown rich through a series of inheritances, and later (56) when he echoes the Vergilian tradition by calling the same man " Mezentius " to identify him as a *contemptor deorum*.

All the analogues here considered from the writers of Greek romance have been more or less graphic, that is, picturable. More nearly logical analogues (such as to appeal primarily to the reason without conjuring up visual impressions) are readily possible, as when Calasiris consoles Chariclea, who blushes to admit that she has fallen in love (Heliod. IV. 10, 5): "know that you are not alone or the first to undergo this experience, but rather you are in company with many distinguished women and with many otherwise sensible virgins. Eros is the greatest of the gods and one who has at times been said to have power over the gods themselves." [20] Nothing very picturable is required by this argument, although specific stories can serve to illustrate it, as for example Apollo and Daphne (cf. Ach. Tat. I. 5, 5-7). Relatively general arguments of the sort could, surely, have been used much more often had the authors felt them desirable.

However, the graphic analogue obviously made a strong appeal to writers of romance, although the essential idea was as old as the "godlike" heroes of Homer. And even during the period when the romance burgeoned, it was not the sole property of that genre. Any

[20] The same type of argument occurs in Chariton (VI. 3, 2), Longus (II. 7, 2), and Achilles Tatius (I. 5, 7). To use the *acta deorum* as justification for one's own deeds is subject to attack in literature at least from the fifth century onward (e.g., Eur. *HF* 1340-46).

kind of narrative which will be read without highly relevant pictures, charts, and diagrams, must be illustrated by verbal means, so that the reader can visualize persons, places, and situations. Myth was known to all. The stories had been sketched with such clear lines by countless tellers that they had inspired innumerable artists to paint their subjects. And those paintings had in turn inspired even more clear-cut narrative presentations (hence often the stories of literature seem to be told with a painting in mind). It is not surprising, then, that the authors of romance, who often claimed to be relating the story of a painting (e.g., Longus and Achilles Tatius), turned to myth when they wished their readers to picture either their heroes and heroines or the situations in which they found themselves.

Northwestern University
16 January 1966

THE TEXT OF OVID'S *AMORES*

Revilo P. Oliver

Only in recent years have we been in a position to examine critically the text tradition of the *Amores*. At the opening of the nineteenth century, Ovid's text was essentially in the state in which it had been left by Heinsius and Burman, who were editors of great learning and discernment, to be sure, but gave us only occasional and sometimes ambiguous information concerning the lections of the comparatively few manuscripts they had at their disposal. Thereafter, although the intensive study of palaeography and the methodology that is most closely associated with the name of Lachmann greatly improved the text of Lucretius and other authors, the effect on the text of Ovid was not progress but regression. For more than a century, "conservative" editors, with the almost fetishistic devotion to "oldest" and "best" manuscripts then in vogue, tried to construct a text of the *Amores* from three mutilated manuscripts of the ninth to eleventh centuries. It is a nice irony that those editors were blissfully unaware that what Housman called "the arsenals of divine vengeance" held in store an older and complete manuscript that was ignored because some librarian had labeled it "saec. XIV."

The first adequate edition of the *Amores* was the meticulously accurate and brilliant work of Franco Munari, published in 1951 and revised in 1955 and 1959.[1] It was followed in 1961 by E. J. Kenney's excellent edition of all of Ovid's amatory poems except the *Heroides* in the Bibliotheca Oxoniensis. The editions by Munari and Kenney, when used in conjunction, report for the first time the readings of some sixty-six manuscripts that had been previously

---

[1] Franco Munari, in the "Biblioteca di Studi Superiori" published by "La Nuova Italia" Editrice in Florence; Munari gives the more complete and detailed apparatus.

contemned on the wild assumption that *recentiores* are always *deteriores.*[2]

We may be confident that Kenney's edition will soon be replaced. For one thing, the editor, despite his fine critical acumen and careful diligence, himself corrupted the text of the *Amores* in two places by inadvertently introducing readings that he neither found in any manuscript nor intended as emendations,[3] thus providing for textual critics an impressive, though painful, lesson in what can happen to a text even when it is copied by a distinguished and careful scholar. In another place, the meaning of the text has been corrupted by an exegetical note in the apparatus which attributes to Ovid Latin for which no parallel can be found outside the debased jargon of the decadence.[4] And finally, after Kenney's edition had gone to press, there was discovered in Berlin—of all places!—a manuscript, Hamiltonianus 471, which was written shortly before or after the opening of the ninth century, and contains, according to preliminary reports, the complete *Amores* together with the *Ars amatoria* and the *Remedia amoris.*[5] It is therefore older by at least

[2] E. J. Kenney uses none of the manuscripts that Munari designates with lower-case letters, and only some of those designated with capital letters; he has, however, collated a number of manuscripts that Munari did not use. The reader, who, I assume, will have both editions before him, should note that Kenney's B, D, and F were not collated by Munari, who uses those sigla to designate other manuscripts, while Kenney's Ab = Munari's G, Ac = F, Ea = E, Ob = O, Va = B, and Vb = X. Note also that Kenney's ω means *recentiores plerique,* while Munari's means *codices omnes.*

[3] These errors, which puzzled many readers and occasioned considerable inquiry, are (together with *rogantia* for *precantia* in *A. A.* I. 709) confessed by Kenney in *CR,* xiv (1964), 13.

[4] In II. 1, 5, *in sponsi facie* is glossed in the apparatus as *coram sponso,* and this is not a slip in Latinity for it is obvious from Kenney's remark in his "Notes on Ovid" (*CQ,* viii [1958], 59) that he understood the line to mean that the *virgo* was to read the poems in the presence of her fiancé! That is a meaning for which, as a glance at the *Thesaurus,* s.v. 'facies,' will quickly show, there is no parallel outside the Itala and writers of the extreme decadence. The phrase is merely one of Ovid's numerous uses of *in* with the ablative to designate the person who is the object of emotion—a poetic extension of a construction that is common in Cicero (to say nothing of other prose writers); I gave a few examples in *CP,* li (1956), 60 f., and liii (1958), 138, in connection with my discussion of the reading in II. 4, 11. The *virgo* is *non frigida in sponsi facie* in precisely the sense in which Ovid in II. 7, 9, denies that he is *frigidus in te* (ablative), and the meaning was properly explained in Némethy's commentary (1907) *ad loc.:* "quae [sc. virgo] movetur pulchritudine sponsi."

[5] First reported by Friedrich Lenz in a "stop-press" supplement to his excellent new edition of the *Remedia amoris* in the Corpus Paravianum (1965). In this appendix, Lenz gives a collation of the Hamiltonianus for the *Remedia,* from which it is clear that the manuscript is closely related to R and appears to have

half a century than any other manuscript now known, and is the *only* manuscript earlier than the twelfth century that contains the whole text.

The present study is offered as a modest contribution to the next edition of the *Amores*.

I

As we should expect, the text tradition has been studied by the scholars to whose collations we owe our present knowledge, Munari [6] and Kenney.[7] To their studies must now be added a long and brilliant article by G. P. Goold.[8]

These investigations make it certain that the known manuscripts fall into two sharply distinct groups, a and β. The former are evidently derived from a manuscript now lost whose readings are preserved by R, a fragmentary manuscript of the late ninth century, by P, which was copied from the now lost portion of R about the beginning of the tenth century, and, with less fidelity, by S, which comes from the eleventh century.[9] To these, of course, future editors will have to add the recently discovered Hamiltonianus, which will probably be recognized as the best representative of a.[10]

The real difficulty is presented by β, which is a group that contains a very large number of manuscripts of comparatively late date derived from a presumably large number of earlier manuscripts now lost. These manuscripts have been so affected by what is called horizontal transmission [11] that Munari tentatively, and Kenney

been copied directly from an exemplar that was in either Beneventan or Visigothic script with little or no division of words. I understand that a complete collation of the Hamiltonianus will soon be published by Franco Munari, and I have not attempted to anticipate his findings for the text of the *Amores*.

6 Franco Munari, "Sugli 'Amores' di Ovidio," *SIFC*, XXIII (1948), 110–52. The article includes a complete collation of R and P, which is indispensable for a close study of the text. A complete collation of S was published by Lenz, *Rendiconti dell'Istituto Lombardo di Scienze e Lettere*, LXIX (1936), 633–56.

7 E. J. Kenney, "The Manuscript Tradition of Ovid's *Amores, Ars amatoria*, and *Remedia amoris*," *CQ*, XII (1962), 1–31, to which I hereinafter refer as "Kenney (1962)." See also his "Notes on Ovid," *CQ*, VIII (1958), 54–66, which I cite as "Kenney (1958)."

8 G. P. Goold, "Amatoria critica," *HSCP*, LXIX (1965), 1–107.

9 For published collations, see n. 6, above. The relation between R and P is most fully explained by Goold, p. 4.

10 On the characteristics of the Hamiltonianus, see Lenz' edition of the *Remedia*, p. 100.

11 The term comes, of course, from Giorgio Pasquali's monumental *Storia della tradizione e critica del testo* (Firenze, 1934; 2a ed., 1952).

definitively, despaired of ever untangling their relationship. Indeed, Kenney (1962) regards β as a "convenient fiction" that designates not a family of manuscripts derived, however remotely, from a single ancestor, but a polyphyletic crowd, "the product of more than one stream of tradition." And as Kenney points out, it is *a priori* highly improbable that only two manuscripts of a work so widely read as Ovid's should have survived the Dark Ages. Most recently, however, Goold not only regards β as a family, but believes that both α and β descend from a single Medieval archetype whose pages were "liberally glossed" with exegetic notes and, presumably, *variae lectiones*.

In addressing ourselves to this problem, we shall, I think, find it profitable to change our perspective by trying to view the tradition from its point of origin.

II

It is now generally accepted that Ovid began to "publish" his *Amores* when, as he says in the *Tristia,* "barba resecta mihi bisve semelve fuit," that is to say, about 25 B.C., when he was eighteen; that, as he also tells us, his poetry won for him immediate celebrity; and that, as is intrinsically probable, he completed the five books of the *Amores* within, at most, a few years after that date.

In an article which I shall not attempt to summarize here,[12] I tried to show that the first edition of the *Amores* in five books must have contained a coherent account of Ovid's liaison with Corinna comparable to Propertius' story of his affair with Cynthia; that in the second edition in three books, issued when Ovid was nearing or had reached middle age, the comparatively few elegies that mention Corinna are scattered among others in an order that deliberately destroys both chronological sequence and consistent portraiture; and that this and other evidence indicates that the second edition was a revision of the first so drastic that we now have no line of verse that we can certainly identify as having appeared in the first edition.

The second edition of the *Amores* was undoubtedy issued many years after the first. The reference to the Sygambri in I. 14, cannot conceivably be earlier than 16 B.C., and it is probably an indication of a date at least nine years later than that, for the reference to that people as a *gens triumphata* would have been outrageous hyperbole

[12] R. P. Oliver, "The First Edition of the *Amores*," *TAPA,* LXXVI (1945), 191–215.

before the tribe, which inflicted a severe defeat on a Roman army in 16, was subdued and partly dispersed by Tiberius about 8 B.C., and the first triumph in which they could decently have been represented as conquered was that which Tiberius was granted in 7 B.C.[13] It is, furthermore, highly improbable that the Sygambri could have become an important source of blonde hair for the wig-makers of Rome before large numbers of them were resettled in Gaul.

At the very earliest, therefore, the second edition was issued when Ovid was thirty-five. At the latest, it appeared before the last book of the *Ars amatoria,* which clearly alludes to this edition;[14] that gives us a date of approximately 1 B.C., when Ovid was forty-two. Even if we make a very generous allowance for hyperbole in Ovid's repeated claim that his youthful songs about Corinna were known and recited *per totum orbem,* copies of the first edition must have been produced in large numbers during the two decades that preceded the appearance of the second edition, and we may be quite sure that that large multitude of widely scattered copies did not simply evaporate when Ovid issued his revision. Indeed, it is likely that the second edition did not entirely displace the first in antiquity any more than Cicero's second edition of his *Academica* supplanted the first.

Some copies of the first edition could have survived, and probably did, for centuries, although papyrus is a relatively perishable material. Furthermore, it is likely that copies of the first edition continued to be made long after the second appeared. There must have been readers who preferred the much longer, probably more coherent, and doubtless less cynical work. Ovid was, throughout the empire, a poet second in popularity only to Vergil.[15] He was so

---

[13] Dio, LV. 6; on the subjugation of the German tribe, see the *Cambridge Ancient History,* x, 363; Pauly-Wissowa, s.v. 'Sugambri,' col. 661.

[14] Since the "collation of the late manuscripts" desiderated in my article of 1945 has now been made partly available by Kenney, I am no longer uncertain about the reading in *A. A.* III. 343: *deue tribus libris.* Incidentally, I now see that this reading, copied as *deuet'b;,* would almost automatically have been transcribed as *de veteribus,* a metrically impossible reading that would almost inevitably (given *amorum* at the end of the line) have been corrected to *de veterum,* the variant that particularly troubled me in my article (p. 194, n. 15). When a collation of the Hamiltonianus becomes available, we shall probably know what R had originally at this point—or should have had; if R were of later date, one would make the obvious suggestion that its reading (*deue cerem*) was the result of confusion between *c* and *t.*

[15] This is obvious from the number of quotations and imitations in verse inscriptions; see the indices to Buecheler and Lommatzsch's *Carmina Latina epigraphica.*

highly esteemed in the time of the elder Pliny that an incomplete poem on the unexciting subject of fish in the Black Sea, reputedly begun by him at Tomis and left unfinished when he died, was in general circulation. Is it likely that those who so admired his work would not have reproduced the youthful elegies, amounting at the very least to more than two books, that the poet's more mature judgment had (rightly or wrongly) rejected?

In short, it is well to remind ourselves that we have no reason to suppose that even so late a writer as Servius, for example, could not have found a text of the first edition of the *Amores,* had he looked for it.

III

The first edition is now lost, of course, but we should not forget it, for it provides us with a datum of considerable importance in literary history. For example, Ovid uses in poems that range from our extant *Amores* to the penultimate book of the *Tristia* phrases and even a complete line apparently taken from the quite minor poet who called himself Lygdamus. This fact has produced a proliferation of theories and arguments, which range from the contention that Lygdamus was a later writer whose elegies were inserted in the Corpus Tibullianum by either accident or a *supercherie littéraire* to an ingenious and plausible hypothesis that Lygdamus was Ovid's elder brother.[16] No one seems to have considered the obvious possibility that Lygdamus borrowed from the first edition of the *Amores,* and that Ovid, when in exile he wrote a line that also appears in Lygdamus, was simply reusing his own property, as it was, indeed, his custom to do.[17]

Modern editions of the *Amores* include as III. 5, an elegy that was circulated widely in the Middle Ages as a separate composition entitled *Somnium.* The manuscript tradition, as studied by Munari and Kenney (1962), makes it virtually certain that this elegy did not appear in any antecedent of the β group, and makes it seem probable that the composition was added to the *Amores* in α and did not appear in the source of that tradition. The poem, however, is undoubtedly ancient; even those who deny its authenticity concede that the Latinity and versification indicate that the author was

[16] Ably presented, with references to earlier discussions, by Max Ponchont in his Budé edition of Tibullus (1924), pp. 122–27.

[17] A few examples are given by Goold, pp. 24–25.

either a contemporary of Ovid's or a *poëta Ovidianus* of the next generation, and the poem is quoted as Ovid's in Servius *auctus, ad Buc.* 6, 54, which proves that it was accepted as authentic in the fourth century—and possibly, if we accept a very plausible theory concerning the derivation of the *auctus* part of the commentary, in the second century.[18] The poem has been pronounced spurious on stylistic grounds, most recently by Kenney (1962), who athetizes it in his edition. The attribution to Ovid has been as vigorously defended, notably by Friedrich Lenz, who found the style and technique perfectly Ovidian,[19] and Georg Luck, in his careful review of Kenney's work, remarks that the arguments against the poem's authenticity "überzeugen mich nicht." [20]

Some of the stylistic details that Kenney adduces are inconclusive,[21] and one, indeed, can be used to counter his argument. With reference to the line "ingenium dominae lena movebit anus," he observes that *"ingenium movere* in the language of Ovid means 'inspire,' not 'corrupt.' " True, and the expression, therefore, is precisely what Kenney's *poëta Ovidianus* would have carefully avoided, while Ovid would not have hesitated to give a sarcastic twist to one of his favorite terms. The expression has point in this elegy only through contrast with its normal use, as in III. 12, 16: "ingenium movit sola Corinna meum." The implication is: The girl arouses my talent for poetry; the *lena* arouses the girl's talent for adultery.

The most telling sylistic argument is that two of Ovid's favorite devices, hyperbaton and repetition, occur more frequently in this elegy than in the other amatory poems, and that two of the repetitions produce a rather heavy emphasis where none seems to be needed. We must admit that this elegy falls below the high level

[18] The theory that much of the added material was derived through Aelius Donatus from Aemilius Asper, who probably wrote in the second century; see Alfred Tomsin, *Étude sur le commentaire virgilien d'Aemilius Asper* (Paris, 1952).

[19] Friedrich Lenz, in Bursian's *Jahresbericht*, ccxxvi (1930), 112–14.

[20] Georg Luck, *Gnomon*, xxxv (1963), 258, n. 2.

[21] I cannot see why *lene sonantis aquae* is "unsuitable in its context" when that context is descriptive of a brook along whose banks the grass grows thickest; and the fact that the phrase appears twice in the *Fasti* may merely show that Ovid was fond of it. The fact that the only parallel to *pastus* used passively occurs in the *Halieutica* does not show that our elegy is spurious; Kenney may be astonished that "there are those who believe that Ovid wrote the *Halieutica*," but those who believe that he did not face a somewhat embarrassing dilemma; cf. *CP*, LIX (1964), 39.

of technical skill and artistic finish that we find in the other *Amores*. Although the poem, as Kenney admits, is "the work of an accomplished poet," the style is inferior to what we expect of Ovid.

The principal objection to the poem is, I think, latent in Munari's comment that if the authenticity cannot be established, "nè Ovidio nè il lettore avrebbero a rammaricarsene." It is an objection not to style, but to subject. There is something juvenile about the solemn young lover who dreams a symbolic dream, consults an *interpres*, and faints at the discovery that his mistress can be unfaithful. That romantic adolescent is not the Ovid of the *Amores*, with his urbane wit, his worldly wise and mild cynicism, and his habit of expressing deep emotion only to follow it with a smile. But the elegy does use an Ovidian symbolism [22] and its defects, especially the striving for pathos in recounting personal emotion, are of the kind commonly found in the writing of youthful poets. We may grant that Ovid would not have included this elegy in our collection, but if I was justified in concluding, twenty years ago, that "no inferences concerning either the style or the character of Ovid in his youth can safely be drawn from the [extant] *Amores*," [23] I do not see how we can overlook the very distinct possibility that this elegy was a part of Ovid's first edition and one of the many that he excluded from the second, excluding it precisely because he felt that it was inferior stylistically and that his woebegone lover was too juvenile to be amusing. If that is what happened, neither the separate transmission of the text nor ancient quotation from the poem as Ovid's should excite any astonishment.

IV

On the basis of our knowledge of ancient books, we can outline in general terms the transmission of the text of our *Amores* in antiquity. The second edition was undoubtedly disseminated in the form of three papyrus *volumina* written in the capital hand that is familiar to everyone from the papyrus fragments of the *Carmen de bello Actiaco*.[24] The words (except proclitics) were separated by *interpuncta*, apices and *i-longae* were used wherever those marks of quantity seemed convenient, and rapid reading was probably facilitated by the fairly elaborate punctuation that appears to have been

[22] Cf. II. 12, 25–26.
[23] Oliver (1945), p. 215.
[24] Cf. Oliver, *TAPA*, LXXXII (1951), 241 f.; Jean Mallon, *Paléographie romaine* (Madrid, 1952), 48–50, 77–80, 173–75.

in general use during the Augustan Age and for some time there-after.[25] And the accuracy with which the professional scribes copied a text was probably proportional to the price at which it was sold.

Like Vergil, Ovid was one of the classics whose works were made available—to those who could pay for the luxury of compact and conveniently portable books—in parchment codices near the end of the first century. We know that in A.D. 85 a purchaser could obtain over the counter a codex containing the fifteen books of the *Metamorphoses*,[26] and it is quite likely that Ovid's amatory elegies were collected to form a companion volume of comparable size. So far as our present knowledge permits us to judge, however, it is unlikely that such a collection would have affected the transmission of the texts to later times. The codices of Martial's time appear to have been *livres de luxe,* roughly comparable to our one-volume Shakespeares on India paper, and to have enjoyed only an ephemeral vogue.[27] To the end of the third century, literary texts were normally—and perhaps, during the greater part of that time, exclusively—transmitted as papyrus *volumina,* each of which, of course, contained a *liber.*

About the time of Hadrian, apices and marks of punctuation become rare or entirely disappear and texts are written in *scriptura continua.*[28] One would suppose that this regression would have greatly increased the likelihood that texts would be miscopied or misunderstood, but I know of no evidence that it did have that effect.

As is well known, Latin literature—or, to be more exact, the part of it that was cherished as classical—was transferred from papyrus *volumina* to parchment codices during the fourth and fifth centuries. We are justified in assuming that our text of the *Amores* was incorporated in codices that resembled the few that have survived of

[25] Studied in "Latin Punctuation in the Classical Age," a doctoral dissertation written at the University of Illinois by E. Otha Wingo (1963); it will be published in the near future.

[26] Martial XIV. 192.

[27] See C. H. Roberts, *The Codex* (London, 1954; repr. from *Proceedings of the British Academy,* XL), pp. 177–82. Roberts notes the significant fact that "in the later years of Martial's literary activity there is no further reference . . . to the parchment codex," and suggests that the apparent failure of so useful an innovation may have been due to "Greek influence in Roman cultural life" in the early second century.

[28] I am inclined to attribute the change to *scriptura continua* primarily to a desire to imitate Greek books, but it may have some relation to the "métamorphose de l'écriture romaine," identified and analyzed by Mallon (pp. 93–104), which took place at approximately the same time.

Vergil, particularly the well-known Palatinus, Romanus, and Mediceus; that is to say, the text was written on vellum in rustic capitals and *scriptura continua,* with no separation of words, unless the purchaser himself *distinxit* by inserting points for his own comfort. Whether the text of Ovid was also reproduced in the far more costly square capitals found in the now fragmentary codices Augusteus and Sangallensis is uncertain: we do not know how common such luxurious books were.

Since the three *volumina* of the *Amores* would form only a small part of a codex, it is only reasonable to assume that in the fourth century the amatory works of Ovid were united to make a codex of respectable dimensions. Such codices probably contained the collection that was found in our oldest extant manuscripts when they were intact, viz.: the *Ars amatoria,* the *Remedia amoris,* the second edition of the *Amores,* and the *Epistulae heroidum.* If the collectors were consistent, they also included the *Medicamina faciei femineae.* Whether they did or not, we do not know. What remains of that work is two fragments of fifty lines each, and the only reasonable inference is that our text comes ultimately from two not contiguous leaves that had twenty-five lines on a page and somehow survived detached from their codex. They *could,* of course, have been leaves from a codex similar to the Palatinus or Mediceus of Vergil.[29]

It is virtually certain that the text of Ovid was never copied in uncials, and improbable that it was copied in semiuncials.[30]

[29] Some very slight support for this conjecture may be found in the circumstance that the first leaf, which contained the opening of the poem, had as many lines as the second; no space, therefore, was taken by the title, and if there was one, it stood in what was normally the upper margin of the page. This, however, opens the further possibility that the first leaf either bore no title at all or had an abbreviated one; the words *faciei femineae,* therefore, may be a Medieval addition.

[30] B. L. Ullman, *Ancient Writing and Its Influence* (New York, 1932), p. 68. Ullman first noted the significance of the fact that although we have a considerable number of uncial manuscripts, none contains the text of a pagan poet. Ullman also calls attention to the "leap" in the text tradition of Vergil from rustic capitals to Carolingian minuscules. A glance through the published volumes of E. A. Lowe's *Codices Latini antiquiores* (I–X) confirms the impression that texts of the pagan poets were not reproduced between the opening of the sixth century and the last decades of the eighth; had copies been made in any considerable number during that period, there seems to be no reason why they should not have survived among the fairly numerous manuscripts that did reach our time. This would suggest that ninth-century manuscripts of such writers cannot be very far from rustic-capital exemplars. The difficulty, of course, lies in the assumption, which we base on the very few ancient codices

Our texts of Vergil seem to have passed from rustic capitals to minuscules of the Carolingian period, thus, in effect, leaping over the intervening centuries of the darkest of Dark Ages. There is a general likelihood that the text of Ovid made the transition in the same way, and that our earliest extant manuscripts are not separated by many intermediaries from texts in rustic capitals.

This brings us to our central problem: How many rustic-capital codices of Ovid's amatory works survived the Dark Ages? When the sun set forever on the Roman Empire, there must have been scores, and probably were hundreds, of such codices, and there is no *physical* reason why such durable books should not all have survived to our time. It is *a priori* improbable that only one out of so many should have reached the ninth century, and even more improbable that if several did survive, only one would have been the source of all later copies. The gravamen of proof must therefore fall on those who would trace our many extant manuscripts ultimately to a single archetype.

V

One test that we can apply is titulature. Some years ago, I collected evidence concerning the form of superscriptions and subscriptions in both *volumina* and codices in antiquity, and I believed the evidence sufficient to trace a pattern of evolution.[31]

If we examine P and S, manuscripts that represent a and contain the parts of the *Amores* where the internal division into books is shown, we find the following as the work of the first hands: [32]

P	S
EXPLICIT LIBER I	INCIPIT LIBER .II.
EXPLICIT LIBER SECUNDUS	Incipit liber tertius

that have survived, that codices in capitals were the normal form in which the classics were preserved in the last century of the Roman Empire. It is possible that such codices were rare *livres de luxe,* which owe their preservation to their beauty, and that the *normal* parchment codex of the period was written in a cursive hand, and that no specimens have survived because no one made an effort to preserve books that lacked aesthetic appeal. This does not seem probable, but it is possible. That Ovid passed through the rustic-capital stage is shown by such errors in P as *et dis* (FIDES), *funtis* (EVNTIS), and, no doubt, most of the confusions of *-et/-it, -es/-is,* listed by Goold (pp. 25 f.), but such misreadings could have been perpetuated through any number of intermediary manuscripts, and so tell us nothing about the date at which the rustic-capital text was copied in minuscules.

[31] R. P. Oliver, "The First Medicean MS of Tacitus and the Titulature of Ancient Books," *TAPA,* LXXXII (1951), 230–61.

[32] I use the collations by Munari and Lenz (see n. 6, above).

Now these subscriptions must go back to what I identified as the simplest and oldest form of internal colophon, that in which the end of a book was indicated by a subscription of the form LIBER·I, with no title for the next book, no recitation of the name of the author or the title of his work, and, of course, without the formulaic *explicit* and *incipit* that are demonstrably late additions to the style of writing colophons in codices. And if my deductions from the admittedly scanty evidence were correct, this means that the subscriptions in P and S come (with, of course, the addition of *explicit* or *incipit*) from a rustic-capital codex that was at least as old as the Palatinus of Vergil, which is usually assigned to the early part of the fourth century. If it had been of later date, it would presumably have added AMORVM at the end of each book, and had it been as late as the Mediceus (late fifth century) it would probably have had at the end of each book the full formulaic colophon that had come into vogue by that time, that is, something like P OVIDI NASONIS | AMORVM LIB· I EXPLICIT· | INCIPIT LIB· II FELICITER.

The end of the *Amores* is missing in P and S, so these manuscripts have no terminal colophon. The beginning is missing in P and there is no title above the opening lines in S, which means that either the title was part of a colophon that appeared on a preceding and now lost folium of S or that S was copied from an exemplar that had no title, having undergone the same kind of mutilation. As a result, of course, a scribe who had as his exemplar either P or S (in their present state) would have had no means of knowing the title of the poetic work that he was copying.

In R, the opening of the *Amores* is preceded by the colophon: P. OVIDI NASONIS LIBER PRIMVS REMEDIORVM | EXPLICIT. INCIPIT EIVSDEM ANIMORVM | LIBER PRIMVS. The Hamiltonianus, which is older, has a colophon which does not have the silly mistake at the end of the second line and is instructive in other ways: P. OUIDI NASONIS REMEDIORŪ EXPLIC̄ LIB· Primus | INC̄IP EIVSDĒ AMORŪ LĪB· Iˢ. Now *primus* must be an expansion of a numeral that stood for *unus*, and it is likely that the notation *lib.* was added after the formulaic *explicit* had been added to the colophon. This suggests that the original form of the colophon consisted of a single word, REMEDIA, or, possibly, REMEDIORVM.[33] This was probably

---

[33] In the Palatinus of Vergil, for example, the end of the eclogues is marked by the single word BVCOLICON; the reader was expected to understand *liber* and to know that there was only one book of them. On the colophons in the Romanus, see p. 252 of the article cited in n. 31 above.

followed, on the same or the next page, by the notation, AMORVM LIB·I. That is precisely the form of colophon and title that we find in the Palatinus. Thus the evidence—tenuous, to be sure, but all that we have—again suggests a date early in the fourth century rather than later.

If we now turn to manuscripts of the β group, we find that all of them, so far as they have been reported, have titles (and corresponding colophons) such as *Incipit ouidius sine titulo* or *Incipit liber ouidii de sine titulo* [!] or *Incipit ille liber cuius non nomen habetur*. From this fact we must draw three deductions, viz.:

1. All these manuscripts are derived ultimately from rustic-capital codices in which the division between books was indicated by the same kind of simple colophon that appeared in the source of α. If there were many such codices, it would be something of a coincidence that they all came from the early fourth century or earlier, but that is all. Presumably it was only chance that preserved for us the Romanus and Mediceus of Vergil instead of two contemporaries of the Palatinus.

2. All are derived from a source or sources in which the text of the *Amores* was not preceded by a title. If there were several sources, that is a greater coincidence, but we need not balk at it. Titles were frequently combined with the colophon of the work that ended on the preceding page, and we can think of several reasons why the portion of a codex that contained the *Amores* could have become separated from the rest.

3. All come from a source or sources in which there was no terminal colophon at the end of the *Amores*. P now has no colophon because the folium that contained the concluding part of the last book has been lost, and S has no colophon because it was copied from an exemplar that had been mutilated by the loss of several folia.[33a] The *recentiores*, however, have the complete text of the last

---

[33a] That S was copied in the eleventh century from an exemplar that was already mutilated is clearly shown by a bit of evidence that has not, perhaps, been sufficiently noted. Its text ends with the *first* word of line 11 of III.9—a word which the scribe entered at some distance to the right of line 10. This fact puzzles Lenz, who, in the discussion preceding his collation (p. 634), suggests several far-fetched hypotheses. The explanation must be that the exemplar of S was produced in a scriptorium in which it was customary to place *custodes* at the bottom of the last page of each quaternion or other gathering to make certain that the gatherings would be bound in the right order. In the codex that became the exemplar of S a quaternion ended with line 10 of III.9, and its scribe accordingly wrote in the lower margin as a *custos* the first word on the first page of the next quaternion, that is, the first word of line 11. That following quaternion was

book, and we cannot resort to the desperate suggestion that their sources had been mutilated in the same way as P and the exemplar of S so that some part of the text has been lost after what is now the last line of the last elegy, because that elegy, with its valediction to amatory poetry, must have concluded the *Amores,* and the last distich of that elegy obviously brings it to a conclusion. To explain the loss of the colophon, therefore, only four hypotheses are possible, viz.: (a) a codex in which the last line of the final elegy came at the bottom of a page, thus making it necessary to write the colophon on the next page, which was lost before any copies were made; (b) a very expensive and ornate codex, probably in square capitals and comparable to the Sangallensis of Vergil, in which a separate page was devoted to the colophon, which page, again, was lost before copies were made; (c) a codex in which the colophon was simply omitted through some oversight of the scribe; and (d) a codex in which the *Amores* ended on a recto which was then so torn that the colophon was lost but the concluding lines of the poem escaped damage. There is nothing inherently impossible in any one of these hypotheses, but what they all have in common is that they require either a very unusual kind of codex or an uncommon accident— or both.

Now all three of the conditions that we have postulated above must have existed simultaneously in the codex or codices from which the many manuscripts of the β group were derived. When we calculate probability, we will all grant that there could have been one such codex, and some of us will grudgingly admit that there could— perhaps!—have been two. Three would require a fantastic number of coincidences.

---

detached from that codex and lost before S was copied. The scribe of S, knowing that his exemplar was incomplete, copied after line 10 the *custos* at the bottom of the page. There is further proof that the exemplar of S was thus mutilated, if Lenz is right when he implies (pp. 634, 637) that the scribe of S (*librarius Sangallensis*) also wrote the note that appears in the upper margin of the first page of the *Amores.* That note assures us that the title of the work is *Sine titulo* for two reasons, first, because Ovid wrote it only to influence his *amica,* and, second, because Ovid, having been accused before Augustus of corrupting Roman womanhood with his poetry, did not dare put his name on it: "non ausus ⟨est⟩ hic apponere titulum." In the Middle Ages, to be sure, ignorance was almost as glib and presumptuous as it is today, but even so, if the scribe of S composed or copied that note, his text must have come from an exemplar that had neither title nor terminal colophon. If he wrote the note, then S, although its text of the *Amores* belongs to the α family, has the absurd title that characterizes the *recentiores.*

Therefore, unless further collations disclose a subgroup of β manuscripts that preserved the title *Amores,* we may legitimately infer that they are all descended from not more than two ancient codices, and that the chances are that they are descended from only one. That one, conceivably, could have been the ancestor of *a,* having been mutilated in some way after *a* was copied.

Titulature, therefore, seems to rule out Kenney's view that β had "probably several" antecedents, and does not disprove Goold's view that only one text survived the Dark Ages.

VI

The surest indication of a common origin is unanimity in omitting portions of the text. If all the manuscripts exhibit one lacuna, it is likely that they have a common ancestor; if they show two, the likelihood becomes a high degree of probability.

The editors mark no lacunae in the *Amores,* but there are two points, I believe, at which we must either decide that some verses have been lost in all of the known manuscripts or accuse Ovid of gross ineptitude.

In II. 13, Ovid, praying for the recovery of Corinna, whose life is endangered by the aftermath of an unskillful abortion, first addresses a long plea (lines 7–16) to Isis. That plea seems to reach its logical climax with the claim that if the goddess interposes her miraculous powers, she will save two lives: "nam vitam dominae tu dabis, illa mihi." In line 19, Ovid begins a prayer to Ilithyia, the classical goddess (identified with Lucina) who traditionally had jurisdiction over pregnancy and parturition. The two prayers, however, are separated by the strange couplet:

> saepe tibi sedit certis operata diebus
> qua tingit laurus Gallica turba tuas.[34]

This couplet no editor has understood. Heinsius frankly declared, "Haec obscurissima sunt & quae Oedipum requirant interpretem," and the modern editors have echoed him.[35] The difficulty is simply this: as the text stands, the antecedent of *tibi* must be Isis, and the couplet is a miserably anticlimactic addition to the plea already

---

[34] The editors accept Heinsius's emendation, *sedit,* which was based on the assumption that the worship of Isis was involved: *dedit* P *meruit* S recentiores plerique *servit* recentiores nonnulli. In the next line: *tingit* P recentiores nonnulli *tangit* S unus e recentioribus *cingit* recentiores plerique.

[35] Munari: "Locus nondum explicatus." Kenney: "Locus obscurissimus."

made—and what have the Galli to do with Isis? The priests of Isis were not eunuchs nor did they, so far as we know, indulge in comparable rites; and Ovid certainly knew that "Gallos, qui se excidere, vocamus." [36] That Ovid should have called the priests of Isis *Galli* is as improbable as that a part of the worship of Isis should be dated by the ceremonies performed by the eunuch hierodules of a rival cult.[37] I do not pretend to be Oedipus, but the only explanation I can see is that between lines 16 and 17 we have lost one or more couplets in which Ovid, having properly concluded his prayer to Isis, turns to the Magna Mater, whose cult, as is well known, attracted light-headed women, did impose ritual incubations or vigils on its votaries, and did have as its most conspicuous feature the insane [38] or crafty exhibitionism of the Galli.[39] In thus turning to three deities, Ovid both attained a certain symmetry and observed an historical sequence. He invokes first Isis, whose alien cult did not become securely lodged in Roman society until after the fall of

[36] *Fasti* IV. 361.

[37] There is no reason to suppose that the priests of Isis were eunuchs or behaved with the frenzy of the Galli, either in Rome or in their native country. (A compendious account of the Egyptian practice may be found in H. Idris Bell's *Cults and Creeds in Graeco-Roman Egypt* [Liverpool, 1954], pp. 60–75.) And even if there was a coincidence in the date of ceremonies, the Galli would not be using *laurūs* belonging to Isis.

[38] *Fasti* IV. 365.

[39] The general nature of the cult and its public ceremonies are, of course, well known; see Kurt Latte, *Römische Religionsgeschichte* (München, 1960), pp. 258–63; Franz Cumont, *Les religions orientales dans le paganisme romain* (3ème éd., Paris, 1929), pp. 73–114; Cyril Bailey, *Phases in the Religion of Ancient Rome* (Berkeley, 1932), pp. 181–85, 197–203. Cumont, speaking of the cult of the Magna Mater, observes (p. 94): "La dévotion féminine surtout trouvait dans ces cérémonies un aliment et une jouissance singulière—car toujours la Grande Mère, déesse féconde et nourricière, fut adorée par les femmes avec prédilection." When Heinsius imagined that the term *Galli* could be applied to priests of Isis, he was thinking in terms of the syncretism of the third century. As early as the time of Domitian it was possible for one woman to combine the offices of *sacerdos, flaminica Divae Iuliae Piae Augustae et Matris Deum Magnae Ideae et Isidis Reginae* (*CIL* IX, 1153 = Dessau, 6487), and by the first quarter of the second century, if not earlier, it was possible for a man to be simultaneously *sacerdos Isidis et Matris Deum* (*CIL*, XI, 3123 = Dessau, 6587), but that was after Caligula had officially admitted Isis to the Roman pantheon and Claudius had ended the official quarantine of the Magna Mater by permitting Roman citizens, presumably not castrated, to become Galli. In the time of Augustus the Galli were certainly eunuchs, as Ovid himself attests (cf. n. 36, above), and the two Oriental cults were competitors; indeed, it is generally believed (Cumont, pp. 88–90) that Claudius relaxed the restrictions on the cult of the Magna Mater for the purpose of offsetting and thus checking the growth of the cult of Isis.

the Republic.[40] He then addresses the Magna Mater, whose cult was notoriously the first Oriental infection brought to Rome.[41] And finally he turns to the native goddess of the classical world.[42]

Unless we suppose that Ovid was both inept as a poet and ignorant of the great difference between two popular cults, we must either indicate a lacuna before lines 17–18 or athetize them as a distich that must have entered the text in the same way as the undoubtedly spurious couplet, I. 13, 31–32.[43]

[40] On the cult of Isis at Rome, see Latte, pp. 282–84; Cumont, pp. 127–58; Bailey, pp. 186–89, 197–200. As is well known, the Senate, despite clamorous agitation among the rabble, tried to prohibit the worship of Isis at Rome by a series of decrees from 58 B.C. to 48 B.C. prohibiting the erection of altars to the Egyptian deities or ordering the destruction of shrines and temples already erected. Cicero in the De natura deorum (III. 19, 47) could still number Isis and Serapis among the gods not accepted at Rome. But although the Triumvirs apparently did not fulfill their pledge, made in 43 B.C., to erect a temple to the immigrant deities, the official recognition thus given to the cult must have accelerated its propagation, and temples privately erected on the outskirts of Rome were probably as popular as an official shrine on the Capitol would have been. The first serious effort to suppress the Egyptian superstition under the Empire was made by Tiberius, but the effect would probably have been transitory, even if Caligula had not given the alien cult a privileged position in the state.

[41] The well-known story of the importation of the Magna Mater should be considered in the light of the penetrating analysis by Theodor Koeves, "Zum Empfang der Magna Mater in Rom" (Historia, XII [1963], 321–47). Koeves has shown that political purposes were at least as important as regard for the supposed Sibylline oracle in procuring the importation, although the precise purposes of the promoters and the extent of their knowledge of the Pessinuntic cult must remain conjectural. Although the Senate tried to quarantine the imported superstition by confining the Galli to their temple except on the days of certain festivals, Romans who felt so inclined, especially women, must always have had access to the temple, and Latte (p. 260) is certainly right in observing that such customs as the mutitationes show that the cult was accepted as respectable "in vornehmen Kreisen."

[42] Ovid, it is needless to say, identified Ilithyia with Lucina (Met. IX. 283 and 294).

[43] The most obvious interpolation in the Amores is also the most instructive. With the exception of the opening and closing couplets, the poem is a monologue in which Ovid expostulates with the dawn, addressing Aurora always in the second person. In the midst of this monologue and as an integral part of the text in all manuscripts of the β class appears the couplet:

quid si non Cephali quondam flagrasset amore?
an putat ignotam nequitiam esse suam?

The shift from the second person to the third makes it obvious that the distich does not belong here, and there is no place in the elegy where the lines would be appropriate; furthermore, the couplet sadly interrupts the thread of thought and awkwardly anticipates the allusions in lines 35 and 39. How did a distich so obviously spurious become part of the text? Some nineteenth-century editors, such as Jahn, seem to have been haunted by a vision of a crafty little monk in a medieval scriptorium who, at every opportunity, slipped some verses of his

Another lacuna is highly probable in the opening elegy of Book III. Tragoedia and Elegia appear before Ovid, and the former exhorts him to abandon amatory verse for higher things. Elegia then expostulates with her rival, whom she addresses directly. Ovid, who is standing by and watching the ladies quarrel, is *huic* in line 44, and in lines 45–48 Elegia, certainly speaking to Tragoedia (*tu ... tuo ... tuo*), makes two points, viz. (a) that she has succeeded where her rival would have been powerless, and (b) that she deserves gratitude for having borne affronts and contumely that haughty Tragoedia would not have endured. Then, surely continuing to address the rival Muse, she documents her first point by observing (lines 49–52) that it was she who persuaded Corinna to overcome difficulties and take risks that she might become Ovid's mistress; Elegia then logically proceeds to prove her second point, thus:

53   a, quotiens foribus duris infixa pependi [44]
            non verita a populo praetereunte legi!
55   quin ego me memini, dum custos saevus abiret,
            ancillae miseram delituisse sinu.
        quid, cum me munus natali misit,[45] at illa
            rupit [46] et adposita barbara mersit [47] aqua?

---

own into a classical text and then rubbed his hands together in glee at his success in putting something over on posterity; and even recently so learned and usually judicious a scholar as Friedrich Lenz could seriously suggest (*Rendiconti dell'Accademia dei Lincei*, XIII [1938], 386–94) that the diabolic interpolator, learned in the niceties of nineteenth-century textual criticism, actually forged his verses so that their absence from the genuine tradition would be explained as loss through homoeoarcton or homoeoteleuton! But even if there were such mischief-makers (which I doubt) and if they concerned themselves with the text of Ovid, this couplet could not be the work of one of them, for the forger would surely have had intelligence enough to put his forgery in the second person instead of using the third and thus making his forgery as obvious as a red patch on a black suit. How then did the couplet enter the text? The only way that I can think of is that the verses came from a margin where they were cited for comparison with the allusion to Aurora's adultery in line 35 or with the mention of her love for Cephalus in line 39. The couplet came, therefore, from another poem on the same subject, and, at the risk of seeming to ride a hobbyhorse of my own, I venture to suggest that it is entirely possible that Ovid did include in his first edition a poem in which he did speak of Aurora in the third person.

[44] Goold has ably shown that it is necessary to read *a* and *infixa* instead of the *vel* and *incisa* that Munari and Kenney accepted from P. In line 56 I also follow Goold in reading *miseram*, although I am aware that *missam* could be defended as contrasting a poem privately sent with the publicly displayed poem of the preceding couplet.

[45] *misit* recentiores omnes *mittis* PS (Munari, Kenney).

[46] *rupit* S recentiores praeter unum omnes *rumpit* P (Munari, Kenney).

[47] *mersit* PS recentiores plerique *misit* recentiores nonnulli *mergit* Housman, unus e recentioribus (Munari, Kenney).

The text, as I have given it above, is perfectly coherent. Elegia, pointing out to Tragoedia what humiliations she has endured ("emerui plus quam tu posse ferendo"), says that she (in the form of a poem written on a sheet of papyrus) has very frequently dangled ignominiously from a nail or other projection set in a door, that she has sometimes lain hidden between the breasts of a slave-woman, and that she has even undergone the ultimate humiliation of being torn up and thrown in the wastebasket.[48] But now we come to the very next line,

59   prima tuae movi felicia semina mentis;
            munus habes, quod te iam petit ista, meum.

As we realize with dismay and shock, the antecedent of *tuae* and the subject of *habes* must be Ovid, not Tragoedia, to whom Elegia was speaking. To cushion the shock, editors have gone back to the preceding distich and read *mittis* with PS, which forces them to read, against the weight of the manuscript evidence, presents instead of perfects in the pentameter. The cushion is but a thin one; we receive a very unpleasant jolt when we come to *mittis* and realize that the subject cannot be Tragoedia, to whom Elegia has thus far been speaking, and have to assume that Elegia has somehow turned away from her rival, leaving her argument unfinished, and addressed Ovid with a statement that is, so far as he is concerned, utterly irrelevant and for which neither he nor the reader has been in any way prepared. Ovid can be abrupt, it is true, but his abruptness is that of a mercurial fancy [49] and never becomes sheer incoherence.

[48] The use of water to destroy papyrus and what had been written on it is amply attested, e.g., Mart. I. 5, 2; IX. 58, 7–8; XIV. 196, 2. It should not be confused with the practice of washing ink from parchment *pugillares* to permit their reuse.

[49] This has sometimes puzzled his editors. In I. 7, 61, all the manuscripts have *tamen*. Bornecque conjectured *tandem;* Munari retained the manuscript reading, defending it by reference to a very dubious statement in Nonius Marcellus (653, 6 Lindsay) that sometimes "tamen significat tandem." Kenney keeps *tamen* with the comment in his apparatus "nondum satis explicatum." What misled the editors, I think, is that Ovid, to produce an abrupt antithesis, omitted *sed* in the next line. But for this, I am sure, they would not have overlooked the fact that *tamen* with its normal adversative force is occasionally used rhetorically with reference to a following, not a preceding, statement. The precise parallel is to be found in Cicero, who *begins* a letter (*Ad Att.* XII. 2) thus: "Hic rumores tamen Murcum perisse naufragio, Asinium delatum vivum in manus militum, . . . sed auctor nullius rei quisquam" ('There are indeed rumors here in Rome that Murcus died in a shipwreck, *etc.*, but there is no authority for any of these statements'). Ovid's use of *tamen* has the same force: 'Thrice indeed I sought to implore her pardon, (but) thrice she repulsed me.'

The *gaucherie* of the text as it stands is, I submit, unworthy of Ovid—nay, it is unworthy of Maximianus. So far as I can see, the only remedy (short of athetizing lines 59–60, which is almost unthinkable) is to postulate the loss between lines 58 and 59 of one or more couplets in which Elegia, having answered her rival, turns to Ovid and tries to persuade him not to abandon her.

Now the same cause (e.g., homoeoarcton) can produce the same lacuna independently in two unrelated manuscripts, but it is unlikely that such a cause would produce two lacunae in each of two unrelated manuscripts, and highly improbable that it would produce the same effect in three or more independent texts.

Here, again, the evidence distinctly favors a single source for both *a* and *β*, and virtually excludes more than one source for the latter.

VII

Another means of determining the relationship of manuscripts is to look for unanimity in error. This is difficult in the *Amores*, for the manuscripts usually provide a wide variety of readings, and, to be rigorously fair, we can use only passages where all agree in one error —not passages where all are corrupt. For example, with Kenney I consider Camp's brilliant emendation, *erro velut*, at II. 10, 9, as palmary and, for all practical purposes, certain, but although all the manuscripts are corrupt, they vary so much among themselves that the corruptions could have arisen independently and cannot therefore be attributed with any confidence to an archetype.[50] We must exclude Greek names and inflections (e.g., *Io,* accusative) that were almost habitually corrupted by scribes, the writing of common variants (e.g., *ut* for *uti* in I. 6, 17), and unusual idioms (e.g., *hâc facere,* 'to work on this [=our] side,' restored by Tyrrell in I. 3, 12) that few scribes would have understood. All the manuscripts have *Terror* for *Error* in I. 2, 35, but the mistake could have been so

---

In III. 2, 9, the editors should punctuate:

Hoc mihi contingat! Sacro de carcere missis

The first three words are an exclamatory wish. This wish, of course, is absurd, for Ovid as a charioteer in the Circus would resemble Swinburne as a contender for the championship in boxing. But his volatile imagination transports him to the chariot and he describes what he *will* do in the race by a series of verbs in the future tense: *insistam, dabo, notabo, stringam, morabor.* This leap of the imagination parallels that in II. 15, 9–26; cf. *CP*, LIII (1958), 103–106. I am deeply gratified that my emendation and reading of that passage is accepted by Goold.

[50] Another good instance is I. 13, 39, where Riese's emendation, *quem mavis*, must be accepted, for reasons now cogently stated by Goold.

easily made by simple dittography of the last letter in the preceding word, *erunt*, that the consensus proves nothing.

When we make these allowances, the indications of a common source of error are few. The most significant is *quinquatria* in I. 8, 65, where Heinsius' emendation, *circum atria* is generally accepted. This is the only corruption that is so manifest that it can be cited without discussion.

At III. 7, 55, both Munari and Kenney quite properly print †*blanda*†. Despite the great ingenuity and authority of Housman, who now has the endorsement of Goold, few will be convinced that *blandā* is an ablative that agrees with *a puellā* in line 53, that is to say, in a sentence that is not only syntactically distinct but is emotionally opposed to the mood of the following distich. Ovid does not devise syntactical puzzles for his readers to solve. All the manuscripts must be corrupt, and the failure of generations of scholars to produce a plausible emendation is a fairly good indication that the corruption is not palaeographic. As Lenz has recently shown, what both logic and Ovidian usage require here is a verb such as *subiit,* which gives both the required meaning and the parallel structure that Ovid habitually uses: *non subiit, non perdidit, non sollicitavit.*[51] We must therefore regard *blanda* as a reading, doubtless imported from the margin,[52] which replaced a quite different word.

[51] Friedrich Lenz, *La Parola del Passato,* XVIII (1965), 376 f.

[52] Lenz suggests that *blanda* came from a marginal gloss that explained the meaning of *optima* in the second half of the line. I think another explanation of the error more likely. What Ovid means by *optima oscula* is clear from line 9 of this poem, and given the Latin terminology for cataglottismatic kisses (*columbari, columbatim*), the margin opposite line 55 could well have quoted II. 6, 56: "oscula dat cupido blanda columba mari." I think it likely that in the archetype the margins not infrequently quoted parallel passages from other erotic poems chiefly, if not entirely, by Ovid. As S. G. Owen pointed out years ago (*CQ,* XXXI [1937], 5), "Interpolations from other parts of the poet's works are frequent in manuscripts of Ovid." Many variants in the *Amores* are most easily explained in this way. In III. 2, 1, for example, the poet, addressing the lady whom he intends to seduce, says "non . . . sedeo studiosus." In *Her.* 16. 33, Paris, addressing Helen, whom he intends to seduce, says "non venio . . . spectator." Now, although there is nothing obscure about the statement *non sedeo studiosus,* some of the recentiores replace it with *non venio spectator,* while others combine the two phrases to produce *non sedeo spectator.* In III. 2, 37 f. we find "faciles . . . ventos, quos faciet . . . mota tabella." A parallel passage, *A. A.,* I, 161, has "tenui ventos movisse tabella." And in the *Amores,* some of the recentiores replace *faciles* with *tenues.* In II. 10, 4, Ovid wrote "duas . . . turpis amo," which would suggest a comparison with III. 12, 5, "coepi solus amare"— and most of the recentiores replace *turpis* with *solus.* Some vestiges of such marginal

In I. 7, 58 all the manuscripts have *abiecta,* which, as I have pointed out elsewhere,[53] cannot be correct, although no satisfactory emendation has thus far been proposed. There is another reading that may represent unanimity in error. In I. 3, Ovid promises Corinna the immortality that poets bestowed on three of Jove's mistresses, Io, Leda, and Europa, and concludes with the well-known lines:

> Nos quoque per totum pariter cantabimur orbem,
> iunctaque semper erunt nomina nostra tuis.

This can be understood only by assuming that although *nos* means *et ego et tu, nostra* means *mea* in antithesis to *tua.* The violence of this change seems to me intolerable, as it did to Francius, who proposed the drastic emendation, *tu quoque . . . cantaberis,* which has been rightly rejected. There is an easy way out of the difficulty, which must surely have occurred to many readers. Of the three ladies whose celebrity Corinna's is to equal, Io became a goddess, Leda was at least the mother of the Dioscuri, and Europa at least gave her name to a third of the world; [54] and all, of course, are associated with Zeus. If Ovid and Corinna become equally known as an example of romantic adultery, their names will be joined with the names of gods, and so, in a sense, with the gods themselves. It is true that Ovid prefers the usual contracted form *dīs,* which he uses forty-four times, but there are seven certain occurrences of *deis: Rem.* 678 (where it was corrupted to *tuis* in two good manuscripts, although that word is meaningless in the context); *Fasti* I. 615; 706; 707; *Trist.* IV. 2, 12; *Ex Pont.* III. 5, 54; IV. 5, 26. The point is, I think, worth considering.

The elder Seneca has preserved (*Cont.* II. 2, 12) the correct reading in II. 11, 10: "et gelidum Borean egelidumque Notum." Now P and S have the absurd reading *et gelidumque Notum,* while manuscripts of the β group offer the various readings *non gelidum* (which

---

citations may remain in the sparse marginalia in capitals found in P. Opposite I. 8, 64 we find the note NOMEN. In that line occurs the phrase "gypsati crimen inane pedis," for which a good parallel would be *A. A.* I. 740, "nomen inane fides." Opposite I. 15, 31, P has TELLVS, which could not have been intended to be a variant reading, and has no perceptible relevance to the context. The line, however, contains the phrase, "dens patientis aratri," which could have suggested quotation of Verg. *Georg.* II. 423: "tellus, cum dente recluditur unco." Opposite I. 2, 35, R has the unintelligible gloss in capital letters HISMA. This could be what is left of a quotation from *Her.* 16. 351: "terror in his . . . maior."

53 Oliver, *CP,* LIII (1958), 138.
54 *Fasti* V. 618.

looks like a marginal definition of a somewhat rare word), *praecipi-tem* (the epithet applied to Notus in line 52 of this poem, and also in I. 7, 16), and *praetepidum* (which may have been suggested by *tepidus* in I. 7, 56 and II. 8, 20).[55] With the text of Seneca before us, the correct reading is obvious, but I wonder whether it would have been so obvious without it. It would probably have been proposed as an emendation, but surely some editors would have objected that the word *egelidus* does not elsewhere occur in Ovid. At all events, no one now doubts but that Seneca quoted accurately.

We should therefore listen to Seneca with respect when he quotes I. 2, 12, with *rursus* in place of the *vidi* that our manuscripts unani-mously have here, probably repeating the verb from the preceding line.[56] Kenney, whose decision was, I suspect, influenced by his view of the manuscript tradition, follows the manuscripts, but *rursus,* which has been accepted by many editors, including Bornecque and Munari, is by far the better reading, as has been conclusively shown by Goold, whose discussion of the passage should settle the matter once and for all. The manuscripts, in short, unanimously preserve a corruption of the text at this point.

In short, we find that both α and β in complete accord preserve at least three false readings (*quinquatria, blanda, vidi*—to which I should not hesitate to add *abiecta*), and it is difficult to believe that these represent mere coincidence—that two or more scribes working independently of one another just happened to make the same mistakes in the same places.

VIII

We have confined our examination to details which (unlike inter-polations, for example) could scarcely be the result of horizontal transmission. In every case, the calculation of probabilities virtually excludes a plurality of sources for the many manuscripts classed as β. Despite the wide diversity of their readings, we must regard them as descended from a single manuscript. What is more, the proba-

[55] Ovid could have coined the adjective *praetepidus;* in II. 3, 6, he uses *prae-tepescere,* probably with the meaning 'to begin to grow warm.'

[56] The note in Kenney's apparatus is sadly misleading and repeats an error made in his article of 1962 (p. 29, n. 2), where he says "Seneca puts *rursus* into the mouth of Porcius Latro." But Seneca (*Cont.* II. 2, 8) is not quoting Porcius Latro; he is quoting Ovid directly to show that Ovid did derive the metaphor from Porcius Latro, whose declamation, which is also quoted by Seneca, does *not* contain the word *rursus.*

bilities greatly favor a common source for α and β. The only contrary indication is that provided by the titulature, but since the titles in β require us to assume either mutilation of a very uncommon kind of manuscript or mutilation of a more ordinary kind of manuscript by a most unusual accident, the source of α could have become the source of β after suffering mutilation.

Our evidence therefore indicates that, in all probability, there was a single archetype. Contrary to what was probable *a priori*, only one codex containing the *Amores* survived the Dark Ages. This means that we shall have to explain all the divergent readings of the many manuscripts as having their origin in either (a) misreading of the archetypal text, (b) choice among *variae lectiones* present in the archetype, (c) importation into the text of words that stood in the margins of the archetype as either exegetical glosses or passages quoted for comparison with Ovid's text at or near that point, or (d) changes intentionally made either to remove a real or imagined corruption or to simplify a difficult passage. The first step must be to determine what *kind* of notations appeared in the margins of the archetype; that is, did the archetype have variant readings or glosses or quotations from other works—or some combination of two, or all three? Such a determination is probably not impossible, but it will require a prolonged and delicate investigation.

University of Illinois
24 January 1966

ADDENDUM

After the foregoing was written, a complete collation of the Hamiltonianus, accompanied by photographic reproductions of twelve pages or portions of pages, became available in Franco Munari's study of that manuscript: *Il codice Hamilton 471 di Ovidio* (Roma, Edizioni di Storia e Letteratura, 1965).

This manuscript, to which Munari gives the designation Y, contains one entirely new reading, *licenda venit* in I. 10, 30, that is unquestionably right, and it furthermore confirms emendations made by Heinsius, Housman, and Kenney (listed by Munari, pp. 62 f.) and readings hitherto attested only by some *recentiores*. But its text is very close to that of P, so that *Y contains every reading that in the foregoing article I have cited from P, either specifically or as included in "all manuscripts."* These readings, furthermore, are all the work of the original scribe. The new manuscript, therefore, does not affect the arguments that I presented above, and suggests no change in the conclusions that I ventured to draw. It does, however, suggest some further considerations relevant to the text tradition of the *Amores*.

Although Lenz, whose palaeographic acumen is well known, did not hesitate (in his edition of the *Remedia*, p. 68) to date the Hamiltonianus "saeculo VIII exeunte vel potius IX ineunte," Munari will affirm no more than that "nella datazione non si può scendere sotto il sec. XI." Munari believes that Y, despite its close affinity with P and R, which were written in France, was written in Italy. If Munari is correct, this indicates a much wider distribution of good texts of the *Amores* in the tenth (if not the ninth) century than we have hitherto supposed. Furthermore, although Munari does not discuss that point, Y abundantly confirms the evidence in P and R that the *a* text was derived from a manuscript in either Visigothic or Beneventan script with little or no division of words that had been copied, perhaps directly, from an ancient codex in rustic capitals and *scriptura continua*. If, as Munari believes, the text of Y was available in Italy at an early date, then, in the absence of any indication of relationship with Spain, an archetype in Beneventan script becomes more likely than one in Visigothic. That would mean that, if, as I have argued above, *a* and *β* have a common source, the only copy of Ovid's amatory works that escaped the Dark Ages was preserved in Italy—perhaps at Monte Cassino.

The internal colophons of Y are of the expanded type, but, with one exception, without *feliciter*. The exception (shown on Munari's Plate I, fig. 1) is of some interest as showing how one scribe understood that formulaic addition: P·OUIDI NASONIS AMORŪ EXPLIC̄ LIBER SECUNDUS. | INCIP̄ EIUSDĒ AMORŪ LIB̄ · III · FELICITER UTERE·Q(*ui*) LEGERIS: It is clear that the internal colophons in Y (with the exception of that scribal addition) were regularized on the model of the external title that I quoted from R above and the terminal colophons that in all probability appeared in R and P when they were intact.

If I am not mistaken, Y also illustrates a procedure that must occasionally, if not frequently, have affected the preservation of medieval manuscripts. It contains, in order, the *Ars, Remedia*, and *Amores*, but the last two folia of the last quaternion are missing, and the last four lines of the *Amores* with the *explicit* are on an inserted leaf in a hand which Munari assigns to the twelfth century. The most likely explanation, it seems to me, is that the codex originally contained other works (probably continuing with the *Heroides*), and that the latter portion was *intentionally* detached. When the codex was thus divided, the last two folia of the split quaternion would naturally go with the second part, since they contained 155 lines of the *Heroides* or whatever work came after the *Amores*, while it would require but a moment's work to copy from them the five lines needed to preserve the end of the *Amores* with the first half of the divided codex. It is quite possible that this intentional splitting and reassembling of codices may have been practiced in the twelfth century as freely as it was in the Renaissance, and I need not remark that however carefully a reassembled codex was bound, single folia were much more likely to become detached and lost or defaced than intact quaternia.

One can see clearly in Y the process of corruption by inept emendation. A man of some learning, whom Munari calls y and assigns to the twelfth century or late eleventh, appears to have read Y with a fairly good manuscript (now lost or possibly yet unnoticed) at hand, but it is possible that he also exercised at times his own ingenuity. In I.3,15, not recognizing the word *desultor,* he changed it to *desertor.* It seems idle to speculate whether he did so because he found that corruption in his other manuscript or because he remembered that Ovid did write *desertor amoris* in *Her.* 19,157 or simply because *desertor* came to his mind as a word that would make sense and fit metrically in place of what he thought was a corruption in Y. In II.11,10, recognizing that *etgelidumque* did not make sense, he changed it to *precipitemque.* There are a number of similar instances, and it does not really matter whether this man (who, if his hand is correctly dated, is earlier than most of the *recentiores* anyway) made the alterations *suo Marte* or copied them from a manuscript in which someone else had already made them on *his* own; the process of corruption is quite clear.

On the other hand, where Y is corrupt and the twelfth-century corrector restores what must be the correct reading, although the correction could not easily have been suggested by the corruption in Y (e.g., *Aeaeaque* in I.8,5, where Y probably had the same error as P, *eaque*) or else presupposes a minutely critical knowledge of Latin that is highly improbable in the twelfth century (e.g., *diducere* for *deducere* in I.7,47, where Y had the unintelligible corruption *deduceretur*), we must deduce that the twelfth-century corrector had at his disposal a manuscript that preserved in these places correct readings from the now lost archetype that were not, so far as we know, preserved in any other manuscript of either family. But it is quite clear that Mr. y, as we may call him, did not make a systematic or even a cursory collation of the manuscript that he had at hand when he went over the text of Y; if he had, he would surely have noticed the omission in Y of some distichs that must have been in the archetype and which it is most unlikely that his independent second manuscript coincidentally also omitted. He evidently turned to that manuscript only when he was puzzled by what he found in Y. On the occasions on which he did consult his second manuscript, he probably followed its authority when it presented a better reading that he understood, but we would do well to remember that he probably would not have been impressed by a correct reading that he did not understand. In other words, if, in the passages that I mentioned above, that manuscript had the correct readings *desultor* and *egelidum*, Mr. y, not understanding the words, could still have made his "corrections" in Y of his own accord. This kind of unsystematic procedure may well have intervened many times in the course of the horizontal transmission that has produced such variety in the *recentiores*.

Thus Y, while providing us with our only complete text of the *a* family and enabling us at last to determine with some certainty what must have been the readings in the ancestor of that family, also provides fresh evidence that that ancestor was not the only descendant of the ancient codex that survived the Dark Ages. This emphasizes again the importance of extracting all the truth we can from the multifarious *recentiores*. Their texts may seem as inextricably intertwined as the strands of the Gordian knot, but we must be more patient than the Conqueror of Asia.

LATIN LYRIC: CRAFT AND SUBJECT

Roy Arthur Swanson

Quidam notus Horatio nomine tantum is not so much one who wearies by prolixity or dullness as he is a troublesome person or nuisance. He really ought to be called a pest instead of a bore. There is no sufficient proof that the pest who bothered Horace was Propertius (in his late teens and not yet patronized by Maecenas). But it can be shown that Horace's distaste for this pest was of substantially the same character as his distaste for the [*Romanus*] *Callimachus,*[1] who may in fact have been Propertius.[2] Our deduction must begin with a closer look at Horace's Satire (I. 9).

Long familiarity with a poem frequently predisposes a student to neglect scrupulously close inspection of it. The opening line of the satire is so familiar to students of Horace's poetry that its inherent complexity is all too infrequently noted:

Ibam forte uia Sacra, sicut meus est mos.

There is certainly something of a contradictory tension between *forte* and *sicut meus est mos,* however slight the emphasis we place upon *forte*. Habit is not a natural complement to chance. That a person *happens* to be acting *by habit* requires some clarification: *Estne Horati mos "ire forte"*? Our translators do not actually provide any; for example,

SMITH PALMER BOVIE: I was walking down the Sacred Way, my usual route. [*Forte* is completely disregarded.]

CASPER J. KRAEMER, JR.: I happened to be going along the Via Sacra, thinking, as is my wont, on some trifle. [Here the translator conjoins *sicut meus est mos* with *nescio quid meditans nugarum* in the second line. This conjunction is a good solution to the problem of translating

[1] *Epist.* II. 2, 100.
[2] Propertius IV. 1, 64.

the passage, but it is not a resolution of the veritable oxymoron in the first line.]

There are other possibilities of translation, of course; for example, "I happened to be going along the Via Sacra, as it is my custom to do on other occasions." That is, the poet has regular business along the Via Sacra but happens at this time, during which he is at leisure, to be doing what at other times, when he is intent on business, he does as a matter of habit. His chance action, in other words, *coincides with* his customary action; but his chance action *is* not, in itself, his customary action.

Ibam forte could merely—and very naturally—anticipate a *cum inuersum* construction, which would serve as an introduction to the main action of the narrative. Horace's *accurrit,* the first word in the third line, is of course a vivid historical present with the full force of such a construction. The chance would then be relative, not to Horace's strolling, but to his being bothered by the pest: "It happened that I was set upon by this fellow while I was going along the Via Sacra, as it is my habit to do." But this explanation does not eliminate the difficulty of reconciling *ibam forte* with *sicut meus est mos,* unless we choose to let the conventional and formulaic character of the two phrases deaden our sensibility to their logical incompatibility. To make this choice is to disregard the ability of the poet to change the prosaic into something rich and strange. In ordinary conversation we are not always attentive to illogicalities: e.g., "I happened to be walking along, as I usually do, when this character comes up to me." But in severely disciplined poetry which produces the effect of ordinary conversation, we are enabled to see colloquial illogicalities in startling perspective and to gain new insights from the poet's purposes in highlighting them.

There are in the first line of Horace's satire (I. 9) other connotations with which translators seldom concern themselves. The name of the famous street is precisely appropriate to the poem's occasion. *Sacer* means 'holy'; it also means 'detestable.' The street is in fact holy because, among other reasons, the Vestal precinct is in its proximity. The street is also detestable on this occasion because of the pest's presence upon it.

Sacer also means 'dedicated.' Horace's *uia sacra* is his dedication to poetry. During this particular walk, he, as the first person of the poem, is totally preoccupied with minor matters of poetry or versification (nescio quid meditans nugarum, totus in illis). The pest intrudes upon this preoccupation and expropriates—or profanes—the poet's thoughts. True to his *uia sacra,* the poet transmutes even this event of interruption into poetry, namely this satire. This poem is as much concerned with the nature of poetry as the "Ars Poetica" is. The pest is a poetaster whose immediate concern with poetry is merely instrumental to personal advancement. He turns the holy path of poetry into a detestable path. Horace's poem presents the profound difference between the two paths, between dedication to poetry and exploitation of poetry. The poet transcends mundanity by presenting it through poetic art. The poetaster sees poetry as mundane, and, in so doing, subsumes poetry to mundanity. Through poetic art Horace presents and thereby transcends the mundanity of the ambitious pest.

By juxtaposing the conventional but logically incompatible *ibam forte* and *sicut meus est mos,* Horace exposes the prosaic vulgarity of the mundane world (cf. his explicit contempt for *profanum vulgus* in *Carm.* III. 1, 1). He uses the language of men who have no feeling for language. Horace can use this language as easily as Catullus can use the language of Furius and Aurelius; and, like Catullus, he can give *lingua uulgaris* an elevation that is untenable by men who lack poetic sensibility. Here the elevation is, in part, achieved through the strategic insertion of *uia Sacra,* with all of its poetic ambiguity, between the formulaic phrases. The Via Sacra brings together both poet and poetaster, both the person who is appreciative of *sanctitudo* and the person who is impervious to it, by providing an avenue common to each; it tolerates social and intellectual disparities. The *uia sacra* of poetry reconciles logical disparities; art brings order out of disorder and confusion; the poet sees connections which the *profanum uulgus* cannot see; and, in his art, the poet makes these connections for the benefit of men who can appreciate them. On the mundane level, Horace speaks of his walking on a street. On the poetic level, he says, "I used to walk by chance on the *uia sacra* of poetry—and be preoccupied with its matters—, as it is now my custom [*or* regular practice] to do." The imperfect tense (ibam) and the present tense (est) contribute, on the mundane level, only colloquial expression; but, on the poetic level, they show a progression from part-time (forte) to full-time (mos) poetic endeavor. In committing himself to the world of poetry, Horace accepts the fact that he must continue to live in the mundane world; and he accepts the difficult task of turning mundanity into poetry.

By an artistic use of connotative elements Horace effects his subtle change of mundanity into poetry. The exclusively mundane element of the first two lines of *Serm.* I. 9 may be translated as follows:

I happened to be going along the Via Sacra, as it is my custom to do when I am intent on important business, thinking about and quite preoccupied with some unimportant business matters.

The poetic element may be translated:

I happened to be going along the Via Sacra, as it is my custom to do when I am bound on business, thinking about and quite preoccupied with some matters of lyric poetry.

A transmutation of the mundane element into the poetic element is achieved through ambiguity. The ambiguity is provided by the word *nugarum,* which connotes both "unimportant business matters" (trifles) and "matters of lyric poetry" (verse). Mundanity hereafter appears in the form of the pest, who is its easily recognizable embodiment, and threatens to occlude poetic transcendence. The images of Vesta and Apollo (deities as the embodiment of transcendence) sustain the poet (as poet); and, of course, Apollo saves the day for poetry.

We can assume that the poet is freed from the ravages of the poetaster in the immediate vicinity of the temple of Apollo. Horace's scene, then, is a stroll westward on the Via Sacra, southwestward off the Via Sacra past the temple of Vesta, southward by way of the Vicus Tuscus toward the Velabrum, into the Forum Holitorium and ending at the temple of Apollo.[3] Fuscus Aristius' hasty flight leaves the poet *sub cultro:* the mention of the knife, ostensibly in connection with circumcision, squares nicely with the proximity of the poet to the Fora Holitorium and Boarium and their vendors' and butchers' knives. The invasive mundanity of the *fora* is juxtaposed to the sanctity of Apollo's temple, as the invasive mundanity of the poetaster is juxtaposed to the *uia sacra* of the poet.

The ambiguity of *uia sacra* now appears to be more complex. It is threefold: the street in the Forum, the way of the poet, and the combination of mundanity (*uia,* the business thoroughfare) and the transcendent (*sacra*). With this phrase as his focus, Horace reconciles the mundane and the transcendent. The *aedes Vestae* is in the marketplace (Forum) and the *aedes Apollonis* is next to marketplaces (Fora Holitorium Boariumque). The lower world of

[3] For this itinerary I am indebted to Professor George E. Duckworth of Princeton University.

the market threatens the higher world of poetry, as the poetaster's incursions bring the poet, figuratively, *sub cultro*. But the higher world sustains the poet, and the poet champions the higher world.

Ibam forte uia sacra[4] is far more poetically effective in its complexity than Lucilius' *ibat forte aries*,[5] which is followed by no such contradictory clause as *sicut meus est mos,* or his *ibat forte domum*,[6] which is an unambiguous statement. Eduard Fraenkel ties the satire and these two Lucilian passages to the tradition of the αἶνος[7] but, rightly, prefers not to note any stylistic or thematic analogy of Horace's lines to those of Lucilius.

Fraenkel examines the dramatic tension in the poem and astutely compares the structure of the *sermo* to that of a tragedy complete with *deus ex machina* (sic me seruauit Apollo). The mock tragic structure is quite true to the nature of satire. He sees the poem's structural parallel in Catullus 10.[8] The correspondences appear to be true, the difference significant[9] and the comparison valid. I, for one, quite agree with Fraenkel's analysis.

Aside from scene and structure, however, *Serm.* I. 9 is, in the substance of its thought, more like Catullus 16. That is, both poems have primarily to do with the poet's dedication to his craft, the poet's *pietas*. Catullus defends his craft against the mundanity of Furius and Aurelius; Horace defends his craft against the mundanity of the pest, who presumes in fact to be a craftsman ("docti sumus"; "quis me scribere pluris / aut citius possit uersus").

Fraenkel observes that in Catullus 10 the poet (as dramatic character) is pleased with himself and suffers a "deserved downfall." We may go on to observe that the drama is in two acts. Act I (ll. 1–8) is informed with seeing (uisum) and seeming (uisum est). Act II (ll. 9–34) is informed with speaking (respondi; inquiunt; inquam; inquit). The poet, as dramatic character, is superior to the situation in Act I, overwhelmed by it in Act II.

The drama in *Serm.* I. 9 is also presented in two acts. Act I (ll. 1–34) begins with *ibam;* Act II (ll. 35–78) begins with *uentum erat.* There is a deserved downfall; but it is the poetaster's, not the

[4] Editorial capitalization of *sacra* tends to lessen our appreciation of the ambiguity.

[5] Diehl, *Poetarum Romanorum veterum reliquiae* (Bonn, 1911), fgt. 246.1.

[6] Diehl, 551.5.

[7] Eduard Fraenkel, *Horace* (Oxford, 1957), pp. 112–13.

[8] Fraenkel, pp. 114–15.

[9] "Horace deliberately paints on a large canvas whereas Catullus chose for his picture a small medallion" (*ibid.*).

poet's. The poet, in fact, is elevated by virtue of Apollo's inter-
cession in his behalf. In both dramas the poet is literally embarrassed by social intercourse which is alien to his craft. In both cases
the poet transcends his embarrassment by means of his craft: to
each poet his craft is more important than social success; each poet
makes a poem of his social embarrassment; the embarrassment is
the subject of the craft; the craft is more important than the subject.
Both poets are victimized: Catullus by the *puella,* Horace by the
pest (ego, ut contendere durum est / cum uictore, sequor). Both
poets remain secure in their craft. Catullus' embarrassment does
not detract from his poetic craft; he remains superior to the *puella*
in his poetic presentation of her. Horace's embarrassment does not
detract from his craft; to the situation in which he finds himself he
remains superior by his poetic presentation of that situation. To
put it another way, the poets' persons are assailable but their craft
is unassailable. The distinction between person and craft in Catullus 16 is also a distinction between subject and craft: a poet's
subjects may be assailable, but his artistic presentation of those
subjects is not. Both Catullus and Horace invoke the importance—
and the security—of their craft, not that of their subject.

   It is, I think, the unassailability of his craft that enables Catullus
to survive the ravages that Lesbia makes upon his person. His
dedication to his craft is more important to him than his dedication
to Lesbia. Whatever the causes of his illness and early death, and
whatever the predisposition to illness and death which Lesbia may
have induced in him, Catullus writes *Furi et Aureli, comites Catulli*
as one whose personal defeat does not detract from his poetic craft
but, instead, becomes its subject.

   In Latin lyric poetry we can distinguish Catullus and Horace
from the elegists precisely in this matter of attention to craftsmanship. To Catullus and Horace craftsmanship is more important than
subject matter. To the elegists subject matter is more important
than craftsmanship. The subject matter of the elegists is love.
Catullus and Horace write poems. The elegists—Tibullus, Propertius, and Ovid in his role of amorist—write, with decidedly few
exceptions, love poems.

   Horace's concern with craft is patent in the "Ars Poetica," in
Serm. I. 9 (as I have attempted to prove), in statements like *quodsi
me lyricis uatibus inseres, / sublimi feriam sidera uertice (Carm.*
I. 1, 35–36, which lines, of course, follow *me doctarum hederae
praemia frontium / dis miscent superis* [ll. 29–30]) and *exegi monu-*

mentum aere perennius (*Carm.* III. 30, 1), and in *Carm.* II. 20. Catullus' concern with craft is explicit in Poem 16 and can be inferred from such works as 6, 10 and 11.

Propertius shows his concern with craft in III. 2,[10] which bears some resemblance to Horace's *Carm.* III. 30 (exegi monumentum . . .) and *Carm.* II. 20 and to Catullus 16 and 11. Like Catullus in Poem 11 and Horace in *Carm.* II. 20, Propertius makes use of geographical references. Poetry's power to elevate, expressed in Catullus 6 (ad caelum lepido uocare uersu)[11] and Horace's *Carm.* I. 1 and III. 30, is similarly expressed here. Line 18 of Propertius (III. 2) reads *carmina erunt formae tot monumenta tuae.* Catullus speaks of *Caesaris monumenta* as he constructs his own monument of poetry. Horace speaks specifically of his own poetic *monumentum perenne.* But Propertius identifies his poetry as a monument to Cynthia. There is a considerable difference between poetry as a monument in itself and poetry as a monument to someone or something.

Poetry, as a monument in itself, celebrates, whatever its subject, only itself; that is to say, it celebrates its Muse. The Muse of poetry is *sub specie diuinitatis,* e.g., Apollo, Venus, Musae, Camenae. Persons (e.g., Lesbia, Cynthia) or things (e.g., phasellus, amor) are *sub specie mundi.* Dante honors the human Beatrice, but he celebrates the divine Beatrice; he celebrates, not *amor,* but the transcendent *Amor che move il sole e l'altre stelle.*

The subjects selected by Catullus and Horace serve their poetry. The poetry of Propertius serves his subject, which, like that of Tibullus and the amorist Ovid, is *amor* (uerus amor nullum nouit habere modum [Prop. II. 15, 30]). Propertius does not worship the Muses; he uses them. He is not their messenger; they are his:

> Mirabar, quidnam uisissent mane Camenae,
>   ante meum stantes sole rubente torum.
> natalis nostrae signum misere puellae
>   et manibus faustos ter crepuere sonos.   (III. 10, 1–4)

They are his intermediaries with love.

---

[10] His estimate of himself as a poet is also presented in III. 1, 3, and 5 and in II. 34b. Of particular importance in these poems is his attention to *amor* and *fama.* His self-appraisal as a poet is presented in IV. 1, 62–64:
> mi folia ex hedera porrige, Bacche, tua,
>   ut nostris tumefacta superbiat Vmbria libris,
> Vmbria Romani patria Callimachi!

[11] Cf. Prop. III. 1, 8–9:
> exactus tenui pumice uersus eat,
>   quo me Fama leuat terra sublimis. . . .

The sense of Propertius (II. 34b) is that poetry must serve love; therefore, love is the only fit subject for verse: *quid Erecthei tibi prosunt carmina lecta? / nil iuuat in magno uester amore senex.*[12]

For Propertius, *Cynthia prima fuit, Cynthia finis erit* (I. 12, 20). Whether he enjoyed her favors or not, Propertius wrote about Cynthia. His prime career in poetry was to write about Cynthia and about his love for her:

> Quaeritis, unde mihi totiens scribantur amores,
>   unde meus ueniat mollis in ora liber.
> non haec Calliope, non haec mihi cantat Apollo.
>   ingenium nobis ipsa puella facit.   (II. 1, 1–4)

The elegist needed a Cynthia, a Delia, a Nemesis or a Corinna as the focus of his disquisition on love. Catullus did not need a Lesbia; he was a poet in spite of, not because of, Lesbia. Catullus and Horace are *poetae pii et docti*. The elegists are *amoris poetae*.

We need not read Propertius IV. 5 very closely to recognize that it is an *ars amatoria*. Perhaps it is cynical and even a form of self-parody; but it is consistent with a specialization in love. Ovid's handbooks of love are the natural and logical successors to the specializations in love worked out by Tibullus, Propertius and Lygdamus. In Latin lyric poetry we move from the *ars poetica* to the *ars amatoria*. One of Catullus' great subjects is love, one of

---

[12] Propertius' book is the book of love. He makes this clear through skillful use of figures. For example, in II. 3 *liber alter erit* (l. 4) is balanced by *uenerit alter amor* (l. 46). Compare II. 25: *unica*, the first word in the first line, is balanced by *una*, the first word in the last line; and *dolori*, the last word in the first line, is balanced by *mala*, the last word in the last line. The balance is like that in an equation. In this poem (II. 3) there is between lines 4 and 46 a striking set of balances, viz., (a) *amor*, (the last word in line 8) : (b) the chiasmus, *nix minio . . . rosae puro lacte* (ll. 11–12) : (c) *scripta* (l. 21): (a) *amor* (the last word in line 24) :: (d) an umbilical sequence of anaphora and homoioteleuton (ll. 25–30) :: (e) *perire* [*Troia*] (l. 34) and *obiret* [*Achilles*] (l. 39): (c) *tabulas* (l. 41): (b) the chiasmus, *Hesperiis . . . Eois . . . Eoos . . . Hesperios* (ll. 43–44): (e) *moriar* (l. 46). The sequence (d) is as follows:

> haec tibi . . . d*iui*
> haec tibi . . . *putes*
>   . . . *dona*
>   . . . *bona*
> . . . Romanis . . . *puellis*
>   Romana . . . I*oui*

The items (a) and (e), in balance, bring together the ideas of love and death and enhance the idea of dying for love. Balances of this kind are very much evident in the craft of Catullus and Horace. But, where we find them, and other figures, in Catullus and Horace, we discover the aesthetic union of form and content; in Propertius and Tibullus they represent an enhancement of subject by craft.

Horace's is Epicureanism. The elegists, in their major endeavors, virtually limit themselves to the subject of love, but they are no more Catullan than they are Horatian.

We admire the distich,

> uidi ego odorati uictura rosaria Paesti
> sub matutino cocta iacere Noto,   (IV. 5, 61 f.)

as we admire "Mignonne, allons voir si la rose," etc. Both Propertius and Ronsard are singing the sensual beauties of love for love's sake. The persuasion of Catullus and Horace is art for art's sake, that of the elegists is art for love's sake.

My concern in this brief essay has been to recognize these different and distinct persuasions in Latin lyric. I shall not attempt to judge their respective values. I wish only to conclude that, by Catullan and Horatian standards, the poet who specializes in a subject must make his craft conform to that subject. This limitation of craft is ultimately pragmatic and scientific: craft is put to special use; love poetry ends in love science. The Golden Latin lyric comes to an end in Ovid. Literary history would have been different, obviously, had the elegists continued to develop the craft of Catullus and Horace instead of developing one of Catullus' subjects. Craft is developed when subjects are put to use. This development, initially pragmatic and scientific, is ultimately poetic. Subject constraining craft produces content with distinguishable form; but, by Catullan and Horatian standards, craft constraining subject produces a union of content and form, the one indistinguishable from the other.

Those critics who would attempt to render value judgments relative to these persuasions should not limit their considerations to matters of style or sincerity.[13] They must judge whether the *uia sacra* or the *uia pietatis* is of more or less value than the *uia profana* or the *uia amoris*. The *pius poeta* and *Musarum sacerdos* travel the same road, the *uia sacra*—the road which, in this century, Robert Graves, as priest of the White Goddess (the Muse), chooses to travel. The *amans* may be spirited, wild and irrational; but he is undeviatingly pragmatic when he uses his craft to cater to his irrationality. This pragmatism culminates in Ovidian amorism. The difference between the *amans* who exploits poetry for a single purpose and the pest who exploits it for a single purpose is merely one of degree. We should doubtless enjoy reading the poems of the pest if he had had

---

[13] E.g., Catullus is the most sincere in love; Tibullus and Propertius are respectively less sincere; and Ovid is the least sincere.

the talent of any of the elegists. Horace would doubtless still have considered him a pest: *fortuna non mutat genus.*[14] The Callimachus of *Epist.* II. 2, 100 is as obnoxious to Horace as the pest of *Serm.* I. 9. If indeed the *quidam notus nomine tantum* and the *quis nisi Callimachus* could be proved to have been one and the same, namely Propertius, there would be no need to argue Horace's attitude toward craft: it would be readily apparent in his unchanged reaction to the ambitious young poetaster who developed a genuine talent for elegy and won the patronage of Maecenas.

Horace's affection for Tibullus can hardly be said to be based upon his friend's poetic talents. In *Epist.* I. 4 he recognizes his critical ability and poetic talent but urges him to look to other of life's pleasures. In *Carm.* I. 33, 1–4 he gently derides Tibullus' poetic preoccupation with love.

> Albi, ne doleas plus nimio memor
> immitis Glycerae neu miserabilis
> decantes elegos, cur tibi iunior
> laesa praeniteat fide. . . .

No ties of friendship, of course, hold down Horace's antipathy to the likes of Propertius; and, if Propertius is reflected in the [*Romanus*] *Callimachus* of *Epist.* II. 2, then the *"doctus"* pest of *Serm.* I. 9 is his prototype.

Macalester College
26 January 1966

---

[14] *Epod.* IV, 6. Note also the lines which follow:

> uidesne, Sacram metiente te uiam
> cum bis trium ulnarum toga,
> ut ora uertat huc et huc euntium
> liberrima indignatio?

Sacram uiam can be as ambiguous here as I have indicated it to be in *Serm.* I. 9.

THE PREAMBLE OF THE EARLY
ATHENA NIKE DECREE

Alan L. Boegehold

The text which is studied here was cut into stone, not written on vellum, and it is documentary, not literary; but even so, an attempt to see the whole of which a fragmentary Greek text was once a part lies well within the great tradition of classical scholarship which Ben Edwin Perry continues to augment.

For students of Greek history, religion, and architecture, the early Athena Nike decree [1] is a document of central importance. Proposed by a man whose name time and chance have partially obliterated, the decree stipulates how the first priestess of Athena Nike is to be appointed, fixes how and what she will be paid, authorizes a door for the sanctuary, and a temple, both to be built to the specifications of Kallikrates, and an altar. A certain Hestiaios, in an amendment to the main motion, creates a four-man committee on finance. These are major provisions, quite enough for a single decree, one might think, and yet, in a definitive collection of historical documents where exegesis is normally spare, one reads that the detailed motion which precedes Hestiaios' amendment is likewise an amendment.[2] If it is true that the stone preserves but two amendments to a decree, it can rationally follow that in the main decree a singularly vast project was authorized. And we have recently been told that the putative vast project "was almost certainly the architectural reorganization of the western approach to the Acropolis." [3] If this

---

[1] *IG* I² 24. For subsequent studies, see M. N. Tod, *GHI²*, No. 40, *SEG*, x, 30, xix, 9; B. D. Meritt and H. T. Wade-Gery, *JHS*, LXXXIII (1963), 109-10.

[2] G. F. Hill, *Sources for Greek History* (rev. by R. Meiggs and A. Andrewes, 1951), B 31. W. B. Dinsmoor in *AJA,* xxvii (1923), 319, proposed the theory which B. D. Meritt elaborated in *Hesperia,* x (1941), 307 ff.

[3] Meritt and Wade-Gery, pp. 109-10. The authors do not describe the stele (or

hypothesis is accepted, it leads in turn easily and naturally to other, larger ones; but before the progression extends itself further, the assumption from which it originates should be re-examined. This assumption is that the letters which can be read in the first two lines on the stone do not permit restoration of a normal preamble.

At the head of any normal Athenian decree passed around the middle of the fifth century B.C., one expects to find the following information: (1) the fact that the decree represents a decision of the Council and the People (recorded by the formula ἔδοξε τῇ βουλῇ καὶ τῷ δήμῳ), (2) the name of the phyle in whose prytany the decree was passed, (3) the name of the secretary, (4) the name of the president, (5) the name (sometimes) of the eponymous archon, (6) the name of the man who proposed the decree. The items and the order in which they are given are not absolutely inflexible, but their regularity is well enough established for major deviations to be unlikely. In the case of the Athena Nike decree, which if dated early might be suspected of showing irregularities, editors have been unable to restore a scheme for the preamble which includes in a satisfactory way all or most of the canonical information. I shall try to show that an adequately paralleled preamble can be restored to the decree without inconsistencies or irregularities. It is a simple solution which has not been proposed heretofore because most editors, evidently, have been misled by a coincidence. Once the coincidence is recognized, its obfuscating influence is soon dissipated.

The photograph (Plate I) shows the inscribed face with which we are concerned, but it is difficult, even for one who has worked with the stone, to see in a photograph all of the crucial letters. For this reason, I print the letters of lines 1 and 2 as a guide to show where letters can be seen on the stone if not in the photograph. A facsimile is not intended.

Line 1   ı   ⸝ ˷

Line 2   ⸜ ˏ ΚΟϨΕΙΓ

On the stone the text is arranged so that its letters are in vertical alignment (*stoichedon*), and in each horizontal line there are twenty-nine letterspaces. The traces of letters in Line 1 fall in the

---

series of stelai?) which carried what we must imagine was a very long text. The stone on which *IG* I² 24 and 25 are inscribed does not seem adequate, even with its upper block in place.

twenty-first, twenty-fourth, and twenty-fifth letterspaces from the left, and here subsists the coincidence that has frustrated attempts to restore a full preamble to the first motion on the stone. The first of these three letters can have been an *iota, tau, upsilon,* or *phi.* The second is definitely a *mu* and the third an *omicron. Mu* is certain because the slanting strokes are long enough to be extended accurately with a straight-edge and when they are extended, they meet to form an angle well above the top of the line in which the letter stands, as only the strokes of *mu* will. The arc from a circular letter in the next space to the right must have been an *omicron,* for in Greek, *theta* does not follow *mu.* One doubtful and two certain letters in a line of twenty-nine would not ordinarily establish any restoration, one moreover which creates awkwardnesses, as this one has, in so many editions. But the three letters in question are and were from the time they were first cut, at the very top of the stone and they fall in precisely the right letter spaces for the regular opening statement, ἔδοχσεν τῆι βολῆι καὶ τῶ]ι [δέ]μο[ι, to begin, as was normal, at the left edge of the stone. This combination of clues, viz., the letters themselves, the spaces and the line in which they stand, and the predictability of the opening words, has made that restoration irresistible for most editors of the text.[4] But it is awkward because there are not enough letterspaces between the restored opening formula and the name of the speaker to restore all the other regular and predictable items such as phyle, secretary and president. Two of these items must be jettisoned or put out-side the stoichedon pattern, both of which solutions have been judged excessive deviations from the normal order.[5]

Hiller was uneasy enough about this awkwardness to accept (" dubitanter ") A. Koerte's restoration:

$$[- - - \, ἐγραμμάτε]υ[εν] \; Mo[ιραγ]$$
$$[ένες \; ἐπεστάτε \; hιππόν]ικος \; εἶπε \; [τῆι]$$

$$(IG \; I^2 \; 24)$$

Koerte was on the right track, but again, given the number of letterspaces available, and even allowing for additional lines above those on the stone, the other necessary items could not be made to

[4] E.g., Prott-Ziehen, *Leges Graecorum Sacrae* (1906), 2.45, No. 11; Dinsmoor, p. 319, R. Schlaifer, *HSCP,* LI (1940), 258; Tod, *loc. cit.*

[5] See Meritt, *Hesperia,* pp. 311 f. His restoration (pp. 313 ff.) includes τῶι δέμοι in the crucial place but removes it from the context of a preamble. He notes an unparalleled inconsistency in his restoration, viz. it entails for the two riders two different kinds of punctuation, both of which can be found in fifth-century decrees but never the two of them in the same decree.

fit the stoichedon pattern.[6] Possibly it was the influence of $τό]_ι$ $[δέ]μο[ι$ which limited Koerte's experimentation with other names. Whatever the case, it is with the arbitrary restoration of a name that the solution lies. Take, for example, the name Kleidemos. It permits the following restoration of the first two lines on the stone:

$$[...^{6}... ἐγραμμάτευε \; Κλε]ί̣[δε]μο[ς \; ἐπε] \; |$$
$$[στάτε - - - ἔρχε - -]α̣υκος \; εἶπε \; [τε̑ι]$$

To recover space for the opening formula and the name of the prytanizing phyle, we turn to an upper stone. This one has never been accessible for learned study and may have ceased to exist in an identifiable form long ago, but there can be no doubt that it did exist. The top of what we must now call the lower stone shows a carefully prepared resting surface; and in the photograph (Plate I) one of the two square cuttings for dowels can be seen. This whole surface slants down from front to back to give added strength to the union of upper and lower stones, once the upper stone, cut to correspond, was set into place and secured by dowels.[7] This joint makes the stele, as we must imagine it to have been, unique.

B. D. Meritt (p. 312) explains correctly why the letters of the first line on the lower stone were cut so close to the top. Normal interlinear spacing on the lower stone is 0.006 m.; the top of the first line is 0.003 m. from the original top of the inscribed face. The natural inference is that a line of text which in size, shape, spacing, and number of letters conformed to those below was cut into the upper stone 0.003 m. up from the join. The result was that normal interlinear spacing was maintained. No doubt the juncture of the two stones manifested itself at most as a hairline running horizontally between the two lines of text. Assume now that the opening formula is restored to this hypothetical line of text on the upper stone. There will be nine unoccupied letter-spaces between the end of the opening formula and the restored word, ἐγραμμάτευεν. It is not important that there are nine letter-spaces, since there might be ten or eight with the restoration of other names in the letterspaces before the restored word ἐπεστάτε. It is important only that the gap is large enough for the restoration of a single Athenian name.

---

[6] I am guessing that this was the source of Hiller's reluctance. He assumes that there was a sculpture on the upper block, and admits the possibility of additional lines of text above those now on the lower stone.

[7] Dinsmoor (p. 319) calls it, "the strongest form of a splice or scarf-joint."

Plate I. IG I² 24.

Plate II. IG I² 78.

Plate III. IG I² 24 (detail). Photograph of C. C. Vermeule.

The decree now lacks only one item, the prytanizing phyle. S. Dow first saw how useful *IG* I² 78 might be in recovering the design of the early Athena Nike decree,[8] and his fruitful observation will be utilized here. The photograph (Plate II) shows the last two letters of the name of the prytanizing phyle and the verb ἐπρυτάνευε. These letters, larger than those in the body of the decree, are not aligned with letters below them and are separated from the opening formula by more than the interlinear spacing observed elsewhere on the stone. Above these larger letters, there is a sculptured relief. The text of the decree,[9] it should be noted, has to do with the cult of Apollo at Athens, and since the text of the Athena Nike decree has also to do with cult matters, it is not inappropriate to use the one monument to recover the original design of the other. Differences between the two [10] are not of a sort that need invalidate such an attempt.

The restored preamble of the early Athena Nike decree can now be represented as follows:

RELIEF SCULPTURE

[ΛΕΟΝΤΙⳞ ΕΓΡΥΤΑΝΕΥΕ]

Lapis superior   [ἔδοχσεν τῆι βολῆι καὶ τôι δέμοι . . .]

Lapis inferior

[- - - ἐγραμμάτευε - -]ι[. .]μο[ς ἐπε]

[στάτε -⁵⁻⁶- ἐρχε Γλ]αυκος εἰπε[τῆι]

κτλ.

Leontis was suggested by Meritt (p. 311). The name *Kleidemos* was useful as an example, but I do not print it here, because other names suit as well. The name of the speaker is plausible.[11] The dotted *upsilon* in his name could also be an *iota*, and the dotted *alpha* could also be a *gamma*. In the letterspace to the left of the dotted *alpha*, there remains toward the bottom enough original surface to exclude certain letters from consideration. Any letter

---

[8] See Schlaifer, pp. 258 f.

[9] On particular aspects of the text, see *SEG*, x, 63, xii, 25, xiii, 6, xvi, 6, xxi, 38.

[10] The Athena decree is opisthographic (*IG* I² 25 is inscribed on the back), the other is not, nor is there evidence that the Apollo decree was inscribed on more than one stone. The Athena decree is also generally thought to be the older of the two by some years (see n. 14, below). Although Meritt (p. 312) faults Schlaifer's evidence for a secretary in rubric form, he approves *IG* I² 78 as evidence for the tribe.

[11] Suggested by Dinsmoor in *Hesperia* (Suppl. 5 [1941], 159 n. 337), *Glaukos* has since been accepted by various editors.

whose vertical stroke runs through the middle of the space (*iota, tau, upsilon,* and *phi*) or any letter with a low horizontal stroke (*beta, epsilon,* and possibly *zeta*) [12] would have had to leave a trace of its sometime existence. The photograph (Plate III), for which I thank Cornelius C. Vermeule, shows the preserved area clearly. It is above the *heta* of ἱιέρεαν in what will now be numbered line 5. I had thought, after careful examination, that a *lambda* would also have had to leave a trace, but a master epigraphist, who examined the stone at my request, was less sure. Other *lambdas* in the inscription stand toward the left of their spaces, and the rising bottom stroke, he felt, conceivably ran above the area that is now preserved.

A small, certain gain results from study of this letterspace. The name *Pataikos,* once suggested (albeit diffidently) as a possible speaker's name, is now definitely excluded from further consideration.[13] On the other hand, speculation concerning the speaker's name will continue, and the name *Glaukos* now seems better established than heretofore, since no other properly attested Athenian name meets every requirement imposed by the traces on the stone.

To speculate further, if Glaukos is the speaker, the archon's name has either five or six letters, like those of, for example, Konon (462/1), Habron (458/7), Krates (434/3), and Eukles (427/6). But the scope of the present inquiry would have to be greatly enlarged to permit full consideration of the possible date of the decree.[14] It is enough at present to hope that the original scheme of the preamble has been recovered.[15]

Brown University
1 February 1966

[12] *Zeta* is questioned because there is not one on the stone to compare. *Delta* is possible because several *deltas* elsewhere in the inscription float above the line.

[13] For *Pataikos,* see Dinsmoor (n. 11, above). *Hipponikos,* suggested by A. Koerte (*Hermes,* XLV [1910], 623 ff.) and subsequently accepted by some, rejected by others, is impossible. After repeated examinations, I am convinced that the diagonal line in stoichos 18 is from an *alpha* or a *gamma*.

[14] For recent discussion concerning the date, see H. B. Mattingly, *Historia,* X (1961), 169 ff., the rejoinder of Meritt and Wade-Gery, pp. 109-10, and Mattingly, *Historia,* XIV (1965), 278 ff. See also W. K. Pritchett on the rule of the three-barred *sigma, BCH,* LXXXIX (1965), 425 ff.

[15] Mr. H. B. Mattingly and Professor F. Mitchel helped me examine the stone; Professor E. Vanderpool improved early versions of the paper with stringent criticism; and Professors S. Dow, B. D. Meritt, and T. L. Shear, Jr., subsequently added valuable suggestions. A grant from the Howard Foundation and a grant-in-aid from the American Council of Learned Societies enabled me to work in Athens in 1964-65.

THE FRAGMENTS OF GREEK
LEXICOGRAPHY IN THE PAPYRI[1]

Mark Naoumides

The importance of the papyrus lexica [2] for the history of ancient Greek lexicography was duly emphasized by W. Crönert, who hailed the publication of the four lexica from Oxyrhynchus (P. Oxy. 1801-1804) as "der wichtigste Zuwachs seit der Herausgabe des Anfangs des Photius." [3] Although not all items listed in the accompanying table (pp. 182-83) [4] could match these four in importance and in the wealth of new classical fragments which they contain, nevertheless they provide us with useful information for a better understanding of ancient lexicography over a period of a millennium, its development as well as its vicissitudes. In attempting an evaluation of these

[1] This article reproduces in revised form the last chapter of my unpublished dissertation, "Greek Lexicography in the Papyri," Urbana (Illinois), 1961.

[2] The term *lexica* is used in this article to indicate alphabetically arranged dictionaries, as contrasted with other types of lexicographic material in which the entries follow the order of the text. These can be termed *paraphrases*, when only a brief literal translation of the lemma is given; *glossaries*, when the linguistic treatment is less trivial and the material more selective; and *commentaries*, when besides the meaning of uncommon words various other points bearing on the text—critical, aesthetic, antiquarian, etc.—are discussed. Finally the term *onomastica* should apply only to lists of words (usually without explanation) arranged in categories according to meaning.

[3] Cf. Crönert's review of *The Oxyrhynchus Papyri*, Part XV (London, 1922), in *Literarisches Centralblatt*, LXXIII (1922), 426.

[4] This list does not include the following papyri: P. Michael. 6 (Pack 2.2123), which was probably (as its editor suggested) part of a Greek-Coptic dictionary; P. Dura-Europos 3 (Pack 2.2135), which is virtually illegible and in my opinion hardly resembles a dictionary; O. Berol. 12605 (Pack 2.2131), which clearly was not a lexicon of any extent despite the fact that it preserves three glosses that appear in alphabetical sequence; P. Oxy. 2328 (Pack 2.2124) and P. Merton 55 (Pack 2.2130), for the arrangement of which we have no evidence; and a number of papyri termed *lexica* (cf. Pack 2.1163, 1166, 1180, 1187, 1191, 1195, 1196, 1198, 1199, 1202), although they do not contain alphabetically arranged dictionaries.

SYSTEMATIC LIST OF PAPYRUS LEXICA

No.	Reference and provenance	Date (century)	Form	Author and contents	Alphabetized by	Corrected	Reference in Pack *
1.	P. Hibeh 175	III B.C.	roll	Anonymus, *variae glossae* (Δε, Ευ)	2 letters		2122
2.	P. Hibeh 5(a) P. Rylands 16a P. Lit. Lond. 186 P. Bad. 180 P. Heidelb. 200 (all from Hibeh)	III/II	roll (verso)	Anonymus, *variae glossae* (Οζ-Ου)	2 letters	yes	1220
3.	P. Freib. inv. no. 12 (prov.: unknown)	II/I	roll (verso)	Anonymus, *variae glossae* (Ου)	2 letters	no	1219
4.	P. Oxy. 1801	A.D. I	roll	Theon (?), Λέξις κωμική (Βα-Βη)	2 letters	partly	2121
5.	P. Rylands 26 (prov.: Oxyrhynchus)	I	roll	Apion (?), *Glossae Homericae* (Ομ-Οπ)	2 letters	partly	1216
6.	Bodl. MS. Gr. class. e. 44 (prov.: unknown)	I	roll	Apollonius Sophista, *Lexicon Homericum* (Εφ-Εχ, Ζα)	2 letters	yes	1217
7.	P. Oxy. 2087	II	roll	Anonymus, Λέξεις Ἀττικαί (Αδ-Αν)	2 letters	no	2120
8.	P. Oxy. 2517	II	codex	Anonymus, *Lexicon Homericum* (Θα-Θρ)	2 letters		(**)
9.	P. Oxy. 1802	II/III	roll (verso)	Anonymus, Ξένως εἰρημένα (Κ, Λα, Μα-Μι)	strict arrangement.	no	2127

No.	Papyrus	Date	Form	Author, Work	Arrangement	Complete	Pack*
10.	P. Rylands 532 (prov.: unknown)	II/III	roll	Harpocration, *Lexicon decem oratorum* (Ka, Ke)	4 letters		458
11.	P. Oxy. 416	III	roll	Anonymus, *Lexicon* (Στ)	2 letters	no	168
12.	P. Oxy. 1804	III	roll	Anonymus, Λέξεις ῥητορικαί (Π, Ρ, Σν)	1 letter	partly	2128
13.	P. Cairo 50208 (prov.: Oxyrhynchus)	III	roll	Anonymus, *Homeric lexicon*, (Εν)	2 letters	partly	1218
14.	P. S. I. 892 (prov.: unknown)	IV	codex	Diogenianus (?), Περι-εργοπένητες (Φυ)	strict arrangement.	no	2125
15.	P. Rainer 7 (prov.: Fayum)	IV/V	codex	Anonymus, Lexicon of Demosthenes *In Midiam* (Δ-Ι)	first sound (κατ' ἀντιστοιχίαν)	partly	308
16.	P. Berol. 5008 (prov.: Fayum)	IV/V	codex	Anonymus, Lexicon of Demosthenes *In Aristocratem* (Μ-Ο)	1 letter (?)	partly	317
17.	P. Oxy. 1803	V	codex	Anonymus, Λέξεις Ἀττικαί (Σ)	1 letter	partly	2126
18.	P. Colt 8 (prov.: Auja el Hafir, anc. Nessana)	VII	codex	St. Cyril, *Lexicon* (Α-Ω)	1 letter	no	2119

* R. A. Pack, *Greek and Latin Literary Texts from Greco-Roman Egypt*, Second revised edition (Ann Arbor, 1965).
** Cf. E. Lobel, *The Oxyrhynchus Papyri*, Part XXX (Egypt Exploration Society, Graeco-Roman Memoirs, No. 44), (London, 1964), pp. 28-30.

findings, I concentrate on questions bearing on some aspects that
have been neglected in the past, mainly because the evidence offered
by our tradition was both scanty and indirect.

The papyri under discussion are for the most part products of
professional bookmaking, as is evidenced by the fact that they are
written in various literary hands either on the recto of papyrus rolls
or on papyrus codices. Of the three lexica written on the verso,
No. 3 has been considered by its editor as a school copy of a lexicon
and No. 9 was probably left incomplete. The size of the papyri
varies from one fragment with remnants of as few as 19 lines (No. 5)
to fragments of eleven leaves preserving parts of 111 lines (No. 18).
Like many other literary papyri, they have a number of casual corrections usually by a hand similar to, if not identical with, that of
the first scribe.

EXTERNAL FORM

The publication of the four Oxyrhynchus papyri made it apparent that ancient lexica had a definite form of arrangement,[5] which
can now be observed in the majority of our papyri (see Plate I.
Note that the plates do not reproduce the manuscripts in their actual
size). Each entry always begins with a new line even when the last
line of the preceding entry is short enough to accommodate the
lemma and even part of its explanation. The lemma protrudes to
the left, while the remaining lines of the entry are indented
(εἴσθεσις). Occasionally the last line of a long entry is even further
indented in relation to the other lines.[6] Sometimes *paragraphi* are
used to mark off an entry or to indicate the presence of a quotation.[7]
In at least two cases (Nos. 6 and 7) the first letter of the lemma is
larger than the rest, a feature which foreshadows the common practice of the Byzantine lexicographers to set off distinctly the first
letter of each lemma with or without different colored ink.

It has passed unnoticed, however, that there existed yet another
type of arrangement, which is found primarily in the earliest and
simplest lexica. In these the glosses are listed one under the other
and, as in the other papyri, a blank space is left between the lemma

---

[5] Cf. B. P. Grenfell and A. S. Hunt, *The Oxyrhynchus Papyri*, Part XV (London
1922), pp. 150-51.

[6] Cf. No. 4 s.v. Βεργαῖον and No. 13 s.v. ἐντυπάς.

[7] Thus regularly in No. 4 and 17, and possibly in No. 5 and 15. *Paragraphi*
were more commonly used in commentaries. Cf. n. 11.

Plate I.   P. Oxy. 1801 (recto).   (Theon's [?] *Lexicon*)

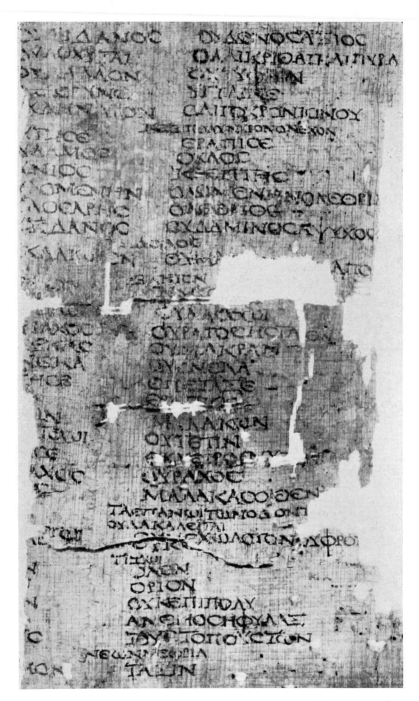

Plate II. P. Freib. 12 (*variae glossae*)

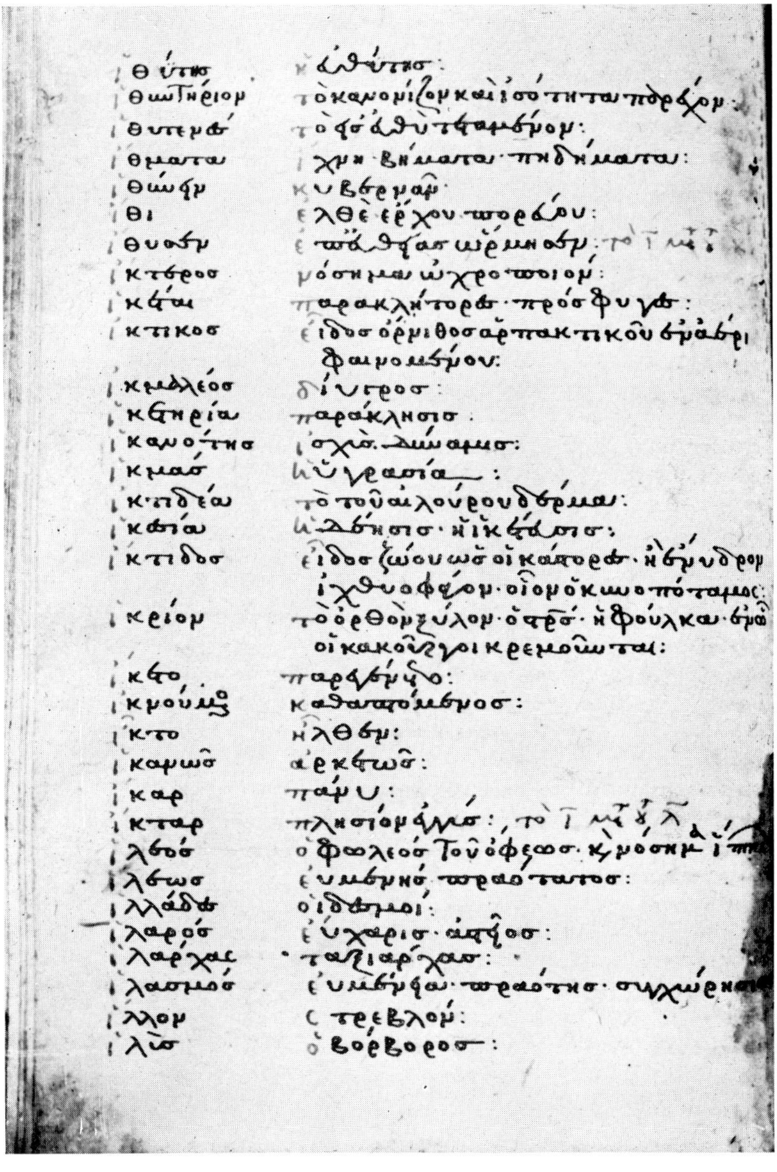

Plate III. Codex Par. gr. 2655, fol. 108ᵛ. (*Lexicon Cyrilli*)

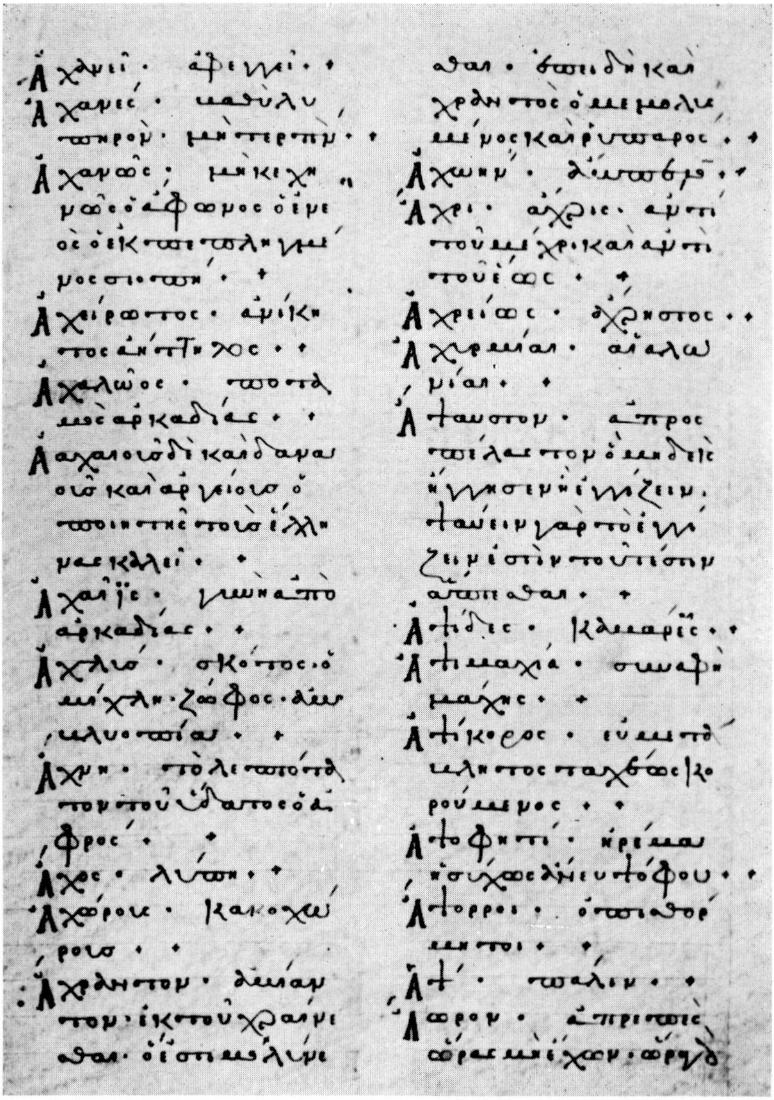

Plate IV. Codex Vat. gr. 2130, fol. 29r. (*Lexicon Cyrilli*)

and the explanation. Gradually, however, a tendency developed to separate further the two elements and eventually resulted in the splitting of each σελίς into two distinct columns, one of which was occupied by the lemmata and the other by the explanations. The culmination of this tendency was already reached in papyrus No. 3, where the two columns are well separated and the explanations are kept within the limits of their own column even when they continue over to a second or a third line (Plate II).

The simplicity of this system and its use in paraphrases as well as in bilingual dictionaries, whether Greek-Latin (also Latin-Greek) or Greek-Coptic,[8] indicate that these lexica originated from lists compiled either by students in the classroom or by adults with a limited knowledge of the vocabulary of poetical or otherwise difficult texts. Their purpose was for study and possibly for memorization.[9] As these lists grew longer, they were alphabetized to facilitate consultation and reference and subsequently introduced into the schools or sold to the general public. Indeed, of our papyri No. 3 was probably a school book while Nos. 1 and 2 could have come from a private library. Other papyrus lexica with this type of arrangement are Nos. 11 and 18 of our tabulation, both of which have short explanations. This system also survived in some of the oldest manuscripts of the *Lexicon* of St. Cyril, a dictionary of similar composition.[10]

A comparison of the two systems clearly shows that the one evolved from the other as the explanation expanded. The transition can be seen in papyrus No. 2, which like the other early lexica abounds in short entries. In the longer entries, however, the scribe

---

[8] Homeric paraphrases: cf. Pack 2.1158, 1180, 1187, 1189, 1192; paraphrases of Cicero's *In Catilinam* and of Virgil's *Aeneid* (with translation into Greek): Pack 2.2922, 2923, 2943, 2950; bilingual Greek-Latin and Latin-Greek glossaries: G. Goetz–G. Gudermann, *Corpus Glossariorum Latinorum*, Vol. II (Leipzig, 1888), especially plates i-iii (manuscripts), and R. Cavenaille, *Corpus Papyrorum Latinarum* (Wiesbaden, 1958), pp. 392-94 (papyri); Greek-Coptic glossaries: Pack 2.2132, 2133, and P. Michael. 6 (above, n. 4).

[9] That memorization of the meaning of rare and obsolete words was part of the students' training in school is well known from the famous fragment of Aristophanes' Δαιταλῆς (fr. 222 Edmonds).

[10] All remarks made here in reference to St. Cyril's *Lexicon* stem from a personal study of the numerous manuscripts of this still unpublished *Lexicon*. The most recent studies on the *Lexicon Cyrilli* are those of A. B. Drachmann, *Die Überlieferung des Cyrillglossars* (Det Kgl. Danske Videnskabernes Selskab. Hist.-filologiske Meddelelser, XXI.5), Copenhagen, 1936; K. Latte, *Hesychii Alexandrini Lexicon*, I (Hauniae, 1953), xliv-li; and P. Burguière, "Cyrilliana," *REG*, LXIII (1961), 345-61, and LXIV (1962), 95-108.

continues the explanation directly below the lemma but leaves an indentation of two or three letters on the left (εἴσθεσις), which makes the lemma appear to protrude into the margin.

The more developed form of arrangement became predominant in the papyrus lexica and can be contrasted with the arrangement common to commentaries, in which the entries are as a rule written consecutively and are separated only by a blank space or a colon. Although there are a few commentaries which have adopted at least some of the above features of the lexica,[11] it seems that in general there was neither pressing need nor established tradition for a clear-cut distinction of the entries in the commentaries, since they were always used side-by-side with the texts to which they pertained.[12] There is only one alphabetically arranged dictionary whose external form resembles that of commentaries (No. 15). But even this exception proves the rule. For this is in reality a commentary turned into a lexicon through the alphabetization of its entries.[13] Its counterpart (No. 16), on the other hand, although of similar origin has the arrangement common to the other lexica.

Both types of arrangement as described above assure for the copyist as well as for the reader a clear distinction of one entry from another and of the lemmata from the explanations. Despite this advantage, both these systems were abandoned in later times in order to save space, and survived only in some manuscripts of the *Lexicon* of St. Cyril (Plates III and IV).[14] The other extant dictionaries are written continuously, and various signs (such as στιγμή, colon or cross) were introduced to mark the end of an entry or of a lemma. Rubrication of the first letter of the lemma also

---

[11] Thus, e.g., P.S.I. 1219 (Pack 2.196) and P. Oxy. 2262 (Pack 2.204) have all the basic characteristics of the alphabetical dictionaries. *Paragraphi* mark off the entries in P. Berlin 9780 (Pack 2.339), P. Berlin 9782 (Pack 2.1393), and P. Oxy. 418 (Pack 2.1164). Sometimes the lines containing the phrase-lemma are longer than those of the explanations, even though the lemma starts in the middle of the line. Cf. P. Oxy. 418 (see above), 1087 (Pack 2.1186), P. Oxy. 2221 (Pack 2.1327), and P. Berlin 9780 (see above).

[12] Cf. Zuntz, "Die Aristophanes-Scholien der Papyri," *Byzantion*, XIV (1939), 547 ff.; and E. G. Turner, "L'érudition alexandrine et les papyrus," *Chronique d'Egypte*, XXXVII (1962), 148 ff.

[13] Thus we find in it entries with comments on stylistic and historical aspects of the speech, which was a feature of the commentaries but not of lexica (see above, n. 2).

[14] For the κατ' εἴσθεσιν arrangement of these manuscripts, cf. A. B. Drachmann, p. 5 (above, n. 10) and A. Turyn, *Codices Graeci Vaticani saeculis XIII et XIV scripti annorumque notis instructi* (Codices e Vaticanis selecti quam simillime expressi, XXVIII), (Vatican City, 1964), 89.

became common. Since, however, the first letter was mechanically inserted after the copy was finished, it was occasionally omitted or added in the wrong place. As a result, some entries were either fused or falsely divided and even transposed to what seemed to be their proper place.[15]

As is attested by our manuscripts, it was customary in Byzantine times to indicate a change of section with rubrics such as ἀρχὴ τοῦ θ', τὸ θ' μετὰ τοῦ α', etc., or with vignettes and other signs. Our papyri, although fragmentary for the most part, testify that this tradition went back to older times. Thus papyrus No. 8 (of the second century A.D.) was supplied with subheadings such as θ' καὶ ο' at the beginning of each two-letter section and in No. 18 a series of long dashes was used to indicate the end of glosses beginning with the same letter.

ALPHABETICAL ARRANGEMENT

Before the discoveries of the papyri, it was commonly believed that the alphabetical arrangement was not used in lexicography before the first century B.C. or even later.[16] Although the oldest dictionary reportedly arranged alphabetically was Zenodotus' "glossary,"[17] scholars had questioned the authenticity of its arrangement and suggested that it was merely given to this collection by a later grammarian who rearranged the glosses.[18] Our papyri, however, leave little doubt that the alphabet was used as a device for arranging lexicographic material as early as Zenodotus' lifetime. The alphabet was already used from much earlier times as a numeral system as well as for musical notation. It has also been established that Callimachus used it as a classificatory device in his

[15] Cf. K. Latte's remarks for the rubricator's errors in the Marcianus of Hesychius (above, n. 10) p. xxx; and pp. xi, xxx for characteristic examples of mistakes due to inadequate separation of entries and/or faulty rubrication.

[16] Cf. L. Cohn, "Griechische Lexikographie," in Müller's *Handbuch für klassischen Altertumswissenschaft*, 4. Auflage, 2. Band, 1. Abteilung (München, 1913), p. 687. Before Cohn, G. Autenrieth ("Griechische Lexikographie," in the same *Handbuch*, 2. Auflage, 2. Band [München, 1890], p. 588) had suggested Apollonius (first century A.D.) as possibly the first author of an alphabetic dictionary.

[17] The alphabetical arrangement of Zenodotus' γλῶσσαι was first suggested by H. Pusch ("Quaestiones Zenodoteae," *Dissertationes Philologicae Halenses*, XI [1890], 192-93), on the basis of the reference to it in the scholia on the *Odyssey*, γ' 444 (cf. Dindorf, *Scholia Graeca in Homeri Odysseam* [Oxford, 1855] I, 162, n. to line 27).

[18] Cf. L. Cohn, p. 685, n. 3 (above, n. 16).

Πίνακες.[19] There is no ground, therefore, to deny the alphabetic arrangement of Zenodotus' γλῶσσαι.

The alphabetical arrangement of the glosses, however, was not as strict as in modern dictionaries. In the oldest of our papyri (see table), the alphabetical arrangement was not observed beyond the second letter of the lemma. In No. 9 the arrangement seems perfect, but since the portion of the text preserved on papyrus is by no means extensive, we are not in a position to determine how consistent it was.

The application of stricter alphabetical order never became general (see table). Hesychius in the Preface to his *Lexicon* still refers to a system of arrangement in which the first four or five letters of the lemma were taken into consideration for the alphabetization, and this was the prevailing system of the κατὰ στοιχεῖον arrangement of Byzantine dictionaries. In most manuscripts of St. Cyril's *Lexicon*, the arrangement is not observed beyond the second letter. Although exceptions may be cited, it seems that as a rule there was a certain relation between the size of a dictionary and the degree of strictness of its alphabetical arrangement. Most of the later papyrus lexica arranged on the basis of the first letter only were small in size with a limited number of glosses under each letter, so that a stricter alphabetical order would seem neither necessary nor worth the effort.

What method was applied in collecting and arranging lexicographic material is not very clear. In the later dictionaries, glosses taken from different sources form distinct groups succeeding one another in the same order from section to section.[20] These groups were dispersed or greatly reduced when rearrangement was made to fit a stricter alphabetical order. In our papyri rarely do we find groups of glosses of common origin. Thus in No. 15 three consecutive entries show such close relationship with the corresponding entries of Harpocration's *Lexicon* that they can safely be attributed to a

---

[19] Cf. Fr. Schmidt, *Die Pinakes des Kallimachos* (Klassisch-Philologische Studien, fasc. 1), (Berlin, 1922), pp. 57-66 and 70-91. See also R. Pfeiffer, *Callimachus*, I (Oxford, 1949), 349, and E. G. Turner, pp. 135 ff. (above, n. 12).

[20] Cf. R. Reitzenstein, *Geschichte der griechischen Etymologika* (Leipzig, 1897), p. 47 for the *Etymologicum genuinum;* W. M. Lindsay, *Nonius Marcellus' Dictionary of Republican Latin* (Oxford, 1901); H. Kleist, *De Philoxeni Grammatici Alexandrini studiis etymologicis* (Gryphiswaldiae, 1865) pp. 16 ff. for Orion's *Etymologicum;* and J. Klein, *Erotiani vocum Hippocraticarum conlectio* (Leipzig, 1865) pp. xvi ff. Similar groups can also be observed in the so-called third Seguerian Lexicon (ed. I. Bekker, *Anecdota Graeca,* I [Berlin, 1814], 117-80).

common source.[21] Likewise in No. 1, three glosses (gl. 5, 6 and 8) seem to have been taken from the first book of the *Iliad* in the same order in which they appear in the papyrus. Some similar grouping of glosses can also be observed in No. 7. But no other distinct groups occur, which seems to indicate that the papyrus dictionaries had been subjected to numerous rearrangements before they were given the form in which they reached us.

Rearrangement of a dictionary to fit a stricter alphabetical order was practiced in later times quite commonly. To the known examples our papyri have added one more, the *Lexicon* of Apollonius the Sophist, which—as is clear from a comparison of the order of the entries preserved in the papyrus fragment with the order of the same entries in the unique manuscript of the dictionary—was rearranged sometime between the first and the tenth centuries. It is noteworthy that in this lexicon even after the rearrangement there are glosses which disturb the stricter order imposed by the reviser. Such inconsistency, also observed in other dictionaries, is always viewed with suspicion as indicating interpolation. But it may equally be due to the method used during rearrangement. As Lindsay has pointed out for Latin glossaries, the copyists arranged the glosses while copying them.[22] As a result, some glosses were omitted or misplaced in the process and the arrangement was never perfect.

The alphabetical arrangement was sometimes affected by pronunciation changes. Thus in Byzantine times, besides the regular arrangement (called κατὰ στοιχεῖον) another based on pronunciation developed and became known as the arrangement κατ᾿ ἀντιστοιχίαν. In accordance with the latter system words beginning with letters identical in pronunciation (e.g., ι, η, and ει; ε and αι; or ο and ω) were classified together, and so were glosses with the same letters in the first syllables.[23] Our papyri again offer possibly the earliest example of such an arrangement. Thus in No. 15 (IV/V century A.D.) the entry εἰσιτήρια is listed after the entry θέμενος τὰ ὅπλα and before ἱεροποιόν, clearly because of iotacism.

---

[21] Cf. my article, "Notes on Literary Papyri," *TAPA*, xciii (1962), 243. Although the papyrus is later than Harpocration, the relationship between the two is not direct, since the papyrus entries are longer than Harpocration's.

[22] W. M. Lindsay and H. J. Thomson, *Ancient Lore in Medieval Latin Glossaries* (St. Andrews University Publications, No. 13), Oxford, 1921.

[23] The best known example of this type of arrangement is the so-called Suda Lexicon. Cf. *Suidae Lexicon*, ed. A. Adler (Lexicographi Graeci, Vol. ı), Leipzig, 1928-1938.

SIZE

An important question in connection with our papyrus lexica is the estimate of their size. Despite their fragmentary state, it is possible to deduce it fairly well in some instances. Thus in the case of No. 18, it is clear that the entire lexicon occupied eleven folios of a papyrus codex in all. The total number of entries, according to the editors, did not exceed 500. The papyrus of Harpocration's *Lexicon* (No. 10) shows such close agreement with the version preserved in our manuscripts as to leave little doubt that the two versions were identical.[24] Since the entire dictionary as we have it is not of an impressive size, we can assume that it did not extend beyond one papyrus roll or two at the most. Another papyrus, that of the *Lexicon Homericum* of Apollonius the Sophist (No. 6), does not contain a single entry beyond those of the extant version which, in all, covers 46 folios in the unique manuscript of this lexicon. And although the preserved entries are more extensive than in the manuscript, the entire lexicon most probably was not much larger. Since our tradition does not assign to it any specific number of "books," it is safe to assume that it did not occupy more than one roll. If No. 14 has indeed preserved a fragment of the *Lexicon* of Diogenianus, this would be the only papyrus lexicon to cover attestedly more than one roll.[25]

As for the other lexica, we can estimate their approximate original size by comparing the number of the entries of the preserved section with the corresponding section of Hesychius' *Lexicon,* which of all preserved dictionaries displays by far the most numerous and closest parallels to our papyrus lexica (see p. 200). Thus we can obtain the relative size of No. 7, which is arranged on the basis of the first two letters of the lemmata. The papyrus fragment has preserved sixteen entries from the beginning of section Αε to the end of section Αμ. In Hesychius, where all but one of the above entries occur, there are 2,945 entries listed in the corresponding sections, or about 180 times the number of those preserved in the papyrus. This is a clear indication, I believe, that the original size of this dictionary was very small. Indeed the entire lexicon would easily be accommodated in not more than a few folios of the *Marcianus* of Hesychius. Applying

[24] Cf. my article, "The Papyrus of the *Lexicon* of Harpocration," *TAPA,* xcii (1961), 384-88.

[25] The original work occupied five books or papyrus rolls. Cf. *Suda Lexicon* s.v. Διογενιανός, and L. Cohn, "Diogenianos" in Pauly-Wissowa, *RE,* v (1903), 778.

the same method, we can establish that the original size of No. 4 did not exceed one roll.[26] The lexica confined to single speeches of Demosthenes (Nos. 15 and 16) could not have been very large, as is shown by the number of entries in some sections. Thus No. 15 has only one entry beginning with H and one beginning with Θ, while the E-section occupied less than a page. No. 16 has preserved no entries beginning with N or Ξ. Of the other papyri, No. 9 clearly did not extend over the entire roll; No. 12 has so many close parallels with the fifth Seguerian Lexicon [27] and shows such great affinity with it both in structure and in the order of the entries that we can assume that the two were most likely of equal size, if not indeed different versions of the same work. If No. 5 is a more complete version of the *Lexicon* ascribed to Apion in our manuscripts, it could not have been more than a few times the size of this Lilliputian dictionary. From the extent of the entries preserved in No. 13 and its limited scope, it seems that this dictionary was not of impressive size either. The length of the three earliest lexica cannot be determined, for the papyrus fragments contain no complete sections that could be compared with those of extant dictionaries. But from their dates, size of entries, and character we can deduce that neither were they very extensive. The same was probably true for No. 11. And in No. 17, the loose alphabetical arrangement may also point to a small dictionary.

On account of the small size of the majority of our papyrus lexica, some scholars have questioned their integrity and have been too eager to consider them epitomized. Such an opinion was held by A. Ludwich in regard to No. 5 (the Apionic lexicon) [28] and by Tolkiehn in regard to No. 6.[29] The integrity of No. 4 has also been questioned by K. Latte, who calls Oxyrhynchus *provinciam compilatorum*.[30]

Such an attitude, in my opinion, is not entirely warranted. Our tradition confirms in the main the evidence furnished by our papyri

[26] Cf. my article, " Ὁ P. Oxy. 1801 καὶ ὁ Θέων," Χάρις Κωνσταντίνῳ I. Βουρβέρῃ (Athens, 1964), pp. 327-35.

[27] Also known as the *Lexicon Bekkerianum* No. 5, ed. I. Bekker, pp. 195-318 (above, n. 20).

[28] A. Ludwich, "Über die Homerischen Glossen Apions," *Philologus,* LXXIV (1917), 208, n. 7.

[29] "Lexikographie" in Pauly-Wissowa, *RE,* XII (1925), 2445. What may have prompted Tolkiehn to such a conclusion was probably the unsuccessful supplements of some lines by the first editor. Cf. my article, p. 245 (above, n. 21).

[30] Latte, p. xlii (above, n. 10). Cf. also my article (above, n. 26).

on this point. Indeed a statistical study of the size of the lexica known to us either directly or indirectly shows that as a rule they were small in contrast with other types of dictionaries, especially the commentaries. Indeed, the size of the latter can occasionally be contrasted directly with that of the alphabetical dictionaries. For a striking example, Harpocration of Argos (II cent. A.D.) composed a commentary on Plato which extended to twenty-four books, while the same author's Platonic lexicon occupied only two books.[31] Likewise, the two lexica on Hippocrates mentioned by Erotianus appear relatively small in contrast with the commentaries on the same author, some of which extended to as many as twenty books in length.[32]

Larger lexica did exist, but even when a lexicon was mentioned as extending to five or ten books (i. e., rolls), its actual size when transferred to a codex was not too large. This is clearly indicated by Photius, who testifies that the following lexica were all included in one manuscript: Timaeus' *Lexicon Platonicum*; Aelius Dionysius' *Voces Atticae* (divided into five books or λόγοι) ; Pausanias' *Lexicon*, which was twice the size of Dionysius'; Boethus' Λέξεων Πλατωνικῶν συναγωγή and Περὶ τῶν παρὰ Πλάτωνι ἀπορουμένων λέξεων ; Dorotheus' Περὶ τῶν ξένως εἰρημένων λέξεων ; and Moeris' *Lexicon Atticum*.[33]

Nor was the size always a sign of erudition. Indeed the most extensive of our papyrus lexica, the *Lexicon* of Diogenianus (see p. 190), although more copious in the number of entries it contains, is less erudite than some of the smaller lexica (e.g., Nos. 4 and 9). The available evidence, therefore, points in general to small-size, easy-to-use lexica and not to bulky reference works. These latter were the exception rather than the rule.[34]

In view of the above, any *a priori* assumption that the small size of a papyrus lexicon is evidence of epitomization should be dismissed, unless it is supported by other considerations. Indeed, deliberate epitomization can be detected, since the method and the

[31] Cf. *Suda Lexicon*, s.v. Ἁρποκρατίων and H. von Arnim, " Harpocration von Argos," in Pauly-Wissowa, *RE*, VII (1912), 2411.

[32] Cf. Erotianus, *Vocum Hippocraticarum collectio*, ed. by E. Nachmanson (Uppsala, 1918), pp. 5-8.

[33] Cf. Photius, *Bibliotheca*, Codd. 151-57. Note besides that Pollion's lexicon, which was double the size of Diogenianus', according to Photius' testimony (*Bibliotheca*, Cod. 149) occupied only one codex.

[34] Such were the dictionaries of Dorotheus of Ascalon (at least 108 books), Pamphilus (95 books), Stephanus Byzantius (at least 52 books), and Phrynichus (38 books). Extensive also were the three anonymous stylistic dictionaries mentioned by Photius (*Bibliotheca*, Codd. 146, 147, 148).

mechanics used by epitomists of lexica are obvious both in the extant epitome of Harpocration's lexicon and in the manuscript version of the *Lexicon Homericum* of Apollonius the Sophist as compared with our papyrus No. 6. In the latter case, although none of the recognizable entries of the papyrus is wanting in the manuscript, the latter's entries are generally shorter than the corresponding entries of the papyrus. The abridgment seems to follow a certain pattern. While each of the papyrus entries has at least one quotation, the manuscript entries are usually deprived of quotations. This was true for almost everything except the explanation proper; that is, the etymologies, the names of grammarians sponsoring a certain view, etc. Even the explanation proper is abbreviated at times when it is unusually long.[35]

CONTENTS

As is shown in the table, the papyrus lexica display a great diversity not only in their method of composition but in their content as well, ranging from dictionaries devoted exclusively to one work of one author (cf. Nos. 15, 16) to the most extensive collection of glosses (No. 14). Lexica of a general character are rare, however, while those of a limited scope are the rule. Thus of our lexica, six are devoted to Attic orators and/or Attic diction, while those that can be classified as Homeric lexica rank second in number. Of a special character are the three Ptolemaic dictionaries (Nos. 1-3), which contain a mixture of Homeric and non-Homeric glosses. On account of their date and type, they can be considered specimens of the collections attributed to the γλωσσογράφοι.[36] Some evidence in support of this theory is provided by No. 2, s.v. ὀνείατα. The explanation given in the papyrus (βρ[ώματα]) is referred to in the Homeric scholia A on Ω′ 367 as originating from the γλωσσογράφοι. Since this explanation finds support neither in the extant

[35] Cf. also my article, pp. 243-47 (above, n. 21). The epitomist, however, was not consistent throughout, as is shown by the fact that this dictionary in its present form has occasionally preserved much valuable information in some of its entries.

[36] Cf. W. Aly, *Mitteilungen aus der Freiburger Papyrussammlung* (Sitzungsberichte der Heidelberger Akademie der Wissenschaften, Phil.-hist. Klasse, Heidelberg 1914), pp. 21-22. On the γλωσσογράφοι, cf. K. Lehrs, *De Aristarchi studiis Homericis* (Lipsiae, 1882³), pp. 36-39; A. Ludwich, *Aristarchs Homerische Textkritik*, II (Leipzig, 1885), 118; and V. de Marco, *Scholia minora in Homeri Iliadem*, Pars prior, Λέξεις Ὁμηρικαί codd. *Urb. CLVII et Selestadiensis CVII*, fasc. primus (Vatican City, 1946), XXII ff.

scholia nor elsewhere in our lexica, it seems logical to assume that at least this papyrus has preserved a fragment of such a collection. The other two could also by analogy of their content and date be attributed to the same source. Since in all three, non-Homeric glosses are found side by side with Homeric (although in smaller proportion to the latter), it can be inferred that the lexica of the γλωσσογράφοι were not exclusively Homeric.

The question of how comprehensive the papyrus lexica were can be raised only in the case of the Homeric lexicon of papyrus No. 8, which has preserved the entire Θο- section. The compiler has left out not only the proper names Θόας, Θόη, Θόων, etc., but also the words θοινηθῆναι (an *hapax legomenon*), θόλος and θόωκος. Nor does it have any entries beginning with Θλ, Θν.[37] It is clear, therefore, that it was not an exhaustive work on Homeric diction. Nonetheless, even this does better than the Homeric lexicon extant in manuscripts,[38] which not only omits the Θλ, Θν glosses but the entire Θο- section as well.

The length and contents of the glosses differ, as expected, from entry to entry and from dictionary to dictionary. Although individual glosses are always made to conform with the scope of each lexicon, some general tendencies can be observed both in the size and in the structure of individual entries. A study of these more than of any other features reveals the limitations of the early lexicographers as well as their concept of lexicography.

One tendency was to list the glosses in the form in which they occurred in a given text and to record the meaning which the lemma had in that particular context. This can be observed quite well in the earliest lexica, where different forms or different meanings of a word may appear as separate entries. Thus No. 2 lists three forms of the adjective ὀθνεῖος successively. No. 3 has double entries for the words οὐτιδανός, οὐλαμός, οὖλος, and οὐρίαχος and lists four different forms of the verb οὐτάζω. But this practice is not limited to these early dictionaries. Thus, No. 13 has two entries (and possibly a third) for the word ἔντεα; No. 18 lists twice the words παναγής and πημαίνω and has three forms of the pronoun σφεῖς as separate entries. The same tendency is occasionally found even in lexica of more scholarly nature. No. 9, for example, has double entries for the words μέροψ and μήτρα; and No. 14 (the *Lexicon* of

Diogenianus) has three separate entries for the word φυή, with the entries listed successively in each case.

Only exceptionally do our papyri contradict this tendency by systematically listing more than one or even all the possible meanings of a word. Such a tendency can be seen especially in the papyrus of the controversial lexicon attributed to the grammarian Apion (No. 5). Each lemma is followed by a letter indicating the number of meanings that the word has in Homer, and citations from the Homeric text are given to illustrate each meaning. A similar tendency, although not as systematic as the above, is seen in No. 17 (s.v. συμφοράν and σῖτος). From a number of later grammatical works originating in the classroom, where all the meanings of a word are given in the form of question and answer,[39] we can infer that such a practice started in the schools and is in reality an outgrowth of daily vocabulary drills and not necessarily a mark of erudition.

A preference for short entries is evidenced in most of our papyri. Indeed, of all the preserved entries in our fragments nearly half occupy only one line and another one-sixth of the whole extend over a second line. Several of our lexica, indeed, list almost exclusively one-line entries. But even in the more advanced dictionaries, one-line and two-line entries are not uncommon and appear side by side with the longer entries (cf. Nos. 4, 6, 9, 12, 15). Since in most cases these glosses appear to be complete, there is no reason to suspect that they have been epitomized. Exceptionally long entries occur mostly in the two lexica that originate from commentaries (Nos. 15 and 16), and only occasionally in the others.[40]

The lemmata do not always consist of one word. Sometimes a small phrase may stand in the place of a lemma, for example, ὄζος Ἄρηος (No. 2), οὖλε γύναι, οὖλος Ἄρης (No. 3), ὡς ἔπος εἰπεῖν, ὦ πόποι, ὦ πέπονες (No. 18); also a number of words preceded by the negative οὐ, e.g., οὐκ ὄθομαι, οὐκ ἀλέγω (No. 2); οὐκ ἀλαόν, οὐ δηναιόν, οὐχ ἑκάς, οὔτε τεῳ, οὐ δήν (No. 3). In the two lexica on Demosthenes' speeches, this is naturally more common. Examples of the same tendency can also be found in the lexica of Hesychius, Harpocration, St. Cyril, etc.[41] In nearly all cases, the first word of the lemma

---

[39] Cf. A. Kopp, *Beiträge zur griechischen Excerpten-Litteratur* (Berlin, 1887), pp. 143 ff.

[40] Cf. No. 6, s.v. Ἐφύρους; No. 9, s. vv. μέλισσαι and μελύγειον; and No. 17, s.v. σῖτον.

[41] Cf. also Photius, *Bibliotheca*, Codd. 145, 158.

counts for the alphabetical arrangement. There is, however, one exception. In the last entry of No. 15, it is not the first word of the phrase-lemma but the third (i.e., the actual word under discussion) that has determined the position of the entry in its present order. But this must have been unique.

The explanation proper, that is, the word or words that specifically define the lemma, forms the heart of the entry and is always present. There is only one instance in which no explanation is offered and the reader is left on his own to infer the meaning from two quotations in which the lemma appears (No. 10, s.v. κατατομή). The general tendency is to limit the explanation proper to as few words as possible.

Discussion of grammatical points and etymological analysis of words are rare. Questions of grammar such as the quantity of a vowel, the spelling, the form of the future, etc., are found solely in the Atticistic lexicon No. 17. Etymologies are occasionally mentioned, in my opinion, for the purpose of clarifying the meaning of the lemma. Some of them were of a very elementary nature and—naturally—correct (e. g., the derivation of ἄκομψος from κομψός in No. 7, of οὖλα from οὖλος in No. 3, and of ἔχματα from (ἐπ) ἔχειν in No. 6). More intricate are two etymologies found in papyrus No. 7 (that of ἀκραιφνές from ἀκεραιοφανές and of ἀλήπεδον [sic] from ἀελεάπεδον), which seem to follow the principles applied to the derivation of words by the ancient philosophers, especially the Stoics. In general, however, etymologies in the papyrus lexica are few in number and brief, always used as a further illustration of the meaning of a given word.

Whenever there were two differing views about the meaning of a word, the lexicographers dutifully listed both (cf. No. 3, s.vv. οὐρίαχος and οὖρος; No. 4, s.v. βέμβιξ; and No. 9, s.vv. Μαργιανοί, Μίθρας). The second view was introduced with some vague expression as ἔνιοι δέ, παρ' ἑτέροις, κατὰ δ' ἄλλους, etc. More rarely did they mention the exponents of the conflicting views (cf. No. 6, s.vv. Ἐφύρους [42] and ζαφελῶς).

QUOTATIONS AND REFERENCES

Sometimes the lexicographers would quote (*in extenso* or abbreviated) a *locus classicus* with the definition of a legal term, the description of an institution, plant, or even the recipe of a rare

[42] With the restorations suggested in my article, p. 246 (above, n. 21).

drink. Thus No. 4 (s.v. βέλεκκοι) takes the description of this plant from an unidentified author of a *Historia Plantarum*. No. 7 (s.v. ἀδικίου) and No. 15 (s.v. διαιτηταί) cite Aristotle's *Ath. Pol.* No. 9 cites Apollodorus (?) (s.v. μέλισσαι) and Glaucus (s.v. μελύγειον), and No. 16, Aristotle and Xenophon's *Laced. Pol.* (s.v. μόραν), Philochorus (s.v. ὅτι Θεμιστοκλῆς ὠστρακίσθη) and Didymus (s.v. ὁ κάτωθεν νόμος).

Besides these occasional quotations, our lexica were more frequently supplied with citations from ancient texts for the purpose of attesting either the source of a gloss or a particular meaning dealt with in the explanation. Lexica which belong to the older type of arrangement are, as a rule, without references or quotations of any kind. In the lexica of the more developed type, however, citations like the above are quite common and are proportionately more numerous than in the extant dictionaries. Since a number of these quotations and references are completely new,[43] our papyri indeed offer an acknowledged service to classical scholarship in general. To the specialist in lexicography, however, quotations or mere references are of special interest since they indicate the type of lexicon in question as well as the sources of the particular glosses and, by analogy, of similar glosses in our extant dictionaries.

While Nos. 4, 6, 9, and 10 (all being lexica of strictly limited scope) contain references taken directly from the source with a given gloss, the addition of references at a later stage is by no means unattested. Hesychius states in his letter to Eulogius that serves as a preface to his *Lexicon* that he supplied Diogenianus' glosses with the references which they lacked. Photius, likewise, gives similar testimony in regard to the (lost) dictionary of Aelius Dionysius (*Bibliotheca*, Cod. 152). But this practice was not confined to later lexicographers. Thus according to Erotianus' testimony (pp. 4 ff., Nachmanson), Bacchius supplied the entries of his glossary to Hippocrates with many references to poets (πολλὰς παραθέμενον . . . μαρτυρίας ποιητῶν) in contrast with his predecessor Xenocritus, who had confined himself to simply explaining the glosses (τὰς τοιαύτας ἐξαπλοῦν φωνάς). Our papyri offer one example which shows the continuity of this practice. Indeed, a comparison of some

---

[43] These come mostly from No. 4 (eight new fragments, seven of which originate from lost comedies or satyr plays and one from the historian Phylarchus—all very incomplete), No. 9 (twenty miscellaneous prose fragments, most of them mere references), No. 16 (seven fragments mostly from ancient historians), and No. 17 (seven new fragments from lost comedies, five of them by Menander).

of the glosses of No. 7 with the corresponding entries in Phrynichus' *Praeparatio Sophistica* reveals that the unknown compiler of this papyrus, when he did not entirely omit Phrynichus' references to poetical works, has purposely replaced them with other references to prose works, in order to be consistent with the scope of his lexicon which was confined to prose diction.[44]

The degree of accuracy of both quotations and references may in some cases be investigated, whenever an extant text is involved. An over-all check shows a rather high degree of inaccuracy in the form of omissions, free adaptations of the text, and faulty references.[45] Not all of these flaws can be blamed on the copyists. Some at least were due to the original compilers and also possibly to their sources,[46] which were not always first-rate. In general, we can distinguish, among our papyrus lexica, those that are more accurate and dependable from those that appear less trustworthy. To the latter class belongs No. 7, which displays six errors of various kinds in the ten quotations and references that it contains. Special attention is needed, however, in determining the nature as well as the origin of the error, since it may, for example, betray a different reading or a different division (or classification) of a work than that known to us. A good example of the latter is offered by No. 9, where reference is made to the eighth book of Aristotle's *De partibus animalium* instead of the ninth of the *Historia animalium*. As W. Crönert has pointed out, our papyrus probably makes reference to Aristotle's text as it was before Andronicus' arrangement.[47] The same, perhaps, may be true in the case of a similar mistake in No. 7, where, s.v. ἀναρριχᾶσθαι, reference is made to Aristotle's *De natura animalium* instead of the *Historia animalium*.

As for errors that may originate from a different reading, the same papyrus (No. 7) again offers an interesting example. Line 33, in a passage taken from Demosthenes' *Contra Boeotum*, instead of ἄλλῳ τινί reads only ἄλλῳ. Since the point made there is that ἄλλος

---

[44] I have discussed this point at more length in my unpublished dissertation (above, n. 1).

[45] Omissions occur in No. 6 (s.v. ἐχώμεθα), No. 17 (s.v. σῖτον), and No. 15 (s.vv. διαιτηταί and πληρωταί); free adaptations of the original text in No. 7 (s.v. ἀδικίου) and 15 (s.v. διαιτηταί); faulty references in No. 7 (s.vv. ἀκταινῶσαι, ἀλλόκοτος, ἄλλον and ἀναρριχᾶσθαι) and 9 (s. vv. μέροψ and μῆτραι).

[46] Thus, e.g., the reference to Plato's *Phaedo* instead of *Leges* in No. 7 (s.v. ἀκταινῶσαι), found also in Phrynichus, *Praeparatio Sophistica* (p. 39. 14 De-Borries). The latter was either the source of the former, or depended on that source.

[47] Crönert, pp. 425-26 (above, n. 3).

is used sometimes instead of τις, the omission seems intentional and may indicate a reading different from that of our manuscripts. Indeed, this new reading could in my opinion be accepted, if we suppose that the τινί of the manuscripts was an explanatory gloss *supra lineam* which was eventually admitted into the text.[48]

THE PAPYRI AND THE LEXICOGRAPHIC TRADITION

Only three of our papyri (Nos. 6, 10, and 18) contain fragments of lexica extant in manuscripts. Nos. 6 and 10 are especially important for evaluating our tradition, because both are almost contemporary with the authors of the respective dictionaries and at least a thousand years older than our manuscripts. Of these, No. 6 has preserved a text fuller than that of the unique manuscript of this lexicon and thus confirms the view expressed before the discovery of this papyrus that the extant version was epitomized.[49] The text of No. 10 is essentially identical with (though in its readings superior to) the "fuller" version of Harpocration's manuscripts (see p. 190). The third papyrus, however, although older by at least two centuries than our earliest manuscripts of the *Lexicon Cyrilli,* has preserved a version clearly inferior to that of the manuscripts.[50] One could also add a fourth example, namely, the Homeric lexicon No. 5, which has been identified with Apion's *Lexicon* and which indeed displays a text fuller than that of the manuscripts, although both the identification and Apion's authorship have been disputed.[51] All the other papyri have preserved fragments of lost dictionaries, some of which can be identified—at least tentatively—with lexica known to us only by reference.

However, a comparison of the individual glosses of all our papyri with those of the extant lexica and scholia shows that only a few of the former are completely or virtually new.[52] Most of them have at least remote parallels to one or more of the lexica on vellum, a fact which indicates that our lexicographic tradition has in one way or

---

[48] The reading τινί is, however, supported by P. Oxy. 1093, which has preserved parts of this speech.

[49] Cf. A. Brosow, *Quomodo sit Apollonius Sophista ex Etymologico Magno explendus atque emendandus* (Diss.), Regimonti Borussorum, 1884.

[50] See K. Latte's remarks, p. 505 (above, n. 10).

[51] See the bibliography listed by Pack, to which add V. de Marco, xxviii ff. (above, n. 36), and K. Latte, p. ix, n. 1.

[52] Such are the glosses ὁπλογενῶν (?), ὀθνιότυμβος, in No. 2; μελῳδία, μέροπες, μιεστήρ, μιθόργ, μιλήχ, and μινῶδες, in No. 9; Μιλτοκύθης, in No. 16; Σάραπις, συναγαγεῖν, συνεθίζεσθαι, and σιωπήσομαι, in No. 17.

another preserved a good percentage of the glosses of lost lexica. This, however, should not serve to minimize the importance of our fragments, since the latter, besides supplying us with quotations from and references to lost works, provide first-hand information about the source of individual glosses and illustrate their history and background.

Of all our lexica on vellum Hesychius has by far the greatest number of parallels to the papyrus glosses. In some cases the closeness of the entries of a papyrus with the corresponding Hesychian glosses is so striking as to imply a direct relationship between the two, as in the case of Nos. 3, 4, 9, and 14, among which there are two of his professed sources. This is also confirmed by the number of parallel glosses to Hesychius which the other papyri display. Naturally Hesychius' glosses are as a rule more concise than those in the papyrus lexica when they are not combined with similar entries of different origin.

Almost all the preserved lexica and scholia offer a number of parallels to individual entries of our papyri. The agreement in some cases is so close as to imply at least a common source. In view of the importance of this question in determining the sources of the extant dictionaries, I give here a list of the most remarkably close parallels to papyrus glosses, dictionary by dictionary.

Harpocration's *Lexicon decem oratorum* offers three such parallels to papyrus No. 15 (ἡγεμὼν συμμορίας, πληρωταί, θέμενος τὰ ὅπλα) and another three to No. 16 (μόραν, ὁδός, ὁ κάτωθεν νόμος). Phrynichus' *Praeparatio Sophistica* has close parallels to four glosses of the contemporary papyrus No. 7 (ἀκταινῶσαι, ἄκομψος, ἀλλόκοτος, ἀναρριχᾶσθαι), while Pollux's *Onomasticon* has only one parallel to the same papyrus (Αἰγιναία δραχμή). Moeris, another lexicographer of the second century A.D., agrees closely with No. 17 in one case (στιφρόν). The fifth Seguerian Lexicon has two glosses in common with No. 7 (ἆθλοι, Αἰάκειον) and three with No. 12 (περίστατοι, πορεῖον, ῥῶπος). The *Lexicon Bachmannianum* [53] agrees with No. 3 s.v. οὐτιδανός and with No. 12 s.vv. ῥυτήρ and σκειράφιον. Similarly, the *Suda Lexicon* agrees with two entries of No. 17 (συμφοράν, σῖτον), which are not found in the sources of the *Suda* extant. The Etymologicum Magnum has a close parallel to the gloss βέλεκκοι of No. 4, and Thomas Magister seems to parallel No. 5, s.v. ὅπλον.

---

[53] Ed. by L. Bachmann, *Anecdota Graeca*, I (Lipsiae, 1828), 1-422; also known as Συναγωγὴ λέξεων χρησίμων, indicated simply as Σ.

The scholia on Homer attributed to Didymus have close parallels to No. 2, especially in three cases (οὖλος Ἄρης, οὕνεκα, οὐκ ἀλέγω) , the scholia on Aristophanes to No. 4 (s.vv. βέμβιξ and Βερέσχεθοι) and those on Thucydides to No. 7 (ἀκραιφνές, ἀμφίβολοι) . Finally, Eustathius in his commentaries on Homer has a wealth of parallels to our papyri of which the following deserve special mention: to No. 6, s.v. ἐχεπευκές; No. 4, s.vv. βέλος, Βέλλερον; No. 7, s.vv. ἄληκτα, ἀμφίβολοι; and to No. 17, s.v. συγγίγνεσθαι.

CONCLUSIONS

First and foremost, the papyrus lexica have enriched our tradition with fragments of lost dictionaries either completely unknown to us or known only indirectly. Most notable in the second category are the first four papyri (Nos. 1-4), which have preserved specimens of lexicographic work of special interest, on which we had only the most vague information. The new discoveries have also enabled us to check and evaluate in part our tradition both by means of the fragments of extant lexica that they have preserved (which antedate our MSS by several centuries) as well as of the glosses which have parallels in the lexica on vellum. Finally, they have offered us first-hand information concerning the external form, arrangement, scope, and even the size of early lexica and have thus supplemented the picture afforded by our tradition in these aspects. And although some of the extant lexica were compiled at dates contemporary with or even earlier than some of our papyri, nevertheless the testimony of the latter is of special importance since our manuscripts are all much later and since, as is known, the dictionaries were not reproduced with the same care as the other ancient texts but were subject to interpolation, epitomization, or rearrangement—to say nothing of the cases in which they were incorporated in whole or in part into later lexica.

The over-all picture of ancient lexicography as it emerges from a study of the papyrus fragments may not be as impressive as one might have expected. Indeed, with the exception of one papyrus (No. 16), which was by no means a typical lexicon, we do not find in our lexica the affluence of learning which presumably characterized the works of a Dorotheus of Ascalon [54] or a Didymus. Even the

---

[54] Cf. Porphyry's comment: ὅλου βιβλίου ἐδέησε Δωροθέῳ τῷ 'Ασκαλωνίτῃ εἰς ἐξήγησιν τοῦ παρ' 'Ομήρῳ κλισίου, quoted by the Homeric scholia B on I 90; cf. G. Dindorf, *Scholia Graeca in Homeri Iliadem*, III (Oxford, 1877), 376.

dictionaries which stand out among the rest, such as Nos. 4, 6, 9 and 10, appear trifling at times. This—unless one chooses to adhere to the disproved theory of epitomization—may of course be accidental. Works of reference or erudition certainly did not then circulate any more commonly than they do now, and this may in part explain their absence from our finds. Such a possibility, however, is balanced by the following considerations: (1) the fact that the works of some well-known grammarians (such as Theon, Apollonius the Sophist, Harpocration and possibly Apion) appear among our papyri; (2) the fairly good distribution of the papyrus lexica in date, provenance and scope; and (3) the parallel testimony of the commentaries found so far in papyri, which for the most part fall short of our expectations even when they are signed by an Aristarchus.[55]

This more sober view of ancient lexicography provided by the papyri should neither lead to a negative attitude toward such study nor minimize its value. Rather it should serve to place in a more realistic perspective the achievements of the ancient grammarians as well as their limitations in grappling with the difficulties that they encountered in their pursuit of scholarship.[56]

University of Illinois
7 February 1966

[55] Cf. the commentary on Herodotus by Aristarchus preserved in P. Amh. 12 (Pack 2.483). Cf. also E. G. Turner's comments on Theon's commentary to Pindar's *Pythians,* in *The Oxyrhynchus Papyri,* part XXXI (London, 1966), pp. 16-17.

[56] Cf. the very instructive article of E. G. Turner, cited above, n. 12.

AVIANUS, FLAVIANUS, THEODOSIUS, AND MACROBIUS

W. Robert Jones

Preceding the text of the fables of Avianus, the older and better manuscripts have a brief dedicatory epistle which begins: *Dubitanti mihi, Theodosi optime, quonam litterarum titulo nostri nominis memoriam mandaremus, fabularum textus occurrit, quod in his urbane concepta falsitas deceat et non incumbat necessitas veritatis. Nam quis tecum de oratione, quis de poemate loqueretur, cum in utroque litterarum genere et Atticos Graeca eruditione superes et Latinitate Romanos?* Near the end of the epistle Theodosius is told: *habes ergo opus, quo animum oblectes, ingenium exerceas, sollicitudinem leves totumque vivendi ordinem cautus agnoscas.*

Although until the nineteenth century Avianus and his fables were sometimes assigned to the second century of our era, it is now universal to attribute the collection to the late fourth century, or the early fifth at the latest. It has become almost as universal to ignore, or to consider erroneous, the statement in four manuscripts that the *Theodosius optimus* is the *imperator* Theodosius.[1] The tenor of the argument has been that there could hardly be anyone, of whose existence we otherwise know nothing, bold enough to address the emperor so abruptly; that no one could have expected Theodosius the emperor to swallow the only bit of flattery, the enormous lie about his Greek learning and his Latinity. The Theodosius addressed, the argument concludes, must be rather Theo-

---

[1] The four (of the nineteen manuscripts containing the epistle) are Reg. 208 of the ninth century; Reg. 1424 of the tenth or eleventh century; Bodl. Rawl. G. 111 and Medic. Plut. lxviii.24 of the eleventh century. Readings of manuscripts are cited or quoted from photostatic copies in the library of the University of Illinois. The epistle above is quoted, though I have modified the punctuation, from Guaglianone's edition (1958).

dosius Macrobius, the erudite author of the *Saturnalia* and the commentary on the *Somnium Scipionis,* and the fabulist someone friendly enough to address him so.[2]

And who might this someone have been? Seven Avianus manuscripts speak, in incipit or title, of the author as *Avienus* (or, in the genitive, *Avieni*), and one has *Fabulae Aviani Festi.*[3] Stylistic considerations make it quite clear, however, that Rufus Festus Avienus, the author of the *Aratea* and the *Descriptio orbis terrae,* cannot have written the fables as well. In Macrobius' *Saturnalia* there appears briefly another Avienus, an *adulescentulus,* who used to look to some as if he might be the fabulist;[4] but the overwhelming preponderance of *Avianus* (or *Aviani*) in the manuscripts, including the best and the oldest, presents great difficulty. Similarly it has been suggested that the fabulist may have been an Avianius, a much commoner name; but in all the fable manuscripts there is no trace of *Avianius* (or *Avianii*).[5]

The title page of Cannegieter's edition of 1731 attributes the fables to Flavius Avianus, the name Flavius being a restoration, the editor tells us, "ex Codicibus vetustis quos inspexerunt Barthius & Vossius."[6] At the end of the eighteenth century Johann Christian Wernsdorf maintained[7] that Avianus' name was probably Flavius

[2] See Robinson Ellis' edition (1887), p. xiv, for an alignment of scholars in the identification of Theodosius. J. Wight and Arnold M. Duff in their edition (Loeb *Minor Latin Poets,* 1934), p. 680, identify the Theodosius as "probably Macrobius Theodosius." Arnold M. Duff, *OCD* s.v. Avianus, writes, presumably under admonitions of brevity: "he dedicated his forty-two fables . . . to Macrobius Theodosius."

[3] *Avienus* or *Avieni* in Reg. 208 of the ninth century; Vat. Lat. 3799 of the tenth century; Bodl. Rawl. G. 111, Paris Lat. 8093, and Medic. Plut. lxviii.24 of the eleventh century; Leiden Voss. L. O. 89 of the twelfth century; Pal. 1573 of the thirteenth century. *Aviani Festi* in Bodl. Auct. F. 2.14 of the early twelfth century. It would seem that the curious, possibly the scribes themselves in some instances, were assigning the fables to someone with whose name or work they were familiar.

[4] So Ellis in his edition (1887), p. xiv, as a "hypothesis," although he continues throughout to use the traditional name.

[5] L. Aurelius Avianius Symmachus Phosphorius, father of Quintus Aurelius Symmachus, in spite of a reputation for *eloquentia* and *doctrina,* wrote faulty verse, as Avianus did not. He can hardly be considered, then, as author of the fables. See Seeck, *RE* 4A (1931), 1142–44 (= Symmachus 14).

[6] P. 262, in Cannegieter's *Dissertatio* following text and commentary. Kaspar Barth's codex of Avianus has been lost, and none of the extant Vossiani of Avianus has *Flavius,* abbreviated or in full, preceding *Avianus*—if indeed we are to assume that Barth and Voss owned the manuscripts in which they found the unusual readings.

[7] *Poetae Latini minores* (5 vols., 1780–99) v, 670 = *Poetae Latini minores ex*

Avianus, since there is a character in Macrobius' *Saturnalia* named Flavianus (of whose identity Wernsdorf was apparently ignorant), "atque id in codicibus antiquis fabularum repertum perperam in duo nomina Flavii Aviani distractum est." Nearly a century after Wernsdorf, Albert Villeneuve pointed out [8] that it was by no means certain that the name Flavius belonged to Avianus, that in fact it had been suggested that the letters F and L which "précèdent dans toutes les anciennes éditions le nom d'Avianus" could in fact have been part of the name of the fabulist, who would then have been Flavianus instead of Flavius Avianus. Villeneuve does not reveal his source for information about early editions, but in fact no known extant manuscripts, and no editions except that of Cannegieter, have *FL,* or *Flavius,* or *Flavii,* preceding *Avianus,* or *Aviani.* Villeneuve did not pursue the identity of his suggested Flavianus; and there, so far as I can discover, the matter rested.

Virius Nicomachus Flavianus,[9] who is called, except in two inscriptions, simply Flavianus, was born about 334. He was a first cousin of Quintus Aurelius Symmachus, ninety-one of whose letters to him are still extant.[10] Flavianus attained the senatorial *munera,* was taken into the *collegium* of the *pontifices,* and in 364 or 365 was named *consularis Siciliae.* His next office, the vicariate of Africa, did not come to him until 376, probably because he remained a pagan. Even after this, several edicts were directed against him, all in the matter of his paganism, and under Gratian he received no more offices. There are no traces of Christianity in the fables of Avianus.

With the accession of Theodosius I, Flavianus was reinstated. Apparently what attracted Theodosius was Flavianus' highly praised scholarship and a literary reputation which he had acquired during his retirement from public life. Flavianus had come to be consid-

---

recensione Wernsdorfiana, in *Bibliotheca classica Latina* ed. N. E. Lemaire, cxxxix (1825), 45.

[8] Albert Villeneuve, *Mém. de l'Acad. des Sciences Inscr. et Belles Lettres de Toulouse,* Ser. 8, Vol. v, 1st sem. (1883), p. 98.

[9] Seeck, *RE* 6 (1909), 2506–11 (= Flavianus 14), presents a great deal more detail than my summary, including references for Flavianus in Macrobius, Symmachus and others.

[10] Book 2 of the *Epistulae* (Symmachus, ed. Seeck, 1883). Amid all the literary matters mentioned, there is nothing specific which might even suggest that Flavianus wrote a collection of fables. Seeck's genealogical tables (p. xl of his edition of Symmachus, col. 1143 of his *RE* Symmachus article) help to clarify the intermarriages among the Symmachi, the Flaviani, and other prominent families.

ered an authority on augural procedure and prophecy. No doubt this phase of his activity, being rather obviously pagan, interested Theodosius little. But it may be significant that in Macrobius' *Saturnalia,* in contrast to the shadowy *adulescentulus* Avienus, Flavianus, renowned in the technique of augury, is granted considerable space to interpret and expound the theological wisdom of Vergil. The fables, though written in Ovidian elegiacs, are full of Vergilian echoes; they have been rightly called the most Vergil-saturated work of antiquity. Perhaps Flavianus was accorded such prominence in the *Saturnalia* for two reasons, his scholarship in matters of ritual and a long-standing fondness for Vergil.

Flavianus' known writings, all of which have been lost, would have been more likely to attract Theodosius. A close friend of the philosopher Eustathius, he edited a book *De dogmatibus philosophorum* and translated Philostratus' life of Apollonius of Tyana. He wrote a treatise on grammar, *De consensu nominum et verborum.* His greatest work was his history, *Annales,* which, as far as it went, was Ammianus Marcellinus' chief source, and which was dedicated to Theodosius.

Flavianus was called to Theodosius' court and was made *quaestor sacri palatii.* He was influential enough to procure the proconsulate of Asia for his older son, Nicomachus Flavianus, who married the daughter of Symmachus, and for his younger son Venustus the administration of an Italian province; in 383 he was himself promoted to the position of *praefectus praetorio Italiae Illyrici et Africae.* In 389 we find his cousin, even the important Quintus Aurelius Symmachus, asking Flavianus to use his influence with Theodosius by personally reading a letter to the emperor. In 391 the pagan Symmachus was designated consul by the Christian Theodosius, and it is generally agreed that his cousin had something to do with the appointment. Flavianus was certainly a man who, given the auspicious occasion, might feel bold enough to address the emperor with nothing more honorific than *Theodosi optime.*

The statement that Theodosius surpasses the Athenians in Greek learning and the Romans in Latinity is not only excessively adulatory; Theodosius was in fact frequently accused of lacking erudition. If we refuse to allow the fabulist an outright tactical lie, or perhaps indulgence in a private joke between personal friends, may we not grant that he may have intended his words in what we may call a passive sense, that Theodosius admired intellectual accomplishments

Plate I. 35A, fol. 35b, Epist. 1-5. Bibliothèque Nationale, Paris. Nouv. acq. lat. 1132, fol. 35r

in others, that he was, by his generous patronage, a scholar by proxy? Sextus Aurelius Victor tells us [11] that it was a part of Theodosius' nature *simplicia ingenia aeque diligere, erudita mirari, sed innoxia.* These qualities certainly describe the fables; perhaps their author knew the emperor and his tastes well.

The further life of Flavianus need not concern us here, for in 394 he deserted Theodosius to follow the usurper Eugenius, because his prophetic vision told him that Eugenius would be victorious and Christianity disappear. In the battle which followed, when he saw that his pagan gift had betrayed him, he committed suicide.

These may be only interesting coincidences in the life of Flavianus, and it is impossible to circumvent Theodosius Macrobius' erudition; the fabulist's flatteries, if addressed to Macrobius, are essentially true, even if somewhat exaggerated. There is, however, one further bit of evidence.

The only extant illustrated manuscript of Avianus, Nouv. acq. lat. 1132 in the Bibliothèque Nationale in Paris, of the late ninth or early tenth century, is a fragment containing only the epistle and the first ten fables. Art historians, most recently Adolf Goldschmidt, have declared that the illustrations are derived from work of the fourth century.[12] Fortunately the illustration preceding the epistle to Theodosius is preserved (see Plate I), but unfortunately the problem is not thereby solved; it is made more complex.

The simple illustration shows two men; not a hint of a letter identifies them. The man at the left has curly hair but no beard; he wears a garment enveloping him from neck to ankles, and shoes; he is seated on a decorated rectangular bench. The man at the right, slightly lower, has bobbed hair and a beard; he is nude to the waist except for his garment which covers his left shoulder and arm, and he is barefoot; he sits in a wicker wingback chair of the type familiar in fourth-century commemorative sculpture; in his extended bare right arm he holds a scroll. According to Goldschmidt, the recipient is Theodosius Macrobius, the older of the two men, since he has a full beard and bobbed hair; he is "clearly the more noble one." Since he holds the scroll, he has just received it. The younger beardless man is, then, the poet. Goldschmidt has assumed a younger unknown poet, in social status inferior to the recipient of his poems.

[11] Sextus Aurelius Victor, *Epitome* 48.
[12] Adolf Goldschmidt, *An early manuscript of the Aesop fables of Avianus and related manuscripts* (1947), pp. 4–9, Pl. 1.

If the two men are rather Flavianus and Macrobius, the matter of age and protocol is not so simple. Then indeed a bearded, presumably older, Flavianus, who, according to Goldschmidt, "like an ancient philosopher or poet . . . sits with crossed legs," must be just about to present a scroll to a younger Macrobius: for Macrobius must have been somewhat younger than Flavianus. If, however, the two men are Flavianus and Theodosius I, then Goldschmidt has undoubtedly reversed poet and recipient: Flavianus, "like an ancient philosopher" (versed in Vergil and augury), still holds the scroll which he is about to present to a man whose coiffure, beardlessness, and garb make him resemble the incontestably identified Theodosius I of the Madrid Missorium,[13] whose appearance is so like that of other emperors of approximately the same period, such as the well-known colossal Constantine of the Conservatori in Rome. At any rate, the bearded figure of the Paris manuscript bears no resemblance to the Madrid Theodosius. If this is true, then, Goldschmidt to the contrary, garb and appearance are no indications of relative age of the two men: Flavianus and Theodosius I must have been very nearly the same age. Theodosius seems never to have been represented with a beard; I can find no evidence of whether either Flavianus or Theodosius Macrobius was bearded or clean-shaven, nor in fact of whether the original illustrator knew anything about the physical appearance or even the identity of the men whose portraits he drew.

If, however, beardlessness does indicate youth, then the search for Avianus, the evidence and the arguments, might be continued another generation or so, and well in to the fifth century. Could the beardless man be the younger Theodosius II, who died in 450? [14] If so, then the poet might be the younger Flavianus, who was first married before 383, but lived until at least 432.[15] The few words of

[13] H. P. L'Orange, *Studien zur Geschichte des spätantiken Porträts* (1933), Pl. 171 (from Delbrück, *Consulardiptychen*, Pl. 62). Even though the sculptured head (L'Orange Pl. 178) from the Theodosius Obelisk at Istanbul is badly mutilated, it appears to bear some resemblance, at least in coiffure, to the beardless figure in Nouv. acq. lat. 1132; but the identification of the Istanbul head as Theodosius is quite uncertain.

[14] We may even rest a little more comfortably, perhaps, in the matter of the Greek learning and the Latinity of the younger Theodosius. At any rate no one seems to have belittled his education.

[15] For the younger Flavianus, see Seeck, *RE* 6 (1909), 2511-13 (= Flavianus 15). The son is commonly referred to as Nicomachus or, like his father, as simply Flavianus. Symmachus' eighty-one letters (Bk. 6, ed. Seeck) to the younger branch of the family (the younger Flavianus married Symmachus' daughter)

the epistle and the considerations of style in the fables themselves remain the same.

It is my hypothesis—which I insist can be only that, in view of the inconclusive evidence, and which I admit is merely a synthesis of earlier partial hypotheses—that the *Fabulae Aviani* were written by Flavianus, probably the older of the two prominent men of that name at the end of the fourth century, and were presented to an emperor Theodosius, probably Theodosius I. Beyond that, *non liquet.* But if the author was Flavianus, then certainly one can understand why this small collection might have been handsomely illustrated,[16] as a de luxe edition, possibly even in a single copy for private use by the emperor only, a book which as a part of the imperial library would be more likely to survive. Could this have been the first quirk of fate which allowed such a mediocre effort to become in the Middle Ages the schoolbook second only to the *Disticha Catonis* in popularity?

The Ohio State University
5 March 1966

[It is with deep regret and a keen sense of loss that we here record the sudden and unexpected death of William Robert Jones on August 6, 1968.
—The Editorial Committee]

---

mention nothing which might refer specifically to fables or the fable collection. Werner Hartke's attempt (*Klio,* Beiheft 45, 1940) to attribute the *Historia Augusta* to the younger Flavianus and the last years of the fourth century leads us once again up a blind alley. The biographical coincidences which strike us for the father are missing for the son. Furthermore, if the younger Flavianus addressed his collection of fables to the older Theodosius, then he probably did so before his father deserted the emperor in 394.

16 Even before Omont called attention (*Bibl. de l'Ec. des Chartes,* LXXXIII [1922], 5–10) to the Paris illustrated Avianus, it was clear that there must have been early illustrated copies of the fables. In many Avianus manuscripts, especially the oldest, individual fables have no titles at all; what titles there are do not follow the general textual affiliations of the manuscripts in which they appear, as if they had been added by copyists to supply a deficiency in archetype or archetypes. Codex 1396 in the Stiftsbibliothek at St. Gall (eleventh or twelfth century), which is allied textually with the oldest extant manuscripts, of the ninth century, has large spaces between fables, but no titles.

ΤΑ ΣΧΕΔΗ ΤΟΥ ΜΥΟΣ:
NEW SOURCES AND TEXT

John-Theophanes Papademetriou

This paper presents three codices, unrecognized so far, which contain the *Schedê tou Myos*,[1] and which contribute considerably to the establishment of a better text. Since this interesting small work has been known and edited on the basis of only two manuscripts,

[1] As the title implies, the work falls into the genre of *schedos* which became very popular in the later centuries of the Byzantine Empire. Du Cange defines the genre thus: " Σχέδος, artis Grammaticae pars ea dicta quam Latini inferioris aevi *Partes* appellant: qua scilicet docentur pueri orationem per *partes* ac verba singula examinare," *Glossarium ad Scriptores Mediae et Infimae Graecitatis*, columns 1503-4; under *schedos* and its derivatives Du Cange cites numerous references in Byzantine Greek authors including one to Anna Comnena (see *Alexias*, ed. B. Leib, vol. III [Paris, 1945], xv, 7, 9, p. 218) in which she seems to imply that the art of schedography was invented during her time. It has been shown, however, that schedography was already flourishing in the early eleventh century; see the discussion and bibliography in Fr. Fuchs, *Die höheren Schulen von Konstantinopel im Mittelalter (Byzantinisches Archiv*, VIII [1926; reprinted Amsterdam, 1964], 44 ff. and 49 ff. and esp. 45, n. 8).
Concerning the nature of schedography see Fuchs (above) and S. D. Papadimitriu, Θεодоръ Продромъ. Историко-литературное изслѣдованіе (Odessa, 1905), pp. 413-36 (see the review by E. Kurtz, *BZ*, XVI [1907], 289-300); also R. Devreesse, *Introduction a l'étude des manuscrits grecs* (Paris, 1954), p. 219; K. Krumbacher, *Geschichte der byzantinischen Litteratur*[2] (München, 1897; repr. New York, 1958), I, 590-93, where older works on the subject are listed; G. Schirò, "La schedografia a Bisanzio nei secoli XI-XII e la scuola dei SS. XL. Martiri," in the *Bollettino della Badia greca di Grottaferrata*, N.S. III (1949), 11-29. Information on various *schedê* is scattered in many manuscript catalogues and also in scholarly studies such as: R. Browning, " The Patriarchal School at Constantinople in the Twelfth Century," *Byzantion*, XXXII (1962), 167-202, and XXXIII (1963), 11-40; N. B. Tomadakis, " Βυζαντινὴ Ὁρολογία. Α'. Ἐκκλησιαστικά τινα βιβλία," *Athena*, LXI (1957), 3-16 and esp. 9-10; S. G. Mercati, " Giambi di Giovanni Tzetze contro una donna schedografa," *BZ*, XLIV (1951), 416-18; C. Gallavotti, " Μονῳδία εἰς τὸν κυρὸν Θεόδωρον τὸν Πρόδρομον," *Studi Bizantini e Neoellenici*, IV (1935), 225; R. Reitzenstein, *Geschichte der griechischen Etymologica* (Leipzig, 1897; reprinted Amsterdam, 1964), 332-35; J. Fr. Boissonade, *Anecdota graeca e codicibus regiis descripsit annotatione illustravit*, IV (Paris, 1829; repr. Hildesheim, 1962), 366-412. A few more studies are mentioned in the notes below.

210

it seems advisable to offer below a new edition which takes into consideration both the old and the new sources. The new manuscripts presented here are:

1. Leidensis Vulcanianus 93
2. Monacensis Miscellaneus Gr. 551
3. Oxoniensis Miscellaneus Gr. 272 (Auct. T. 5. 10).

The choice of the subject of this article for this volume is not accidental, but rather reflects the fruitful influence of Ben Edwin Perry on my work. My interest in fables and late Byzantine literature dates from the time I wrote my Ph.D. thesis under his learned and generous guidance. It is indicative of his character that he has continued to take a keen interest in my work and allowed me to resort to his erudition with the same generosity which he displayed in my student years. Thus, it is a pleasurable duty to dedicate this small offering to the man without whose influence and guidance it would not have been written.

In recent years other scholars have called attention to the existence of a fable in two of the three codices without, however, any knowledge of the identity of the text or of its editions. Evelyn Jamison in her book on Admiral Eugenios of Palermo [2] pointed out that the Oxoniensis after the Greek text of the *Fables of Bidpai* [3] "concludes with a story about Cat and Mice [*sic*] which does not seem to belong to the Bidpai family of Fables." Even more recently L.-O. Sjöberg [4] noted the presence of the text in both the Oxoniensis and the Monacensis (the latter manuscript, too, includes the Greek text of *Bidpai*), but was not able to identify it. Nevertheless, Sjöberg concurs with Jamison, although he does not refer to her work, in

---

[2] Evelyn Jamison, *Admiral Eugenios of Sicily, His Life and Work and the Authorship of the Epistola ad Petrum and the Historia Hugonis Falcandi Siculi.* Published for the British Academy, Oxford University Press (London, 1957), p. 13, n. 1.

[3] For the Greek text of the *Fables of Bidpai* and relevant bibliography, see my dissertation, *Studies in the Manuscript Tradition of Stephanites kai Ichnelates,* (Urbana, 1960) (distributed in Xerox copies by University Microfilms, Inc., Ann Arbor, Mich.); also, my article "The Sources and the Character of *Del Governo de' Regni,*" *TAPA,* xcii (1961), 422-39; also, Sjöberg's book, mentioned below, n. 4. The most complete text was edited by Vittorio Puntoni, ΣΤΕ-ΦΑΝΙΤΗΣ ΚΑΙ ΙΧΝΗΛΑΤΗΣ, *quattro recensioni della versione Greca del Kitāb Kalilah wa-Dimnah* (the Arabic title in Arabic characters), in the *Pubblicazioni della Società Asiatica Italiana,* ii (Roma-Firenze-Torino, 1889).

[4] Lars-Olof Sjöberg, *Stephanites und Ichnelates, Überlieferungsgeschichte und Text* (translated into German by Hans-Georg Richert), *Acta Universitatis Upsaliensis, Studia Graeca Upsaliensia,* ii (Stockholm-Göteborg-Uppsala, 1962), 35-36.

considering it as independent from the text of *Bidpai*. Furthermore, he adds (p. 36) that "der Text ist, so weit ich weiß, unveröffentlicht." The existence of the text in the Leidensis has passed unnoticed probably because the latest cataloguer, at least, seems to have confused it with the text of *Bidpai* to which it is appended in the manuscript.[5]

The text, however, has undergone three editions and Krumbacher also accords it an extensive summary in his handbook.[6] The *editio princeps* was made by J. Fr. Boissonade in 1829 [7] on the basis of Parisinus Gr. 2652, a fifteenth-century manuscript [8] which Boissonade considered a *codex unicus*, as indeed it was for a long time. Boissonade attributed the work to Theodoros Prodromos, relying on the title of the text in his manuscript. Boissonade's text was reprinted with only a few alterations (recorded below in the *apparatus criticus*) by K. N. Sathas in 1894.[9] The last edition of the text was made in 1905 by K. Horna,[10] who discovered the text in another and older manuscript, Vaticanus Gr. 711, dating from the end of the fourteenth century,[11] and used it as the basis of his edition. In establishing his text Horna availed himself of Boissonade's emendations and of the text of Parisinus, which he knew from a collation of H. Omont.[12] Horna's work improved the text considerably and showed that each of the two parts of the text was concluded by a few dodecasyllabic verses. Boissonade, working with a more corrupt text, had mistaken the verses for prose. In Horna's manuscript neither Prodromos nor anyone else is credited with the composition of *Schedê* and this led Horna to dispute the generally accepted attribution of the work to Th. Prodromos. Moreover, he pointed

---

[5] P. C. Molhuysen, *Bibliothecae Universitatis Leidensis Codices Manuscripti, I. Codices Vulcaniani* (Leyden, 1910), in describing Codex Vulcanianus 93 (pp. 36-37), states that fols. 1-112ᵛ contain the text of *Stephanites*. In fact, however, *Stephanites* ends near the bottom of fol. 109ʳ; the text of *Schedê* follows immediately and continues through fol. 112ᵛ with no indication in the codex that a different text starts.

[6] K. Krumbacher, II, 757.

[7] J. Fr. Boissonade, *Anecdota graeca e codicibus regiis*, I, 429-35.

[8] H. Omont, *Inventaire sommaire des manuscrits grecs de la Bibliothèque Nationale et des autres bibliothèques de Paris et des Départements, III. Ancien fonds grec* (Paris, 1888), 19.

[9] K. N. Satha, Μεσαιωνικὴ Βιβλιοθήκη ἢ Συλλογὴ 'Ανεκδότων Μνημείων τῆς 'Ελληνικῆς 'Ιστορίας, Vol. VII (Venice, 1894), pp. ριδ'-ριξ'.

[10] K. Horna, *Analekten zur byzantinischen Literatur*, (Wien, 1905), pp. 12-16.

[11] See R. Devreesse, *Codices Vaticani Graeci, III. Codices 604-866* (Vatican, 1950), p. 196.

[12] Horna, p. 14.

out that in terms of style, the *Schedê* does not follow the manner of Prodromos, but rather that of Manasses and his imitators.[13] Finally, Horna maintained that a whole lengthy paragraph which occurs both in the *Schedê* and in a work of Manasses—*Ecphrasis Telluris*—indicates that the same person must have written both literary works.[14] Thus, Horna concluded that Manasses was the most likely author of the *Schedê*. The problem of the authorship has been discussed subsequently by other scholars and more recently by S. G. Mercati.[15] The various views, however, fall outside the scope of this paper. Suffice it to note here that the whole case for Prodromos has rested on the evidence of the title in the Parisinus which reads τοῦ σοφωτάτου κυροῦ θεοδώρου τοῦ προδρόμου σχέδη μυός.[16] In the three new manuscripts, however, no mention is made of Prodromos or of any other author.

The character of the text has also been a disputed point. Boissonade viewed it as a "tenuissimum opusculum" written as an exercise for scholastic purposes. Krumbacher saw it as a humorous parody of Holy Scripture and calls it *Maushumoreske,* an appellation that reappears as the title of Horna's study. Sathas considers it as the key to the satirical play of Prodromos, *Galeomachia.* Mercati and Festa [17] deny the satirical character of the work and point to its very title and to the introductions preceding its two

[13] Horna first presented his views before his edition of the *Schedê* in a footnote to his article, "Das Hodoiporikon des Konstantin Manasses," *BZ*, XIII (1904), 324, n. 1.

[14] There is indeed such a repetition indicated in the *Apparatus Criticus* below. The first to observe it was P. Maas, "Rhythmisches zu der Kunstprosa des Konstantinos Manasses," *BZ*, XI (1902), 511, n. 1. Maas, however, suggested a different conclusion from Horna, namely, that Manasses had plagiarized Prodromos.

[15] S. G. Mercati, "Intorno agli ΣΧΕΔΗ ΜΥΟΣ," *Studi Bizantini*, II (Roma, 1927), 13-17. See now, however, Hunger's work listed at the end of n. 18 (p. 218).

[16] It may be useful for future students of the *Schedê* and save them unnecessary doubts to note here that in the photographs of the Parisinus originally studied for this paper, absolutely no trace of title or name of author appears at the top of the text. It was only because scholars of the erudition of Boissonade, Omont, Mercati and Horna have either asserted or implied the existence of a title that I felt compelled to examine the codex itself. Indeed, at the very top of fol. 110, above even the folio number, the title and author appear in faded red characters which somehow failed to make even a trace on the photographs. The substance of the inscription on top of the text is repeated in the index of the manuscript written by a more recent hand: θεοδώρου τοῦ πτοχοπροδρόμου σχέδη μυός.

[17] Mercati, "Intorno . . . ," pp. 13-17; N. Festa, "Note preliminari su Longibardos," *BZ*, XVI (1907), 452.

parts as proof that it is merely a scholastic exercise to be used in the classroom.

Mercati and Festa, however, in opposing Krumbacher's and Horna's view of the *Schedê* as *Maushumoreske,* create an issue where none need exist. There is no doubt that, as Boissonade had already pointed out, the *Schedê* has the form and the purpose of a school exercise. The very title *Schedê* leaves no doubt. But there is also no reason why a school exercise cannot be a satirical work of literary merit. This is clearly the case here. A variety of circumstances can become the occasion for the creation of a literary work and here a school exercise has provided it. Even a casual reading of the text reveals the intent of the author to construct an amusing dialogue by placing in an unexpected humorous context scriptural texts familiar from their liturgical use, but with enough taste to avoid unpleasant shock or sacrilege. Humor arises in a typical fashion from the absurdity of the situation and the contrast with the solemn language employed. Further entertainment is achieved by the exalted language the Mouse uses to describe its condition (ll. 25-36) and by occasional words which to the ear have double meaning or by puns (e.g., ll. 52-53, 81, 83). That this entertainment is offered in the form of a school exercise is rather a compliment to the ingenuity of the author than cause for a scholarly dispute.[18]

[18] It is perhaps strange that no one has attempted to define the scholastic purposes of the work. If it is a *schedos,* what is it supposed to teach? The answer to the question has to be speculative but such speculation may contribute to the solution of the problem of the authorship. The problems that a student would have to solve seem to be largely similar to those which confront the editor. The students could have been expected to recognize the few verses that conclude the prose in both parts of the *Schedê;* they could also be drilled on some rare words included in the text such as υἱωτο in line 50. But the main problem would be to recognize and identify the numerous literary allusions and quotations contained in the text—not an easy task, as evidenced by the increase of such identifications in each successive edition of the *Schedê,* including the present one. If this is so, then the presence in *Schedê* of a whole passage from *Ecphrasis Telluris* of Manasses is no plagiarism and anybody could have decided that its inclusion was legitimate and, indeed, an indirect sign of the author's esteem for Manasses. Of course, Manasses too could have elected to use a paragraph from one of his earlier works. In either case no question of plagiarism is involved. Yet many of the arguments concerning the authorship of the work rest on the issue of plagiarism (see a summary of the various arguments in Mercati, n. 15, above).

A moral lesson too, although not a profound one, may also be drawn from the *Schedê.* The final argument of the Cat before devouring the Mouse is, in substance, "since you are a monk I might have spared you if you were wearing your special garb; now, though, that you have come out without it I will devour

The five manuscripts which preserve the *Schedē* do not present a uniform tradition. The oldest one, the Vaticanus (=V),[19] seems to contain the best text in most cases although not in all. Its closest congener is the Monacensis (=M), which dates from the fifteenth century.[20] The Monacensis, however, contains a far less trustworthy text because it has clearly undergone a deliberate revision in which it suffered certain losses and underwent linguistic revision. Thus, the entire proem to the second *schedos* (ll. 47-48), which all the other codices preserve, is missing and as a result the two parts are fused into one continuous text. In terms of specific readings, M often presents an incorrect variant radically different from the reading of the other manuscripts. The following examples illustrate the point:

Line
429,2   παραβολήν M: συσσίτιον ceteri codd.
431,5   τροφαῖς M: τρυφαῖς   "   "
433,17   σφόδρα M: τέλους   "   "

Some other examples of the same kind appear in lines 430,8; 431,4; 432,7; 432,15; etc. (see the *apparatus criticus*).

There are also a few omissions in M which do not occur in the other manuscripts; e.g., in line 435,6, M omits the phrase ἀπὸ τῆς κέλλης σου which all the other manuscripts preserve. Occasionally, M gives a better reading where all the other manuscripts seem to err; e.g., in line 435,3, M reads μοναχικήν where the reading of the other manuscripts μοναδικήν makes no sense.

The kinship between M and V is not such as to allow us to consider them copies of the same manuscript. As the stemma below indicates, at least one intermediate link must have intervened between M and its common ancestor with V. The effect of deliberate revision lessens the value of M for the reconstruction of the text but does not cancel it completely. Where M agrees with V it is obvious

you." Would not this be a simple and humorous way of giving a lesson to young monks who wore civilian clothes outside the school compound? If this view is accepted, then the author would be more likely to have been a master in a school for young monks or novices. However, if the moral suggested above is not the one intended, then the fable has no moral and this would be a most unusual instance for that period. [Note 18 continued on p. 218.]

[19] For the text of V, I have relied totally on Horna's collation (verified by S. G. Mercati) as presented through his edition. MLO I have studied in photographs.

[20] See I. Hardt, *Catalogus codicum manuscriptorum Bibliothecae Regiae Bavaricae*, v (München, 1812), 378.

that the reading represents the hyparchetype from which they both descend. This is important because the preponderance of the evidence points to their hyparchetype as the better one of the two assumed in the stemma.

The Leidensis (=L), written in the fifteenth century, presents striking similarities with the Oxoniensis (=O), a manuscript of the sixteenth century.[21] A close examination of the two codices has revealed beyond any reasonable doubt that O is a copy of L and, therefore, its variants may be excluded from the *apparatus* of the text. L contains nineteen corrections *in margine* which were written by a second hand and, actually, the same one that wrote O. All the corrections except one are almost purely orthographical. Although both L and O contain numerous misspellings (as a rule the same ones in both manuscripts) the spelling of the words as corrected in the margin of L is exactly the spelling with which they appear in O regardless of whether it is better or not. The one correction which is a little more serious concerns the very first occurrence in L of the word αἰλουρὶς (= feminine form) which is corrected in the margin into αἴλουρος (= masculine form). In O the word appears throughout the text [22] as ὁ αἴλουρος and this change of gender accounts for a series of differences between L and O. Naturally, the scribe of O had to use the masculine forms in all cases where feminine forms in L modified the word ἡ αἰλουρίς. Furthermore, O contains at least two errors that could not have arisen in any other way except in the process of copying L. On fol. 110ʳ of L, in the passage corresponding to 429,8, the initial two letters of what should have been the word ὀσμὴ have been completely obliterated. As a result the passage as it reads in L has absolutely no meaning. Nevertheless, the same corrupt reading appears only in O. Also, on fol. 111ʳ of L, in the passage corresponding to 431,15, the ι of the phrase καὶ ἑξῆς has been distorted by excessive ink in such a way that it strongly resembles a θ and thus the phrase appears as if it were καθεξῆς, which is precisely the reading that O contains. Finally, the texts of L and O are almost identical even in spelling. All the deviations of O from

21 See H. O. Coxe, *Catalogi codicum Manuscriptorum Bibliothecae Bodleianae, pars prima recensionem codicum Graecorum continens* (Oxford, 1853), 814.

22 There are some exceptions to this rule. Influenced, obviously, by his exemplar (=L) the copyist wrote sometimes αἰλουρὶς as on fol. 142ʳ in the passage corresponding to line 61, and other times he wrote as on fol. 142ᵛ (line 73) κυρία (as L reads) instead of κύριε which consistency on his part would have required.

the text of L are of minor character and all of them can be easily explained as usual copyist's errors or as slight "improvements" effected by the scribe of O, who had displayed in the margin of L his penchant for "improvements." Under these circumstances we may safely consider O as a copy of L and not belabor the point by citing the very numerous cases where the two manuscripts give a common reading clearly different from the one preserved in the rest of the codices. For this reason we may exclude from the *apparatus criticus* not only the variants of O but also the marginalia of L.[23]

The value of L for the establishment of the text of the *Schedê* lies primarily in the fact that it represents a distinctly different line of tradition from V and M. There are no serious lacunae, as in M, and there is a host of readings that differ greatly from the readings of V or M. Unfortunately, however, the text of L has suffered deterioration, as indicated by its many obviously incorrect readings (see the *apparatus criticus*). The mistakes of L cannot be attributed to its copyist. The abundant mispellings and the retention of readings which make no sense but would be easy to correct (e.g., 432,11 ἔφης instead of ἔφη; 430,18 μεγαληγορῶς instead of μεγαληγορῶν; 433.14 ἀνεστόμα instead of ἀνὰ στόμα) show that the scribe was not well educated and copied what he saw without attempting to improve it.

The variants of L agree more often with the Parisinus than with V or M. Despite its mistakes, L is still a useful source providing confirmation of the reading of the other codices and, where they differ, assisting in the selection of the genuine reading. On some rare occasions L seems to preserve the best reading (e.g., l. 432,1).

The last manuscript to be dealt with is the Parisinus (= P), which dates from the fifteenth century. P is a valuable source for the text, preserving many correct readings not found in V, M, or L. Its closest relative among the extant manuscripts seems to be L, but the relation is not very close. There are readings suggesting that P and L had a remote common hyparchetype. Such is the error in 431,13 where P and L read χαίτας while V and M read τρίχας. The evidence is, however, inconclusive and the place given to P in the stemma below is tentative.

From the above discussion of the manuscripts of *Schedê* it becomes evident that the best one is V. The superiority of V, however, is

---

[23] The demonstration of O as a copy of L has a bearing also upon the problem of the provenance of O and upon the Greek text of *Bidpai* included in both codices. These subjects, however, will be examined in another paper.

not such as to eliminate the need to weigh carefully the evidence of the other codices whenever they differ from V. In the text printed below, the reading of V has usually been retained, particularly when confirmed by either P or L which represent the other branch in the transmission of the text. In numerous instances, however, the reading of one or more of the other codices has been adopted.

As a conclusion to this discussion of the manuscript tradition of *Schedê* the following stemma is suggested:

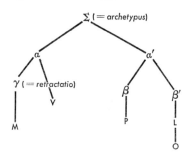

NOTES: Σ = archetype; α = a descendant of Σ which is the hyparchetype of γ and V; α′ = a manuscript (= hyparchetype) intervening between the archetype Σ and the exemplars of P and L; β = the exemplar of P; β′ = a manuscript or series of manuscripts from which L descends; γ = the exemplar of M in which the *retractatio* preserved in M was made.

CONSPECTUS SIGLORUM

L = Codex Leidensis Vulcanianus 93, fols. 109^v-112^v, saec. XV

M = Codex Monacensis Miscellaneus Gr. 551, fols. 99^v-101^r, saec. XV

(O = Oxoniensis Miscellaneus Gr. 272, fols. 140^v-143^r, saec. XVI. Cf. *infra*, n. 24)

P = Parisinus Graecus 2652, fols. 110^r-114^v, saec. XV

V = Vaticanus Graecus 711, fols. 72^r-77^v, saec. XIV exeuntis

/ = spatium litterae

+ = littera erasa

[Note 18 *continued* from p. 215.]

On the satirical element of the *Schedê* we now have also the stimulating analysis of H. Hunger in *Der byzantinische Katz-Mäuse-Krieg: Theodoros Prodromos, Katomyomachia. Einleitung, Text und Übersetzung*, in the series *Byzantina Vindobonensia, herausgegeben vom Kunsthistorischen und dem Institut für Byzantinistik der Universität Wien* (III [Graz-Wien-Köln, 1968], 59-60). Hunger's book appeared while this article was in page proof and could not be considered here fully. I am grateful to Prof. H.-G. Beck for calling my attention to the appearance of this interesting study.

TEXT

ΤΑ ΣΧΕΔΗ ΤΟΥ ΜΥΟΣ [24]

I

429,1 Εἰ βούλεσθε, ὦ παῖδες, τραφῆναι τήμερον λογικῶς, ἰδοὺ ὁ
μῦς ὑμῖν τὸ συσσίτιον δίδωσιν. Οἴδατε δὲ ὡς τὸ ζῷον λίχνον
ἐστὶ καὶ κατὰ τὸν Ποιητὴν ἐμβασίχυτρον.

5 Διόπερ καί που τῶν παλαιῶν τις ἄριστον κατα|σκευασάμενος καὶ   5
τοὺς ἑταίρους αὐτοῦ συγκαλέσας πρὸς ἑστίασιν ἀνεκέκλιτο· ἡ τῶν
βρωμάτων δέ, ἡ μᾶλλον εἰπεῖν, ἡ τῆς σαρκοφαγίας ὀσμὴ τὰς
10 γνάθους ὑπέσαινε τοῦ μυός. ἔνθεν τοι καὶ μετὰ τὸ τε|λεσθῆναι
τὸ ἁβρὸν ἐκεῖνο τῶν φίλων ἑστίαμα τοῖς λειψάνοις ὁ μῦς ὀξέως
ἐπέδραμε· καὶ ἐπιδραμὼν τῶν μὲν ἄλλων ὑπερεφρόνησε καὶ παρῆλ-   10
θεν ὡς ἄχρηστα καὶ ἀφῆκεν ὡς ἄβρωτα καὶ οὐδὲ βλέπειν προσ-
15 εποιήσατο, ὅλος δὲ τοῦ κρανίου τῆς τρίγλης ἐγένετο.|ἦν γὰρ ἐκεῖσε
μάλα πολλὰ καὶ διάφορα λείψανα· ἦν ἐκεῖσε καὶ γεράνου κνήμη
430,1 καὶ ῥάχις λαγὼ | καὶ πέρδικος σκέλος καὶ ἐν τοῖς ὀστέοις λεπτὰ
σαρκία περιεσῴζετο· ἦν ἐκεῖσε καὶ τρίγλης ἀγλαομόρφου κρανίον   15
καὶ τούτῳ φέρων ὁ μῦς ἐπέρριψεν ἑαυτόν. καὶ ἦν ὁμοῦ λιχνευό-
5 μενος καὶ φοβούμενος· ἅμα τὸ | στόμα ὑπήνοιγε καὶ ἅμα ὑπό-
τρομος ἀνεπόδιζεν. ἡ μὲν γαστὴρ ἤπειγεν εἰς τροφήν, τὸ δὲ δέος
ἔτρεπεν εἰς φυγήν· τὸ μὲν ὀρεκτικὸν ἀνηρέθιζεν, ἀλλ᾽ ἀντεπεῖχε
τὸ δειλοκάρδιον· ἅμα ἐπέτρεχε καὶ ἅμα ἀπέτρεχε· καὶ ὡς ἐδώδι-   20

---

1 Τὰ σχέδη τοῦ μυός. V: τοῦ σοφωτάτου κυροῦ θεοδώρου τοῦ προδρόμου σχέδη μυός P
ἀπὸ τῶν ποιητικῶν, μύθος. περὶ τοῦ μυὸς καὶ τῆς αἰλουρίδος M nullus titulus L(O) ||
2 βούλεσθαι L || σήμερον Sathas || 3 ὑμῖν τὸ συσσίτιον Boissonade: ὑμῖν τὸ
συσσίτειον V ὑμῖν τὸ συσσίον P ἡμῖν τὸ συσίτιον L τὴν παραβολὴν ὑμῖν M
οἴκαδε L || δὲ VPL: γὰρ M || 4 conf. Batrachom. v. 137 || 5 τίς τῶν παλαιῶν M ||
6 ἑτέρους VL || ἀνεκέκλιτο scripsi: ἀνακέκλιτο V Horna ἀνακέκλοιντο M
ἀνεκέκλιντο P Boissonade || 6-7 ἡ τῶν βροτῶν δὲ M τῶν
βρωμάτων δέ PL || 7 ἡ om. L || 7-8 δς μὴ τοὺς γνάθους P ++μὴ vel //μὴ τὰς
γνάθους L || ὑπέσαιμε L -σενε P || 10 ὑπέδραμε L || 12 δλος V: ὅλως cett. ||
ἐγίνετο V περιεγένετο L || ἦν γὰρ ἐκεῖσε scripsi: ἦσαν γὰρ (δ᾽ M) ἐκεῖσε VM
ἦν (γὰρ P) ἐκεῖ PL || 13 ἐκεῖσε VM ἐκεῖ PL || 14 ῥάχις λαγὼ Horna conf.
Manasses Ecphrasis Telluris 120: ῥάχις λαγωοῦ M ῥάχις λαγωοῦ ῥᾶχις V ἦν ἐκεῖ
καὶ ῥάχις(-χης L) λαγωοῦ PL || καὶ ἐν VL: καὶ M κἂν P || 15 ἦν ἐκεῖσε V: ἦν
ἐκεῖ cett. || 16 τούτῳ em. Boissonade conf. Manasses Ecphrasis Telluris 134:
τοῦτο codd. || 17 ἀπήνοιγε L || 19 ἀντεπεῖχε V: ἀνταπεῖχε (-η- Lpc) cett. ||
20 ἀπέτρεχε VP: ὑπέτρεχε M ἐπέτρεμε L || 20-21 ἐδώσημον M ||

[24] The merely orthographical errors of the manuscripts are not recorded in
the *apparatus* except for those which could conceivably be significant for the
relation of the codices. As already explained (above, p. 217), the variants of O
and the *marginalia* of L are not included. One exception was allowed in order
to record the absence of any title for *Schedê* in O.

The numbers in the left margin refer to the *editio princeps* of Boissonade.
Numbers in the *apparatus* refer to the lines of my text, indicated in the right
margin.

10 μον ἤθελε καὶ ὡς πολέμιον ἔφευγεν. ὑπώ|πτευε γάρ, μή πού τις
κατοικίδιος αἰλουρὶς τοῖς ὀστέοις ἐμπερικρύπτοιτο. ὅμως δὲ τὸ
δέος ὀψέ ποτε ἀποτιναξάμενος τῷ κρανίῳ τῆς τρίγλης ἐνέπιπτε.
καὶ ἦν ἰδεῖν τὸν μῦν ἐπιγανύμενον καὶ χορεύοντα καὶ μονονουχὶ

15 τὰ τοιαῦτα καυχώμενόν τε | καὶ λέγοντα· " Ἀρά που καὶ   25
βασιλεὺς τοιαύταις τρυφαῖς ἐναγάλλεται; καὶ ποῦ τοσαύτην παν-
δαισίαν ἀπραγματεύτως εὑρήσειε; " ταῦτά πως ὁ μῦς καθ᾽ ἑαυτὸν
μεγαληγορῶν καὶ τῇ κεφαλῇ τῆς τρίγλης περιχορεύων καὶ πυκνὰ

20 πυκνὰ τοῖς ὀδοῦσι δάκνων αὐ|τὴν καί, " Ὦ τῆς εὐτυχίας," βοῶν,
" ὅτι περ οὐδὲ τὰ τῆς θαλάττης κάλλιστά με λανθάνουσι βρώ-   30
ματα. βαβαὶ τῆς ταχυτῆτος, ἧς ἐπλούτησα, καὶ δυνάμεως, ἧς οὐδ᾽

431,1 Αἴας, οὐδ᾽ Ἀχιλλεύς, οὐδὲ Μενέ|λαοί τινες, οὐδὲ Νέστορες ηὐτύ-
χησαν πώποτε, οὓς ἡ ποίησις σοφῶς κατηγλάισε. ταῖς κορυφαῖς
τῶν μετεώρων οἰκημάτων ἀναθρῴσκων καὶ αὖθις ἐκεῖθεν ταχινῶς

5 κατερχόμενος μονονουχὶ βασιλεύω γῆς καὶ | θαλάττης καὶ πάσαις   35
ἄλλαις τρυφαῖς ὑπάρχω κατάκομος." ταῦτα λέγων ὁ δυστυχὴς
ἐκεῖνος μῦς καὶ πλείω φθεγγόμενος σοβαρῶς, ἐξαίφνης, ὅπερ
δέδοικεν, ἔπαθεν· ἡ γὰρ αἰλουρίς ποθεν ἐκπηδήσασα τοῦτον

10 συνέλαβε· καὶ οὕτω παίγνιον ταύτης ἔμ|προσθεν ὁ δείλαιος
προὔκειτο τῆς συμφορᾶς τῷ πάθει νικώμενος. καὶ ὁ πρὶν ὑπερή-   40
φανος μῦς ἀμφοτέραις χερσὶ τοῦ γενείου ἐδράττετο καὶ τὰς τοῦ
πώγονος τρίχας προρρίζους ἀνέσπα καὶ δάκρυσι τοὔδαφος ἅπαν
κατέβρεχεν.

15   Ἀλλ᾽ εἰ δοκεῖ στήσωμεν ὧδε τὸν λόγον,
        ὡς καὶ καθεξῆς μυὸς ἐκ τῶν βρωμάτων   45
        τραφῆτε, παῖδες, τῇ λογικῇ δυνάμει.

22 ἐμπερικρύπτετο P   ἐμπεριεκρύπτετο ci. Boissonade || 24 ἰδεῖν ἐκεῖσε P ||
μονονουχὶ P || 25 τὰ om. V || 26 καὶ ποῦ τις P καὶ που τίς M || 27 ἀπραγματεύτων
P || εὑρήσειε ML: ἐξεῦρε V   εὑρήσεις P   εὑρήσει vel εὑρήσειε ci.
Boissonade   εὑρήσει Sathas || 27-28 καθ᾽ ἑαυτὸν μεγαληγορῶν (-ρῶς L) VL:
μεγαληγορῶν καθ᾽ ἑαυτὸν M   πρὸς ἑαυτὸν μεγαληγορῶν P || 28 τῆς κεφαλῆς τῆς
τρίγλης M || 28-29 πυκνὰ P   πικνὰ πικνὰ M || 29 τῆς om. P || 31 ἧς alt.
VML: εἰς P || 32 εὐτήχησαν ML || 34 ταχεινὸς L ταχεινῶς V || 35 κατεχό-
μενος M || μετερχόμενος P || μονονουχὶ P || βασιλεύων V || γῆς καὶ M: καὶ cett.
|| θαλάσσης M 36 τροφαῖς M || ὑπάρχων V || κατς κοσμος P κατάκοσμος
ci. Boissonade || 37 ἐξ (ἔξ L) αἴφνης ML || 38 τούτου PL || 39 οὕτως M || 40 τὸ
πάθος L || 42 τρίχας VM: χαίτας PL || προρρίζους om. M || 44 στήσομεν P ||
45 ὡς καὶ ἑξῆς L ||

II

Ἰδοὺ καὶ σήμερον ἁβρὸν ὑμῖν τὸ ἑστίαμα ἡ τοῦ μυὸς εὐτρεπίσειε τράπεζα.

432,1 Ὡς γὰρ ἐκεῖνον εἶχεν ἐντὸς τῶν ἀρκύων ἡ αἰλουρὶς καὶ κατέ-
παιζεν, ἠρώτα τοῦτον, τίνος πατρὸς καὶ μητρὸς ὕωτο παῖς καὶ τίς   50
ὁ βίος καὶ ἡ πρᾶξις, καὶ ἁπλῶς εἰπεῖν, ἀρχῆς ἀπ᾽ ἄκρης τὰ περὶ
5 τούτου | ἠρώτα μαθεῖν. καὶ ὁ δυστυχὴς εὐθὺς συγκεκομμένῳ τῷ
ἄσθματι, " Οὐ δύναμαι, κυρία μου," ἔφη, " πλησίον ὁρῶν σε τἀμὰ
ἀτρόμῳ λόγῳ διατρανοῦν. ἀλλ᾽ εἰ βούλει, μικρὸν ἀναχώρησον καὶ
10 οὕτω φιλαλήθως ἐρῶ σοι πάντα τὰ κατ᾽ ἐμέ." ἡ δὲ | βλοσυρῶς   55
αὐτὸν βλέψασα, " Ἵνα τί, κάκιστε τῶν μυῶν," ἔφη, " δολίως
φθέγγῃ βουλόμενος ἀπατῆσαί με ; ἢ γοῦν φθέγγου τὰ σά, ἢ κατά-
βρωμα ἤδη γένῃ καὶ σπάραγμα." ὁ δ᾽ αὐτίκα δακρύων, " Ἐγώ,
15 κυρία μου," ἔφη, " Ἐλαιοπότης κικλήσκομαι, | ὁ δέ γε πατὴρ   60
Λαρδοφάγος καὶ ἡ μήτηρ Παστόλειχος." ὑπολαβοῦσα δ᾽ αὖθις ἡ
αἰλουρὶς ἠρώτα τὸν μῦν· " Καὶ τί σου τὸ τοσοῦτον δάκρυον ; καὶ
433,1 ποῦ δακρύειν μεμάθηκας ; μὴ καὶ παρ᾽ ὑμῖν εἰσιν ἀσκηταὶ προσ|ευ-
χόμενοι καὶ δακρύοντες καὶ τούτων εἷς καὶ αὐτός ; καὶ ποῦ ἡ
ἐπωμίς ἐστιν, ὅπερ λέγουσι παραμάνδυον ; ποῦ ἡ κίδαρις ; ποῦ
ὁ μανδύας ; ποῦ τὰ τῶν ποδῶν σου σανδάλια ; " ὁ δὲ μῦς ἐθέλων   65
5 | ἑαυτὸν δικαιοῦν καὶ ὅσιον ἐμφαίνειν ὡς τὰ πολλά, ὡς ἂν ἀπο-
δράσῃ τὸν κίνδυνον, " Ἐγώ, κυρία μου," ἔφη, " τῶν παρ᾽ ἡμῖν
μοναχῶν πέλω καθηγεμὼν καὶ σχήματι μεγάλῳ κοσμοῦμαι καὶ
κίδαρις ἐμοὶ καὶ μανδύας καὶ τὰ λοιπά· κανόνα δὲ τοῖς ὑπ᾽ ἐμὲ
10 | κατέστησα ἀκριβῆ, ὡς δὶς τοῦ σαββάτου εὔχεσθαί σε ὡς ἀγαθήν."   70

47-48 om. M ‖ 47 ἀμβρὸν L ‖ ὑμῖν τὸ ἑστίαμα VP: ἡμῖν τὸ ἑστίαμα L   ἡμῖν
ἑστίαμα Sathas ‖ εὐτρεπίσειε V: εὐτρεπήσειε L   εὐτρέπειε L (sed Horna et Omont
leg. εὐτρέπεισε) P   εὐτρεπίσειε Mercati ‖ 49 ὡς VPL: /ς M ‖
ἐντὸς τῶν ἀρκύων ἡ αἰλουρὶς ML: ἐντὸς σαρκίων ἡ αἰλουρὶς V   ἡ αἰλουρὶς ἐντὸς τῶν
ἀρκύων P ‖ 50 ὕωτο V: υἵατο P   πέφυκε M   ὑπάρχεις L ‖ 51 πατρὶς P ‖
εἰπεῖν om. L ‖ ἀρχῆς ἀπ᾽ ἄκρης: conf. Lycophr. Alexandra v. 2 ‖ 52 τούτων
M ‖ post δυστυχὴς add. ἐκεῖνος V Horna ‖ συγκεκομμένῳ P   συγκεκομμένω
ML ‖ 53 ἄσ/ματι L ‖ ὁρᾶν M   τὰ ἐμὰ L ‖ 54 διακενοῦν M ‖ 55 οὕτως V ‖
56 αὐτὸν VPL.: πρὸς αὐτὸν M ‖ κάκιστε VPL: ὦ κάκιστε M   ἔφης L ‖ 57
φθέγγῃ V: φθέγγη L   φθέγγει PM ‖ γοῦν VPL: τοίνυν M ‖ 58 γένῃ V: γένη
L   γίνη MP ‖ δ᾽ V: δὲ MPL ‖ 59 κικλήσκομαι V: λ (κ^{pe}) ικλή-
σκομαι   κεκλήσκομαι ML ‖ 60 ἡ δὲ μήτηρ M ‖ 61 ποῦ om. L ‖
63 τούτως M ‖ εἷς V: εἷς MP   εἷς ὑπάρχεις L ‖ 64 ὅπερ VPL: ὃ M ‖ 65
μανδύας P   μανδίας L ‖ ἐθέλων in marg. V ‖ 66 ὡς ἂν VML: ὠτὰν P ‖
ἀποδράσει L   —ση PM ‖ 69 μανδυίας P   μανδίας L ‖ κανόνα δὲ MPL: καὶ
κανόνα δὲ V ‖ 70 ἀγαθὴ M ‖

ἡ δέ, "Καὶ μεμάθηκας," φησί, "ψαλτήριον ψάλλειν καὶ εὐχὰς
ἀναπέμπειν καὶ ἄπερ πέλει τοῖς μοναχοῖς συνήθεια ἀκριβής;"

15　καὶ ὃς εὐθὺς τὸν ψαλμὸν ἀνὰ στόμα ἐλάμβανε· "Κυρία|μου, μὴ
τῷ θυμῷ σου ἐλέγξῃς με, μηδὲ τῇ ὀργῇ σου παιδεύσῃς με.
ἐκακώθην καὶ ἐταπεινώθην ἕως τέλους." καὶ αὖθις, "Ἡ καρδία　　75
μου ἐταράχθη καὶ δειλία θανάτου ἐπέπεσεν ἐπ' ἐμέ, ὅτι αἱ ἀνομίαι
20　μου ὑπερῆραν τὴν κεφαλήν μου.| ἐβραγχίασα κράζων, ὠλιγώθην
434,1　καὶ ἐσίγησα καὶ ἡ ἀλγηδών μου ἐνώπιόν μού ἐστι διὰ παντός, καὶ
οἱ φοβερισμοί σου ἐξετάραξάν με, καὶ τὰ λοιπά."

5　Ἡ δὲ αἰλουρὶς αὖθίς φησιν, "Ἐκεῖνο δὲ πῶς οὐ | ψάλλεις; τό,　80
Ἔλαιον θέλω καὶ οὐ θυσίαν, βούτυρον βοῶν καὶ γάλα προβάτων
μετὰ στέατος ἀρνῶν· καί, Ἀγαπητά μοι ταῦτα ὑπὲρ μέλι· καί,
Ἐν ἐλαίῳ πίονι ἔχρισα καὶ ἐλίπανα τὴν κεφαλήν μου, καὶ τὰ
10　ἑξῆς." ὁ δὲ ἰδών, ὅτι οὐκ ὠφελεῖ, | ἀλλὰ μᾶλλον καταγινώσκεται,
"Ταῦτα," φησίν, "ἐγώ, κυρία μου, ἐφυλαξάμην ἐκ νεότητός μου　85
καὶ οὐκ ἔφαγον οὔτε μέλι, οὔτε γάλα, οὔτε βούτυρον, ἀλλὰ μόνον
τῶν τῆς θαλάττης ἀγνῶν βραχέως καθάπτομαι, ἵνα φθάσω τῶν
ἀρετῶν τὸ ἀκρότατον." |

15　Ἡ δὲ αἰλουρὶς ταῦτά φησι; "Καὶ τίς ἄλλος, εἰ μὴ σύ, ὦ
435,1　καθηγούμενε τῶν μυῶν, τοὺς τῶν μονα|χῶν ταλάρους ἀναδιφᾷ　90
καὶ κατεσθίει ὅ, τι περ ἄρα καὶ τύχοι; τίς τὰς ἐλαιοδόχους κανδήλας
ἀποκενοῖ; καὶ εἰ μὲν τὴν μοναχικήν σου στολὴν ἐνεδέδυσο, ἐνετρά-
5　πην ἂν κἀγὼ καὶ ἐδυσωπήθην διὰ τὸ σχῆμά|σου· ἐπεὶ δ' ἄτερ τῶν
μοναχικῶν ἀμφίων σου ἐξῆλθες ἀπὸ τῆς κέλλης σου, τὸ στόμα
μου γενήσεται τάφος σου,　　　　　　　　　　　　　　95

ὡς ἂν ἐκεῖσε τῶν προσευχῶν τὰ γέρα
λήψῃ πρεπόντως, ὦ μυῶν καθηγέτα."

71 φησὶ om. MPL || 72 πέλει om. L　πέλλει MP || ἀκριβῆ PL || 73 ἀναστόμα
P　ἀνὰ τὸ στόμα MV　ἀνεστόμα L || post μου add. λέγων L || 73-74 conf.
Psalm. 6, 2 et 37, 2 || 74 ἐλέγχῃς Sathas || 75-76 conf. Psalm. 37, 7 et 9 et postea
54, 5 || 75 καὶ ἐκακώθην M || τέλους VPL: σφόδρα M || ἡ καρδία μου om. L ||
76-77 conf. Psalm. 37, 4 || 77 ἐβραγχίασα V　ἐβραχίασα cett. conf. Psalm. 68, 3
|| ὠλιγώθην L: ὀλιγώθην VM　ἐλιγώθην P　conf. Psalm. 106, 39 || 78 conf.
Psalm. 37, 18 || 78-79 καὶ οἱ VPL: καὶ om. M || 79 φοβερι/σμοῖς L　conf.
Psalm. 87, 16 || 80 ἐκεῖνο δὲ VPM: ἐκεῖ L || 81-82 conf. Ose. 6, 7 et postea
Deuter. 32, 14 || 81 ἔλεον P　ἔλεον̅ᾱⁱ M || 82 ὑπὲρ μέλι: conf. Psalm. 18, 11 ||
83 καὶ ἐν ἐλαίῳ M: καὶ ἐλαίω L　ἐν ἐλαίῳ V　ἐν ἐλέω P　conf. Psalm. 88, 21;
91, 11; 22, 6 || 84 ὠφελῇ P conf. Psalm. 88, 23 || 85 ταῦτα φησίν (-ν om. V)
ἐγὼ κυρία μου MV: ἐγὼ κυρία μου ἔφη P　ταῦτα ἔφη πάντα κυρία μου fortasse
recte L　conf. Marc. 10, 20 || 86 καὶ οὐκ ἔφαγον—ἀλλὰ VMP: καὶ οὔτε στέαρ·
οὔτε μέλι· οὔτε γάλα· οὔτε κρέας· οὔτε τυρὸν εἰσῆλθεν ἐν τῷ στόματί μου· ἀλλὰ L ||
86-87 μόνον τῶν τῆς ML: μόνων τῶν τῆς V　μόνον τῆς τῆς P || 87 ἀγνότων L ||
ἅπτομαι V　καθάπτειμαι P || 88 εἰς τὸ ἀκρότατον L || 89 τοῦτο P　αὖθις L
τούτῳ fortasse recte Boissonade || φησί om. L || σύ VMP: σὲ L || 90 τοὺς τα-
λάρους τῶν μοναχῶν M || ἀναδιφᾶς L || 91 ὅτι περ ἄρα καὶ τύχοι V: ὅτι περ ἄρα
καὶ τύχει ML　ἄρα καὶ τύχει P || τὰς τῶν ἐλαιοδόχων M || 92 μοναδικήν VPL
edd. || σου om. L || ἐνεδύσω P || 93 κἀγὼ om. M || δὲ MLP || 94 μοναχικῶν
scripsi: μοναδικῶν VPL edd. om. M || ἀπὸ τῆς κέλλης σου om. M || 95 γενήσῃ
P || 96 ὡσὰν ἐκεῖθεν M　ὡς ἂν ἐκεῖ P || τῶν προσεχόντων L || 97 λείψει P
λείψῃ̅η M

University of Colorado
4 March 1966

NICETAS OF HERACLEA AND
BYZANTINE GRAMMATICAL DOCTRINE

Antonio Tovar

In 1830, J. F. Boissonade published[1] a grammatical poem to which he gave the title Ἀνωνύμου στίχοι περὶ γραμματικῆς. He refrained from attributing it to any author, saying in a note: " Quem sit ad auctorem referendus libellus non dixerim; diuinabit alius." In studying the collections of the University of Salamanca, I was able to identify one item contained in Codex M 229 of that library with this poem,[2] and at Salamanca its title bears one of the usual forms of Nicetas of Heraclea's name: Τοῦ ἡρακλείας.[3] τῶν συντάξεων τῶν

[1] J. F. Boissonade, *Anecdota graeca e codicibus regiis*, II (Paris, 1830; repr. Hildesheim 1962), pp. 340-93. Boissonade took his text from two Paris MSS, 2599 fol. 4 ff. and 1630 fol. 255 ff. (in this last, the sections on prepositions, ll. 724-1055, are omitted).

[2] *Catalogus codicum Graecorum Uniuersitatis Salamantinae* (Acta Salmanticensia, 1963), p. 44; cf. Chr. Baur, *Initia Patrum,* II (Città del Vaticano, 1955), 376. This manuscript also contains the commentary of Manuel Moschopoulos on Hesiod's *Works and Days,* the first book of Philostratus' *Images,* and an introduction to the *Treatise on Method for Rhetoric* attributed to Hermogenes; it carries at the end the name of Lianoro de' Lianori, copyist, collector of manuscripts, and former student of Theodorus Gaza and Guarino da Verona. I do not know if the codex was written by him; on this scholar see E. Cosenza, *Biographical and Bibliographical Dictionary of the Italian Humanists* (Boston, 1962), III, 1983, V, 1007 f. The Salamanca manuscript has to be dated earlier than the end of the fifteenth century (as I did in my *Catalogus*), probably in the sixties. The book belonged to Fernán Núñez de Guzmán (Pintianus), who wrote Latin marginal notes and studied the text, correcting many of its faults.

[3] See for this title J. Sickenberger, " Die Lukaskatene des Niketas von Herakleia," *Texte und Untersuchungen,* XXII, 4 (1902), 14. The title ὁ τοῦ τῶν Σερρῶν, which is often given to Nicetas (Sickenberger, pp. 13 ff.) and led to the erroneous opinion that he was a metropolitan of Serres (so the old writers, as M. le Quien, *Oriens Christianus,* I [Paris, 1740], 1111; Fabricius-Harles, *Bibl. Graeca,* VII [Hamburg, 1801,] 750), has been explained as owing to his being a nephew of a bishop of Serres (Sickenberger, p. 17; H.-G. Beck, *Kirche und theologische Literatur im byzantinischen Reich* [München, 1959], p. 651, J.

τεσσάρων τοῦ λόγου μερῶν ὀνόματος, ῥήματος, προθέσεως καὶ ἐπιρρήματος.[4] Thus the supposedly unedited [5] poem of Salamanca has been identified, and the anonymous text of Boissonade finds its author.

There is no reason to doubt the authorship as it is stated by the Salamanca manuscript. A comparison of our poem with the literary works of Nicetas of Heraclea proves not only that it is analogous to the rest of his profane works, but also that it is the most important item among them. Furthermore, it casts, as I believe, new light on the teaching of grammar at a moment of Byzantine history.

The list of Nicetas' profane writings consists of the *Duodecim deorum epitheta* edited by W. F. A. Studemund; [6] the *Rhythmi de marium fluuiorum lacuum montium urbium gentium lapidum nominibus* published by L. Cohn; [7] Cohn, after establishing the sources for the *Rhythmi,* adds (pp. 661 ff.) extracts from Nicetas' *Canon de orthographia.* More similar to our poem than the *Rhythmi* or κοντάκια,[8] whose music is that of church hymns, are the Στίχοι περὶ γραμματικῆς also published by Boissonade,[9] 100 iambic verses on the declension of certain nouns in *n,* which is attributed to Michael Psellos in another manuscript.[10] To these works R. Browning [11] adds another unedited grammatical poem with title varying in the manuscripts and the following incipit, Πέδον τιθηνὸν ἀκριβοῦ.

Our syntactical poem is, indeed, no masterpiece, to our taste, but it is an interesting document for the history of Byzantine education at a moment when, in the midst of extremely critical revolutions in the Empire and the Church, there is a real revival of the culture.

Darrouzès, *REB,* xviii, 179-84). As R. Browning has shown in his important paper, "The Patriarchal School at Constantinople in the Twelfth Century" (*Byzantion,* xxxii [1962], 167-201, xxxiii [1963], 11-40; see xxxii, 172, xxxiii, 16), Nicetas' uncle was named Stephanos.

[4] The title has lost the indication of the author in the Paris MS A in being transferred after the eight lines of the preface. The title in Boissonade has Περὶ συντάξεως instead of Τῶν συντάξεων of the Salamanca MS.

[5] C. H. Graux and A. Martin, *Notices sommaires des manuscrits grecs d'Espagne et de Portugal* (Paris, 1892), p. 174. These authors tentatively attributed the poem to Nicetas of Serres, that is, of Heraclea (see my n. 3).

[6] W. F. A. Studemund, ed., *Anecdota uaria,* i (Berlin, 1886), 257-83.

[7] L. Cohn, *Neue Jahrbücher für Philologie und Pädagogik,* cxxxiii (1886), 649 ff.

[8] So termed by F. Fuchs, "Die höheren Schulen von Konstantinopel im Mittelalter," *Byzantinisches Archiv,* Heft 8 (Leipzig-Berlin, 1926), p. 32.

[9] J. F. Boissonade, *Anecdota,* iii (Paris, 1831), 323-27.

[10] Bodleian-Baroccianus, see K. Krumbacher, *Geschichte der byzantinischen Literatur* (München, 1897), pp. 587 f.

[11] R. Browning, *Byzantion,* xxxiii, 15.

As N. Iorga says,[12] referring to these disastrous times, " une fraîche brise de renaissance soufflait sur les miasmes de ce vieux Byzance."

It is in this same atmosphere that Michael Psellos had flourished. Cynical, learned, eloquent, in love with the Platonic philosophy,[13] Psellos was an older contemporary of Nicetas, whom we think he greets as λογιώτατε ἀδελφέ in a very curious letter.[14] In it Psellos teases the Master of the Patriarchal School for not having accepted the imperial gift of the κλητώριον,[15] a rejection which he interprets as a sign of yet greater greediness. This letter reveals the jealousy between the two schools.[16] Perhaps we can see here how envious Psellos was of Nicetas' advancement in imperial favor.

After Michael Psellos, John Xiphilinos (Patriarch of Constantinople 1064-1075), Constantine Likhoudes, John Patrikios,[17] and other prominent figures, Nicetas of Heraclea deserves a distinguished place. But he, with Theophylact, the future bishop of Ochrida, belongs to a younger generation, and devotes himself to ecclesiastical studies. He, " der berühmte Katenist," as H.-G. Beck says,[18] " mag unter den Bischöfen der Stadt von Herakleia hervorgehoben werden." Most of his activity was devoted to the exegesis of the Bible and commentary on Gregory of Nazianzus; [19] he was almost the last author of "chains": on the Psalms, on the Gospels of

---

[12] N. Iorga, *Histoire de la vie Byzantine*, II (Bucharest, 1934), 209. See also A. A. Vasiliev, *History of the Byzantine Empire* (Madison, 1952), pp. 366 ff.

[13] Iorga, pp. 231 f.

[14] K. N. Sathas, *Mesaionike Bibliotheke*, v (Venice, 1876), 428-30. The letter is addressed to τῷ Μαΐστωρι τῶν Χαλκοπρατίων and no name is found in it. Its date being unknown, the attribution to Nicetas as addressee remains conjectural.

[15] According to Suidas (III, 1799 Adler) this means βασιλικὴ τράπεζα, and perhaps it refers to some imperial largess of which I do not know; nor do we get any help from the definition of the word in the Μέγα λεξικόν of D Demetrakos, v (Athens, 1939), 3994: ἐπίσημον γεῦμα παρατιθέμενον ἐν τοῖς ἀνακτόροις τοῦ Βυζαντίου. Mrs. R. Kahane, who was kind enough to help me in many questions, calls my attention to Ph. Koukules, Βυζαντινῶν βίος καὶ πολιτισμός, v (Athens, 1952), 188, 201 f.

[16] Thus those sentences would gain significance in which Psellos (429) reproaches Nicetas that, if he seeks continuous and full imperial favor, he ought to teach a full curriculum, including philosophy. When, a few years later (in 1082), John Italikos, the successor of Psellos, is brought before the Holy Synod and accused as a Platonician and heretic (cf. L. Bréhier, *Byzantion*, III, 76), these are perhaps only later developments of that rivalry between the secular and the ecclesiastical school.

[17] L. Bréhier, *Vie et mort de Byzance* (Paris, 1950), pp. 272, 275; *idem, La civilisation byzantine* (Paris, 1950), p. 456; Fuchs, p. 25 (above, n. 8).

[18] Beck, p. 161 (above, n. 3).

[19] A list of Nicetas' works is included in R. Browning, *Byzantion*, XXXIII, 15 f.; see also Beck, pp. 651 f., 416, and A. Ehrhard in Krumbacher, pp. 211 f., 215 f.

Matthew, John and Luke (this last one had influence also in the West, on the *Catena aurea* of Aquinas); another catena on the Epistles of Paul is a proof of his activity in this field. After him the catenae become scarce, and it is evident that dogmatic interest supersedes exegesis.[20] He commented extensively on sixteen sermons of Gregory.[21] Probably belonging to him is a work on canon law which carries his name, the thirteen Ἐρωταποκρίσεις addressed to a bishop suffragan of Heraclea.[22] An important speech of Nicetas [23] against the orthodoxy of bishop Eustratius was published for the first time a few years ago.[24]

Beck [25] suggested 1030 and 1100 as very probable years for the birth and death of Nicetas. But we know now, through the speech against Eustratius, that he was still alive in 1117. It seems that the date of his appearance as οἰκουμενικὸς διδάσκαλος, once put at 1080,[26] also must be deferred by a few years. R. Browning [27] thinks it should be in some year after 1092.

The Patriarchal school won importance, probably, later than the secular institutions fostered by Constantine Monomachos. After a parenthesis of more than two centuries Nicetas of Heraclea received the title of οἰκουμενικὸς διδάσκαλος as head of the Patriarchal School.[28] Some years later he occupied a position which could be compared to that of Michael Psellos, head of the school of Philosophy at the Portico of Achilles,[29] and of John Xiphilinos at the school of Law at St. George of Mangana.[30] Nicetas had previously been teacher at the school τῶν Χαλκοπρατείων, that is, the Patriarchal School.[31]

---

[20] Beck, p. 654.

[21] A. Ehrhard in Krumbacher, p. 138.

[22] Perhaps still deserving of consideration is the hypothesis of Le Quien, p. 1113 (above, n. 3), who thinks that the author of this work is a second Nicetas, of a later time.

[23] Λόγος τοῦ θεοφιλεστάτου μητροπολίτου Ἡρακλείας κυροῦ Νικήτα τοῦ Σερρῶν ἀπολογητικὸς καὶ ἐλεγκτικός, πῶς καὶ διὰ ποίαν αἰτίαν οὐ προσδέχεται τὸν Νικαίας.

[24] P. Joannou, *Byzantion*, XXVIII, 1-30. See for another manuscript J. Darrouzès, *REB*, XVIII, 180 f.

[25] Beck, p. 651.

[26] Fuchs, p. 48.

[27] Browning, *Byzantion*, XXXIII, 39.

[28] Fuchs, p. 36; F. Schemmel, in his paper "Die Schulen von Konstantinopel" (*PW*, XLIII, 1178), is wrong in placing the restoration of the *oikoumenikos didaskalos* in the twelfth century. This same writer says that Eustratius, the Aristotelian commentator, was πρώξιμος at the school τῆς νέας ἐκκλησίας.

[29] Fuchs, pp. 28 f.; F. Schemmel, p. 1181.

[30] Fuchs, pp. 25, 29; Schemmel, p. 1179.

[31] Fuchs, pp. 36 ff., 49.

As for Nicetas' career we know that he was deacon and *skeuo-phylax* [32] at the Great Church. Browning (p. 17) supposes justi-fiably that the importance of this last office obliges us to place it in his more advanced years, leaving those of Nicetas' youth for his teaching. His career as a teacher has two stages: he was first πρώξιμος [33] after 1071, according to J. Darrouzès (*REB* xviii, 183), and then διδάσκαλος τοῦ εὐαγγελίου, that is, οἰκουμενικὸς διδάσκαλος. It seems very probable, as Beck says,[34] that most of his writings belong to the time when he was teaching at the Patriarchal School.

J. Sickenberger [35] has tried to recover some biographical notices from two letters of Theophylact of Bulgaria to Nicetas.[36] Theo-phylact felt extremely unhappy about his banishment from the capital to his see at Ochrida, and Sickenberger supposes that Nicetas may have written some consolation to him. But the infor-mation is very scanty, both because of the highly rhetorical style of Theophylact and because of the uncertain text of the letters.[37]

All that we know for certain is that when Theophylact was arch-bishop of Ochrida [38] Nicetas still was διδάσκαλος τῆς μεγάλης ἐκκλησίας,

[32] Cf. F. Dölger, *Lex. für Theologie und Kirche*, ix, 818.

[33] We accept from Fuchs (p. 49), the suggestion that the title πρώξιμος means Vice-Rector, and must be inferior to that of διδάσκαλος οἰκουμενικός or τοῦ εὐαγγελίου. Possibly the title πρώξιμος was absorbed by the Church school, since, according to F. Schemmel (p. 1179), πρώξιμος was used at the Bardas University in the ninth century for the teacher of grammar.

[34] Beck, p. 651.

[35] Sickenberger, pp. 4 f. (above, n. 3).

[36] The first letter (*MPG*, cxxvi, 373) consists of complaints, and is really not very understandable; notice the sentence: οἱ δ' ἐμοὶ μὲν ἀδελφοὶ σοὶ δὲ μαθηταὶ προσκυνοῦσι τὴν σὴν τιμιότητα. The second (*ibid.* p. 509) is very short, but must be read together with the one preceding it, and corresponds to the time in which Theophylact was very bitter about his residence in Ochrida. Still another letter (*ibid.* pp. 436 f.) addressed τῷ διδασκάλῳ τῆς μεγάλης ἐκκλησίας, asking for help in enigmatic terms, must be added to the documents of the correspond-ence between Theophylact and Nicetas of Heraclea: the reference πυθοῦ τοῦ μαθητοῦ σου, τοῦ ἐμοῦ ἀδελφοῦ must be compared to that sentence of the first letter transcribed above (see P. Gautier, *REB*, xxi, 168 for Theophylact's brothers). A letter τῷ χαρτοφύλακι κυρίῳ Νικήτᾳ (*MPG*, cxxvi, 417 ff.), which could be addressed to our Nicetas, is not mentioned by Sickenberger, and it is really a difficult document: it shows great deference and the addressee is informed about dark intrigues. If we put this letter together with the other one τῷ χαρτοφύλακι (*MPG*, cxxvi, 436), which seems simultaneous with that τῷ διδασκάλῳ τῆς μεγάλης ἐκκλησίας, it seems that there were at the same time at least two different Nicetases (cf. J. Darrouzès, *REB*, xviii, 194 Addition).

[37] Cf. Alice Leroy-Molinghem (*Byzantion*, xiii, 253 ff.), who gives convincing examples of the unreliability of the printed editions (the most recent, that in Migne).

[38] He was appointed to that see in 1088-1089, as P. Gautier (*REB*, xxi, 159 ff.) has proved.

and only later, we do not know when, did he become the bishop of Heraclea.

Two more letters of Nicetas Stethatos to our Nicetas on theological subjects have been published,[39] but their content as evidence for his biography is minimal.

Our grammatical poem, if not a very enjoyable piece of poetry, serves to bring Nicetas of Heraclea closer to us, and to show him in one aspect of his professorial activity.[40] To appreciate the poem we have to take into account the tastes of the eleventh century at Byzantium. As all the aspects of life were ruled by traditional ideals, our poem is a mnemotechnical device to teach grammar—the grammar of a language which was out of use, but which every educated person was supposed to write and speak with all the complicated rules of fifteen centuries earlier. To write abstracts of the traditional grammar in iambic or political verses is characteristic of Byzantine literature,[41] especially in these centuries. The definitions of the grammar were enough while the usages of the classical language were living. Now the students needed to be taught the constructions, and this need was met by treatises on syntax or special dictionaries, or by syntactical additions to the old ones.

In our poem the teacher addresses a boy who is no doubt of most noble birth: he is called εὐγενής (l. 1), but he is still a beginner (ἀτελής, 22) for whom the syntax of four parts of speech is adequate. He will therefore be taught first concerning the noun, not the whole of the syntax of the noun, but only that of its cases, since the construction of the noun with the other parts is more appropriate for the more advanced σχεδογράφοι,[42] whose study seems more interesting to the author (φιληδῶ τῇ τῶν σχεδῶν μελέτῃ, 178).

[39] Sickenberger, pp. 8 ff.

[40] Our poem is probably a document for the activities of the Patriarchal school, of which, as Georgina Buckler (in *Byzantium*, edited by N. H. Baynes and H. St. L. B. Moss [Oxford, 1948], p. 218) says, "No history can be written, for our sources are totally inadequate."

[41] Krumbacher, p. 580.

[42] Lines 23 ff.:

> Τὸ δ' ὄνομα διδάξω σε πρῶτον ὡς δεῖ συντάσσειν,
> οὐχὶ πρὸς πάντα τὰ λοιπὰ μέρη, πρὸς δὲ τὰς πτώσεις.
> Ἡ γὰρ πρὸς ταύτας τῶν μερῶν σύνταξις τῶν τοῦ λόγου
> τοῖς σχεδογράφοις κατὰ σὲ τῶν ἀναγκαιοτάτων.

Boissonade explains the term and compares verse 428, in which the author dissuades the student from competing with ἀρίστοις σχεδογράφοις. Anna Comnena (*Alexiad* XV. 7; 2.293 f. Reifferscheid) speaks of the composition of σχέδη beside the study of ἐρωτήσεις at the grammar school in the Monastery of the Iberians. Cf. also Krumbacher (p. 590 ff.), who says that this practical method

Perhaps it is only courtesy on the part of the author to suppose that his pupil is well disposed toward these studies (ῥάθυμος πρὸς λόγους, 102), for more than once the teacher demands his attention either because he supposes he is distracted, or because the question becomes difficult: καὶ σκόπει μοι τὸν λόγον (82), τήρει μοι τὴν σύνταξιν (255), οὐκ ἄχαρις φανήσομαι, λοιπὸν ἀκροατέον (388), τὰς δὲ προθέσεις γίνωσκε (724), σκόπει μοι (1052 and 1054), λέγε μοι (1080).

He accuses his student of νωθρεία (390) and, as if he were scolding him, uses a series of compounds to reprimand the youth (555 ff.):

> φρονεῖς τὰ μὴ καθήκοντα, καταφρονεῖς μαστίγων,
> ὑπερφρονεῖς κολάσεων, περιφρονεῖς αἰκίας,
> ἀντιφρονεῖς τοῖς ἀγαθοῖς καὶ συμφρονεῖς τοῖς φαύλοις.

On other occasions he gives the student good counsel, always in the form of examples (1077 f.):

> ἐκτέον πόνων λέγομεν, φευκτέον τὴν ἀργίαν,
> τῆς ἀτοπίας ἄπαγε . . .

Once he appears to be indulgent with the student (590):

> ἀλλ' ἅλις τῆς δριμύτητος τοῦ λόγου καὶ πικρίας,

but he continues implacably with his lists. Sometimes the poem seems rude toward the student, but besides the fact that our standards are very different, the teacher repeats topics which are more traditional than real.[43]

The poem makes really no pretense of being a masterwork. In the introductory lines it is planned as the fruit of the labor of one night (l. 5):

> γένοιτο μικρὸς τῆς μιᾶς νυκτὸς πόνος.[44]

---

of learning grammar developed especially toward the end of the eleventh century. How the method was fixed can be seen in the treatise of Manuel Moschopoulos (Περὶ σχεδῶν [Paris, 1545]): a series of short texts, to be learned by heart, is provided with comments on morphology, etymology, etc. Another meaning of the word is in Ed. Kurtz, *BZ*, xvi, 299 f.: "Schedographia as orthographic rules."

[43] Thus for instance ὡς ἐναντίος βλέπεις με (439), εὑρίσκω σε σκληρότατον (446), ἀλγῶ τὴν φρένα βλέπων σε τοὺς λόγους μὴ ποθοῦντα (471); allusions to whips are made (l. 500, 513, 613), the student is reprimanded for his bad habits, his laziness, etc. (476 ff.).

[44] This is evidently one of the proofs of authenticity for Nicetas' authorship, since with this can be compared the opening lines of his other poem in Boissonade (*Anecd.*, iii, 323):

> Καιρὸς μὲν ὕπνου, καὶ καθεύδειν ἦν δέον,
> ἀλλ' οὖν δι' ὑμᾶς, παῖδες, ἀγρυπνητέον·
> ἡ νὺξ δὲ τοῦ νῦ λῆξιν ἐξεταζέτω.

(i.e., "let the night be devoted to the study of nouns ending in nu").

It is play for the author, a κούφισμα τῆς λύπης, a relief from sadness. This mixture, as he believes, of study and play, is "a pledge of his love for the boy" (12).

Nicetas enters into his subject with a definition of the sentence (13 f.) which is taken from Dionysius Thrax,[45] as Boissonade opportunely notices:

> λέξεων τοίνυν πέφυκε παράθεσις ὁ λόγος
> σημαίνουσα διάνοιαν, ὦ νέε, πληρεστάτην.

But although at first sight we might think that he is simply going to put some textbook into verse, and he confesses to his pupil that the explanation of the grammatical terms must be sought in Dionysius,[46] he writes a kind of rhapsody of grammatical material he knows mostly by heart. Besides that, he has at hand lexicographical material, some repertories of constructions of nouns, verbs, prepositions and adverbs.

It is therefore not easy to establish the source. Boissonade, in publishing the text, made several important comparisons. Some sections, whose dependence on textbooks seems established, can be assigned with some confidence: thus the lines on comparatives and superlatives (35-42) correspond to Dionysius 27 f.; the genitive (or dative) construction of the words called πρός τι is briefly stated by Dionysius 35, but, as Boissonade notices, the scholia to this author can be compared to our poem.[47] The construction of agent nouns (defined in Dion. 46) is explained in lines 49-51;[48] the epithets (52-59) depend on the definition by Dionysius 34, but the examples seem to be developed by Nicetas from his memory.

The next sections (60-74), on the construction of compounds with ὁμο- or words meaning equality, could be derived from lexi-

---

[45] We quote Dionysius according to the pages of the edition of Uhlig: compare (22) λόγος δέ ἐστι πεζῆς λέξεως σύνθεσις διάνοιαν αὐτοτελῆ δηλοῦσα.

[46] Line 27 ff.:

> Εἰ δὲ τυχὸν καὶ χρήσομαι δεινότητι ῥημάτων,
> μὴ βουληθῆς κακίσαι με τῆς ἀσαφείας χάριν·
> ὁ Θρᾷξ γὰρ Διονύσιος τὰς φύσεις τούτων πάντων
> καὶ τὰς τομὰς παρέδωκεν ὡς πρὸς εἰσαγομένους.

As G. Uhlig says (preface to Dionysius Thrax, *Ars grammatica* [Leipzig, 1883], p. VI) this grammarian "regnabat in scholis Graecis ab altero saeculo usque ad duodecimum certe post Christum."

[47] See the Scholia Londinensia in A. Hilgard, *Schol. in Dionysium* (Leipzig, 1901), 533₂₅. Line 48 of our poem is wrong in substituting the instrumental dative for the possessive dative πατὴρ αὐτῷ or the dative depending on such adjectives as ἴσος of the scholia.

[48] The example κριτής could have been suggested by *Schol.* 243₂₈ Hilgard.

cographic sources. In lines 75-78 Nicetas adds to the ἐθνικὰ ὀνόματα (cf. Dion. 38) the term τοπικά which is new, not found in the scholia.[49]

With line 79 the most extensive section of the poem begins, up to line 723, devoted to the verbal constructions. It is divided into two parts: simple (80-383) and compound verbs. Nicetas seems to have personal reasons for giving the verb more importance: it is most essential for the perfection of the sentence (79 ff.). He reacts against the traditional doctrine [50] that the noun is more important than the verb.

His definition of active and passive verbs (103 ff.) is traditional, and corresponds to Apollonius Dyscolus 345₁₆ Uhlig or *Schol. in Dionys.* 401₁₂ Hilgard. So far as I know, the term ἀντιπάθεια for the reciprocal character of verbs, as used in line 123, is new, and represents a concept of Nicetas' which apparently did not find continuation.

The sections on the verbs of feeling (128 ff.) and passion (142 ff.) depend on traditional doctrine (cf. Apollonius 416-18, 406₄, 408₁ Uhlig). The same is true of the verbs of ruling (line 149 ff.) and some others which he calls, as in a casual remark of Apollonius (422₁₇ Uhlig), σημαντικὰ περιποίησιν [51] πραγμάτων (line 161 ff.), which can be compared to the same grammarian (419 f., 422₁₀). Verbs of praising (166 ff.) correspond to Apollonius 406₆.

Nicetas calls διπλαῖ συντάξεις the different constructions of the same verb with different meanings (179 ff.) ; and here begins the promiscuous use of lexicographical sources. Boissonade in his edition compares with this part of the poem the syntactical lexicon published by I. Bekker,[52] Suidas,[53] another treatise Περὶ τῆς τῶν ῥημάτων συντάξεως κατὰ τοὺς παλαιούς,[54] another *Fragmentum lexici Graeci* and a treatise Περὶ τῆς συντάξεως τῶν ῥημάτων πρὸς τὰ ὀνόματα.[55] He quotes also an unedited lexicon from the Paris codex 1630.

---

[49] See *Schol. in Dion.* 238₂₂, 393₁₄ Hilgard.

[50] Cf. Georgii Choerobosci *Proleg. in Theodosii Alexandrini canones* (ed. Hilgard; Leipzig, 1889) 105₂.

[51] Cf. τὰ περὶ ποίησιν in the Περὶ τῆς τῶν ῥημάτων συντάξεως κατὰ τοὺς παλαιούς (Bachmann, *Anecd.*, ii) 314₂₈.

[52] I. Bekker, *Anecdota Graeca*, ɪ (Berlin, 1814), 117-80.

[53] A. Adler in her edition of this dictionary (ɪ, XXX) quotes two syntactical lexica among its sources.

[54] Edited by L. Bachmann, *Anecdota*, ɪɪ (Leipzig, 1828), 287-316.

[55] Edited both by G. Hermann from a manuscript of Augsburg in his *De emendanda ratione Graecae grammaticae* (Leipzig, 1801), pp. 319-52, 353-421. The attribution of the *Fragmentum* to Nicephoros Gregoras seems to be con-

Nicetas uses his memory, which seems as rich as his lexica at hand. The verbal section of Nicetas' poem must be taken together with the syntactical lexica or special monographs on construction, and only in connection with them can it be appreciated.

The section on the prepositions (724-989) follows the order of Dionysius (cf. 71 Uhlig), but again syntactical sources are used not only to give examples, but also to mark less usual constructions. The observations on the use of prepositions to form compounds (990-1054) seem not to be found elsewhere, but the terms παράθεσις 'construction' and σύνθεσις 'composition' are read in the London (and Madrid) scholia to Dionysius (464₃₄ Hilgard).

The final short notes on some adverbs (1055-87) do not depend on Dionysius, though some have correspondences in his scholia, as the κατωμοτικά (cf. 434₇ Hilgard). In considering as adverbs the nominal forms in -τέον (l. 1063 ff.), Nicetas follows the customary ideas (cf. Dionys. 85 Uhlig). The term χωρισμοῦ (for adverbs of separation), as different from τοπικά, which is not found in Dionysius, appears in the later tradition, as in the commentary of Heliodorus.[56]

APPENDIX I

VARIANTS IN THE SALAMANCA MANUSCRIPT

We offer a selection of readings of this manuscript. In general, it is not particularly good; and it shares, or perhaps increases, the faults of the Paris codices. But sometimes it has excellent readings, arousing our interest. The Salamantinus agrees sometimes with one of the Parisian manuscripts, sometimes with the other.[57] But it is independent, and shows a different line of transmission. Thus lines 71 f. are inverted; also 584 f. (interesting in connection with the fact that 585 is missing in B and the inversion corrected in our MS with letters at the margin), 594 f. The missing lines (179, 332 with A, 431 f., 436 f., 513, 527-30, 538, 551, 566, 624, 706, 787, 918, 969, 998, 1054 f.) seem to prove that the Salamantinus is a different redaction. The same is proved by added verses: 379a λωβῶμαι σοὶ λυμαίνομαι καὶ λοιδοροῦμαι λέγε — 625a τοῖς ταπεινοῖς προσκλίνου δὲ καὶ τούτους ἐπικλίνου — 716a see below, n. 70 — 867a φέρω κινῶ καὶ μελετῶ φαντάζομαι καὶ γράφω.

---

firmed by the largely coincident Περὶ γραμματικῆς attributed to him in the MS 303 of the Holy Synod, and edited by C. F. Matthaei, *Anecdota Graeca* (Moscow, 1775), pp. 1 ff.

[56] *Schol. in Dionys.* 100₉ Hilgard.

[57] It agrees with A in lines 119, 193, 196, 216, 230, 240, 247, 285, 303, omission of line 332, 334 (with a slight difference), 384, 452, 479, 487, 489 f., 563, 591, 623, 634, 704, 709, 1056; with B in lines 11, 12, 16, 34, 69, 77, 146, 190, 224, 258, 396, 447, 491, 523, 584, 653, 686 (with a slight difference).

We give the variants of major interest, putting an exclamation point after those which improve the printed text: 2 τρόχον! — 69 ἰσοπλατεῖς ἰσοβαφεῖς (?) ἰσομετρ᾽ [58] ἰσομήκοις (?) — 133 εἰ γὰρ — 136 τὸ βρόχον (emend πικρόν instead of μικρόν) — 142 ἐκ (for τοῦ) — ἀπελάσουσιν! — 222 ἀμνημονεῖ (corrected from the text of Dem. *Phil.* II, 12 p. 69) — 227 τὸ φόβον — 252 εἴπω — 265 τὸ γὰρ (as AB; it is possible to maintain the text with the emendation of Pintianus σημαῖνον) — 285 προσευχῇ — 287 τουτὶ σὺν Λιβανίῳ ! — 299 ὕπνων ! — 311 οἴνου ! — 315 σημαῖνον ! — 328 προσέβλεψαˑι ! — 329 αὐτὰς ἐνδύεσθαι ὁ παῖς ! — 334 ὁ μέγας οὕτως εἶπεν — 368 καὶ τοῦτο — 380 πολλαχοῦ — 387 συνθήκην λόγου — 393 παιδείαν — 394 ἀμελεῖν φιλοῦντας — 401 μισῶν — 418 στέργοντα — 420 ἀσπάζῃ — 433 καταφρονῶ τὸν τόπον δὲ τὸ διδα-σκαλεῖον ! — 439 ἐναντίος ! — 433 συμβλέπεις — 445 περιλαλῶν ! — 446 σκληρό-τερον ! — 463 γελᾷς δὲ σὺ τοὺς θέλοντας ὡς — 470 πειράζω σε διδάσκω καὶ σοῦ καταπειράζω — 523 εἰ (instead of οὐ) — 533 ἐπιπνέω(ν) [59] — 540 f. instead of the two verses the Salamantinus has οὐκ ἀποδοκιμάζομαι τοῖς φίλοις τῇ νωθρείᾳ — 550 αἰσίαις μυστηπόλων — 554 τῶν ψόγους ! — 567 μοι (for μὴ) — 587 ἀναλαμβάνειν ! — 588 παραλαμβάνων ! — 597 ἀποδίδομαι ! — 600 ἐφῆκε — ἐφεῖτο — 632 προυφέρω τῶν λοιπῶν — 655 κατάβαλε — ὑπερβάλου — 674 παρε-δρεύειν — προκαθῆσθαι (almost coinciding with Boissonade's correction) — θέλε — 676 τούτων χάρις — 705 ἐξελασθείς — 724 γίνωσκε ! — 746 κακῶν ! — 786 σημαίνειν βούλεται ὁ καὶ μικρογραφεῖται — 809 συσταυρωθέντα — 823 ἄρχοντα — τὸν κρατοῦντα — 881 χειλέων — 932 σημαντική ! — 958 τέθεικεν — 977 ἐπί σε (which seems better than ἐπίσης) — 993 προσακτέον — 1001 ἔξοικος (instead of ἐξώλης) — 1005 πρόδρομον — πρόβολον — 1020 δεικνύει (with the margin of A) — 1027 παράβλεψις ! — 1071 τὰ ! — 1074 Τληπολέμου ! — 1081 συντάττοις — 1082 σὺν τούτῳ (for συντάττεις).

APPENDIX II

IDENTITY OF THE STUDENT ADDRESSED

Can we identify the noble boy to whom our poem was dedicated? Since Michael Psellos composed mnemotechnical poems for his imperial student, the future Michael the Seventh,[60] and, as we are going to see, still a later composition in the same style was written for someone in the palace of Alexis the Third, there are probabilities in favor of the idea that our poem was dedicated to the prince Constantine Ducas, the son of Michael the Seventh and Maria of Alania.[61]

Born about 1074, the education of Constantine was entrusted to Theo-

[58] Boissonade comments in his note that he does not like this form; notice that our manuscript gives it without any accent, like B.

[59] ν added in the Salamantinus by Pintianus.

[60] *Expositio Cantici canticorum, MPG*, CXXII, 537 ff. (combination of comments taken from fathers and mnemotechnical verses); *De dogmate, ibid.* pp. 811 ff. (163 lines); *Synopsis legum, ibid.* pp. 923 ff. (1047 lines); *Inscriptiones psalmorum* in *Scripta minora* I, 389-400 Kurtz-Drexel. To these can be added *De hexahemero* in *Scripta minora* I, 401-10 and the *Lehrgedicht zum Messopfer* published by P. Joannou, *BZ*, LI, 1-9 (257 lines), not dedicated to Michael.

[61] See B. Leib, "Un basileus ignoré—Constantin Doucas," *Byzantinoslavica*, XVII (1956), 341-59.

phylact.[62] His teaching must have lasted only a few months, but his plan was probably to convert the unlucky prince into a scholar, in the most unfavorable Byzantine sense of the word, as Psellos had done with the boy's father, the unfortunate Michael the Seventh.[63]

We possess a document, the Παιδεία βασιλική [64] in which Theophylact, at the start of his teaching,[65] explains to the young man the duties of a king. Unfortunately the rhetorical tone of the work does not reveal what the education consisted of. Theophylact, his vanity elated at being "teacher of the prince" (καθηγητὴς τοῦ βασιλέως, I 2, PG cxxvi.253), in eulogizing Constantine's qualities is less enthusiastic than his betrothed Anna Comnena,[66] but he extols his mental abilities. Only vague praise is given to the dethroned father of the prince (I 6, 260), but he devotes the half of the first, or panegyric, part of his speech to the Empress Maria. No allusions to Alexis are made. The second part is a kind of Prince's Mirror, in which the virtues of being a ruler, and some of the dangers, such as becoming a tyrant, are commented upon.[67]

It is not possible to say that Constantine Ducas was actually educated at the school of Theophylact.[68] The Παιδεία βασιλική was soon followed by a speech of the same teacher, in which he advised the Emperor to proclaim as heir his own son John,[69] to the detriment of Constantine's rights.

Are we entitled to believe that it was at this moment that Constantine was entrusted to Nicetas? Thus the tone of the poem is quite different from the Παιδεία βασιλική. Our student is already a youth.[70] The line in which Nicetas tells his pupil

μὴ συνοικήσῃς γυναικί, φαμέν, στωμυλωτάτῃ (716),

would indicate that, if the student was Constantine, his betrothal to Anna Comnena had been broken off.

---

[62] Cf. on this author P. Gautier, "Le discours de Théophylacte de Bulgarie à l'autocrator Aléxis Ier Comnène (6 janvier 1088)," REB, xx, 93-130 and "L'episcopat de Théophylacte Héphaistos archevêque de Bulgarie, Notes chronologiques et biographiques," REB, xxi, 159-78.

[63] The grandfather of the boy, the Emperor Constantine Ducas (1059-1067) is counted among the companions of Psellos at the school (cf. L. Bréhier, Byzantion, iii, 75).

[64] MPG, cxxvi, 253-86.

[65] About 1088-1089 (correcting Chalandon's date of 1090), as P. Gautier (REB, xx, 106) says.

[66] See her descriptions in the Alexiad I. 10 (1.35 Reifferscheid), 12 (1.41), and III. 1 (1.93 f.).

[67] See on the sources, especially of the second, or paraenetic, part, K. Praechter, BZ, i, 399 ff.

[68] It is true that we have the affirmation, "Constantine Ducas was the ornament of a school kept by archbishop Theophylact," made by Georgina Buckler, Byzantium, ed. by Baynes and Moss (Oxford, 1948), p. 201. But does her information come from some reference, which I could not locate, on Constantine's attendance at the Patriarchal School?

[69] B. Leib, Byzantinoslavica, xvii, 356; P. Gautier, REB, xx, 93 ff.

[70] Constantine would be 14 years old. So the verse 716a, which is missing in A, would not be impossible:

μὴ προσοικήσῃς φθονερῷ, μὴ παροικήσῃς πόρνῃ.

APPENDIX III

THE DATE OF BOISSONADE'S ORTHOGRAPHICAL LEXICON, ANECD., IV, 366 FF.

Another poetico-grammatical piece, on spelling, is the lexicon which Boissonade edited and christened Λεξικὸν σχεδογραφικόν, a title which does not seem appropriate. It is in the same meter and style as the poems of Psellos and Nicetas to which we have referred. Krumbacher's scepticism [71] about the invocation (l. 55)

ἄνασσα Ἄννα, σκόπει,

as really being directed to Anna Comnena, is perfectly right. Boissonade and Krumbacher have wrongly supposed that the poem quotes an unknown Angelus Comnenus.

What its author wrote (l. 185) is

ἔτης καὶ ὁ πολίτης γάρ, Ἄγγελος Κομνηνός τε,

that is, " ἔτης means certainly citizen, as (for instance) Angelos and Comnenos." This would put the reference at a time when the imperial family of the Comnenoi could be put on a par with that of the Angeloi.[72] These circumstances fit best the time of Alexis the Third (1195-1203), the grandson of Constantine Angelos and Theodora Comnena, who carried the double surname of Angelos Comnenos.[73] The Anna alluded to would be not Anna Comnena, but the widow of Alexis the Second and Andronicus the First, whose " presence in the palace suggests that she had accepted some office in it under Isaac and Maria," [74] and, we may suppose, still later.

University of Illinois
27 April 1966

---

[71] Krumbacher, *Byzant. Lit.*, p. 591.

[72] Constantine Angelos, who married Theodora, the youngest sister of Anna Comnena, came from Philadelphia, from an inferior family; it was his handsome figure that inclined Theodora to a love marriage (F. Chalandon, *Les Comnènes*, II, *Jean II Comnène et Manuel I Comnène* [Paris, 1912; repr. New York, 1960], 27 and 217).

[73] Vasiliev, *Hist. of the Byz. Empire*, p. 439.

[74] Joseph McCabe, *The Empresses of Constantinople* (London, 1913), p. 249.

TO DRAW A LABYRINTH

John L. Heller and Stewart S. Cairns

I. INTRODUCTION

Twenty years ago, the former of the writers named above [1] published an account of a peculiar geometric figure, which he entitled "Labyrinth or Troy Town?" [2] Often associated with the legendary Cretan labyrinth, it also occurred in many other contexts both ancient and modern. He attempted to show that the figure, once invented, must have been spread by diffusion from the eastern Mediterranean to western and northern Europe, not the reverse, and that its original and prevailing use was not to represent anything of historical or religious significance, but merely to provide a pastime for children and other ingenious people. It was, he thought, the simple construction of an apparently complex and literally amazing figure which kept it alive over the centuries in a semipopular rather than a learned tradition. Since that time, however, new evidence has appeared, both from Greece and from western Europe, and further discussion is needed, particularly about the origin of the figure. We now offer the following analysis, partly mathematical and partly historical, speculative indeed but hardly literary, in honor of a distinguished colleague who has himself been greatly interested in problems of literary origins and the diffusion of texts between East and West.

More or less symmetrical, whether in circular or rectangular form, and composed mostly of parallel lines (Fig. 1), the figure has the property of attracting the eye of the beholder to an exterior opening, offering a path to be traced between the lines and leading him

---

[1] Heller is responsible for the first and fourth sections of the article, Cairns for the second, and Heller and Cairns jointly for the third.

[2] J. L. Heller, *Classical Journal,* XLII (1946), 123–39; hereafter *CJ,* with reference to pages or figures.

ultimately to an interior pocket diametrically opposite the opening. At no point in the path is there any obstacle or any divergence. The path leads infallibly to the pocket and—most remarkably—conducts the viewer's eye or finger—or pencil—through every part of the figure, after several turns around the ends of lines. *All the space within the figure is covered in one continuous path.*

The rectangular form occurs on a graffito from Pompeii (*CIL* IV.2331 and Pl. 38.1) with the label: Labyrinthus; hic habitat Minotaurus. Both the square and the rounded forms appear on coins of Cnossos in the Hellenistic period (iv–iii centuries B.C.), presumably as a symbol of the legendary labyrinth, to which the first extant literary reference had been made by Pherecydes at the beginning of the fifth century (*Fragmente der griechischen Historiker*, ed. Jacoby, Vol. I, Pherecydes Frg. 148), and to which allusion had been made by means of a figure of the Minotaur on the obverse of earlier coins

Figure 1. Seven-walled labyrinths, round and square forms.

from Cnossos.[3] Association with the labyrinth is maintained by means of inscriptions or figures of Theseus and the Minotaur in later appearances of the design in mosaic floors of Roman date, and on walls or floors of medieval churches, and in drawings in manuscripts.[4] These are usually completely symmetrical and multiaxial designs, whose relationship to the original figure is not yet clear (see Fig. 3).

The figure also appears, however, in many other contexts and places: as a penitential pathway on the floors of medieval and modern churches, in various turf or pebble structures in northern Europe, where dances and games are said to have been performed

[3] A convenient selection of coins from the British Museum is illustrated in the very useful book of W. H. Matthews, *Mazes and Labyrinths* (London, 1922), Figs. 20–31. Abbreviated to Mt., we will need to cite it frequently. See also B. G. Head, *Historia Numorum* (Oxford, 1911), pp. 461–62; W. Wroth, *Catalogue of the Greek Coins of Crete and the Aegean Islands* [in the British Museum] (London, 1886), *passim*.

[4] See, e.g., Mt., Figs. 33–37; *CJ*, Figs. 2–4.

in it, and even in America, where the figure was known among the Hopi Indians of Southern Arizona, though not in pre-Columbian times. Here it was associated with their hero Tcuoho, who once led them from the underworld through a spiral hole.[5] In Europe the figure was most often associated with a city of classical or Biblical tradition, Troy, Jericho, Nineveh, even (in Finland) the heavenly city ("St. Peter's Game"). In antiquity the figure had also appeared without connection with the labyrinth, once without any association at all, merely as a design scratched on a concealed surface of a gable-sima from the Acropolis,[6] and once on an Etruscan vase of the late seventh century, where it is labelled TRVIA, i.e. Troy. Since the figure on the vase is attached to a pair of horsemen (see below, Fig. 22, for part of the scene), it has aroused great discussion as possibly reflecting an equestrian game, the *Troiae lusus,* known in late Republican Rome and ascribed by Virgil (*Aen.* V.545–603) to the followers of Aeneas.[7]

The elder Pliny had evidently seen the figure outlined in mosaic floors or on children's playgrounds and used for games involving walking or running, but he carefully distinguishes it from the labyrinth of legend, in which one could lose one's way. He describes the children's figure (*N.H.* XXXVI, 85, ut in pavimentis puerorumve ludicris campestris videmus) as *brevi lacinia milia passuum plura ambulationis continentem*—an apt characterization of the figure's special property.

Given the figure's varying associations, the question then arose, what did it represent? Did it have some model in nature, real or imagined? or did it represent merely itself, a challenging design? And how account for its distribution in space and time? Given its complexity, it seemed not likely to have been invented more than once, and its spread must have been due to diffusion from some center. Where was the center, and by what sort of experimentation could the figure have been invented?

[5] See Mt. *passim;* and especially H. S. Colton, "Troy Town on the Hopi Mesas," *Scientific Monthly,* LVIII (1944), 129–34.

[6] See E. Buschor, *Die Tondächer der Akropolis,* I, (Berlin und Leipzig, 1929), 45–46; and R. Eilmann, *Labyrinthos* (Athens, 1931), abb. 5 and p. 9, who dates the tile *ca.* 400 B.C., contemporary with the earlier coins from Cnossos.

[7] The definitive publication of the vase is by G. Q. Giglioli, "L'oinochoe di Tragliatella," *Studi Etruschi,* III (1929), 111–59. For bibliography on the game and other discussions of the figure, see E. Mehl, "Troiaspiel," *RE,* suppl. VIII (1956), cols. 888–905; a few supplements in my article, "A Labyrinth from Pylos?" *AJA,* LXV (1961), 57–62.

In 1946, then, Heller attempted an answer to these questions, on the basis of a simple method for drawing the figure revealed in an article by the American anthropologist, H. S. Colton.[8] After laying out a framework composed of a cross with angle brackets and corner dots, one proceeds to join the upper tip of the cross to the upper end of an adjacent angle bracket [9] by a short line, curved or straight (see Fig. 2); then to join the next two points on either side by a line parallel to the first line, and so on regularly until the complete figure is generated, as the reader can determine with his pencil.

A more symmetrical figure can be produced if the horizontal of the cross is staggered as in Figure 3a, resulting in a design cut in turf and known in Wales as "Caerdroia," i.e. Troy Town (Mt. Fig. 70; *CJ* Fig. 6). Or, if the staggered cross is split down the middle and the left-hand side is transferred to the right side of a rectangle, we get a figure which Meyer called a double meander-turn, since if one regards the path and not the intervening walls,

Figure 2. Construction from 16-point central cross, angle brackets, and corner dots.

it does resemble a meander.[10] This in turn can be bent around a corner and compounded with connecting lanes in such a way as to produce highly elaborate figures, such as one known from a mosaic floor of late Roman date found at Sousse (ancient Hadrumetum) in Tunisia (Mt. Fig. 37, *CJ* Fig. 19), with a path leading all the way through the figure to a central pocket.

[8] See n. 5, above. The construction of the figure had been neglected by previous theorists. To my present knowledge, it had been published before 1944 on only two occasions: in an article by L.-I. Ringbom, "Trojalek och Tranedans" *Finskt Museum,* xlv [1938], 68–106), which Mehl (n. 7, above) knew only at second hand, and by the Finnish scholar J. R. Aspelin, "Jatulintarhat Suomen rantamailla," *Suomen muinaismuitoyhdistyksen Aikakauskirja (Finska fornmin-nesföreningens Tidskrift,* ii [1877]), 155–64, which Mehl did not know at all. To these we must add the medievalist W. Meyer, "Ein Labyrinth mit Versen" (*Sitzungsb. d. Akad. d. Wissenschaften zu München* [1882], ii, 267–300, with a Nachtrag, p. 400). Meyer, however, used a quite different construction.

[9] On which side is immaterial, but in this article we choose to orient the central pocket invariably to the right of the upper vertical of the cross.

[10] Meyer, pp. 268 ff. Meyer thought that the cruciform labyrinths were developments from this meander-turn, but the reverse seems more likely; see p. 259, below.

Heller suggested that this surprisingly simple method of drawing the figure was responsible for its continuity over many generations and in many areas in both an artistic tradition, where it was usually associated with the Cretan labyrinth, and in a popular tradition, where it might be named for various cities but was usually connected with games or dances. He also suggested that whatever symbolic meanings, mythological associations, or ritualistic performances (i.e., dances) have been attached to the figure are probably secondary, and that the figure itself was only a geometrical curiosity which, once invented, was passed along from person to person in a simple drawing game, consisting of three steps. (1) The figure, constructed in secret on the ground or a tablet or any convenient material, would

Figure 3. (a) Staggered cross and "Caerdroia." (b) Double meander-turn and segment similar to mosaic at Sousse.

be shown to an acquaintance, its mystery enhanced by giving it the name of a fabulous structure suggesting the idea of penetration. (2) The friend would be asked to trace his way from the opening to the interior. This would be easy, but then the first boy would (3) erase the figure and challenge the beholder to reproduce it. Not many could do this, unless shown, but probably the secret was revealed only to a few specially favored friends.[11]

[11] My language here borrows from a second article, *AJA*, LXV (1961), 59. The game had been described by Aspelin (as reported by Ringbom in connection with his Fig. 4 = Aspelin Fig. 5) under the caption "att rita labyrint," from which we draw the title of the present article. In the previous article (*AJA*), I had made the point that a name was needed for the cruciform figure to distinguish it from other figures of similar general appearance but different structure, and that the name might well be "labyrinth," whether or not it represented the Cretan labyrinth—if there ever was one such as the legend makes it out to be.

As for the origin of the figure, Heller noted that a not unattractive design could be produced from a simple cross with four dots and no angle brackets, a skeleton which would also yield a swastika (Fig. 4). He therefore concluded (*CJ* p. 137) that the figure was perhaps "invented by Anatolian artists experimenting with meander and swastika, in the period corresponding to the Dark Ages in Greece (1000–750 B.C.)."

This was a good guess, but the date was not early enough. Twelve years later the figure turned up on the reverse of a linear B tablet found at Pylos [12] and datable *ca.* 1200 B.C. The reverse bore no legend and had no discernible relation to the writing on the obverse. It was evidently the doodle of an idle scribe, produced in the same manner as the design scratched on the Athenian tile and in much the same rectangular form. Heller then produced a second article comparing the new find with the other occurrences of the design and noting certain anomalies in the structure of the figure on the tablet, and especially on the tile, which suggested that the central

Figure 4. Eight-point cross, three-walled labyrinth, and swastika.

cross was not always drawn first.[13] Nevertheless the theory of a drawing game involving the cruciform figure was maintained, and diffusion from east to west was reaffirmed. Meanwhile, further examples in the west were becoming known, of figures carved or pecked on rocky surfaces in Spain, Wales, and northern Italy. These include spiral designs, like that of a burial cairn at Bryn Celli Ddu (Fig. 5a)[14] with an easily defended path leading to the center, and another notable figure (Fig. 5b) which, using folded spirals, resembles our labyrinth but is actually a maze with three paths, only one of which leads to the center. This figure was found among numerous rock-carvings in the Val Camonica of the Italian Alps and was dated by Anati in the late Bronze or early Iron Age.[15]

[12] See M. Lang, *AJA*, LXII (1958), 175–91 and Plate 46, on Cn 1287.

[13] Heller, *AJA*, LXV (1961), 57–62 and Plate 33; see Figs. 5–6 and 9–10 for photographs of the tablet and the tile and drawings of the central portion of each.

[14] My drawing is schematized from W. F. J. Knight, *Cumaean Gates* (Oxford, 1936), Fig. 12.

[15] E. Anati, "Prehistoric Art in the Alps," *Scientific American*, CCII (January 1960), 54; cf. my discussion, *AJA*, LXV (1961), 62.

Anati's subsequent book shows a few simpler spiral designs with oculi at the center but also another from the same area but somewhat later in date which, though misdrawn in a few particulars because of a crack in the rock, is unmistakably our labyrinth with its central cross.[16] The Hollywood stone at Dublin, with a perfect example of the labyrinth in the rounded form, has long been known but has received more attention recently during its sojourn at the World's Fair in New York. At least one of its admirers sees in it matters of mysterious significance for the human psyche.[17] Finally, a paper read at a Colloquium on Mycenaean Studies held at Cambridge, April 8–12, 1965, studies the design of the early labyrinths from Pylos and elsewhere and suggests, most ingeniously, that the double-axe symbol was indeed once a part of the figure, which was a kind of artisan's hallmark.[18]

(a)   (b)

Figure 5. (a) Bryn Celli Ddu Spiral and (b) Val Camonica folded spiral maze.

[16] E. Anati, *Val Camonica* (New York, 1961, trans. from the French ed.), figures on pp. 216, 217, 222 (spiral maze), and 226 (labyrinth). In a personal letter, Anati has stated his opinion that the labyrinth figure is quite late, not earlier than the sixth century B.C.; in doing so, he probably had the Etruscan vase in mind. I would guess that whoever drew the earlier spiral maze (Fig. 5, above) had also seen the figure in the round form (as on the Etruscan vase) and was trying to reproduce it from memory, working with the traditional spirals but using only one continuous line, whereas the labyrinth requires two lines.

[17] On the Hollywood stone and the Spanish petroglyphs, see E. MacWhite, *Estudios sobre las relaciones atlanticas de la peninsula hispanica en la edad de bronce* (Madrid, 1951), p. 26, Fig. 2, and p. 35. But the stone was an isolated find, and others have dated it to the medieval period; see G. H. Orpen, *Journ. Royal Soc. Antiquarians of Ireland*, LIII (1923), 177–89, and LIX (1929), 176–79. A typology of labyrinths was attempted by L. Monteagudo (*Cuadernos de Estudios Gallegos*, VII [1952], 301–306), but it is quite superficial, not recognizing the basic structure. For the enthusiast, see G. N. Russell, "Secrets of the Labyrinth," in the *Irish Times* for 16 December 1964.

[18] See *Nestor*, p. 385 (May 1965), listing a paper by L. J. D. Richardson, "The Origin of the Labyrinth, PY Cn 1287." I am greatly indebted to the kindness of the author in allowing me to see a copy of his typescript and figures; see now *Proc. Fourth Intern. Colloquium on Mycenaean Studies, Cambridge 1965* (Cambridge, 1966), pp. 285–96.

This new material has compelled the writer to reconsider his former opinions. He hopes to show that the figure was not, after all, built up from the cross (though the cross is an essential part of the design) but was rather a development of the spiral using two continuous lines instead of a single line. Before indulging this speculation, however, we turn to a mathematical analysis. Given the figure with the cross, as illustrated above, can we generalize its construction and specify the conditions which limit the production of a unicursal figure? And what possible variants can it have?

II. THE LABYRINTH L_n

A *linear graph* is a finite set of points, called *vertices* of the graph, and curves, called *edges* of the graph, where (1) each edge joins two vertices (its *endpoints*) but passes through no vertex and (2) two edges may have one or both vertices in common but do not intersect at any other point. An edge and a vertex are said to be *incident* if the vertex is an endpoint of the edge. We will understand that a vertex is *removable* if it is incident with just two edges, and that vertices may be inserted in curves, dividing them into edges. Thus a circle can be considered a linear graph, since we could divide it into two edges by a pair of vertices on it.

A *labyrinth* is a graph in a plane, suggesting the floor plan of a more or less intricate system of corridors and possibly chambers and entrances. Figure 6 represents a labyrinth with one entrance and one corridor, traced by a dotted line to its end, a sort of cul de sac.

We consider only graphs in a plane. Given such a graph, the rest of the plane falls into a set of connected regions, of which one is unbounded, or infinite. This is the only region, unless a closed curve can be found in the graph, in which case there is at least one bounded region, and the graph is said to *separate* the plane. The solid lines in Figure 1 represent a graph which does not separate the plane.

Various puzzles are associated with labyrinths. The question whether a labyrinth can be traced completely, as in Figure 6, is the question whether, regarded as a graph, it separates the plane. If it does, one might seek to discover how many regions there are, separated from one another by the graph, or one might seek the shortest path between two given points along corridors of the labyrinth.

One may also ask whether a labyrinth is *unicursal,* in the sense that its corridors can be completely traced by a continuous path which, though it may intersect itself, does not trace any segment of a corridor more than once. The seven bridges of Koenigsberg, schematically shown in Figure 7 with the two islands and stretches of river bank, form a labyrinth which is not unicursal. The question of unicursality for a labyrinth is best studied in terms of such graphs as are exemplified in Figures 6 and 7 by the dotted lines representing "walks" along the various "corridors" (bridges and banks in this case). The great Swiss mathematician Leonhard Euler (1707–83), stimulated by the Seven Bridges Puzzle, proved the general theorem that a connected graph is unicursal if, and only if, either (1) each of its vertices is incident with an even number of edges, or (2) exactly two of them are incident with an odd number of edges.[19] This was

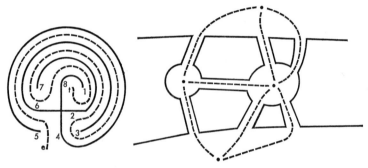

Figure 6.
The labyrinth L_0.

Figure 7.
The seven bridges of Koenigsberg.

but one of several important results whereby Euler laid a foundation for the subsequent development, largely during the twentieth century, of modern topology. From it, one deduces that no promenade can cross each of the seven bridges of Koenigsberg exactly once, since the dotted graph in Figure 7 has four vertices each incident with an odd number of edges.

Imagine the edges of a graph in the plane to be made of stretchable and shrinkable string, with knots at the vertices. Two graphs are *equivalent* if one can be deformed into the other in the plane by moving vertices about, keeping them distinct, and bending,

[19] Euler's first memoir on the theory of unicursal curves ("Solutio problematis ad geometriam situs pertinentis") was published in the *Commentarii Academiae scientiarum imperialis petropolitanae*, VIII (1736), 128–40. See also W. W. R. Ball, *Mathematical Recreations and Essays* (11th ed., rev. by H. S. M. Coxeter; London, 1940), pp. 242–66.

stretching, and shrinking the edges, but never lifting them from the plane or allowing them to intersect or touch one another except at vertices. Removable vertices can be disregarded. Known results imply that equivalent graphs agree in the number of regions into which they separate the plane and in unicursality properties. The labyrinth in Figure 6 is equivalent to the letter X.

We next study briefly the connectedness properties of a class of labyrinths including the historic labyrinths discussed above by Heller. His description of them suggested to the present writer the mathematical definition used below, though as he points out (later), it is extremely unlikely to conform to early methods of drawing labyrinths.

Let x and y be two diameters of a circle C. The circle is used for expository purposes and will form no part of the labyrinth. Let a, b, c, d denote the midpoints, in cyclic order (Fig. 8), of the four arcs into which x and y divide C. For expository convenience, we take x to be vertical, y horizontal, and (a, b, c, d) in clockwise order with a in the upper right arc of C.

A. The inner arcs of L_n. Let n be an arbitrary non-negative integer $(0, 1, 2, ...)$. In each of the four sectors into which x and y divide the interior of C, let n non-intersecting arcs be inserted, arranged and denoted as in Figure 8c, by $(a_1, . . ., a_n)$, $(b_1, . . ., b_n)$, $(c_1, . . ., c_n)$, and $(d_1, . . ., d_n)$. If $n=0$, no arcs at all are to be inserted. We refer to these $4n$ arcs and the diameters x and y as the *inner arcs* of a labyrinth L_n, whose definition we presently complete. The notation is such that a radius from a to the center of C crosses $(a_1, . . ., a_n)$ in the order named, and similarly for b, c, and d.

B. The special points. By the *special points* of L_n we will mean a, b, c, d and the endpoints of the inner arcs just defined. Since there are $4n+2$ inner arcs, there are $8n+8$ special points. A labyrinth L_n will be made up of the inner arcs and a set of *outer arcs,* outside C, joining the special points in pairs.

C. The outer arcs. Let the special points be numbered $(1, 2, . . ., 8n+8)$, starting with an arbitrary one of them and proceeding clockwise. Let two special points be joined by an outer arc if, and only if, the sum of their numbers is $8n+9$. The shortest of the arcs should join 1 and $8n+8$, forming a sort of cul de sac (Figs. 6, 9a, 9b) about the midpoint, t (for terminus), of the short arc of C joining 1 and $8n+8$. The point of C diametrically opposite t will be denoted by e, for entrance. It is halfway between $4n+4$ and $4n+5$, which should be joined by the longest outer arc. The outer arcs are to be almost "parallel," as suggested by Figures 6 and 9, and none of them should intersect the half-line from e outside and normal to C. This puts e in the entrance to L_n.

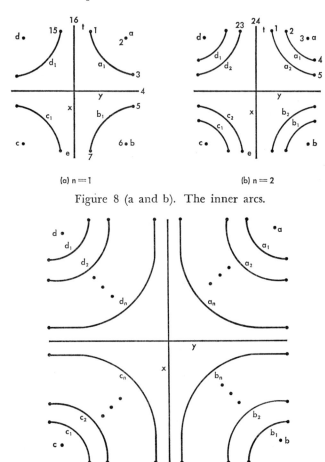

(a) $n = 1$ (b) $n = 2$

Figure 8 (a and b). The inner arcs.

Figure 8(c). The inner arcs of L_n.

In Figure 6, where $n = 0$, a dotted line goes from e to t through the entire labyrinth L_0. In Figure 9a, a dotted line with the same property could be drawn. These two labyrinths are thus both connected and unicursal. So is every labyrinth L_1. Each of them has its entrance next to x or y or next to a, b, c, or d. Each of them is equivalent to the graph consisting of x and y alone. In Figure 9a, for example, one can think of the top half of x as being stretched and bent around so as to cover a^1 and then continued to d, and similarly for the rest of the figure.

The labyrinth L_2 of Figure 9b, on the other hand, separates the plane. A path, indicated by the hatched lines, leads from e to t, but no path leads from e to a, b, c, or d. The graph in Figure 9b falls into two connected parts: (1) a part equivalent to the letter X, containing diameters x and y extended to a, b, c, and d, and (2) a simple curve enclosing this topological X.

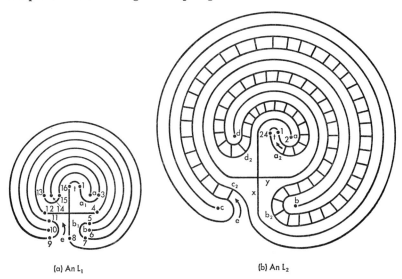

(a) An L_1 (b) An L_2

Figure 9. Examples of an L_1 and an L_2.

By drawing diagrams, one can verify that the other two essentially different types of labyrinth L_2 are connected and unicursal. One of them has its entrance next to a, b, c, or d, and the other has it next to one of the diameters x and y.

D. Paths on a labyrinth L_n. A *path* on L_n will mean a maximal sequence of inner and outer arcs, each two consecutive members of which have a common endpoint.

E. Theorem. A path is either a closed curve or else a curve joining two of the points (a, b, c, d). Inner and outer arcs alternate on a path.

Proof. The endpoints of the inner and outer arcs are special points. Each of the four special points (a, b, c, d) is endpoint of one outer arc and no inner arc. Each of the other $8n+4$ special

points is endpoint of just one inner and just one outer arc, hence
is a removable vertex. These two properties imply the theorem.

F. Corollary. There are exactly two paths on L_n with endpoints.
Each joins two of the points (a, b, c, d).

Proof. A path from $a, b, c,$ or d commences with an outer arc and
continues with alternating inner and outer arcs. Since there are only
a finite number of inner and outer arcs, such a path must have a
final arc. It must therefore join one of the points (a, b, c, d) to
another of these points.

G. A particular L_n. Given n, the inner arcs are determined. The
outer arcs, hence the labyrinth L_n, depend on the special point designated as 1. We analyze the particular L_n in which 1 numbers the
endpoint of a_n next to x. Otherwise expressed, this L_n has its entrance, e, just to the left of the bottom of x. See, for example, the
L_0 of Figure 6 and the L_1 of Figure 9a, which is one of the ancient
forms.

H. The numbers of the special points. For the L_n of Definition
(G), the special points are numbered as follows:

$a = n+1, b = 3n+3, c = 5n+5, d = 7n+7$, and the endpoints of the
inner arcs are given by the following table:

Arc	End points		
x	$4n+4$	and $8n+8$	
y	$2n+2$	and $6n+6$	
a_k	$n+1-k$	and $n+1+k$	$(k = 1, \ldots, n)$
b_k	$3n+3-k$	and $3n+3+k$	
c_k	$5n+5-k$	and $5n+5+k$	
d_k	$7n+7-k$	and $7n+7+k$	

I. Theorem. The graph L_n is a topological X. It consists of two
curves, one from a to c, the other from b to d. They intersect only
where x and y intersect.

This result will follow from lemmas dealing separately with the
cases where n is odd and where n is even.

J. Lemma. If n is odd, the inner arcs on the path from a are as
follows, in the order of their occurrence: $d_1 a_2 d_3 a_4 \ldots a_{n-1} d_n y$
$b_n c_{n-1} \ldots c_4 b_3 c_2 b_1$. That is, the odd-numbered d's alternate
with the even-numbered a's in order of increasing indices until d_n
is reached. Then comes y and an alternation of odd-numbered b's
with even-numbered c's in order of decreasing indices to b_1, which
is joined to c by an outer arc.

Proof. By (C) and (H), an outer arc joins $a = n+1$ to $7n+8$, since
these numbers sum to $8n+9$. By the table of endpoints of inner

arcs, $7n+8$ is an endpoint of d_1, whose other endpoint is $7n+6$. This starts a recurrent process. Suppose, that, in tracing the path from a, we have just traversed an inner arc d_k and are at the special point $7n+7-k$. Then, (C) and (H) imply that $7n+7-k$ is joined by an outer arc to $n+2+k$, which is an endpoint of a_{k+1}. From $n+2+k$, we go along the inner arc a_{k+1} to $n-k$ and from there to $7n+9+k$, which is on d_{k+2}. For $k=1$, we deduce that the next inner arc on the path is $a_{k+1}=a_2$, and the next is $d_{k+2}=d_3$, and so on until we reach the endpoint of d_n numbered $7n-n+7=6n+7$. From there, an outer arc goes to $2n+2$, an endpoint of y, by (H). Along y we proceed to its other endpoint, $6n+6$, from which an outer arc goes to $2n+3$, an end of b_n. The remainder of the demonstration follows this same pattern.

K. Lemma. If n is odd, the path from b terminates at d and passes along the following inner arcs in the order named: $c_1\, b_2\, c_3$ . . . $b_{n-1}\, c_n\, x\, a_n\, d_{n-1}$. . . . $a_3\, d_2\, a_1$. It then continues along an outer arc to d.

The proof is like that of (J).

L. Lemma. If n is even, the two paths from a to c and b to d are specified by the order of the inner arcs on them as follows, where we also list the endpoints of the paths

$$a\ d_1\, a_2\, d_3\ .\ .\ .\ d_{n-1}\, a_n\, x\, c_n\, b_{n-1}\ .\ .\ .\ b_3\, c_2\, b_1\, c$$
$$b\ c_1\, b_2\, c_3\ .\ .\ .\ c_{n-1}\, b_n\, y\, d_n\, a_{n-1}\ .\ .\ .\ d_3\, a_2\, d_1\, d.$$

The proof is like those of (J) and (K) combined.

Theorem (I) follows from Lemmas (J), (K), and (L).

M. Corollary. The particular graph L_n of Definition (G) defines a labyrinth with a single corridor, unicursally traceable from e to t as in the special cases of Figures 6 and 9a.

To see this, let a line start from near a and go along the corridor keeping closer to the left wall than to the right. Let it be continued until it emerges at the entrance, near e, then let it go around the outside, re-enter and retrace the labyrinth, still staying closer to the left wall than to the right, and returning to its starting point. This yields a single closed curve bordering a strip about the arms of the topological X, as is seen with the aid of Lemmas (J), (K), and (L). The corollary is now evident.

By the methods used above, any labyrinth L_n could be analyzed and general theorems proved as to how their structures depend on the number n and the special point which is chosen as number 1.

In the case of an L_2, for example, the labyrinth will be unicursal only if the points are numbered so that the entrance is next to an axis (x or y) or to a midpoint (a, b, c, or d). When L_n is not unicursal, we have what we may call an *incomplete* labyrinth, because a path from e to t does not traverse the entire figure.

The labyrinth L_0 (Fig. 6) is embedded in the L_2 of Figure 9b in the following sense. If the closed curve of the L_2 is removed, L_0 remains. The reader may verify that an arbitrary L_n can be similarly embedded in an incomplete labyrinth as follows. Between each consecutive pair of the $8n+8$ special points of the given L_n, let two new special points be inserted. This implies the corresponding insertion of $2n+2$ new inner arcs in each of the four sections within C. Let the point t for the new, enveloping labyrinth be the same as for L_n. The outer arcs of the new labyrinth, which has $24n+24$ special points, include as a subset those of L_n, since the endpoints of each of the latter are equally spaced from t.

III. VARIANT LABYRINTHS: A TYPOLOGY

Returning to the historical problem, we first comment on the actual occurrence of examples of L_n. By far the greatest number and all the early examples, from the Pylos tablet to the Pompeian graffito, have just one inner arc in each quadrant. We may call this the normal type. Matthews' ample illustration of medieval and modern examples shows one case of L_2, a pebble structure at Wisby on the island of Gotland.[20] This is unicursal; Cairns' "incomplete" labyrinth (Fig. 9b) is not actually attested. There is one case of $n=3$, the large turf structure known as "Troy Town" in Oxfordshire (Mt. Fig. 69; CJ Fig. 7). But there is no example of $n=0$, and Heller now renounces his guess about the swastika (Fig. 4).

Cairns' definition of L_n rightly excludes figures which do not have four midpoints, yet some such actually do exist. Compare a six-walled figure and a five-walled figure on coins from Cnossos, and a nine-walled figure carved on a Danish stone cross (Fig. 10).[21] We may call these figures "false" labyrinths. Otherwise resembling the figure with the central cross, they offer a path which is blocked before it reaches the central point, as the reader can determine with

[20] Mt. (above, n. 3), Fig. 126. A few others are known from Finland and Germany; see Ringbom, (above, n. 8), Figs. 2, 7, and 8.

[21] For the coins, see Wroth (above, n. 3), Pl. 6.8 and 5.13–15; for the cross, Mt., Fig. 128 (CJ Fig. 8). Matthews reproduced the figure from O. Worm, *Danicorum monumentorum libri sex* (Hafniae, 1651), p. 213.

his pencil. The four midpoints are essential, since if one or more is omitted there will be a closed curve, separating the plane, provided the central cross is present.

Figures based on the staggered cross, like the "Caerdroia" of Figure 3a or a perfectly circular drawing from a medieval manuscript illustrated by Meyer (Fig. 3; *CJ* Fig. 4) or the pavement labyrinth shown in Figure 16 (p. 256), are not covered explicitly by Cairns' definition of L_n, but it could easily be extended to include them, since the segment of x in the staggered cross which joins the two halves of y can be reduced to zero without affecting the number or position of the special points. On the other hand, there are other unicursal figures which do not have the central cross, like the complex design of the mosaic from Sousse, based on what Meyer called

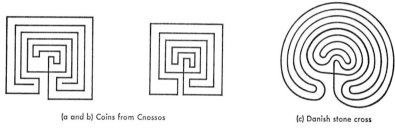

(a and b) Coins from Cnossos   (c) Danish stone cross

Figure 10. False labyrinths, with central cross but lacking some or all midpoints.

a "double meander turn" (Fig. 3b). These labyrinths are developed on a different principle from L_n, and we may call them "meshed combs" (Fig. 17c). Many such are found in medieval churches, laid out on the pavement as penitential pathways, like a famous one at Chartres (Mt. Fig. 47). The path through the meshed combs becomes a continuous folded line, moving back and forth and in and out through all the various parts of a circle (or other symmetrical figure) until it reaches the center. Though many of these figures, like the mosaic at Sousse, are identified by inscriptions with the legendary labyrinth,[22] we would describe them, according to the structure of the walls (or lines that separate the folds of the pathways), as compounded meshed combs or meander-units.

We also call attention to true mazes, which offer a choice of paths, some of them blind alleys. Many such have existed, from the pre-

[22] See also Mt., pp. 56–57 for medieval examples.

historic Val Camonica (Fig. 5) to Hampton Court [23]—and modern laboratories of psychology. They have been greatly favored in the topiary art of landscape gardeners.

Our catalogue now runs as follows:

A. Figures not unicursal
   1. Mazes, of many shapes and designs
   2. With central cross
      a. False labyrinths
      b. Incomplete labyrinths of type L_2
B. Unicursal figures
   1. Labyrinths with central cross (L_n)
      a. Normal type L_1
      b. L_2 and L_3 known but rare and late (medieval)
      c. L_0 possible, but not known

2. Meshed combs, often compounded in symmetrical designs, mostly medieval but known in antiquity; compare the decoration on an Ionic amphora.[24]

And we must not forget to add

3. Spirals, as at Bryn Celli Ddu (Fig. 5); compare an attractive design, formerly cut in turf and known as "The Walls of Troy" at a place in Cumberland (Mt. Fig. 68), which begins on the outside with a simple spiral but concludes at a center or boss from which *two* spiralling lines cause the unicursal path to reverse itself and come back to the boss. If the boss is lengthened, however, and the lines are straightened a bit, it will be seen that what we have is half a labyrinth of type L_2, lacking (that is) the lower half of x and finished on the outside with a spiral.

This last example should warn us that we have not yet exhausted the possibilities of unicursal figures which are variants of the central cross. They are not analyzed by Cairns (for the good reason that Heller did not ask him to consider them), but his methods could be extended to analyze them, and they should be regarded as true but variant labyrinths.

A first class includes figures with the central cross but with the number n of inner arcs varying from one quadrant to another, much as the Cumberland figure (Fig. 11) varies in its inner and outer halves. Let the reader complete the following, noting the descriptive

---

[23] Mt., Fig. 111; see also Fig. 66 for an attractive maze cut in turf at Hilton, Hunts.

[24] Eilmann (n. 6, above), abb. 7; cf. *AJA*, LXV (1961), Pl. 33, Fig. 19.

formulas in the legends in Figure 12. Still other variants could be laid out, and many of them will be unicursal, but none of them is known to exist historically.

A second class includes figures which do not have a central cross but are characterized by other sorts of lines radiating from one or more centers, resulting in more than four sectors or in just three sectors. A great variety of these can easily be imagined, and not all of them will be unicursal. We give only a few examples, noting that again it is not necessary that n be constant (Fig. 13). It will be noted that some of these figures, if they are to be unicursal, result in a

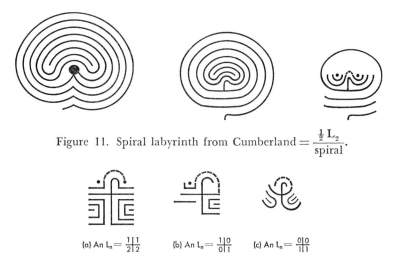

Figure 11. Spiral labyrinth from Cumberland $= \dfrac{\frac{1}{2} L_2}{\text{spiral}}$.

(a) An $L_n = \frac{1|1}{2|2}$ (b) An $L_n = \frac{1|0}{0|1}$ (c) An $L_n = \frac{0|0}{1|1}$

Figure 12. Variant labyrinths with central cross but n not constant.

spiral either at the entrance or at the terminus. The same result, however, will be achieved with some of the regular labyrinths of type L_1 or L_2 (or L_n), if the first outer arc connects a midpoint with an adjacent special point (Fig. 8b, above). In these cases we will have spirals both at the entrance and at the terminus, as the reader can determine for himself. At any rate, topological methods can be applied to analyze these variant labyrinths. Though no historical example of the figures above is known, it will be observed that Figure 13d, where $n=1$, has exactly the same structure as the Cumberland spiral labyrinth (Fig. 11), where $n=2$.

A minimum defining condition for these variant labyrinths is that there must be at least one point from which at least three walls radiate. If there is just one Y junction, there will be three sectors, one of which generally contains a spiral. But we have not yet finished our exposition of variant labyrinths. In order to do so, we now consider a unicursal labyrinth of most peculiar form that is known historically. As a consequence, we think it will be seen that we can have labyrinths with only two sectors.

We reproduce from Matthews (Fig. 125) a stone or pebble structure which Aspelin had seen on an island not far from Borgo in Finland.[25] The path leads first to the inner sector, moving through it first (Fig. 14a) in a counterclockwise spiral, then reversing to clockwise and emerging to the right-hand outer sector. From there it moves back and forth to the left-hand outer sector, reaching a terminus in the central loop of the left-hand sector; it has traversed every part of the figure. If we regularize the labyrinth, as indicated in Figure 14b, giving it a vertical x axis and half of a horizontal y axis, it can be analyzed as a variant labyrinth with three sectors and

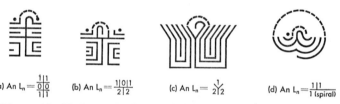

(a) An $L_n = \dfrac{1|1}{\underset{1|1}{0|0}}$ (b) An $L_n = \dfrac{1|0|1}{2|2}$ (c) An $L_n = \dfrac{\backslash|/}{2\backslash 2}$ (d) An $L_n = \dfrac{1|1}{1 \text{ (spiral)}}$

Figure 13. Variant labyrinths without central cross, n varying.

n respectively equal to 2, 4, 4. But it has the further peculiarity that one of the sectors has no midpoint while a second has two midpoints. If this peculiarity can be generalized, we will have a third class of variant labyrinths.

We begin by reducing the number of inner arcs in the preceding figure, as in Figure 15a. Then we construct a figure (b) based on a Y and another (c) on the familiar X of type L_1, taking care to place the two midpoints in such a way as to leave room for an intervening line, and to join the second midpoint by an outer arc to the next special point at its left. In all cases we get a unicursal figure with a double spiral in the central sector, causing the path to reverse itself and lead into a second sector, while the terminus is at one side, in the sector which has no midpoint. Lastly, having in mind the upper right sector of Figure 15c, we try to construct a single

[25] J. R. Aspelin, "Steinlabyrinthe in Finnland," *Ztschr. f. Ethnologie,* IX (1877), Verhandlungen, 439–41.

three-sided sector (d) with two midpoints similarly placed, and by following the usual rules to join all the special points, we discover that an outer sector is generated which contains the terminus, at a point adjacent to the entrance. This is a variant labyrinth based on a U, with two sectors and without so much as a Y junction.

If the path is left open at the terminus, however, or if it stops at the end of the left-hand vertical side, at the point marked by the arrow in Figure 15d, then we have the basic unit of what Meyer called a double meander-turn and we have called a development of

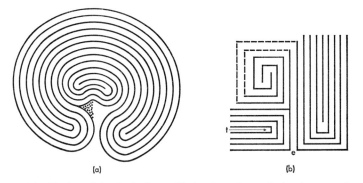

(a)   (b)

Figure 14. Variant labyrinth from Finland and regularization: an $L_n = \dfrac{2}{4}\Big|\,4.$

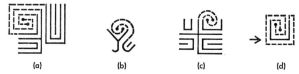

(a)   (b)   (c)   (d)

Figure 15. Variant labyrinths, two midpoints in one sector, none in another.

meshed combs (p. 251, cf. 258). That is, this unit can be extended by adding other similar units which can be arranged, using curved or bent lines and connecting pathways, in elaborate designs like the mosaic from Sousse, with an entrance on the outside and a terminus in the center. In itself, however, the unit differs from the other labyrinths we have considered, in that it has two entrances and no terminus. The path leads through the entire figure, but it does not stop at the center or anywhere else.

The difference between this unit and the other labyrinths is neatly illustrated by a figure which Meyer (pp. 297–98 and Fig. 11) constructed to show the development of the "Wunderkreise der Turnschulen" and which he compared to a labyrinth (his Fig. 6; cf. Mt. Fig. 56) found on the pavement of a ruined church at Toussaints-sur-Marne (Fig. 16a). His Wunderkreis has two openings (Fig. 16b). According to tradition, races were run in this figure, which was usually rounded to avoid sharp turns, by boys stationed at each opening. It will be seen that each boy would have to run through the entire figure without stopping (except for a shock when he met the other boy!), and would emerge at the other opening. Meyer thought that his figure was developed from the labyrinth by removing the exterior axis and opening a new entrance (z in his

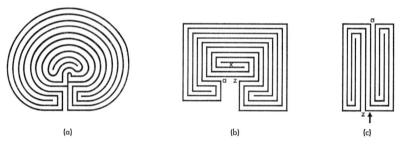

(a)   (b)   (c)

Figure 16. (a) Labyrinth at Toussaints, (b) a Wunderkreis, (c) a pair of meander-units.

drawing) into what used to be the last path. But inspection of the two figures will show that the exterior axis of (a) can still be regarded as present in (b), as the first vertical wall to the right of the main opening. Actually there is no simple way by which (a), an L_2 with staggered cross, can be altered into (b). The latter is, rather, an arrangement of two of our basic units (Meyer's meander turns) so positioned that the openings are adjacent to each other. Compare the vertical regularization in (c), made by standing the outer sector upright, with the opening z outside its lower left corner, and then placing the elongated inner sector on its left, with the other opening, a, on the opposite side. The Wunderkreis is a *Kreis*, wondrous indeed, but not a *Kreuz*. On the other hand, if the left-hand unit of (c) had been terminated by a vertical line above the arrow and the rest of the figure were discarded, we would have the variant labyrinth of Figure 15d, inverted.

IV. ORIGIN OF THE LABYRINTH

Notwithstanding the convenience of the central cross, inner arcs, and midpoints as a skeleton from which anyone may construct a labyrinth and a mathematician may analyze it topologically, it does not seem likely that the person who first constructed our labyrinth began with such a framework. It works, magically, to produce an attractive geometrical figure which is elegant in its unicursality. Once the figure became known, the value of the generating skeleton would be realized, but unless the figure were known in advance and the procedure for generating it had been memorized, it is hard to see why anyone should start with a cross and midpoints, to take the simplest form of the figure. This form is in fact lacking historically. Moreover, the earliest recorded form, on the Pylos tablet, does not seem to have used midpoints as a guide ("The evidence for dots is almost non-existent," Lang cited in *AJA,* LXV [1961], 59), and another early form, on the Athenian tile, does not seem to have begun with the central cross (*AJA,* LXV, 60); and if the artist of the Etruscan vase used inner arcs as a guide, he placed them very irregularly (Mt. Fig. 135; *CJ* Fig. 10; see Fig. 22, below). We must therefore look for other methods of drawing the figure.

Unless a precise model for our labyrinth can be found in nature, we must suppose that whoever invented it was trying to produce a figure which would have some special attraction for a viewer, including himself. Given the desire for geometrical elegance, such as that to be seen in a simple circle or set of concentric circles, the second idea which was essential to the invention of the figure was that of penetration by means of a continuous path. A spiral, obviously, would satisfy the twin desires for elegance and penetration (cf. Figs. 5 and 11), and we will suggest below that our figure was in fact invented in an effort to dress up or elaborate a simple spiral; but first we should examine the possibilities of some other figures.

Neither the meander nor the swastika conveys any idea of penetration, and we rule them out. Curiously, a combination of the two, what we may call a swastika-meander, also appears on coins of Cnossos of the fourth century B.C., just when the labyrinth figure makes its appearance there, and the meander is often associated with the Minotaur on earlier coins and in vase paintings. But inspection of the meander-swastika (Fig. 17a)[26] shows that whatever

[26] Mt., Fig. 23; compare his discussion on p. 44, and, for a vase painting, Fig. 38; but for this kylix and others like it, the reference to the labyrinth has

paths there are lead nowhere; they are soon blocked. And it does not seem at all likely that a swastika could have been elaborated as in Figure 4, above.

A nest of boxes or circles with openings leading to the interior would invite penetration, but there would be more than one path to the center even if there is only one opening in each box (Fig. 17b).

Two parallel lines of course provide a path that is continuous but hardly interesting. If, however, three or more parallel lines are used, and the first, third, and subsequent odd lines are connected at the top while the even lines are connected at the bottom, then a path will be generated that is interesting, first a U, then an S on its side, then a serpentine, as more lines are added (Fig. 17c). The path does not lead to a center, but if several such units, which we have called

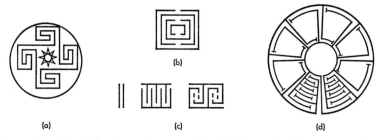

Figure 17. (a) Coin from Cnossos. (b, c) Figures inviting penetration. (d) Mosaic at Cormerod.

"meshed combs," [27] are placed side by side and bent around a square or circle, the path can be continued from one unit to another until it does reach a center. Compare an elaborate mosaic pavement at Cormerod (Switzerland) illustrated by Matthews (Fig. 36), which also has a representation of Theseus and the Minotaur in the center. The principle of connected units (Fig. 17d) is the same as what is seen in the meander-units at the right of Figure 3b above. Moreover, if the parallel lines forming the teeth of the combs are angled off toward each other in pairs (Fig. 17c), then the meander-unit itself will soon develop (Fig. 3b; cf. 15a).

But the meander-unit differs from our labyrinth precisely in that the former has two openings and the latter only one (compare

been doubted by G. W. Elderkin ("Meander or Labyrinth," *AJA*, xiv [1910], 185–90). But see also P. Lehmann, "The Meander Door: A Labyrinthine Symbol," *AJA*, lxx (1966), 192.

[27] See *AJA*, lxv (1961), Pl. 33, Fig. 12, and p. 62.

Fig. 16c with 15d). The path of the latter leads to a dead end, usually at the center (though not so in the variants of Figs. 14 and 15). The path in the former also leads through every part of the figure, but emerges at the opposite side and can be traversed in either direction—hence races in the Wunderkreis (Fig. 16b and c). A single labyrinth provides a path to a center, whereas with meander turns or meshed combs the historical examples require several compounded units bent around a square or circle in order to bring the path to a center. It is true, of course, that this aim could have been accomplished by bending a single unit, a meander turn (Fig. 18a) or meshed combs (18b); or if Meyer's double meander turn (Fig. 3b) is laid out with the upper brackets vertical (18c) and then the upper opening is closed and the usual pairs of special points are connected, we get precisely the labyrinth with staggered cross (18d); compare the rounded form of "Caerdroia" (Fig. 3a). Chronologically, how-

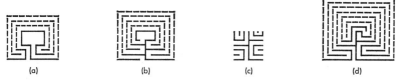

(a)   (b)   (c)   (d)

Figure 18. Labyrinths made from bent meander-units or meshed combs.

ever, all these figures are late,[28] as compared with the numerous examples of L_1 with the central cross. The classic form of the labyrinth could hardly have been developed in this way.

We therefore return to the spiral. We suggest that someone studying its path to a center asked himself what would happen if at some point a second line were introduced, branching off from the spiral (Figure 19a).[29] How could the two lines be continued, more or less symmetrically, in such a way as not to block the existing path and not to introduce a second path? The choice is quite simple. If the second line continues in the same direction as the first (19b), a second path is introduced, and it is blocked. But if it turns in the opposite direction and is carried outside the end of the first line (19c), there is only one path and it is continuous. This result might

---

[28] A coin of Cnossos has the same form as Fig. 18a (see E. Babelon, *Traité des monnaies grecques et romaines*, *II*, Pt. 3 [Paris, 1916], Pl. 250.12); another (250.9) has one more wall, i.e., half of a staggered cross.

[29] For ease in drawing, we illustrate with angular forms. The actual experimenter may well have been using ropes or strings; compare Cairns, above, p. 244.

have satisfied most people, but our inventor asked one more question. Observing that the end of one line is enclosed within a loop of the other, would the figure not be more interesting if both ends were enclosed in loops? Instead of ending the inner (spiral) line at the left of the vertical, let him double it back, leaving room for the other line to be placed inside it (19d). Now, taking up the other line, there is one way and only one way by which it can be brought to end inside the loop of the first line: it must now turn in the same direction as the first line, follow it on the outside and then turn to the inside, forming its loop, and end on the same side of the vertical from which it started (19e).

This movement of two lines, each line ending within a loop of the other, is the real secret of the labyrinth (or so we think). Compare Cairns' demonstration (above, I-L) that the graph L_n is a topological X consisting of just two curves, intersecting only where x and y intersect. So far, of course, we have only the outer half of

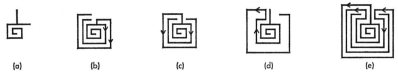

Figure 19. Experiments adding a second line to a spiral.

the figure, finished on the inside with a spiral,[30] but having discovered this much, our inventor would surely go on to apply his secret to the inside of the figure.

Let us suppose he is producing his figure with strings, as Cairns has suggested anyone may do (p. 244). The inside of his structure is shown in Figure 20a. What can he do if he extends the central vertical string downward, crossing the horizontal line? Let us turn the outside strings to one side and let the former single inside string dangle, as in Figure 20b. Our inventor now takes the newly extended string and lays it out as in 20c, taking care to leave room, as he had done on the outside, for the other string to loop around its end and come to an end, in turn, within its loop (20d). Then picking up the outer strings he can restore them to their former position, always remembering his rule: each string (or line, if he is now drawing) must come to an end within a loop of the other.

Once the figure became known and had been studied by artists and geometricians, the central cross, angle brackets (i.e., loops), and

[30] Compare Figs. 11 and 13d for the reverse procedure; but we must suppose that in the process of invention the spiral preceded the labyrinth and was therefore on the inside.

dots (line ends) would have been abstracted from it and used for the regular construction of a truly amazing design. Variants such as the staggered cross would be introduced to render the figure more symmetrical, and meander-units might be developed from them. But I suspect this did not happen for some time. The inventor (to pursue our conjectures) had proceeded by trial and error with a second line to elaborate the idea of penetration suggested by a spiral, and the idea of spiral motion may have persisted after the spiral itself had been removed from the figure. Compare Figure 21, showing a probable method of drawing the figure once its secret had been learned. One starts with the first line (or string), laying it out as in (a) with a loop to the right and the end on the left, rather like a shepherd's crook or our question-mark. The second line is then

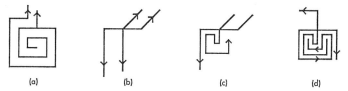

Figure 20. Experiments transforming the inner spiral to a labyrinth.

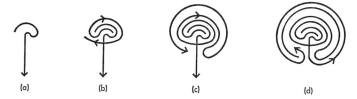

Figure 21. Loop and end, second end within loop, and spiralling motion.

inserted inside the loop and its loop is made around the end of the first line (b); then it continues clockwise in two spiralling revolutions (b and c), until it forms its outer loop at the lower right and then ends on the other side, space having been left for the first line to follow it first, counter-clockwise, and then to form its loop, doubling around the end of the second line and coming to its end inside the loop at the right (20d). A little practice with this method of drawing the figure will convince anyone, we think, that this is both an easy and a satisfying way of producing it.[31] Or if one chooses

[31] One could start elsewhere in the figure, of course. See *AJA*, LXV (1961), 59–61, for my reconstruction of the drawings on the tablet from Pylos and on the Athenian tile, and *CJ*, XLII (1946), 131–32, for Von Petrikovits' reconstruction of the movements of the *Troiae lusus*. But, once started, the lines are generally continued without interruption to their ends and without much help from either central cross or angle brackets.

to place the crook horizontally, pointing downward, and to add a short vertical line as a guide (Fig. 22a) and then to insert the second line, working from the inside outward and continuing it after the interruption caused by the vertical line (22b), he will then understand the apparent irregularities of the labyrinth on the Etruscan vase.

The central framework, then, was not so fundamental as I once thought, nor am I so certain that the drawing game posited above was present from the beginning. As Professor Eric Turner has remarked in a letter, it seems odd to think of "sophisticated persons in Mycenaean Greece playing tricks on each other." As for the date of the figure's discovery, however, and the direction of its diffusion (for so complex a design is not likely to have been invented more than once), the evidence so far available compels us to suppose that the figure was invented in Greece at least as early as the end of the

(a)   (b)

Figure 22. Labyrinth "Truia" on Etruscan vase and (a, b) layout therefor.

thirteenth century B.C. and spread subsequently to Etruscan Italy and thence to central and northern Europe, the British Isles, and Spain. For large objects found in isolation, like the Hollywood stone, simply cannot be dated with any degree of certainty, whereas all the tablets found at Pylos must be dated to the year in which the palace was burned and the tablets, consequently, were baked. Diffusion westward from Mycenaean Greece has been traced for other objects and should occasion no surprise.[32]

Finally, I am tempted to suggest that a not unlikely natural model for spirals and the idea of penetration to a fearsome center could be found in the orb webs typical of certain spiders. See the illustrations in the article by B. J. Kaston, *Natural History*, LXXV, 4 (April 1966), 26–33.

University of Illinois
24 April 1966

[32] See especially the convincing details assembled by H. Hencken, "Herzsprung Shields and Greek Trade," *AJA*, LIV (1950), 295–309; also S. Piggott, *Ancient Europe* (Chicago, 1965), 136–39.

ATHLETIC FESTIVALS IN GREECE AND THEIR ROMAN PATRONS IN THE SECOND CENTURY B.C.

Rachel Sargent Robinson

The evidence to be cited below will, I hope, throw some light on the condition of festival games in Greece during a period which has been passed over with only brief mention in publications about Greek athletics.[1] The general assumption seems to have been that Greece, a small land, upset by many military campaigns throughout its length and breadth during much of this period, must necessarily have allowed its athletic meetings to fade into insignificance.

Three well-worn pieces of evidence from the two centuries in question, strengthened by one from the following century, have been used by some writers to support their statements that it was in the second and first centuries before the Christian era that games in Greece went through their "blackest period."[2] But the burning of Corinth by Mummius, the temporary transfer to Rome by Sulla of all Olympic competitions (save one), the widespread looting of art treasures from festival shrines,[3] and the apparent demoralization of games during Nero's one year in Greece, though well attested by ancient writers, are selective evidence. They furnish only the shadows of a picture which was, on the whole, more bright than

[1] This article was planned as a supplement to Chapter VII of my *Sources for the History of Greek Athletics* (1955), to be incorporated in a section of the revised and enlarged edition of that book, now in preparation. I am happy to offer the present part, on the second century only, as an affectionate tribute to my old friend Professor Perry.

[2] E. N. Gardiner, *Athletics in the Ancient World* (Oxford, 1930), p. 46; *Olympia* (Oxford, 1925), pp. 152–53.

[3] See O. Vessberg (*Studien zur Kunstgeschichte der Römischen Republik* [Lund, 1941], pp. 26–79) for a collection of the literary evidence about the plundering of Greek art by Romans during the republic.

dark. Indeed, to judge from such primary inscriptional evidence [4] as I have examined and from the literary sources (for the most part secondary), the athletic festivals, in some cases with an ever-lengthening program of musical and literary events, appear to have survived all the vicissitudes which Greece as a whole experienced in those two centuries and were in better condition at the end than most other departments of Greek life.[5]

The evidence is plain that from the beginning of the second century before Christ, Roman leaders in Greece on urgent military business took time to visit Greek athletic centers for political or for personal reasons and that their visits there left the Greeks with gratitude for favors received. Those favors often gave evidence of a personal interest in the welfare of the shrine and exceeded the bounds of "political expediency"—a tag so often used by writers in evaluating Roman acts of generosity toward shrines at Olympia, Delphi, and the like.

First, Titus Quinctius Flamininus, victor over King Philip, made a personal appearance at the Isthmian festival near Corinth (196 B.C.) and had his herald address the crowds there from all over the Greek world (Livy XXXII, 1) with a breath-taking announcement of the liberation of most of Greece, including Epirus, from Macedonian control.[6] The joy of the Greeks (Aetolians excepted) was

---

[4] A complete collection of the epigraphical evidence for all aspects of the games and of athletic life in Greece during the second and first centuries is greatly to be desired. L. Moretti once promised such a study in the preface (p. X) of his *Iscrizioni Agonistiche Greche* (Roma, 1953). As it is, his volume is a uniquely useful collection, with commentary, of ninety inscriptions about victor athletes, ranging in date from the sixth century B.C. to the late third century of the Christian era.

However, only thirteen inscriptions of Professor Moretti's collection belong to the period presently under discussion. Six of them date from 200–146 B.C.; the remaining seven (down to 20 B.C.) are grouped in the first part of his Chapter IV, entitled "La Romanizzazione degli Agoni" (Romanization of the Games, if that is the meaning of his word). But Professor Moretti does not explain, in his otherwise excellent chapter, in what particulars the Greek games were "Romanized." I have found no evidence that they were. The new or revised name given to a number of them, *Romaia*, seems to have indicated, in my opinion, "games in honor of the goddess Roma," while the games themselves remained essentially Greek. In the completed chapter I shall return to this topic more than once.

[5] J. A. O. Larsen's *Roman Greece* (Baltimore, 1938) has proved very useful as a reference work for this chapter because of his thoughtful analysis of conditions in general throughout Greece, especially the financial ones during this period. S. Accame's *Il Dominio Romano in Grecia* (Roma, 1946) has also been helpful.

[6] See N. Lewis and M. Reinhold (*Roman Civilization* [N.Y., 1955], I, 172–76) for an English translation of the passages in Livy which describe not only the liberation speech but all of Flamininus' activities in connection with Philip V.

unbounded and the response was characteristic. For in Thessaly, Panhellenic, four-year games sacred to Zeus "Giver of Freedom" were inaugurated and given the name *Eleutheria* (Freedom games).[7] Before the end of the next decade, this young and brilliant Flamininus had been chosen president of the Nemean games where he had made a second announcement of the freedom of remaining portions of Greece, chiefly Argos; at Delphi he had dedicated silver shields and his own long one with appropriate verses. And, as is now known from an inscription at last deciphered from a monument base,[8] he was honored there with a large bronze statue of himself; while in Chalcis the finest gymnasium had been dedicated to Flamininus, wherein his statue was placed (*IG*, XII, 9, 931) and inscribed to "Titus, Savior and Benefactor." It is possible that it was at that time that the Euboean Council renamed their old Demetria games, now calling them *Romaia* (games in honor of Roma), as is hinted in an inscription (*IG*, XII 9, 899, line 13).[9]

Next, it was the management of the Delphi sanctuary with its oracle and its Pythian games who learned what benefits the kindly solicitude of a Roman general could confer upon it. Manius Acilius Glabrio had been sent out from Rome (191 B.C.) to cope with the problem of King Antiochus and his Asian troops in Greece. After a successful campaign, Glabrio, in the course of settling the score with the Aetolian league (a strong supporter of Antiochus), found an occasion to display an amazing concern for Delphi. By forthright measures he freed Delphi completely from control by the Aetolian League, even relieved it, as it appears, of some of its obligations to the old Amphictyonic council; besides independence, Glabrio granted the sanctuary freedom from tribute to Rome and substantially increased its resources. For he confiscated the forty or more houses, together with outlying landholdings, which belonged to

---

For other details about Flamininus in Greece see Plutarch, *Life of Titus* [i.e., Flamininus]: Ch. X (at Corinth); XII, 2 (at Nemean festival); XII, 6 (at Delphi); XVI (honors at Chalcis).

[7] The inscriptional evidence for the *Eleutheria* games (IG, IX, part 2, 508, 525, 526, 528, 529, 534, 537) has been discussed by I. C. Ringwood (pp. 15–21) in her Columbia University doctoral dissertation (1927) entitled *Agonistic Features of Local Greek Festivals Chiefly from Inscriptional Evidence* [includes non-Attic mainland and adjacent islands, except Euboea].

[8] See H. Pomtow's discussion, *Klio*, XVI (1920), 117–19. For coins which depict Flamininus' head and a marble head recently identified as a portrait of Flamininus, see F. Chamoux in *BCH*, LXXXIX (1965), 214–24 (nine illus.).

[9] See Mrs. Ringwood-Arnold's article, a continuation of her doctoral dissertation, entitled "Local Festivals of Euboea Chiefly from Inscriptional Evidence," *AJA*, XXXIII (1929), 385–92, esp. p. 390.

outsiders (chiefly Aetolians) who had been living at Delphi. These he presented to "the temple and to the city of the Delphians." The story of Glabrio at Delphi, like that of Sulla at Oropus, rests upon the primary evidence of an inscription which preserves the Senate's official report of its ratification of Glabrio's measures in behalf of Delphi and of the details of those measures.[10] In line six of the inscription there is the statement that the Delphians, while waiting for their second embassy to return with the final news from Rome, "celebrated games in honor of the Romans." This is an early instance of games called *Romaia*—a name which a little later was commonly affixed to games throughout the Greek world by grateful Greeks.

It must not be imagined that Glabrio's reverence for Apollo's temple and the Pythian games at Delphi was a new emotion for Romans. For ancient writers have reported traditions that specially appointed groups of Romans were sent to seek the advice of Delphi's oracle at the beginning of the fourth century;[11] while at nearby Caere (ancient Agylla), an Etruscan community some twenty-seven miles from Rome, games patterned on the Pythian games had been instituted in the late sixth century B.C. by order of the Delphic oracle. Herodotus is our authority for the games at Caere (I. 167), and he mentions that they were still in existence in his day, a century later. Naturally the Romans of that time would have learned much about the oracle of Apollo and its games from those Etruscan neighbors.

Fulvius Nobilior, a man of consular rank who had been associated with Glabrio in the Aetolian campaign and was active in the groups sent to the Peloponnesus, like the other Roman generals in Greece, quite evidently devoted some time to becoming acquainted with the athletic competitions at Greek games. For as a novelty for his fellow Romans, Fulvius in 186 initiated the custom of importing to Rome a group of Greek athletes to perform at his triumphal games (Livy XXXIX. 22, 2).

Twenty years after Glabrio's action in behalf of Delphi, the

[10] See Larsen (pp. 284–86; esp. p. 285) for his translation of a portion of those letters sent from Rome (189–88 B.C.), which were found inscribed on the base of a monument to Glabrio. The Greek text of the letters (those sent to Delphi and the one sent by the praetor to the Amphictyonic League) has been published by M. Holleaux in *BCH*, LIV (1930), 39.

An important discussion of this "Freeing of Delphi by the Romans" may be found in *Klio*, XVI (1920), 109–40, by Professor Pomtow.

[11] Livy V. 15, 3 and 16, 9; Plut. *Camillus* 8.

famous Lucius Aemilius Paulus, at sixty years of age, was dispatched to the Greece of his dreams to put an end to the troublesome third Macedonian War. Once arrived in Greece, Paulus made use of the interval before he could assume command in order to travel as a tourist to all the famous places in Greece, especially the sites of the Panhellenic games. And Livy (XLV. 27 and 28) preserves the story of how this Roman general and ex-consul stood gazing in rapt awe at Phidias' celebrated statue of Zeus at Olympia and "then ordered a sacrifice to be prepared, just as large a one as he would have offered on the Capitoline had he been in Rome."

To return to Paulus' campaign against the Macedonians, only two weeks were necessary for this experienced general to crush King Perseus and his followers in the battle of Pydna (168 B.C.). After that victory, Paulus to honor his Greek guests at the celebration in Amphipolis in 167 went to a great deal of trouble to arrange Greek-type games with Greek athletes gathered from all around the Greek world. The affair, according to Livy (XLV. 32, 8), moved so smoothly that the invited Greeks were amazed that one of the Romans, all novices in the matter of Greek athletic competitions, could succeed so well in such an undertaking.

Plutarch, a Greek himself (A.D. 46–120?), passes on a tradition, more than two hundred years old, that Flamininus, Aemilius Paulus, and Manius Acilius [Glabrio] not only spared the Greek sanctuaries but even made gifts to them and greatly increased their honor and dignity (*Sulla* XII. 6).

Twenty years after their defeat of the Macedonian Perseus, the Romans, reluctantly, were forced to use military measures against the fickle Greeks—campaigns fomented by acts of the Achaean League.

In the course of this brief war, as is well attested, Lucius Mummius did burn Corinth [12] on orders from the Roman Senate (146

[12] While such harsh treatment was frequently experienced by cities in Asia Minor or in Spain at the hands of victorious Romans, it was rarely the case in cities on the mainland of Greece. For Rome's type of government in Greece see Accame (n. 5, above), esp. pp. 78 and 161.

Strabo (VIII. 6, 23) cites a trivial reason for the destruction of this great commercial center: "The Corinthians, when they were subject to Philip, not only sided with him in his quarrel with the Romans but individually behaved so contemptuously toward the Romans that certain persons ventured to pour down filth upon the Roman ambassadors passing their houses" (trans. Jones, Loeb Classical Library).

But Mommsen would have us believe that competition in trade led to the burning of Corinth (*History of Rome*, Bk. IV [trans. Dickson, p. 49]): "The

B.C.), and he did carelessly allow his friends and his soldiers to pillage its art treasures, even permitting soldiers—so it is reported— to lay priceless paintings on the ground so as to use them as game-boards. The historian Polybius was with Mummius and related this as an eyewitness, according to a fragment preserved from his history (frg. XXXIX. 12 Hultsch).

But just as well attested are other acts of Mummius which have not been so often quoted.[13] Although he seized Corinthian land-holdings outside the city limits and pronounced them henceforth to be property of the Roman state (*ager publicus*), he did exclude from that confiscation the one section which included the site of the Isthmian festival. He not only saved that shrine for the Greeks but he repaired the establishment there and allowed nearby Sicyon, a steadfast friend of the Romans, to assume its management. So, as a result of Mummius' thoughtful planning, the Isthmian games, probably without any lengthy interruption, resumed their programs under Sicyonian control and continued for a full century, undis-turbed by the fate of Corinth. They were transferred back to Corinth's control only when Julius Caesar arranged for that city to be rebuilt.

Further, in the days following the completion of those arrange-ments with Sicyon, Mummius too is reported to have paid visits to Olympia and Delphi and to have presented those shrines with valu-able gifts (for Olympia's see Pausan. V. 10, 5 and 24, 4).[14] Afterward, he made a tour of Greek cities, "being received everywhere with tokens of honor and gratitude," according to his friend and admirer, the Greek Polybius.[15] Such a welcome may have represented genuine

---

destruction of Corinth by no means proceeded from the brutality of any single individual, least of all of Mummius, but was a measure deliberated and resolved on by the Roman senate: *we shall not err, if we recognize it as the work of the mercantile party,* which even thus early began to interfere in politics by the side of the aristocracy proper, *and which in destroying Corinth got rid of a commercial rival"* (italics mine).

[13] In addition to the passage from Strabo cited above, the evidence for Mummius is taken chiefly from the following sources: Polybius, Fragments of Bk. XXXIX. 13–18 (Hultsch); Livy, *Epitome* 52; Plutarch, *Philopoemen* 21, 6; Pausan. II. 2; Zonaras XI. 31 (Dindorf [1869] pp. 337–38). An inscription from Nemea published by D. Bradeen (*Hesperia*, xxxv [1966], 326–39) mentions Mum-mius' visit to Nemea as an arbitrator.

[14] See also *Die Inschriften von Olympia,* ed. Dittenberger-Purgold (in Curtius-Adler, *Olympia,* v), 278–81.

[15] In so trustingly citing Polybius (a primary source, but preserved largely in fragments of later writers) for information about Mummius in Greece, I align myself with Livy who wrote in his *History* (XXXIII. 10, 10) regarding Flami-

feelings on the part of the Greeks since Mummius had not only saved one of their Panhellenic festivals but had assisted in saving also all statues and memorials of the late Philopoemen of Megalopolis, a statesman and general highly esteemed throughout much of Greece. Other Romans had strongly urged their total destruction since Philopoemen had been at times hostile to the Roman cause (Plut. *Philopoemen,* 21, 6).

Thus it is clear that the major Panhellenic games continued along their normal path during the first half-century after the Romans arrived; and that Roman leaders of importance who had come to Greece on serious missions accorded their managing directors a sympathetic treatment. But can we be certain that the many well-known but distinctly minor athletic festivals remained financially able to maintain their schedules? And in a troubled Greece, did the vigor of athletic spirit remain sufficient to interest enough suitable competitors to enter their contests?

Very brief allusions to victories won in such contests are found in several inscriptions of the period, but the inscribed fragments of a pair of monuments, one found at Delos, the other in Athens, conveniently provide a long list of games which were of such importance that they attracted one of the foremost athletes of that day. The monuments honored a Menodorus of Athens for his thirty-two victories in the pancratium and wrestling; won, so it seems, at sixteen festivals, all on the mainland of Greece with the exception of the one on Delos.

The fragments of the Athenian monument (*IG,* II/III² 3147 and 3150) acquired new importance when additional fragments of it were found in the Agora excavations of 1933–34. S. Dow [16] was thereafter able to make a plausible restoration of the inscription by closely analyzing all of the Athenian fragments in the light of the very similar and better preserved words on the Delos fragments.[17] From internal evidence he has reached the conclusion that Menodorus'

---

ninus' victory: "I have given my account, not because the numbers are the smallest [i.e., 8,000 Macedonians killed; 5,000 captured at Cynoscephalae in 197 B.C.] but because I have followed Polybius, *an authority worthy of credence* on all matters of Roman history and *especially on occurrences in Greece"* (italics mine).

[16] S. Dow, *Hesperia,* IV (1935), 81–89. See also Moretti (*IAG* [n. 4, above], No. 51, pp. 131–38) for a discussion of every phase of this inscription. His views differ in some respects from Professor Dow's.

[17] The Delos fragments had been published previously by Professors L. Bizard and P. Roussel, *BCH,* XXXI (1907), 432–35.

listed victories extended from about 150 to 125 B.C. They appeared in neat, vertical rows on the monuments; each entry with both the name of the contest and its site (unless the latter was a familiar one) enclosed in a carved wreath whose foliage resembled that of the wreath customarily awarded there. It is apparent from the sites listed that Menodorus completed a real circuit of Greece in his athletic jaunts: (1) *Eleusinia* (Eleusis); (2) *Panathenaea* (Athens); (3) *Olympian* (Elis); (4) *Soteria* (Delphi); (5) *Nemean* (Argolis); (6) *Pythian* (Delphi); (7) *Eleutheria* (Plataea); (8) *Heracleia* (Chalcis); (9) *Delia* (Delos); (10) *Romaia* (Chalcis); (11) *Heraia* (Argos); (12) *Lykaia* (Arcadia); (13) *Heracleia* (Thebes); (14) *Naä* (Dodona); (15) *Trophonia* (Livadia); (16) *Nymphaia* (Apollonia).

Our inscription concerns only one man who proved victor in one or at the most two contests of each festival mentioned. We must not lose sight of the fact that a large number of youths proficient in athletic competitions would have had to present themselves at these sites before a full roster of competitors for all events could be selected. Besides, there is the possibility that other games were held in Greece which Menodorus did not enter, for one reason or another.

In addition to the honors granted Menodorus at the site of the games there are listed in the inscriptions also the four honorary wreaths presented to him by the cities of Athens, Thebes, and Rhodes and by King Ariarathes (*d.* in 130 B.C.). This of course is an indication that in this period athletes victorious in games were still the darlings of the Greek public, as they always had been, in days of peace or of war.

A stone block found near Argos has yielded an inscription [18] which lists victories in foot-racing won by an Achaean, name unknown. Seventeen festivals (including the four famous Panhellenic games) figure in the list, and the Achaean's peformances, so it has been estimated, occurred in the years between 200–180 B.C. In other words the festivals named are, very likely, the principal minor games usually held during the years when the Romans were first engaged in Greece. Their sites, according to Moretti's interpretation, were (in the order named): Argos, Livadia, Athens, Eleusis, Arcadia, Oropos, Plataea, Aetolia, Thebes, Sicyon, Chalcis, Delphi, Olympia, Nemea, Corinth (Isthmian). If their sites are compared with those at which Menodorus won, it will be clear that the pattern of such

[18] See Moretti in *IAG* (n. 4, above), No. 45, for the Greek text of this inscription (also published in *SEG*, xi, 338).

Greek festivals had not changed much after more than fifty years of Roman activity in Greece.

The fact that in this century eminent Romans sent to Greece on various important missions made every effort also to visit the celebrated sanctuaries in charge of sacred athletic festivals is one to be expected. In this era, Romans of their social rank, when boys at home, had of course heard tales about Greek athletic prowess from their tutors who were enslaved Greeks in their fathers' households. There is the further possibility that the older of those Romans might have acquired a taste for the pleasant recreation of viewing athletic contests when on tours of duty in southern Italy, where many a town was mindful of its Greek origins. And, besides, it should be remembered that games regularly held in honor of a god had been a normal part of Roman life since the days of Tarquin, the duty of providing them for the public falling to magistrates and generals. But since the Greek games were quite a different form of entertainment their novel features would be bound to attract the Roman visitors.

But there was undoubtedly something deeper than an athletic program which stirred those Romans and inspired them to seek ways and means by which such establishments could remain a permanent and solvent part of Greek life. It is possible that those Philhellenists who came to Greece on official business found at last in the attractive sites of the sacred festivals something of the Greece which they had long idealized. The air of tradition, of stability, of rigid laws of ancient origin, and of perfection of ritual detail must have been singularly compatible with the Roman temperament. In addition, during social gatherings in the groves before the games began, business matters could be discussed in a more friendly atmosphere than had been possible at more formal conferences in cities. At the sight of spectators from all over the Greek world sitting in harmony on a grassy hillside and meekly bowing to the will of the all-powerful Hellenic judges (*Hellanodikai*), the Roman visitors could perhaps forget for a moment all their prior chagrin and disappointment at having found the Greeks to be so wavering and impractical in their cities and leagues, and an undependable folk in political dealings not only with themselves as representatives of Rome but with each other in their own rival parties and associations.

University of Cincinnati
4 May 1966

COMMODIAN AND HIS VERSE

Kenneth M. Abbott

The publication by J. Martin in 1960 of the first really critical edition of Commodian since Dombart's monumental publication of 1887 in the Vienna corpus is a rare event.[1] It is, to be sure, an event which is unlikely to be celebrated, and if it could be called long-awaited—Martin's text was finished forty-five years after his first article on Commodian—one could hardly say that it was eagerly anticipated. Commodian, so far as he is known at all in modern times, has a limited notoriety as the bad boy of Latin metrics, his form being mentioned as "barbarous" or "rugged" or "semi-literate" dactylic hexameter or occasionally termed "accentual" hexameter. Nor is there any evidence that if Commodian has interested few in modern times there was a time when things were different.

We have two works, one certainly and one almost certainly by his hand, each surviving in a single manuscript. This paucity of evidence for a Christian author as compared with the hordes of manuscripts of such authors as St. Jerome and St. Augustine is certainly significant.

In the so-called decree of Pope Gelasius, *De libris recipiendis et non recipiendis* (possibly of the year A.D. 496)[2] *Opuscula Commodiani* are listed among the rejects, while Gennadius, *De viris inlustribus* XV,[3] writing at the end of the fifth century, disapproves of

---

[1] Commodiani Carmina Cura et Studio Iosephi Martin (Corpus Christianorum, Series Latina, CXXVIII, Turnholti, 1960). Martin's *Praefatio* (v-xxxii) is very complete and gives in brief his final conclusions on all essential points with full bibliography down to June 1958. A full discussion of major points he had published in *Traditio*, xiii (1957), 1–71. J. Perret's important article, "Prosodie et Métrique chez Commodien" (*Pallas*, v [1957], 27–42), was not available to Martin, and indeed came into my hands very late; see n. 21, below.

[2] *MPL*, lix, 163, quoted and discussed by Martin, *Praef.* 5; cf. Jülicher in *RE*, iv, 773.

[3] Ed. Richardson, *TU*, xiv, 1 (1896), 67: "Commodianus dum inter saeculares

272

his style—"*mediocri sermone*"—his form—"*quasi versu*"—, and his theology—"*vili satis et crasso . . . sensu.*" In spite of all this, and even if we concede that Commodian wrote what one of my Italian teachers persisted in calling an "illegible book," if his theology— with two resurrections and two Antichrists—is to say the least erratic, and if the virulence of his attacks on the Jews is on all counts puzzling, still the question of Commodian's place in the history of Late Latin as a language and the problem of the drift of late spoken Latin into Romance are matters of some genuine interest. Does Commodian in fact give evidence of the disappearance of Latin quantitative distinctions and if so at what period?

This, of course, brings up three good questions at once: Who was Commodian, when did he live, and where was he writing? And to these three questions there are still, in spite of considerable thoughtful or sometimes imaginative work by various scholars, no clear answers. Or perhaps too many clear answers. Dombart and Martin in their editions both plump for the middle of the third century A.D. or not later than the fourth (not after 312—Martin). The Oxford Classical Dictionary assigns him to the fifth century, and Schanz-Hosius-Krüger give 566 as the date for the completion of the works.

Direct information about him is very scanty. He closes his second book of *Instructiones* (II. 35 Martin; II. 39 Dombart) with a reverse acrostic reading *Commodianus Mendicus Christi,* and the title of this poem reads *Nomen Gasei.* This may be and has been emended to read *Gazaei,* which would make the author a native of Gaza in Palestine, but others [4] have interpreted the word as a variant of a Syriac form meaning "poet" and thus assigned the author a birthplace in Syria. The second work, the so-called *Carmen,* which has lost its title as well as the author's name, has a subscription: (BM Add. 43460 f. 197) *Explicit tractat(us) S(an)c(t)i Ep(i)sc(opi)* with

---

litteras etiam nostras legit, occasionem accepit fidei. Factus itaque christianus et uolens aliquid studiorum suorum muneris offerre Christo, suae salutis auctori, scripsit mediocri sermone quasi uersu aduersus paganos. Et quia parum nostrarum adtigerat litterarum, magis illorum destruere potuit dogmata quam nostra firmare. Unde et de diuinis repromissionibus aduersus illos agens uili satis et crasso ut ita dixerim sensu disseruit, illis stuporem, nobis desperationem incutiens Tertullianum et Lactantium et Papiam auctores secutus. Moralem sane doctrinam et maxime uoluntariae paupertatis amorem optime prosecutus studentibus inculcauit."

[4] First persuasively argued by M. Christ. Sigwalt, *Biblische Zeitschrift*, IX (1911), 243; cf. Martin *Praef.* xi, and, for rejection of other suggestions from Semitic, *Traditio,* XIII, 35.

traces of letters below it which can no longer be certainly read.[5] One can therefore find on high authority that Commodian was born somewhere in Syria, or in Gaza, or in Illyria, and that he was a bishop in Carthage, or Illyria, or within the Rhone valley, specifically at Arles. Or as Martin contends, dismissing arguments supporting these views as mostly not worth a fig (non flocci, as he puts it [Praef. xi], forgetting his verb) he may have been a resident of Rome, on equally inadequate grounds.

The only external evidence for Commodian, then, is in the Gelasian decree already mentioned and in Gennadius. But the papal list gives no clue as to his date. Gennadius does appear to classify Commodian with fifth-century authors, but whether or not he was correct in doing so is debatable. Whether he had good reason for citing Lactantius as one of Commodian's authorities is a rather crucial point, but no conclusive evidence has yet been adduced to show such indebtedness on Commodian's part.

The problem then remains that Commodian's Christian vocabulary, his perhaps somewhat erratic views on theological questions and the fervor of his attacks on the Jews all suggest an early date,[6] while the state of his language (a matter much more difficult and uncertain than even Martin suspects)[7] has appeared to suggest a late

---

[5] All that is certain is that no additional information is to be expected here. Dombart reports "de A . . . co", Martin (p. xxiv) could read only d. The British Museum kindly provided me with a photograph under ultraviolet light, which seems to bring out d^e AQINCO (Q and C quite uncertain) but it is in a quite different hand, is three lines below the explicit in a mended section and seems to have nothing to do with our text.

[6] See also Klaus Thraede, "Beiträge zur Datierung Commodians," Jahrbuch für Antike u. Christentum, II (1959), 90–114.

[7] Praef. xiv: "Neque tamen in hac re magni momenti esse credas, quod propria Commodiani sermonis vocabula non nisi apud unum aut alterum posterioris aetatis cuiusdam, quantum hodie affirmare possumus, scriptorem leguntur (plus valent constructiones), cum singula cotidiani sermonis vel etiam vulgaris monumenta adhuc diligentius et plane non iam sint explorata, neve Commodiani sermonem, patrium non fuisse Latinum sed Syrum obliviscaris." Aside from the question of foreign influence, which is anything but proved and is not in any case very helpful, the problem here is not so much a lack of sufficient study but rather that "Vulgar Latin" as we know it is not so much a particular language spoken at certain times and places but a series of deviations from a standard language (cf. V. Väänänen, Introduction au Latin Vulgaire [Paris, 1963], pp. 3–6, and Leumann-Hofmann-Szantyr, Lateinische Grammatik, Allgemeiner Teil [München, 1965], pp. 46*–49*). Some of these deviations, such as apparent confusion of accusative and ablative after verbs of motion, begin rather early and are not altogether colloquial, and most are long continued into manuscripts where they may displace correct readings. Thus, Instr. I. 34, 1 indomita cervia ("vulgär ganz spät" Leumann-Stolz[5] 204) is more likely to be a mistake for indomita

(i.e., fifth- or sixth-century) date. If we could be sure that Claudius Marius Victorius in fact cites Commodian, as his most recent editor P. Hovingh suggests,[8] we would have a *terminus post quem non* in the fourth century. But uncertainty here and the fact that Commodian's so-called rhythmic (i.e., non-quantitative) hexameter is so far, at least, without a history make a really close date unconvincing. The weight of evidence, if I may state summarily conclusions on which argument is here irrelevant, would support Martin's principal views; that is, that Commodian was writing no earlier than the second half of the third century and no later than the early fourth, that whether or not he was born in Syria (that *gasaeus* was ever intelligible Latin for *poeta* is hard to believe), he was living and composing in the west and not the east, as a Christian layman converted from paganism but not as a bishop, and that his Christian vocabulary is not to be interpreted in the light of later technical distinctions.[9] That Commodian's attacks on Jewish proselytizing thus remain without an intelligible historical context is something of a puzzle, to which I am not able to offer a satisfactory solution.

In any case, if we are to come down to the contents of Commodian's work, once again there are no sure indices of date. His works consist of a series of *Instructiones* in two books, 80 rather short pieces in a rough-hewn imitation of dactylic hexameter, all but two of them acrostics and the remaining two abecedaria or alphabet poems, understanding that I use the word 'poem' merely for want of a better word, as I shall shortly try to demonstrate. In these pieces (totaling altogether 1,257 lines), Commodian, on his own account a pagan redeemed after an early life spent in ignorance of Christianity, endeavors to instruct those who are still ignorant of the truth, that is, of course, Christian truth as he understands it. The first 21 pieces, which Martin now counts as Book I,[10] are addressed to those

---

cervix, and *storia* for *historia* at *Carmen* 151 is too common as a manuscript misspelling (as *storiarum, codd., Rhet. ad Her.* IV. 7) to give one much confidence in it here. Martin's excellent collection of material in his valuable *Index Verborum et Locutionum* (pp. 213–67) needs careful sifting.

[8] *Corpus Christianorum*, CXXVII (1960), Index pp. 271–72.

[9] Recent work has tended to confirm a third-century date—as Thraede (note 6); Ant. Salvatore, *Orpheus*, VII (1960), 161–87; J. Gagé, *Rev. d'Hist. et de Phil. Religieuses*, XLI (1961), 355–78 and *Rev. de l'Hist. des Religions*, CLIX (1961), 131–33, although L. Hermann, *Latomus*, XX (1961), 312–21 is persuaded that the *Carmen* was composed between 416 and 421.

[10] He thus includes in Bk. I the first four pieces which the MS assigns to Bk. II. His scheme is thus more logical, but whether it is more logical than the MS or more logical than Commodian I am not sure.

who still worship the pagan gods, and consist of brief attacks, intended to be satirical, on pagan myths or cult practices, followed (Martin's Book II) by a series of brief injunctions to the back-sliding, unconvinced, or inadequate Christians, in particular to those who are Judaizing or who fall prey to the pretensions of the Jews, *qui iudaeidiant* as he spells it (I.37), the *fanatici* or 'shrine-haunters.'

There are three themes interspersed in these injunctions to a Christian life: attacks on the pagan gods, who were really not gods at all but men of ancient times, attacks on the Jews, who, he thinks, are misleading Christians into endangering their souls, and the imminence of Judgment with the obvious message, "Repent before it is too late." Two of these themes he weaves together in his second work, the *Carmen de duobus populis* as Martin now calls it,[11] a rather long (1,060-line) survey of his views of Christian doctrine for the unlearned, in which the Jews, after first a pagan and then a Jewish antichrist, will be saved only long enough to see the triumph of the crucified Christ and then be condemned to eternal hell-fire. Of these themes, the theology and the violent reaction against the Jews are too individual to be of much help in a plausible date. The attacks on the pagan gods, on the other hand, are too traditional to be of much service. Commodian's Euhemerism (or rationalism) is perhaps more irrational than most, and he can provide an "explanation" of a thoroughly fantastic mythological tale so preposterous as to exceed the probable limits of human gullibility.[12] But the degree of silliness of a rather silly theory hardly depends on history.

Wanting other evidence, then, the state of Commodian's language should give some clues, and in fact his habit of writing in acrostics does give some control as to how he spelled, at least—a matter on which the best of manuscripts are usually unreliable. The headings, as borne out by the initial letters of his lines, seem to show a spelling more or less classical: *ae* and *e* are distinguished, except in one word, *eramen* 'bronze' (*Instr.* II. 5 (9), 19), and though he apparently

---

[11] Martin's objections to the older title, *Carmen Apologeticum*, and a proposed *Carmen de Antechristo* (so spelled in the acrostic *Instr.* I. 41) are sound enough (*Praef.* viii–x). His new title, from the opening of the penultimate line of the poem (1059), is a plausible conjecture, but of course only a conjecture.

[12] E.g., of Saturnus (I. 4) that he was a god who swallowed his children is, to be sure, a rather tall tale, but to assert, as Commodian does (I. 5): *Rex fuit in terris, in monte natus Olympo* is to force the reader to assume that any woman would pick the top of a rugged and unoccupied mountain to have a baby. Anyone who could believe that could believe anything.

pronounced -ae as -e,[13] he does distinguish -ae as a long vowel;[14] -tia and -cia seem to be distinct from each other;[15] final -m of the accusative case is written, whether or not or how pronounced; di- before a vowel is pronounced as z-, and in an alphabet poem so spelled.[16] There is no indication anywhere in the headings nor in much of the text of a breakdown of the case system. Vulgar Latin traces are certainly to be found in his manuscripts and in impressive quantity.[17] Yet on the whole and in sum, making allowances for variations in editors' choices, there is little that is really remarkable for the third or fourth century in Commodian's language and grammar. But it is exactly here that another problem arises.

Both the *Instructiones* and the *Carmen,* as I have said, come down in one manuscript apiece. It was once well said by a French palae- ographer that there is no such thing as a good manuscript, and there is much truth in that. No manuscript, however good its read- ings may be by and large, is without some errors of eye or hand or ear, not to speak of bad habits of spelling. The British Museum MS of the *Carmen,* perhaps of the eighth century, has serious gaps and quite enough faults, but is on the whole a fairly good manuscript. But of the former Cheltenham MS of the ninth century (Berlin lat. 167), upon which the *Instructiones* rely entirely, one can only say that if there are no really good manuscripts, there are certainly some very bad manuscripts, and this is one. The scribe of MS C was faithless both in little and in much. He confuses not only things which scribes often confuse (such as final *m, h, c* & *t, ui* & *iu, ni, nu, prae, per, pro, quod* and *quid,* and the like) but he confuses things which could not in theory possibly be confused, leaves out words, omits lines, reverses letters, and then often corrects what is bad to what is worse. If in these 70-odd years since Dombart we have had an impressive gain in knowledge about Late and

[13] *Instr.* II. 4 (8) shows a primitive form of rhyme (properly homoeoteleuton) in which all 12 lines end in -e except lines 9 (*ruinae*) and 11 (*terrae*).

[14] *caelo, aevo* and the like are acceptable line closes, where Commodian de- mands a penultimate long syllable, cf. p. 281.

[15] At *Instr.* II. 19 the MS title is *De Zelo Concupiscentiae* and it seems wise to emend *cum* at the beginning of line 18 with Haupt, Hanssen, Heraeus, and Vernier to *tu,* rather than, with Martin, the title to *Concupiscenciae.*

[16] *Instr.* I. 35, 23 *Zabolicam legem* . . . .

[17] The title and acrostic of *Instr.* I. 25 seems certain as *Qui timent et non credent,* which apparently shows the not uncommon confusion of verbs in *-ĕre* and *-ēre.* Cf. e.g., Väänänen, pp. 314 and 317. At *Instr.* II. 19, 9, however, *si credeas* of the MS has no other support and is likely to be a mistake for *sic redeas*—so Dombart.

Vulgar Latin, and if the *Thesaurus Linguae Latinae,* so far as it has reached, is indispensable, textual criticism has not developed and probably cannot develop techniques to support an editor who is forced to rely on one manuscript. Where comparative material is lacking, the editor is in fact thrown back on Richard Bentley's *ratio et res ipsa.* Nor, as far as *ratio* goes, has there been any conspicuous human gain since the eighteenth century. So that if Martin's changes from Dombart's text (I exclude spelling and punctuation) average, as they do, one in 6.48 lines in the *Carmen* but one in 3½ (3.39) lines in the *Instructiones,* very few of these come from more accurate reports of manuscript readings, most from a more lenient view of Commodian's Latinity and even more from the diminished confidence in the capacity of an editor to go much beyond his manuscript evidence. Where, as in the case of the *Instructiones,* that evidence is patently unreliable, the chances of recovering anything like the author's text are remote, and purely palaeographical corrections are of little help—they can remove surface errors, but where deep corruption exists simple retouches are futile.

For an example (and I think a very fair one) of the problems remaining in the *Instructiones,* the manuscript text of I. 9 on Mercury will have to suffice.

> Mercurius vester fiat *cum araballo* depictus
> 2 Et galea *et pallam* pinnatus et cetera nudus.
> Rem video miram, deum ⟨cum⟩ saccello volare:
> 4 Currite pauperculi cum gremio quo volat ille,
> Ut sacculum effundat, vos extunc estote parati.
> 6 Respicite pictum, quoniam vobis hic ab alto
> Iactabit nummos: vos tunc saltate securi.
> 8 Vane, non insanis, colere deos pictos in axe?
> *siui ue es (supra lin.) escis* cum besteis perge morari.

1 abolla *Oehler,* saraballo *Ludwig, Dombart,* arabylo *Martin*
2 et pileum *Oehler,* aut pileum *Rigaltius,* et ala *Ludwig,* et planta *Dombart*
9 vivere nescis *edd.,* vir esse nescis *Dombart,* vivere recte nescis *Martin, i.e.* viv're

Here the method of composition is characteristic of Commodian, and one which would normally be thought of as an Old Latin method or one characteristic of later prose; that is, the line is a clause or sentence, and the thought, instead of being developed by any method of suggestion if not logic, in which a) leads to b) which leads to c), is accumulated by building up blocks of clauses. This makes things harder than usual, but with lines 1 and 2 we at least have a very strong clue. *Nudus* in line 2 tells us clearly that whatever Mercury had on he should have had more of it.

Thus the emendation *abolla,* a cloak, which not only would make it a little difficult for Mercury to fly, but, since it hung from neck to ankle, denies Mercury the opportunity to shock even the most prudish in line 2, is unfortunate. Dombart, in most circumstances a learned and judicious man, let the dictionary get the upper hand and supposed *saraballo,* wide oriental trousers, which not only would provide a most inappropriate decency to Mercury in Commodian's eyes, but would really look a little odd on a Greek deity. Martin has done a little better; he got *arabylo,* a kind of boot, into line 1, saving Mercury's nudism for line 2. Unfortunately here he did not follow earlier editors, who knew that Mercury was represented with a winged helmet and sandals, but intended—the printer did not get the cue and printed Dombart's text—to write *et galea et palla,* that is, represented with a sandal, helmet and cloak, covered with feathers, otherwise bare. Actually there is no doubt that the first line should read *aryballo,* with a purse, with which Mercury is frequently represented, and in the second line with a helmet and a cloak rolled up around his shoulders—*et galea, et palla, pinnatus,* but otherwise quite naked, as a Greek athlete would normally be represented. In the last line, where corruption has crept in again, Martin's suggestion is one syllable too long and would require syncope of *vivere,* which is unexceptionable French but not very likely if indeed possible for Late Latin. Dombart's reading is possible but not attractive and I should suggest, *si vivere vis* (or *velis*) *escis,* if you wish to live by bait (i.e., by taking bait), go live among the beasts, whom Commodian regards, at II. 3, 1, as living subject to being enticed by men with lures. But here, as in many other passages, possible conjectures have merely a greater or smaller degree of probability, and the amount of guidance we can get from Commodian's rhythmic form is obviously crucial.

As to the nature of this *"quasi-versus"* opinions quite naturally have varied. Since there is no history of this type to guide us, conclusions can be and have been drawn only by inspection and examination of the text as far as we can determine it. And if opinions vary in regarding this as an essentially accentual verse, or one partly accentual and partly quite free, ranging to the opposite view that Commodian was attempting to write quantitative verse so far as he was able, there seems to be no course open except to examine the problem anew, attempting to make as few assumptions as possible.

First of all, it is very clear from the first line of the *Praefatio,* in Martin's text, *Prima praefatio nostra viam erranti demonstrat,* that it does indeed somewhat resemble the dactylic hexameter, but an attempt to scan it fails at the first line. Where the fifth foot should be we have instead three long syllables—not even a close facsimile of a dactyl. And at line 4, *Ego similiter erravi tempore multo,* even the most feather-witted student set to commit a dactylic hexameter would have sufficient prudence not to open a line with six short syllables. But if quantity here has loudly said no, accent is no less negative. In the opening of these lines violations of accent are more numerous than violations of quantity, so that if the line as a whole is not truly quantitative, it is not accentual either. Where there is any kind of consistent structure, it is in a rather surprising direction. A student trained in biological observations—say in how to describe fish—might "scientifically" describe the normal dactylic hexameter with normal third-foot caesura as a phrase of possibly five but usually six or seven syllables up to caesura, followed by a phrase of usually eight or nine or possibly ten syllables to line close. But this scheme, however it might have been arrived at, is Commodian's measure in essence, and any line which falls short of or exceeds this measure before or after caesura requires correction. So far, then, Commodian's line falls within the limits of the dactylic hexameter as to syllable count and caesura, although it is no longer either dactylic or hexameter, lacking any fixed points of recurrence of rhythm except at line ends. Here, of course, relics, at least, of the stylistic rules of the hexameter are still conspicuous. Here too the line closes almost invariably with a word of two or three syllables, and in the *Carmen,* where the text is more certain, I find only ten notable exceptions in 1,060 lines,[18] one of these a proper noun and the others apparently deliberate closes with a word of four or five syllables. More than this, however, the old stylistic rule against beginning the fifth foot with a word ending appears to be still in force, so that the regular accentual pattern of the last two feet of

---

[18] Monosyllabic closes are *fas est* (ll. 124, 712) and *res est* (l. 131), and possibly *elige quam vis* (699; better *quamvis?*). Aphaeresis with *est* (*sola est* 102, *repleta est* 225, *resecta est* 262, *a Summo est* 320, *sanata est* 652) is hardly in point. Notable are: *conditionis* 121, *magnificatur* 349, *nesciebamus* 373, *Deuteronomium* 429, *inposuisti* 444, *derelinques* 447, *clarificabor* 463, *vituperatur* 592, *adorabunt* 744, *pseudopropheta* 985.

the dactylic hexameter is retained. There are, to be sure, exceptions, as in line 6 of *Instr.* I. 9 cited above, but they are not numerous enough to exceed the limits of choice as to coincidence and non-coincidence of accent and verse beat at the close of the dactylic hexameter. If the net result of all this is to be sure to preserve the characteristic ending, it is nevertheless not true to say that accent replaces quantity in establishing the close of the line. Line endings such as *suá sponte currunt, deós adoraṛe, rádīce Iesse, aúgēre quaerunt, lūgere plaudent, ín fine nobis, ín monte Síon, dé illo clamant,*[19] infrequent as they are (I count some 29 violations of word or possible phrase accent in 1,060 lines), are quite enough to show that we are dealing with a stylistic rule, an operation of choice, and not a law of the form. Accent is acquiring domination over quantity, but it has not displaced it. The clausula then begins on an accented syllable or on a long syllable, but curiously, by Commodian's rule, the next to the last syllable of the line, the opening of the old sixth foot, should be a long syllable. That Commodian does in fact insist upon its being so is apparent in the composition itself; the line may close with *egit* but not *agit, fecit* but not *facit, fuere, fuisse,* but not *fuit, videtur* but not *videt.* Thus it is also that he all too often weakens the effect of his lines by closing with such relatively inert forms as *unde, inde, forte, esse, ille, iste* and the like. Martin, to be sure, has contested the rule,[20] but his list of exceptions for the *Carmen* contains 19 items, two of which are emendations of modern editors, three are proper nouns, five normal Late Latin variant scansions. Of the remainder, four are cases of *aqua,* no doubt the VL *acqua* with long first syllable of the *Appen-*

---

[19] Martin (*Praef.* xvi-xviii) cites some 17 from both works. He would apparently read *aúgĕre, práebĕre, lúgĕre* (xvii) for which he has little warrant on his own statement (xvi) "*cum ictus dactylici pedis quinti vitetur quidem cadens in monosyllabum aut verbi plurium syllabarum ultimam neque tamen vetetur, . . .*" My objection is not to the possibility (cf. n. 17) but to the cogency of the evidence.

[20] It was strongly supported by W. Meyer (*Anfang und Ursprung der lateinischen und griechischen rhythmischen Dichtung* [Abh. d. Münchener Akad. d. Wiss. 17,2, 1885], 288 ff.), who dealt with only the *Carmen* as having a text sufficiently sure for sound conclusions. Of Martin's list of counterexamples (from both works) *eritis* (four times) and *feceritis* (once) are, as he knows, variant scansions; *Sion* (twice) and *Deuteronomium* are proper nouns; *latebra* (twice) and *patre* (four times) are standard in Late Latin; *Syrus* (*Carm.* 823) and *magum* (396) are modern emendations; if they cannot be scanned with first syllable long (they can be: cf. *Syrus,* Cl. Mar. Vict. II, 315; *TLL* on *magus*), they are false emendations. At *Instr.* I. 20, 3 *tităno* ("calce *vel* gypso") should probably be *Titano*—so edd.

dix Probi (112), which still survives in Italian. We are thus left with two for the *Carmen: réfugant* (761) which should probably with W. Meyer be emended to *refutant, quoque* (lengthening before -*qu?*) and *tertio die* of the resurrection of Christ. Thus with one certain violation in 1,060 lines we are well justified in affirming that Commodian treats the last two syllables of the line as a spondee. And even if we add the relatively uncertain text of the *Instructiones* we do not have a certain total of more than five arbitrary lengthenings in 2,317 lines.

In sum, then, we have with Commodian not really a precursor of Romance versification nor a type ever very widespread or influential. It is what Gennadius had called it, composition *quasi versu,* or, from a Latin point of view, not verse at all but a kind of prosepoetry with a clausula of five syllables, varying in metrical form but opening usually with an accented syllable and closing with a spondee. That Commodian was in fact insensitive to quantities is refuted by his handling of the final foot, nor indeed would it be likely in the third or early fourth century or in an author who shows influence, even if not much to his profit, of Lucretius and Virgil.[21]

[21] J. Perret's ingenious and penetrating article (see above, n. 1) became available to me only after this paper was written. Perret's method is to test for correctness or falsity of scansions for each type of word at each point of the line, using Dombart's text of the *Carmen* as a base. My general conclusions do not greatly differ from his on the following points: (a) that Commodian's line is an experiment which does not follow the rules of dactylic hexameter and that it does not have a (quantitative) rhythm except for those who have the rhythm of classical hexameter in their heads, and (b) that this was not a "popular" verse derived from a loss of quantitative distinctions, but that at least in open accented syllables Commodian distinguished quantity. Perret's evidence then indicates, as does mine, that Commodian is not insensitive to quantity, but that his departures from it, where they do occur, are deliberate. On the other hand, I am not at all persuaded that Commodian retains the quantity of the accented syllable and of the closed syllable as a metrical base, nor that he regards final and pretonic syllables as of indifferent quantity.

Where I differ from Perret is hardly in the nature of the facts, which he has tested and presented admirably, but rather in the assumption that Commodian was using quantity in any fashion as the *base* of a rhythmic structure. Line openings such as *Instr.* I. 1, 4: *Ego similiter erravi* appear to me to be pure prose, but if we concede considerable freedom as to line openings, line closes must surely be significant. Deviations from quantity in the clausulae of this *Praefatio,* which totals 9 lines, are: *erranti dēmonstrat* (1), *saeculī meta* (2), *insciīs ipsis* (5), *legendŏ de lege* (6), *civică turba* (7), *instruŏ verum* (9). The futility of assuming shortening of final *o,* common as that is, is shown by line 6, nor is there real evidence here for assuming any shortening at all. The form of clausula we see here appears to be $\smile$ xx $\underset{\smile}{'}$x. Yet further tests will show that the first syllable *need* not be long but may instead be accented, such as *deos oratis, Instr.* I. 3, 15; *neque colantur, Instr.* I. 2, 13. Deviation here is too frequent

It is perhaps also in this direction of prose-poetry that in the contact of final vowel with initial vowel in the last five syllables, where the rhythm gives a basis for test, Commodian's rule is, not elision but rather, as in dé illo, hiatus. In this position, in only one line of the *Carmen* is elision required and even that is not certain (849 consurgere in ira; [in] *Hanssen*).

We then come to the conclusion that we are here dealing not so much with the collapse of a metrical form as with an attempt to use a new form for what the author felt, even if others did not, was a new message to which he could contribute his earnestness and fervor. No doubt for one of Commodian's limited talents and uncertain taste it was a mistake. But it is not only in the sciences that experiments often fail.

The Ohio State University
25 April 1966

---

to allow us to assume lengthening of *neque* (before -*qu* Perret) or implausibly of *deus*, where the vowel in hiatus was drifting toward -*i*- and was certainly not lengthening but shortening. If we thus correct to x́xx -x́, we have what appears to me, and I take it Martin, the range of variation, excluding the "spondaic line," five cases of which (*Instr.* I. 17, 9 and II. 2, 8; *Carmen* 265, 423, 890) Martin admits. Commodian strongly prefers a long syllable in the opening of the clausula and avoids syllables "long by position" in the second and third positions, but these are preferences, not absolutely required. *Structura⟨m⟩ gerebat* (*Instr.* I. 10, 7) and *structura⟨s⟩ secutus* (Martin, or *structura⟨m⟩ secutus* Dombart) seem, for instance, absolutely necessary corrections and even the striking *suá sponte currunt* (*Instr.* I. 8, 3) does not necessarily require correction—cf. Martin, *Praef.* xvi. In sum, evidence about the state of quantitative oppositions in the third and fourth century A.D. is scattered and conflicting and I dissent from drawing any wide conclusions from the uncertain evidence of Commodian's composition.

LATIN PROSE RHYTHM IN THE LATE MIDDLE AGES AND RENAISSANCE

Harris Fletcher

About a century ago those studies began to appear which led to an understanding of the prosodic developments in Latin prose and verse after about 1400. This brief paper attempts to pull together what we now know about the development of that prosody, and, perhaps most important, to urge application of that knowledge to the Latin prose written by Europeans between that date and 1800. To understand what is meant by the term, prose rhythm, a glance at its history in the West is necessary. One of the earliest manifestations of the term seems to be connected with the somewhat misunderstood word, *clausula*. This word was defined in sixteenth- and seventeenth-century Latin lexicons, and in Du Cange, as, e.g., Littleton, 1693, "a little sentence which doth conclude." But the word had somehow very early acquired a special meaning in connection with prosody. Such a connection begins to appear at least as early as Cicero. In the *Orator* (215, trans. by Hubbell, Loeb, pp. 486–87), he stated:

Sed sunt clausulae plures, quae numerose et iucunde cadant. Nam et creticus, qui est e longa et brevi et longa, et eius aequalis paean, qui spatio par est, syllaba longior, qui commodissime putatur in solutam orationem illigari, cum sit duplex—nam aut e longa est et tribus brevibus, qui numerus in primo viget, iacet in extremo, aut e totidem brevibus et longa, in quem optime cadere censent veteres.

There are many clausulae which have a pleasing rhythmical cadence; the cretic, for example, made up of a long, a short, and a long (–ᴜ–) and its equivalent the paean (—ᴜᴜᴜ or ᴜᴜᴜ—) which takes the same time but has one more syllable; and which is thought most convenient to insert into prose, since it has two forms: either it takes the form of a long syllable followed by three shorts, which is strong at the beginning, but weak at the end of a sentence; or of three shorts and a long, which the ancients consider the best cadence.

284

A little later he was careful to explain (216, Loeb, p. 488–89):

Sed hos cum in clausulis pedes nomino, non loquor de uno pede extremo: adiungo, quod minimum sit, proximum superiorem, saepe etiam tertium.

In mentioning these feet as used in clausulae, I am not speaking only of the last foot; I include at least the next to the last, and often the one before that.

Again, in *De Oratore* (III. 193, trans. Rackham, Loeb p. 152–55), Cicero stated:

Duo enim aut tres sunt fere extremi servandi et notandi pedes, si modo non breviora et praecisa erunt superiora;

For there are perhaps two or three feet that ought to be kept for sentence endings, and thrown into relief, provided the preceding rhythms are not too short and jerky.

Many other passages in Cicero's works could be cited; but the above will suffice to show how early the Roman rhetoricians and prosodists were aware of the effectiveness of a concluding cadence and its patterns made up of graceful rhythms. The subject has been dealt with by Georg Wuest (1879) and Tadeusz Zielinski (1904: 1920). Quintilian, systematizing Cicero's scattered rhetorical statements, set forth the features of the Roman oration, seeing it entirely as a prose exercise. He devoted the entire fourth chapter of the ninth book of the *Institutio oratoria* to the discussion of the artistry and attractiveness of basing sentence structure on rhythm in an oration, following Cicero of course. His account of the *clausulae* led directly to his account of how these should be arranged.

There was a well-developed *cursus* in Greek prose; but so different are the Greek and Latin languages that it would profit us little here to chart those sets of cadences found in the writers of classical Greek prose. We must concentrate on the rhythmical patterns found in many Latin prose writers of the late Middle Ages and of the Renaissance. It was Léonce Couture (*Le cursus ou rhythm prosaique dans la liturgie . . . du 3 siècle à la renaissance* [Paris, 1891]) who pointed out that, taken directly from classical Latin prose writers, the *cursus* had been widely used in ecclesiastical writings of the fifth and sixth centuries, then disappeared for a time, only to reappear in the eleventh century and continue for generations. More searching was the account of the practice in Latin prose by Dom Andre Mocquereau ("L'influence de l'accent tonique et du cursus sur la structure mélodique et rythmique de la phrase Grégorienne. Le cursus et la psalmodie," *Paléographie musicale,*

3 [1892] and 4 [1894]). In this latter part, he defined *cursus* as (my translation):

certain harmonious series of words and syllables which the Greek and Latin prose writers used at the end of phrases or sentences, or as part of them in order to secure measured cadences with an agreeable effect for the ear. If this arrangement of syllables is based on quantity, the cursus is said to be metrical; if based on accent and number of syllables, the cursus is rhythmic or tonic.

Mocquereau went on to say that the existence of the rhythmic and metrical *cursus,* indeed, of each kind, has long been known, and he then cited the principal writers who have traced its history, or examined its nature and kinds. He then supplied a list of references, arranged in more or less chronological order, beginning with Charles Thurot (1868), laying particular stress on the works of Noël Valois Joseph Louis Havet, and pointing out that the rules for the *cursus* had been traced by Cicero and Quintilian. Mocquereau then proceeded to expound his principal interest, or the use of the *cursus* in medieval liturgical literature, beginning largely in the Gregorian chant, then continuing on indefinitely.

The resurgence or reappearance of the use of set, rhythmical patterns in Latin prose is fairly clear today, thanks to the efforts of these scholars, who began to publish their findings about the middle of the nineteenth century. Especially valuable for examples was the work of Ludwig Rockinger (1863), who transcribed texts by seventeen different writers who dealt with various formalized instructions and rules for Latin composition. These works are chiefly manuals of prose forms, principally the *dictamen* (closely defined by Alberich of Monte Cassino), and the epistle. Almost any form or statement involving the structure of Latin prose found in those manuals has been included by Rockinger.

Valois, in his *De arte scribendi epistolas* (Paris, 1880), especially in his final chapter, *De numero,* brought together the rules of both *dictamen* and epistle, and in addition indicated what had taken place. The term, *cursus,* though coming rather late to mean approximately what *clausula* or a summary or ending phrase had once seemed to mean, was early used almost solely to indicate the way in which the words literally "ran on," as it were. The term, *clausula,* on the other hand, regularly occurred in Rockinger's manuals with the meaning of recurrent metrical and rhythmical patterns contained in or at the end of clauses and sentences. This meaning is found at least as early as Diomedes the grammarian (fourth century), and, because it so occurs, there arises the suspicion that the entire matter of prose rhythms was one in which the scholars of ancient Alexandria had a hand. It may even have been during that early period when a separation was forced between the Greek and the Latin rhythms, for the prose structures of the two languages were so different that such a separation became mandatory. The quantitative stresses of Latin diverged so much from the qualitative-quantitative stresses of Greek that further uses of the *cursus* became almost completely different. But in this summary account of prose rhythms we cannot be concerned with Greek prose, except for a few passing references to it. We must deal only with those found in the Latin prose of the later Middle Ages and in the Renaissance, in so far as these can be traced.

We may now perhaps set forth some definitions. Cicero long ago pointed out that in his orations he tried to conclude his phrases, clauses, and sentences with particularly harmonious endings, by having long and short syllables arranged in an orderly and pleasing fashion. This feature of his orations, as already stated, received the name of *cursus*. Vacanard (1905) stated approximately the same definition of the *cursus* when he wrote: *une marche accélerée du discourse, qui s'arrètait sur une cadence agréable*—a flow (*marche*) of discourse that is ended with an agreeable cadence, just as Quintilian *(Inst. orat.* IX. 4, 70) had stated that *salvus est cursus*. Vacanard went on to point out that a writer of the twelfth century gave the name of *cursus* to the style of St. Leo the Great, which he praised for its grace and elegance, noting that it moved rapidly and clearly. Buono-Compagno (thirteenth century) stated that the *cursus* was *artificiosa dictionum structura*—an easy and harmonious combination of words, artfully made. The detailed rules by which these authors of the twelfth and thirteenth centuries produced their *dictamina* show clearly that the medieval *cursus* had come to mean a way of effectively arranging the beginning, the body, and the ending of whole sentences and phrases according to what had become the rules of harmony, or more precisely as Ponce le Provençal had put it: *Cursus est matrimonium spondeorum cum dactilis perlatione lepida celebratum*—an agreeable union or mixture of dactyls and spondees. (A spondee was a polysyllabic word accented on the penult; a dactyl was a polysyllabic word accented on the antepenult.) However, at first the arrangement of the internal phrases concerned the early grammarians much less than the final cadences. Vacanard's agreement with Mocquereau, whose definition he quoted, can be our final definition, and from about the eleventh or twelfth century onward, *cursus* meant certain harmonious and pleasing arrangements (Vacanard called them *successions*) of words and syllables that were employed consciously and artfully by both Greek and Latin prose writers in order to secure an agreeably measured cadence. As stated herein earlier, if such arrangements were based on quantity, the *cursus* was said to be metrical. If they were based on accent and number of syllables, the *cursus* was said to be rhythmical. As the Latin language of the late Middle Ages and the Renaissance was ruled entirely by the laws of quantity and accent, the cursus naturally arose from the combination of those two elements.

A few details might be helpful here. Quantitatively, syllables are distinguished as long, short, and common. In duration, the long syllable is worth two short syllables. Grouping syllables according to their different time-values makes the metrical foot. By measure then, there are three different kinds of feet, of which the most used are: the dactylic in which the measure is in the ratio of two to two: example, the dactyl itself (–ᴜᴜ), the anapest (ᴜᴜ–), the spondee (– –); and the one that might also occur, the pyrrhic (ᴜᴜ).

The iambic measure (ratio of two to one) included the iambic (ᴜ–) and the trochee or choreus (–ᴜ), the latter name being used at first especially for the trochee that resolved itself into the tribrach (ᴜᴜᴜ).

The third kind of feet by measure includes the molossus (– – –), the major ionic (– –ᴜᴜ), and the minor ionic (ᴜᴜ– –). Since all the above kinds of measures in Latin prosody, deriving in name if not precisely in nature from Greek prosody, are well known, it is unnecessary to do more than merely list them.

Accent—concurring or not with the meter, and often to its detriment—was absolutely required from classical times, and always exerted great influence on the cadences of Latin stresses. Accent is the inflection by the voice placed particularly on a syllable to give that syllable more acuity or force, and inevitably some variation in pitch will result. In a way, inflection forms the soul of a word, just as the soul of the voice is said to depend on pitch. Quantity makes up the material of the word: accent is its logical element. Without accent, the elements of a word are merely juxtaposed. Accent unites them, giving them life and meaning. Every Latin word having its own distinct meaning by itself therefore contains an accented syllable. For centuries grammarians have been agreed on this point, even monosyllables carrying an accent, with a few exceptions, such as conjunctions heading a phrase and prepositions and adverbial prepositions when they immediately precede the words which they govern. Words of two syllables are always accented on the first syllable, whether that syllable be long or short. Because of this fact, it will readily be seen how there will be agreement with the quantity in dissyllabic words. Final syllables never carry the accent; indeed, these syllables tend to be absorbed and lost. Whether the words are iambic (u–) or spondaic (––), the first syllable will be accented by the voice and dominate the second, in spite of the quantity. The first syllable is tonic, the second atonic; the first is strong, the second is weak. In words of three or more syllables, the inflection of the voice is marked on the penult or on the antepenult, according as the penult is long or short. If long, it carries the accent; if short, the antepenult takes the accent. Words of four syllables, accented on the penult, call for a most important statement. Cicero, with Quintilian following him, declared that, with no exceptions, a word can have only one accented syllable. But their "law" has been greatly modified, not without reason, by subsequent writers. However, not until the nineteenth century was the principle formulated by Gaston Paris (1839–1903) and since then accepted that vocal stresses have their way, and that most long words have or may have secondary stresses or accents even in classical Latin. This became so common that probably even in Cicero's day the rule was often broken, especially when the word was used orally, whether in formal or informal discourse. Paris even allowed for tertiary accents, and one has only to read any Latin passage with feeling to discover what was meant.

For dead languages such as classical Greek and Latin, the above rules and schemes work out very well because rules can be formulated and then imposed arbitrarily on the ways in which words must be read aloud or pronounced in context. But for a living language, such rigid rules can scarcely be imposed, and adherence to them is impossible, because no two readers will phrase and read a passage of prose, or even of verse in a living language exactly alike. In such reading, pronunciations which cannot be standardized will inevitably enter into the reading. The same element causes difficulty in trying to make Latin verse or prose conform to Greek rules. Greek, with its change in pitch or in the very quality of its vowels when spoken, differs widely in this respect from Latin, for which language not much claim has ever been made for change in pitch of the same vowels. Sharpening of the vowel in Greek is definitely marked by the acute accent. That is, in Greek, for any of the systems used to catch prose rhythms, there will be both qualitative and quantitative stresses affecting and even making up the rhythms. In Latin, on the other hand, the stresses are quantitative only, to such an extent that the ancient accent marks mean something quite different from what they mean in Greek, if they retain any accentual meaning at all. Most modern settings of Latin texts omit accent marks almost entirely. In the same way, French accent marks have a different significance from what the same marks have in Greek. There are French accent marks which are merely that; others may indicate the former presence of a letter now omitted; and still others are used to mark a difference in the word from the sense or meaning of the same word without the accent mark. These French marks usually occur by rule and under special conditions, none of which involves pitch and sometimes not even quantity.

As a final word on the matter of these prose rhythms, the quickest and most enlightening way into an understanding of how they were made to operate in the Latin prose written at almost any time between 1100 and as late as 1800 is to look at the section labeled *Prosodia* in a Latin grammar as common as Lily's was in England. In this and in similar handbooks of grammar, no distinction whatever is made between poetic and prosaic meters and rhythms until the entire subject of prosody is fully developed. Only after that exposition has been completed did Lily, for instance, turn to *carmina*. All the basic statements concerning prosody pertain equally to prose and verse—or in general, to all Latin composition—"making Latin" as the exercise was so aptly called in English.

There remains now only the emphasis on the need to try to follow the rhythms in the Latin prose by some of the major writers of the Renaissance in order to discover how far such writers knew and applied the rules of the *cursus, clausula,* and other manifestations of writing according to prosodic regulations, which were long forgotten, then revived as the West became more acutely aware of what the ancients had been doing. For Melville, Buchanan, and even Milton, attention has been paid to the prosody of their Latin poems. What is needed are studies equally devoted to the excellent prose of these same masters of Latin composition, almost any of which might serve as models to show how these prosodic rules were used. Writers from Sir Thomas More (1478–1535) to and through John Milton (1608–74) or Sir Isaac Newton (1642–1727) and even later Latin prose writers would admirably serve such purposes. Ciceronianism and the Ciceronians should be tested, not only by Nizolius, but also by their use of such prosodic rules as those described originally by Cicero.

University of Illinois
15 August 1965

CUPRA, MATUTA, AND VENILIA
PYRGENSIS

Robert E. A. Palmer

The three deities which concern us here do not belong to the first rank of divine beings. They have much in common and illustrate the process of syncretism among the disparate peoples of ancient Italy. The two Italic goddesses, Mater Matuta and Mater or Dea Cupra, have strikingly similar semantic beginnings. The third goddess does not appear to originate with the Indo-European speakers of Italy. Rather, as our title suggests, she belonged to Pyrgi, port of Etruscan Caere.

According to Varro (*LL* V. 159) a section of Rome called Vicus Ciprius took its name from the Sabine adjective *ciprus* 'good,' which he refers to the good omen met there by Sabine settlers.[1] Besides Varro's attestation the same adjective is found applied to the Umbrian goddess Cubra Mater for whom a fountain and a cistern were restored.[2] The emperor Hadrian himself restored the precinct of Dea Cupra at the town of Cupra Maritima in coastal Picenum.[3] Cupra Maritima took its name from Dea Cupra whose shrine appeared to Strabo to be an Etruscan foundation with Etruscan rites for the goddess whom he likened to Hera.[4] The shrine itself was situated on the sea.[5] The etruscanization of Cupra's

[1] For other suggestions see J. Collart, "Varron De lingua latina Livre V" *Publ. Fac. Lettres Univ. Strasbourg,* CXXII (1954), p. 247.
[2] See C. D. Buck, *A Grammar of Oscan and Umbrian* 2 (Chicago, 1928), No. 83; E. Vetter, *Handbuch der italischen Dialekte,* I (Heidelberg, 1953), No. 233; and A. Ernout, *Le dialecte ombrien* (Paris, 1961), No. 4, p. 49 and p. 80 *s.v.* bia. The dedication comes from near Foligno.
[3] *CIL,* IX, 5294.
[4] Strabo V. 241c.
[5] Silius Italicus VIII. 432: "litoreae fumant altaria Cuprae."

cult must be later than its foundation [6] unless Cupra, an Italic goddess, was borrowed by Etruscans and then established in Cupra Maritima as Strabo says. The good goddess and good mother of Picenum and Umbria have in common their association with sea and spring water. Perhaps Strabo's antiquarian sense suggested Cupra had been worshipped by the Etruscans. Beyond doubt Dea Cupra was the eponym of Cupra Maritima. Furthermore, the emperor's restoration confirms her local pre-eminence. Since the *ciprius* of Vicus Ciprius is an adjective derived from an adjective, it may well have referred to a deity called Ciprus or Cipra in Rome. When we discuss the *sororium tigillum* we shall note the suitability of such a Roman goddess in that section of archaic Rome.

The Latin adjective *matuta* bears a close semantic resemblance to *cupra*. It is related to the archaic adjective for 'good' *manis/manus* which yielded the adverb *mane* 'in good time', 'in the morning.' [7] The application of *man-* to the morning hours is as old as the Roman praenomen Manius.[8] Although in literature Lucretius is the first to use Matuta to signify the dawn,[9] the semantic development of *mane* from the same root admits the assumption that *matuta* might have been applied to the morning hours long before Lucretius. Linguistically the goddess Mater Matuta could have been either a good goddess or goddess of sunrise. Yet the cult of Mater Matuta and her syncretism suggest something else again.

The oldest known Italian temples of Matuta stood in Rome and Satricum. The Satrican temple was quite ancient but we know nothing of its cult.[10] According to tradition the sixth king of Rome, Servius Tullius, first built the temple for Roman Matuta which was rebuilt after Etruscan Veii's defeat in 396 by the conqueror Furius Camillus.[11] Livy explains that Camillus had vowed the new temple

[6] G. De Sanctis, *Storia dei Romani,* I² (Florence, 1956), 425.

[7] A. Ernout and A. Meillet, *Dictionnaire étymologique de la langue latine* 4 (Paris, 1959), *s. vv.* mane, Manes, manis, maturus, Matuta.

[8] H. Petersen, "The Numeral Praenomina of the Romans," *TAPA,* XCIII (1963), 353. We dissent from his interpretation of the relative times involved in naming Lucius and Manius. *Lux* is not 'dawn' but 'daylight' as opposed to night, and *mane,* at most, is the whole morning or, if we follow Lucretius (next note), only the dawn. Petersen takes *lux* for *prima lux,* by definition only early daylight. The gentilic name Aurelius (cf. Manilius) is the Sabine parallel. See Ernout-Meillet (n. 7), *s.v.* aurora, Latin's Indo-European word for dawn.

[9] Lucretius, *Rer. Nat.* V. 656-57. Cf. Priscian in Keil's *Grammatici Latini,* II (Leipzig, 1864), 76.

[10] Livy VI. 32-33, VII. 27, 5-9, XXVIII. 11, 2. See De Sanctis (n. 6) p. 271.

[11] Livy V. 19, 6, V. 23, 7; Ovid *Fasti* VI. 479-80; Plutarch *Cam.* 5. On Mater

in return for victory over Veii.[12] Camillus dedicated it at the same time he installed on the Aventine Hill Juno Regina, tutelary deity of Veii. Both acts concern affairs of state or, to be more precise, the event of warfare. Surely Cupra, too, enjoyed political prominence, inasmuch as she had lent her name to a community. Furthermore, it is worth remarking that in a sense Rome's quarrel with Veii amounted to strife over the waterway of the upper Tiber River. If we see the contention in this light, the vow to Matuta is appropriate when we set beside it Cupra's patronage of spring and sea. The diplomatic ramifications of the vow and subsequent dedication extend to Caere and reinforce this aspect of Mater Matuta's associations (see p. 301).

The Roman cult of Mater Matuta is partially known. Her festival, the Matralia on the eleventh day of June, apparently takes its name from the worshipping *matres* rather than the worshipped *mater,* since *mater* as a title is incidental and probably employed for the sake of alliterative assonance.[13] The mothers prepared a meal [14] which was offered for their "brothers' and sisters' " children according to the ancient interpretation.[15] H. J. Rose supposes that our ancient authorities misunderstood the term *pueri sororii,* who in fact were merely pubescent children of both sexes.[16] The rites

Matuta and her temple see G. Wissowa, *Religion und Kultus der Römer* [2] (Munich, 1912) pp. 110-12; Link, *RE,* 14.2 (1930) cols. 2326-29; H. Lyngby, "Die Tempel der Fortuna und der Mater Matuta am Forum Boarium in Rom," *Historische Studien,* 358 (1939); F. Bömer, *P. Ovidius Naso. Die Fasten,* II (Heidelberg, 1958), on VI. 475; K. Latte, *Römische Religionsgeschichte* (Munich, 1960), pp. 97-98; R. M. Ogilvie, *A Commentary on Livy Books 1-5* (Oxford, 1965), on V. 23, 7.

[12] Livy V. 19, 6. Ogilvie (n. 11) believes this act reflects Roman conciliation of the Satricans. As we shall see, the Romans had equally good reasons for conciliating the Caeritans of Etruria who held Matuta's counterpart in high esteem.

[13] For cult practices see Ovid *Fasti* VI. 473-568; Plutarch *Cam.* 5, *Quaest. Rom.* 16-17; Tertullian *Monog.* 17, 3. For discussion see the literature cited in n. 11. Examples of similar assonance are Mater Mursina (*CIL,* I[2], 580 = *ILS* 9233 = *ILLRP* 6) and Dea Dia. Of course no certain proof can be adduced that Matralia comes from the *matres.* Lupercalia and Paganalia are the only other examples of old feast days which may have been named after the participants. The *mater* of Mater Matuta is secondary as Pales Matuta suggests (see p. 306).

[14] Varro *LL* V. 106 and Ovid *Fasti* VI. 473-568. Full citations in A. Degrassi, *Inscriptiones Italiae,* 13.2, pp. 468-69, with some discussion.

[15] Ovid *Fasti* VI. 559-61 and Plutarch *Cam.* 5, *Quaest. Rom.* 16-17.

[16] H. J. Rose, "De religionibus antiquis quaestiunculae tres," *Mnemosyne,* LIII (1925), 406-14; "Two Roman Rites," *CQ,* XXVIII (1934), 156-58; and "Mana in Greece and Rome," *Harvard Theological Rev.,* XLII (1949), 165-72. Degrassi (n. 14) delineates the arguments for and against Rose's interpretation, and notes

for such youth are to be related to the *sororium tigillum* and were held on the first day of October. Near the beam (*tigillum*) stood the altars of Juno Sororia and Janus Curiatius. By inference from Janus' epithet we assume these were rites of initiation of the youth into the archaic curias.[17] When we consider later a similar Milesian institution, we shall see cause to exclude the young girls from rites which are mentioned only in connection with a male anyway. Although the cult of Mater Matuta is not connected by the ancients with the *sororium tigillum* and its rites of purification, certain indications do uphold Rose's suggestion. First of all, Janus bore the epithet Matutinus Pater.[18] Secondly, the *sororium tigillum* stood at Acilius' intersection (*compitum*) where one of the cross-streets was Vicus Ciprius.[19] If we are correct in assuming this quarter was named after a Ciprus or, more likely, a Cipra, we discern a likely cult association of *sororii* and two 'good' deities. A part of the mothers' rites for Matuta comprised the beating of a single slave girl and the exclusion of all other slave girls. Either this exclusion appertains to the protection of the citizen vis-à-vis the foreigner because it was a ceremony for new citizens, or it betokens Roman superiority over the enemy (thus a new temple for Mater Matuta was still a fitting gesture in 397 B.C.), or the mothers of sons signalled the exclusion of their female offspring by manhandling a female slave.[20] Finally, according to Augustine, Varro considered Matuta

which modern students of the problem do and which do not follow Rose. Although we do not find ourselves in agreement with Rose on all points, we consider his explanation satisfactory. Bömer (n. 11) objects to Rose's etymology (but see Ernout and Meillet [n. 7] s. vv. soror, frater) and argues that both sources cannot be wrong in speaking of the nieces and nephews. Both Ovid and Plutarch, however, do rely on one source, Verrius Flaccus.

[17] Livy I. 26, 13, on which see Ogilvie (n. 11); Dionysius of Halicarnassus, Ant. Rom. III. 22, 6-10; Festus 380, 399L; Degrassi (n. 14), pp. 515-16. On Janus and the sororium tigillum see L. A. Holland "Janus and the Bridge," Papers and Monographs of the American Academy in Rome, XXI (1961), pp. 77-91.

[18] Horace Serm. II. 6, 20-23. It may not be a cult title; see Latte (n. 11), p. 136, n. 3. However, Horace uses it jestingly as if it were. See Holland (n. 17) p. 143, who seems to consider it a cult epithet.

[19] Degrassi (n. 14), pp. 515-16; Dion. Hal. III. 22, 8. See S. B. Platner and T. Ashby, A Topographical Dictionary of Ancient Rome (Oxford, 1929), s.v. Vicus Ciprius, sororium tigillum; G. Lugli, Roma antica (Rome, 1946), who has it charted on pl. VII.

[20] Above, n. 13. On the practice in general, see H. Wagenvoort, Roman Dynamism (Oxford, 1947), pp. 138-68; on the exclusion of women, pp. 169-75, esp. p. 173 on the exclusion of virgins and unmarried women. To the magical aspects of the argument must be added the fact that the boys are being initiated into the curias. It is one thing for mothers (a status worth emphasizing) to

the goddess of maturing grain.[21] However, Matuta's cult gives not the slightest evidence of agricultural relations.[22]

Outside of Rome and Satricum, where we know she had temples, Mater Matuta was honored at Pisaurum, Cora, Praeneste, and Beirut in ways which invite our attention. The oldest surviving dedications come from Pisaurum on the Adriatic coast. Of fourteen dedicatory inscriptions from this area two concern Mater Matuta.[23] One was dedicated by two *matronae*. Furthermore, the *matronae Pisaurenses* set up a cippus to Juno Regina, evidently the same goddess installed on the Aventine when the Roman Matuta received a new temple from Camillus. A man set up a cippus to the Divi Novensides and another man a cippus to Feronia. The offering to Diana was made by a woman. Otherwise, there survive simple dedications to Apollo, Fides, Juno, Juno Lucina, Salus, Liber and Diva Marica.[24] At Cora two or possibly three inscriptions concerning Matuta have been found. A woman offered the goddess a statue of Jupiter, [25] and a *magistra,* evidently of Matuta's cult, made a donation.[26] On the latter stone is a much older inscription by a woman and *consuplicatrices*.[27] This woman may have been the *magistra* of a fellowship of Matuta's suppliants. At Praeneste Matuta's cult was also led by a *magistra*.[28] From the neighborhood of Syrian Beirut comes the dedication of an altar to Mater Matuta,

---

conduct a ceremony for their sons and another thing for mothers to include their daughters. Once a connection between *sororii/sororiae* and *soror* has been undone (so Rose, n. 16), there is no compelling reason to follow Verrius Flaccus and retain an emphasis on the sex of the slaves, so long as it is not the sex of the officiants that was important, but their relationship to *pueri sororii*.

[21] Augustine *CD* IV. 8. Rose makes much of the Varronian "etymology" which is, to say the least, not at all precise. Neither adjective, *maturus* or **matutus,* is derived from the other; they have a common root.

[22] Cf. Festus 109, 112, 154-55L. On the subject see H. Le Bonniec, *Le culte de Cérès à Rome* (Paris, 1958), pp. 131-32. At Agone a bronze tablet in Oscan was set up wherein were mentioned the statues for *Maatúis Kerriiúis* which Buck (n. 2), No. 45, translates into Latin *Matis Cerealibus* and dates to *ca.* 250 B.C. It must be noted that the same adjective is also applied to Hercules and that *Maatúis* is masculine. On these gods of Agone see Le Bonniec, pp. 40-45.

[23] *CIL,* I², 372 = XI 6294 = *ILS* 2974 = *ILLRP* 17; *CIL,* I², 379 = XI 6301 = *ILS* 2981 = *ILLRP* 24.

[24] See *ILLRP* 13-26 and Degrassi's comment; *ILS* 2970-83. The fourteenth cippus has lost the god's name; its dedicant was also a woman. We shall say more below (p. 298) on Diva Marica.

[25] *CIL,* x, 8416 = *ILS* 3487.

[26] *CIL,* x, 6511 = *ILS* 3488.

[27] *CIL,* I², 1512 = X 6518 = *ILS* 6273 = *ILLRP* 301. The noun *consuplicatrix* is preserved by Varro *LL* VII. 66.

[28] *CIL,* xIV, 2997 = *ILS* 3489; cf. xIV, 3006.

the donation of which was prompted by an oracle of Juno.[29] Who the oracular Juno was cannot be ascertained. However, we shall meet this oriental Mater Matuta in the guise of Leukothea. At Rome, Matuta may be linked to Juno Regina and Juno Sororia, at Cora with Jupiter, at Pisaurum with Juno Regina, Juno, and Juno Lucina, among others, and at Beirut with an oracular Juno. At Cupra Maritima, Dea Cupra was likened to Hera, Juno's Greek counterpart.

The Beirut dedication raises the question of Matuta's identity in syncretism. Now that Phoenician religion has merited a place in any discussion of early Italian syncretism (see p. 300), we may first deal with her oriental syncretism cast in Greek terms although far removed in time and place. From Syria we read a curious dedication of Menneas son of Beeliabes to the Leukothea who evidently belonged to the local community.[30] This monument was raised on behalf of Trajan's well-being (*soteria*). Thus it may belong to roughly the same era as the Beirut dedication, if our date for that can be accepted as nearly accurate (n. 29). A second Greek inscription was set up by a Roman official in Massilia: "Titus Porcius Cornelianus, priest of Leukothea and son of the most eminent Aelianus, the prophet." The style 'most eminent' suggests to the editors a date in the third century A.D. The god of the prophet is not mentioned, but Isis has been conjectured.[31] However, the Beirut dedication would indicate that the prophet could have served the goddess named Juno in Latin, if this Leukothea was associated with the same Syrian cult. Although Leukothea herself delivered oracles among the Greeks (see p. 298), we do not know of any prophet who served her. Therefore, the Leukothea mentioned

[29] *CIL*, III, 6680 = *ILS* 3490 (3489 by error): "Matri Matutae Flavia T(iti) fil(ia) Nicolais Saddane L(ucii) Antisti Veteris ex responso deae Iunonis aram fecit dedicavitque." The Antistii were prominent during the early principate and supplied consuls in 30, 6 B.C., and A.D. 23, 26, 46, 50, 55 and 96. This man was probably a freedman or descendant of a freedman. The wife's Roman name suggests a date after A.D. 100, that is, a generation or two after Vespasian and Titus operated in Syria. She has a Roman, Greek, and Syrian name.

[30] *IGRRP* III. 1075 and Dittenberger *OGIS* No. 611, who has a full commentary. The inscription may present cult problems of Leukothea which do not concern us here. See L. R. Farnell ("Ino-Leukothea," *JHS*, XXXVI [1916], 42), who translates most of the inscription. It must be said in passing that Farnell and his predecessors do not demonstrate that the cult practice under discussion has anything to do with the Greek Leukothea. The dedicant is not Greek and, unlike Flavia (n. 29), makes little effort to be Greek other than to write in Greek.

[31] *IGRRP* I. 10 with comments.

in Massilia may be oriental but need not be referred to the Syrian goddess.

Before examining the western cult of Leukothea, Matuta's Greek counterpart, we would do well to observe in what association Matuta is found at Rome and Pisaurum. Her analogue, Cupra, evinces definite affinities with water. Furthermore, Diva Marica stands out as an outlander among the thirteen deities honored at coastal Pisaurum.[32] For Marica is otherwise attested only in coastal Minturnae at the mouth of the Liris River where she guarded the coast.[33] Very probably her name means 'goddess of the sea' (*marica* < *mare*). Mythologically Marica was related to Circe, but in cult with *Pontia Aphrodite,* Aphrodite of the Sea, whose shrine lay next to Marica's at Minturnae.[34] Since the Pisauran dedication to Marica remains unparalleled outside of Minturnae, we assume that the dedicant had Minturnan affinities and, furthermore, that he thought the dedication appropriate because of Pisaurum's coastal site at the mouth of the Pisaurus River. Of the Roman deities to whom dedications were made at Pisaurum only Mater Matuta has the slightest connection with the sea. At Rome her temple was situated near the Tiber River, which means close to Rome's waterway and docks.[35] The site of the temple lay outside the old pomerium.[36] Unless Matuta can be shown to be mainly a foreign goddess or bellicose deity, the proximity of her temple to the river admits the possibility that she was concerned with the waters of the Tiber. When we discuss later Pales Matuta, we shall see further reason to connect Matuta with water.

The only syncretism of Matuta which the ancients expressed was an identification with Leukothea, a Greek water goddess.[37] Leu-

---

[32] *CIL,* I², 374 = *XI* 6296 = *ILS* 2976 = *ILLRP* 19.

[33] *CIL,* I², 2438 = *ILLRP* 216; *ILS* 9264; Vergil *Aen.* VII. 45-48; Horace *Carm.* III. 17, 7; Livy XXVII. 37, 2-3; Lucan II. 424; Martial XIII. 83; Servius on *Aen.* VII. 47, XII. 164.

[34] Servius *ibid.*

[35] For the site of the temple see Platner-Ashby (n. 19) *s.v.* Mater Matuta; Lugli (n. 19) pp. 544-45 with pl. IX. 553-54, 561, 576, 584; Lyngby (n. 11) *passim;* Ogilvie (n. 11) on Livy V. 23, 7; and Holland (n. 17) pp. 173-74. For the port at Rome see Platner-Ashby *s.v.* Navalia; Lugli pp. 576-77; J. Le Gall, *Le Tibre fleuve de Rome dans l'antiquité* (Paris 1953), pp. 103-11. None of the historical *navalia* goes back to the foundation of Matuta's temple. Its situation alone suggests the likelihood of association with the Tiber.

[36] Lugli (n. 19), pp. 400-406 with pl. VII.

[37] On Leukothea see Schirmer in Roscher's *Lexicon,* II, 2011-17; L. R. Farnell (n. 30), pp. 36-44. The latter considers her a chthonian deity. As we shall see, both the evidence which he uses and which he misses allow us to consider her

kothea had a cult in Lakonia near Epidaurus Limera at a deep lake into which a believer might throw barley cakes whereby he could learn his fortune. Her worshippers on the road to Thalamai slept on the ground in her sanctuary and she would reveal to them true things in dreams.[38] On the island of Samos a spring bore the name Leukothea.[39] At Miletus Leukothea's phantom (*phasma*) appeared to Smikros through whom she bade the Milesian to give her a cult and gymnastic contests for boys.[40] Although the Greek word *paides* is used in this aetiology, the meaning of *Smikros* and the character of gymnastic games preclude the participation of girls. In its purpose the cult resembles the Roman rites for *sororii*. When Plutarch saw similarity (not sameness) in the cult practice of Roman Matuta and Chaeroneian Leukothea, he remarked how the Greek warder with whip in hand forbade admission within the sacred precinct to any Aetolian or slave of either sex.[41] This act surely displays an exclusion of alien and enemy from the Greek shrine for which there is the comparable Roman evidence discussed earlier.

Our chief concern here is Leukothea's cult in Magna Graecia. Evidently there was confusion about her major, if not sole, cult due to misunderstanding of her name. In the bay of Dorian Poseidonia/ Paestum lay the island called either Leukothea or Leucosia. The latter name was applied to the island because, so say the ancient authors, the figure in question was a siren, or a cousin of Aeneas buried there where a temple to the Sirens stood.[42] However, the former name, Leukothea, is also given to the island.[43] The two names are probably the same. Leucosia is the Lakonian form of Leukothea.[44] Since the Greek Leukothea was established in

---

a water goddess, no matter what her beginnings. There is no doubt that Leukothea had connections in mythology with Ino and in cult with water.

[38] Pausanias III. 23, 8, III. 26, 1, on which see Frazer.

[39] Pliny *NH* V. 135.

[40] Konon in Photius *Bibl.* 186.33 (= Jacoby *FGrHist* Vol. 1, Konon F 1.33). Smikros then became the father of Branchos from whom the prophetic Branchidae. See Heeg in Roscher's *Lexicon*, IV, 1082-83.

[41] Plutarch *QR* 16, *Cam.* 5.

[42] Lykophron *Alex.* 722-23 and Schol. Vet. *ad loc.*; [Aristotle] *Mir. Ausc.* 839a, 103; Strabo VI. 252, VI. 258c, Pliny *NH* III. 85, Dion. Hal. I. 53, 2; cf. Ovid *Metam.* XV. 708. See G. Giannelli (*Culti e miti della Magna Grecia*[2] [Florence 1963], pp. 131-32), who notes that the story of the sirens goes back to Timaeus; Giannelli pays no heed to the evidence for Leukothea.

[43] Mela II. 7, 121, Pliny *NH* III. 83, Martianus Capella VI. 644.

[44] For the Lakonian change of θ to σ see Fr. Bechtel, *Die griechischen Dialekte*, II (Berlin, 1923), 302-303; C. D. Buck, *The Greek Dialects*[2] (Chicago, 1955), p. 59, who notes σιῶ for θεοῦ. The writer owes the suggestion of their identity to L. W. Daly.

Lakonia,[45] we assume the siren Leukosia was born of uncertainty about the Lakonian form. Leukosia may also have been worshipped on the promontory immediately south of Poseidonia since both mountain and headland bear the name Licosa today. South of modern Licosa lay ancient Elea/Velia. According to an anecdote, the citizens of Elea asked Xenophanes whether they should sacrifice to Leukothea (*sic*) and mourn her or not. He replied it was not fitting to mourn a goddess or sacrifice to a mortal.[46] The mourning attests an early belief of the goddess' burial in or near Elea. This goes to prove the lateness of the story of Leucosia the Siren and of the cousin of Aeneas by the same name.

At Rome the only syncretism of Mater Matuta connects her with Leukothea whom the Romans could have known from southern Italy. Cicero first makes this identification but he certainly did not invent it.[47] In addition, Leukothea was also identified with the Tiburtine spring goddess Albunea who was associated with a local oracle.[48] Albunea apparently merited the identification by translation of *leuk-* to Italic *alb-*. However, such a comprehension of the two names would have been inappropriate if Leukothea had not herself been concerned with water and had not had oracular powers (see p. 298).[49]

Modern discussions of Roman Mater Matuta usually cite the Leukothea of Pyrgi whose temple was sacked by Dionysius of Syracuse in 384/3. From Leukothea's enormous wealth Dionysius took 1,000 talents and realized 500 talents from the booty taken from Pyrgi, Caere's port.[50] One Greek source assigns this temple to

[45] Above, n. 38. Pausanias calls her Ino, I suspect, because she was Leukosia in Lakonia and this troubled him.

[46] Aristotle *Rhet.* 1400b, 27. The story is variously told after Aristotle; see Diels-Kranz *Fr Vorsok.*[11] Xenophanes A 13.

[47] Cicero *Nat. Deor.* III. 19, 48, *Tusc. Disp.* I. 12, 28. He refers the source of the identification to *nostri;* he is discussing mortals who had become immortal. The syncretism is acknowledged by Ovid, Plutarch, Servius, and Priscian (notes 9, 13). See G. De Sanctis, *Storia dei Romani*, iv (Pt. 2), (Florence, 1953), pp. 230-32 and Bömer (n. 11) on *Fasti* VI. 475 for discussion and bibliography.

[48] Servius on *Aen.* VII. 83, 84. For Albunea see Vergil *Aen.* VII. 81 ff., Horace *Carm.* I. 7, 12.

[49] Lyngby (n. 11), pp. 42 ff. equates Albunea with Matuta on the basis of two glossators (Loewe *CGL*, ii, 14, ii, 359). This is a mistake because no author makes the equation; probably the glossators merely found Albunea identified with Leukothea (cf. Servius in n. 48) and then went on to identify her with Leukothea's usual Latin counterpart, Mater Matuta. There is no evidence of an oracular Mater Matuta. The request of Pales Matuta (see n. 78) was made under special circumstances.

[50] Diodorus Siculus XV. 14, 3-4; [Aristotle] *Oec.* 1349b, 33; Polyaenus V. 2, 20-21; Aelian *Var. Hist.* 1.20.

Eilithyia, the Greek goddess of childbirth,[51] an inappropriate attribution under the circumstances. Today we know much more about
this temple, near which three gold plaques were discovered in 1964.
Two of the plaques are inscribed in Etruscan, the third in a Semitic
language.[52] The Semitic inscription now appears to be rather Phoenician than Punic, and to record the event of an oracle of Astarte.[53]
The following new translation of the Phoenician text has been
communicated to me by Joseph A. Fitzmyer, S.J.:

> To the Lady Astarte (is dedicated) this shrine, which Thebariye' Velanaś,
> the king of Kayśriye', constructed and which he donated in the month of
> the sacrifices to the sun as a gift in the temple. *And I built it* because
> Astarte requested (it) from *me* (in) the third year of *my* reign, in the
> month of KRR, on the day of the burial of the deity. And may the years
> of the statue of the deity in her temple be years like *the stars of 'El* (or:
> *like these stars*).[54]

This new translation at once makes clear that the shrine of Astarte
was only a part of the temple (precinct?) as a whole. Therefore,
Astarte need not be identified with the Leukothea of Pyrgi. Secondly, the "burial of the deity" recalls the Eleate practice of mourning Leucothea and the belief in the burial of some goddess on the
island of Leucosia/Leukothea.

Etruscan Inscription A mentions Unial-Astres, a syncretism of
Astarte and Italic Juno.[55] Already we have remarked the coinci-

[51] Strabo V. 226c, who calls the foundation Pelasgian; cf. at n. 4, above. He
speaks as if the temple still stood, but this would be impossible, according to
the investigation of the archaeologists. See Colonna, n. 52. See Q. F. Maule and
H. R. W. Smith, "Votive Religion at Caere," *Univ. Calif. Publ. Class. Arch.*, IV
(1959), 75-88.

[52] See G. Colonna, G. Garbini and M. Pallottino, "Scavi nel santuario di Pyrgi,"
Archaeologia Classica, XVI (1964), 49-117; Pallottino, "Nuova luce sulla storia di
Roma arcaica dalle lamine d'oro di Pyrgi," *Studi Romani*, XIII (1965), 1-13;
G. Colonna, "The Sanctuary at Pyrgi in Etruria," *Archaeology*, XIX (1966), 11-23.
The first and third articles have photographs of the plaques.

[53] J. Ferron, "Quelques remarques à propos de l'inscription phénicienne de
Pyrgi," *Oriens Antiquus*, IV (1965), 181-98, with a comparative alphabet on p. 197;
G. Garbini, "Considerazioni sull'iscrizione punica di Pyrgi," *ibid.* pp. 35-52, in
which G. Levi dela Vida (pp. 49-52) suggests an oracle similar to that of
Aphrodite on Cyprus.

[54] Translations in italics are "uncertain *mea quidem sententia*," says Father
Fitzmyer, who delivered the results of his research at the meetings of the
American Oriental Society in Philadelphia, April 19-21, 1966, under the title
"Some Observations on the Phoenician Inscription from Pyrgi." His text, trans-
lation, commentary, and bibliography are forthcoming in the *Journal of the
American Oriental Society*. The present writer owes much to Father Fitzmyer's
wisdom so generously imparted.

[55] See Pallottino (n. 52), *Arch. Class.* pp. 76-117. The present writer will deal
with this and other syncretisms elsewhere, since it directly concerns Juno, not
Matuta.

dence of Camillus' vow to Matuta during the Veientine war. At that time Caere, Etruria's greatest power, either aided Rome or preserved Etruscan neutrality in the face of Veii's annihilation.[56] It seems very likely indeed that Camillus' vow was a diplomatic gesture to the Caeritans through conciliation of their great seaport goddess. Hence, we presume that Matuta had by that time already been equated with the Etruscan goddess whom the Greeks call Leukothea. In connection with the request of Astarte for the shrine in the Pyrgan temple we recall the dream epiphanies of Lakonian Leukothea in Lakonia, her phantom at Miletus speaking to Smikros and, above all, the Matuta-Leukothea to whom one Syrian woman set up a dedication as a result of an oracle of Juno. None of these indications, however, points to a total identification of Juno and her counterparts with Matuta and her counterparts. For now it suffices to sum up the similarities and associations of Juno and Mater Matuta. At Rome Matuta and, perhaps, Cipra may be related in function to Juno Sororia. Coincidence in time at Rome and in place at Pisaurum link Mater Matuta with Juno Regina. The food prepared for the Roman Matralia is paralleled by references to suppers or dining facilities for Juno in one form or another.[57] Besides dedications to Juno Regina at Pisaurum, two Matuta dedications were found along with one to Juno and another to Juno Lucina. The latter was equated with Eilithyia,[58] the goddess perhaps wrongly connected by one authority with the Pyrgan temple which Dionysius robbed. Cupra of Cupra Maritima enjoyed an Etruscan cult which made her resemble Hera, the Romans' Juno.

The temple of Pyrgi could hardly have been closer to the sea. Its excavated remains are awash. Its proximity to the sea in a port town evidently invited both native and foreign merchants to make offerings, which would account for its great wealth. On the other hand, the Romans seem purposely to have kept foreigners out of Mater Matuta's temple. Had it once been likewise attractive? We should not be greatly surprised by the presence of Astarte in the Pyrgan temple under such circumstances. Now we must turn our

[56] See M. Sordi, *I rapporti romano-ceriti e l'origine della civitas sine suffragio* (Rome, 1960), *passim,* and A. Alföldi, *Early Rome and the Latins* (Ann Arbor, 1965), pp. 340-42.

[57] Varro *LL* V. 106 (Matralia); Dion. Hal. II. 23, II. 50, 3; Festus 18, 56L (J. Quiritis); *ius Papirianum* in Macrobius *Sat.* III. 11, 5-6 (J. Populona); Varro *LL* V. 162 (J. Sispes of Lanuvium).

[58] Horace *CS* 13-16; Ovid *Metam.* IX. 281-300. See Bömer (n. 11) on *Fasti* VI. 475. See above, n. 51.

attention to the Etruscan goddess whom the Greeks knew as Leukothea and the Romans as Matuta. Whatever her name may be, her
function is clear enough. She belongs to the sea.

The Romans have preserved the name of the Pyrgan goddess
whom the Greeks call Leukothea. She is the sea goddess or nymph
Venilia. Varro derives her name from *venire* or *ventus:* "Neptunus,
quod mare terras obnubit ut nubes caelum, ab nuptu, id est oper-
tione, ut antiqui, a quo nuptiae, nuptus dictus. Salacia Neptuni
ab salo. Venilia a veniendo ac vento illo, quem Plautus dicit, 'Quod
ille dixit, qui secundo vento vectus est tranquillo mari, Ventum
gaudeo.' " [59] Vergil, however, makes Venilia the divine mother of
Aeneas' Rutulian enemy Turnus.[60] Servius and Servius Danielis
explain Vergil's *diva Venilia mater* as follows:

hoc ad Veneris obtrectationem dicit 'cui diva Venilia mater': nam Venilia
nympha est. Pilumnum autem avum Turni ideo dicit, ut a vicino nobilis
genere esse videatur, sicut est Aeneas: nam paulo post dictura est ipsa Iuno
Pilumnusque illi quartus pater. sane hanc Veniliam quidam Salacium
accipiunt, Neptuni uxorem: Salacium a salo, Veniliam quod veniam det
n < avi > g < a > ntibus.[61]

Here Venilia is either a nymph, or the same as Neptune's wife
Salacia or the goddess of pardon (*venia*).

The phrase *Salacia Neptuni* is partially explained as a form of
address to deities. Such 'prayers' were construed as evidence of
divine spouses.[62]

The Scholia Veronensia on Aeneid X.78 offer yet more information on Venilia:

1 [Deam Venilia]m alii Venerem, quod in mari nata sit, alii Nympham
　　quam Graeci Βούνην vocant.
2 [Varro Rerum Divin]arum XIIII de Dis Certis: Spes cum conciliata non
　　frustra esset et eveniss(et)
3 [Veniliae sacrifica]bantur, quam deam cum Neptuno coniungunt. Multi
　　[hanc accipiunt Pyrg]ens(em) quo Cae-
4 [r- . . . .] differre

1 Deam Venilia]m *Keil* βουνηνη *Cod. Ver.* βούνην *Palmer alii alia.* 2 Varro
Rerum Divin]arum *Hermann.* 2/3 eveniss(et) [Veniliae sacrifica]bantur *Preller.*
3 [hanc accipiunt Pyrg]ens(em) *Palmer, quod lacuna 17-20 litt.* 3/4 Cae| [r-*sive
fortasse* Cae| [ret- *Palmer* ens(is) quo cae(cis) *Keil.*

[59] *LL* V. 72. Cf. Augustine *CD* IV. 11, quoted below, and VII. 22: "Venilia,
inquit [*sc.* Varro], unda est, quae ad litus venit; Salacia, quae in salum redit."
[60] *Aen.* X. 76.
[61] On *Aen.* X. 76. The etymology of Venilia from *venia* is not found in Varro.
For the manuscripts' *negentibus* Thilo suggests in the apparatus n<avi>
g<a>ntibus and *egentibus.*
[62] Gellius XIII. 23, 1-2. As we shall see, their proper name is *indigitamenta.*

The Βούνην is suggested as correction of a dittography of η. The Greek goddess Byne is named in place of Leukothea by Lykophron and lexicographers.[63] *Bounene* is nonsense. Augustine in using Varro supplies the relationship of Spes to Venilia: "de pavore infantum Paventia nuncupetur, de spe, quae venit, Venilia, de voluptate Volupia . . ." [64] In line 3 *hanc accipiunt* is supplied from Servius Danielis, just quoted. From Byne we arrive at Leukothea whence we restore [*Pyrg*]*ens(em) quo Cae*[*r-;* either the town of Caere or the residents, Caerites, would follow therefrom. In this commentary on the Aeneid we see that Venilia is either Venus, making an alliteratively assonant pair, or the nymph B(o)yne, or the goddess of hope (see p. 308). Both Venus and Byne are new to the interpretation of Venilia, mother of Turnus. First, we note that such a relation may not have been found in Varro's *Antiquities of Divine Affairs*. In the volume entitled *De Dis Certis* Varro concerns himself with the proper forms of address to the gods which the Romans called *indigitamenta*. These Varro took from the pontifical books.[65] Gellius' list of such titles, which he says comes from priestly books and old speeches, must derive from the pontifical books through Varro.[66] Varro does discuss nymphs in the volume on *Dei Certi* [67] and may have discussed deities with toponyms or epithets [68] such as a Pyrgensis. However, there is a more likely source of the [*Pyrg*]*ens(em) quo Cae*[*r-* in the Scholia Veronensia than Varro, in whose works and in those of Christian authors depending on him we find nothing to connect Venilia with Pyrgi. The scholia alone preserve the two extant fragments of Verrius Flaccus' *Rerum Etru-*

[63] Lykophron *Alex.* 107, 757, on which see Tzetzes. Jessen, *RE* 3.1 col. 1107, suggests Βύνην. Although sometimes diligent in the transmission of Greek, these scholia preserve substantive mistakes as on *Buc.* III. 30, VI. 9, *Geor.* II. 93 (?), *Aen.* I. 247, II. 305, III. 693, VI. 696, VII. 341, IX. 362, and IX. 387. Our text and apparatus of the scholia Veronensia are based on those of H. Hagen's *Appendix Serviana*, being *Servii Grammatici qui feruntur in Vergilii carmina commentarii* Vol. 3, fasc. 2 (Leipzig, 1902).

[64] *CD* IV. 11; see n. 68. The verb *venit* belongs to the Varronian etymology. Varro's peculiar use of *eveniss(et)*, i.e., "when hope had been successfully conciliated and had been realized," probably rests on his etymology. For *spes* see page 308.

[65] Servius on *Geor.* I. 21, *Aen.* II. 141.

[66] Gellius XIII. 23, 1-2; he cites the fourteenth book, *De Dis Certis*, III. 16, 5-11, XV. 30, 5-7. Venilia is absent from Gellius' list of *indigitamenta* evidently because *salacia* was an *indigitamentum* of Neptune and *venilia* was not.

[67] Servius Dan. on *Aen.* XII. 139.

[68] Tertullian *Ad Nat.* II. 8, 6; cf. II. 9, 3, and II. 11, 10: "<Habent et Pave>ntinam pavoris, spei Veniliam, voluptatis Volupiam, etc."

scarum which are found only in the commentary on *Aeneid* Book X.
On *Aeneid* X.183 the scholiast offers the archaic name of Caere
Cisra and possibly a connection between Ardea (Turnus' town) and
Caere.[69] Unfortunately the word *Ardea* does not fully survive.
Nevertheless, Verrius did most certainly discuss Caere from an
antiquarian's point of view. If the mention of Caere under these
circumstances does not suffice to link Venilia to the Etruscans of
Pyrgi and Caere, there is a possible link within the Aeneid itself.
Turnus sought alliance with Mezentius, king of Caere, who imposed
on the Ardeates or Latins a tribute in wine.[70] To Vergil's mind the
Caeritan lord was a natural ally of the Rutulian Turnus of Ardea.
What would be more natural than that Turnus' mother be Venilia
from Pyrgi? Of course Vergil does not come right out and say so.

For Vergil and Ovid [71] Venilia was a character of myth and
legend; she had no cult among the Romans so far as we know.[72]
All authors agree Venilia was divine. Varro relates her to Neptune
and to Spes. In the Servian commentaries she is a nymph. The
Veronensian scholiast identifies her with Byne, another name of
Leukothea. If our restoration of these scholia is near what had
been written, Venilia was the goddess of Pyrgi likened to Leukothea.
Independent of the literary tradition is the name of the island
Venaria off the Etruscan coast [73] which recalls the name-giving of
Leukothea/Leucosia off the Lucanian coast. Venilia was certainly
known to Latin commentators as a goddess who could be connected
with the sea. Although the cult terms *venia* and *spes* are attached
to Venilia, we appear to have no Italic cult.[74] This absence might
be explained by the fact that Venilia was not an Italic goddess. The
word *venilia* seems to be an Etruscan gentilic.[75] But this does not

[69] Schol. Ver. on *Aen.* X. 183, X. 200 = frr. 1 and 2 in Peter's *HRR*.

[70] The story is told as early as Cato's *Origines* fr. 12P; see Livy I. 2, Dion.
Hal. I. 64; Vergil *Aen.* VII. 647 ff. *et passim.* See Alföldi (n. 56), pp. 209-11 for
a discussion of the tradition and its evidence.

[71] *Metam.* XIV. 334, where Venilia is the wife of Ionian Janus and mother of
Canens; see page 306.

[72] See Wissowa (n. 11) pp. 107, 226.

[73] Pliny *NH* III. 81, Martianus Capella VI. 644. For the formation compare
Columbaria and Menaria, other islands in this area.

[74] Lyngby ([n. 11] p. 27) and others believe Leukothea of Pyrgi was Tethys,
or Minerva. It is curious, then, that none of the Greek authors who mention
the temple call the goddess by either her etruscanized Greek name or Athena,
a well-known equivalent of Minerva. No Roman mentions the temple at Pyrgi
which had been destroyed in the third century B.C.

[75] Latte ([n. 11], p. 58) who follows Schulze. To the citation of names add
(M. Buffa, *Nuova raccolta di iscrizioni etrusche* [Florence, 1935], No. 1022) a

necessarily mean Venilia was goddess of that clan. Rather, it may mean the Romans rendered her name into Latin under the influence of the personal name.

Ovid's *Metamorphoses* XIV.332-34 reveals certain evidence for making Venilia a sea-goddess and connecting her with Matuta:

> spretis tamen omnibus unam
> ille colit nymphen, quam quondam in colle Palati
> dicitur Ionio peperisse Venilia Iano.

Ovid is telling the story of Picus' courtship of Canens, nymph daughter of Venilia and Ionian Janus. At first glance, however, Ionian Janus and Venilia, whom Vergil had already named the mother of Turnus, make no sense in the context. For one thing Ovid himself admits Janus had no Greek counterpart.[76] But here the adjective *Ionius* is not used of the people or the land by Ovid; here he is speaking of the Ionian Sea to the south of Italy and to the west of Greece.[77] Ionian Janus is the Italian gateway to the Ionian Sea, Brundisium. In 267 B.C. the consul M. Atilius Regulus conquered the Sallentini of the Peninsula's heel and took Brundisium. He paid the price of victory with a *templum* to Pales.[78] The Veronensian Scholia further inform us that this Pales was Pales Matuta:

'Magna Pales' potest communi [sensu intellegi] et magnis * * * cuius relligionem Ro[mulus] coli statuit et cuius die Romam condidit, id est Palilibus. Sic et alibi poeta: Nunc veneranda P[ales. Appellatur] et Pales Matuta, cuius templum Atilius Regulus vovit ἀντιδιαστέλλων, unde Magna Mat[er dicta est].[79]

Ovid's Venilia of the Palatine Hill can be no other than Pales Matuta. The Ionian Janus refers to Atilius Regulus' victory which presumably was effected with the support of some marine deity at

---

Venelus of Capua, and (K. Olzscha, "Interpretation der Agramer Mumienbinde," *Klio, Beiheft* 40 [1939], p. 58, where he discusses *Venala*) an Etruscan double genitive of a praenomen. Such forms led to new formation of gentilics. See H. Rix, *Das etruskische Cognomen* (Wiesbaden, 1963), pp. 294, 299, 331 f., and p. 400 of the index for names beginning *Ven-*. With these compare Vergil's Venulus, the ally of Turnus, in *Aen.* VIII. 9, XI. 242, XI. 742.

[76] *Fasti* I. 90.

[77] *Metam.* XI. 48-51 (where he connects it with Sallentum), 699-701. For the extent of the Ionian Sea see Strabo VI. 281c (cf. VI. 283), Mela II. 7, 115, Pliny *NH* III. 100.

[78] Florus I. 15, 20: "Sallentini Picentibus additi caputque regionis Brundisium inclito portu M. Atilio duce. et in hoc certamine victoriae pretium templum sibi pastoria Pales ultro poposcit." Cf. Schol. Bern. on *Geor.* III. 1.

[79] On *Geor.* III. 1. All three notices must go back to Livy's lost Book XV.

Italy's exit to the East. The Romans celebrated Pales' feast on 21 April. Of Parilia Ovid writes (*Fasti* IV.728-30):

> udaque roratas laurea misit aquas.
> mota dea est operique favet: navalibus exit
> puppis, habent ventos iam mea vela suos.

Is not the conceit of the poet's song, sailing like a ship from port, acknowledgment of a Pales' interest in the sea? And again Ovid (*Fasti* IV.777-78):

> his dea placanda est, haec tu conversus ad ortus
> dic quater et vivo perlue rore manus!

The *vivo rore* like the *roratas aquas* is purificatory,[80] and belongs to the cult of Parilia. Furthermore, Pales may have been connected with fresh waters, as Ovid implies (*Fasti* IV.759-60):

> tu, dea, pro nobis fontes fontanaque placa
> numina, tu sparsos per nemus omne deos!

Given Ovid's poetic practice, we are in no position to evaluate precisely the relation of Pales to the waters. Besides this April festival of Pales the Fasti Antiates Maiores mention sacrifice to the two Pales on 7 July. This sacrifice has been related to the *templum* of Pales given by Atilius Regulus.[81] The Ovidian reference to Venilia of the Palatine Hill now secures the inference of the site of the *templum* there. Florus, who first mentions this shrine, does distinguish between *templum* and *aedes*.[82] Hence there probably never was any temple (i.e., *aedes*) to Pales Matuta on the Palatine but only the precinct (i.e., *templum*) which all three sources cite.[83] The inappropriate citation of Magna Mater in the Scholia Veronensia concerning Pales Magna and Pales Matuta explains why the precinct of Pales Matuta seems to disappear from later references to the Palatine Hill. The temple (*aedes*) of the Pergamene Magna Mater was built on the land formerly dedicated to Pales Matuta.[84]

[80] See Bömer (n. 11) on *Fasti* II. 35.
[81] For Parilia or the two Pales see Wissowa (n. 11), pp. 199-201, Latte (n. 11), p. 87-88, and Degrassi (n. 14), pp. 443-45, 479, and Bömer (n. 11) on *Fasti* IV. 721 ff.
[82] Cf. Florus I. 14, 19 *aedes* of Tellus and I. 15, 20 *templum* of Pales.
[83] See Platner-Ashby (n. 19) s.v. Pales, templum. They and others mistake *templum* for *aedes* even though they wonder about the ancients' failure to mention a temple.
[84] Shortly after 204 B.C. the goddess was temporarily housed in the Palatine temple of Victory (Livy XXIX. 14, 5-14, cf. XXIX. 11, 5-8). See Platner-Ashby (n. 19) s.v. Magna Mater, aedes. The erection of this temple within the pomerium can be explained in this fashion. Atilius Regulus gave a precinct to Pales Matuta

One question remains to be answered. Why had Atilius vowed a temple to Pales Matuta at the request of the goddess during a war with the Sallentines and Brundisines? The region around Tarentum where Atilius fought was a rich producer of wool. Pales had become the god of flocks and Parilia a feast for purifying the flocks. Matuta had already been likened to the sea goddess of Pyrgi. The pair, Pales and Matuta, seemed to oversee the sources of livelihood in Calabria and Sallentum. Since both were old deities and since one had a Roman hill named after him or her, they could severally or together be installed within the pomerium.[85]

Without Atilius Regulus and his precinct for Pales Matuta, whom Ovid equates with Venilia, wife of the Ionian Janus, we cannot understand Varro's identification of Venilia with Spes.[86] It was apparently Varro who first confused Atilius Regulus with A. Atilius Calatinus, or Caiatinus, consul in 258 and 254, praetor in 257, dictator in 249 and censor in 247 B.C.[87] During the first Punic War this contemporary of Regulus dedicated a temple to Spes in the Forum Holitorium. Not only did the temple rise beside the Tiber but many of the official deeds of Atilius Calatinus in the war concerned naval warware.[88] Rome's hope in the war lay in control of the sea. Unless we compare Pales Matuta, Venilia and Spes in the light of the careers of the two Atilii, we cannot comprehend the Varronian supposition that Venilia and Spes were related to each other. Hence to Varro the *templum* of Atilius (Regulus) belonged to Venilia whom Ovid situates on the Palatine Hill. In contrast, the annalistic tradition reflected by Florus and the two scholia names Pales and Pales Matuta the deity of the *templum*.

In this study we have attempted to define the syncretism of the good goddess, Matuta, and her semantic analogue Cupra among

---

on the Palatine Hill because of Pales. Likening her to Mater Matuta the Romans gave over the precinct to Mater Magna. The Romans had already admitted a "foreign" god under Regulus.

[85] On Pales and Pales Matuta in this context, see V. Basanoff, "Evocatio: Étude d'un rituel militaire romain," *Bibl. École Hautes Études: Sciences Rel.,* LXI (1947), Ch. IV *et passim.*

[86] In Augustine at n. 64, Tertullian in n. 68.

[87] See T. R. S. Broughton, *The Magistrates of the Roman Republic,* I (New York, 1951), *s. aa.* for his career.

[88] Cicero *Leg.* II. 11, 28 (cf. *Nat. Deor.* II. 61), Tacitus *Ann.* II. 49. See Platner-Ashby (n. 19) *s.v.* Spes, aedes; and Le Gall (n. 35) pp. 105-10. For the site of the temple, Livy XL. 51, 6: post Spei ad Tiberim. On the career of Atilius see Broughton (n. 87) and Klebs *RE* 2.2 cols. 2079-81. The Atilii were especially naval strategists.

Italic speakers, and to suggest the true identity of Venilia. All three had connections with the waters of spring, river, and sea. The relative development of the syncretism may be established on these lines. The two Italian goddesses, Matuta and Cupra, watched over waters. The latter even became the eponym of a coastal community. In the early fourth century, at least, Camillus reckoned a gift to Matuta a boon to Caere's marine goddess who was Leukothea in Greek minds. Over one hundred years later under similar circumstances Atilius Regulus honored Pales Matuta who had requested a precinct in Rome. The antiquarian Varro believed she was Venilia whose name he derived from *venire* and *ventus* and whom he confused with Spes because two Atilii had severally honored Venilia and Spes within the same generation and for similar reasons. Venilia is most likely the Etruscan divinity from Pyrgi and the very goddess Greeks likened to Leukothea or Leukosia, worshipped in the southern waters of the Tyrrhenian Sea. From this link of Venilia and Matuta came the identification of Matuta with Leukothea. At Rome and Miletus these goddesses shared concern for the initiation of adolescent boys into the civic fabric. Such a role required the exclusion or abuse of the alien at Rome and Chaeronia. Finally, Cupra, Matuta, and Venilia of Pyrgi appear to have enjoyed religious associations with Juno. In Etruria and in Syria the water goddesses are linked to Juno-Astarte and Juno, respectively, by oracle.[89]

University of Pennsylvania
3 May 1966

[89] The writer thanks L. W. Daly for reading this paper and suggesting improvements. The conclusions are the writer's.

AMICUM SUUM BEN EDWIN PERRY PLURIMUM VALERE

Iubet

Kevin Guinagh

Quis satis laudet meritum magistri,
Quis brevi enarret monumenta amici
Qui fuit cultor prope fontem aquarum
     Pieriarum.

Per suam vitam monito poetae
Laete oboedivit studiisque Graecis
Se die noctuque bene applicavit
     Totus in illis.

Per dies longos animo volenti
Impiger stirpes veterum petivit,
Lineas scrutans, simul explicansque
     Significatum.

Maximum curae et meditationis
Dedit illi qui Phrygius [1] ferarum
Fabulas finxit ratiocinantum
     More virorum.

Diviti autumno segeti coloni
Invidet pauper; simili modo et nos
Saepe miramur socii laborem
     Ingeniumque.

Gloria clarus meruit sedere
Sub sua fico meditans peracta;
Attamen sumit nova pensa felix,
     Fortis, acutus.

Mayaguez, Puerto Rico
2 February 1966

---

[1] Immo Thrax (quod hoc versu dicere non est facile); vide nunc ipsum **Perry**, *Babrius and Phaedrus* (1965), p. xl.—Edd.

DATE DUE